WHEN CORPORATIONS RULE THE WORLD

Other Books by David C. Korten

Agenda for a New Economy

Bureaucracy and the Poor

Casebook for Family Planning Management

Community Management

Getting to the 21st Century

The Great Turning

People-Centered Development

Planned Change in a Traditional Society

Population and Social Development Management

The Post-Corporate World

When Corporations Rule the World

WHEN
CORPORATIONS
RULE THE
WORLD

— 20TH ANNIVERSARY EDITION —

David C. Korten

Berrett–Koehler Publishers, Inc.
a BK Currents book

Berrett-Koehler Publishers, Inc.
1333 Broadway, Suite 1000
Oakland, CA 94612-1921
Tel: (510) 817-2277 | Fax: (510) 817-2278 | www.bkconnection.com

ORDERING INFORMATION
Quantity sales. Special discounts are available on quantity purchases by corporations, associations, and others. For details, contact the "Special Sales Department" at the Berrett-Koehler address above.
Individual sales. Berrett-Koehler publications are available through most bookstores. They can also be ordered directly from Berrett-Koehler: Tel: (800) 929-2929; Fax: (802) 864-7626; www.bkconnection.com.
Orders for college textbook/course adoption use. Please contact Berrett-Koehler: Tel: (800) 929-2929; Fax: (802) 864-7626.
Orders by US trade bookstores and wholesalers. Please contact Ingram Publisher Services, Tel: (800) 509-4887; Fax: (800) 838-1149; E-mail: customer.service@ingrampublisherservices.com; or visit www.ingrampublisherservices.com/Ordering for details about electronic ordering.

Berrett-Koehler and the BK logo are registered trademarks of Berrett-Koehler Publishers, Inc.

Printed in the United States of America.

Berrett-Koehler books are printed on long-lasting acid-free paper. When it is available, we choose paper that has been manufactured by environmentally responsible processes. These may include using trees grown in sustainable forests, incorporating recycled paper, minimizing chlorine in bleaching, or recycling the energy produced at the paper mill.

Library of Congress Cataloging-in-Publication Data

Korten, David C.
    When corporations rule the world / David C. Korten. — 20th anniversary edition.
        pages   cm
    Includes bibliographical references.
    ISBN 978-1-62656-287-5 (pbk.)
        1. Corporations—Political aspects.   2. Industries—Environmental aspects.
3. Industrialization—Social aspects.   4. Big business.   5. Power (Social sciences)
6. Business and politics.   7. International business enterprises.   8. International economic relations.   9. Sustainable development.   I. Title.
    HD2326.K647   2015
    322'.3—dc23   2015008552

Third Edition

20 19 18 17 16 15 | 10 9 8 7 6 5 4 3 2 1

Produced and designed by BookMatters, edited by Karen Seriguchi, proofed by Janet Blake, indexed by Leonard Rosenbaum, and cover designed by Steven Pisano.

To two great teachers,
Professors Robert North and Willis Harman,
who taught me to question conventional wisdom
and opened my eyes to possibilities that changed my life.

To my life partner, Dr. Frances F. Korten, who shares the incredible
journey on a road less traveled.

and

To Smitu Kothari,
friend, colleague, and one of India's leading intellectuals,
who advised me that to truly serve the cause of the world's poor,
I should return home to the United States from Asia
and teach my fellow Americans
what I had learned abroad about the source of their poverty.
Heeding his advice, I returned and wrote
When Corporations Rule the World.

Those who own the country should govern it.

John Jay, first chief justice of the United States

The arc of the moral universe is long, but it bends towards justice.

Martin Luther King Jr.

The worship of the ancient golden calf has returned in a new and ruthless guise in the idolatry of money and the dictatorship of an impersonal economy lacking a truly human purpose.

Pope Francis, *Apostolic Exhortation Evangelii Gaudium*

In spite of current ads and slogans, the world doesn't change one person at a time. It changes as networks of relationships form among people who share a common cause and vision of what's possible. . . . We don't need to convince large numbers of people to change; instead, we need to connect with kindred spirits.

Margaret Wheatley and Deborah Frieze,

"How Large-Scale Change Really Happens"

CONTENTS

A Choice for Life

Money flows faster. Financial bubbles inflate.
Economists assure us we grow richer.

Electronic gadgets and entertainments distract us.
Real-world families and communities disintegrate.
Earth and democracy die.

Ruled by soulless corporations
that value money more than life,
we get more money, less life.

We face an epic choice:
People power or corporate power;
living communities or corporate colonies;
democracy or corporatocracy;
more life for all or more money for the few.

Humanity awakens to long-forgotten truths.
We are living beings born of and nurtured by a living Earth.
Real wealth is living wealth.
Money is just a number.
We find true happiness in the joy of living and contributing
as members of caring families and communities.

We have the right and the means
to replace a life-destroying suicide economy
ruled by money-seeking corporate robots
with living economies
grounded in the foundational principles
of democracy, real-market economies, and living systems.

Many millions of people are engaging.
They reconnect with one another and the rest of nature.
They rebuild living communities, democracy, and economies
in which people cooperate to make a living
rather than compete to make a killing.

A Personal Journey

I think there are good reasons for suggesting that the modern age has ended. Today, many things indicate that we are going through a transitional period, when it seems that something is on the way out, and something else is painfully being born. It is as if something were crumbling, decaying and exhausting itself, while something else, still indistinct, were arising from the rubble.

—VÁCLAV HAVEL,
president of the Czech Republic

As a young man, I decided I would devote my life to ending world poverty. To that end I spent thirty years of my life as a development worker in Africa, Latin America, and Asia. I saw extraordinary changes in the world—especially in Asia, where I lived from 1978 to 1992.

During my first visit to Asia as a student in 1961, I experienced many cities as dingy and remote. By the time I returned permanently to the United States in 1992 to share with fellow Americans the lessons of my experience, these same cities were sporting luxurious modern airports, superhighways crowded with late-model cars, five-star hotels, gated residential communities, and air-conditioned mega shopping malls stocked with state-of-the-art electronics and elegant designer clothing from all over the world.

Such signs of progress in what we once called underdeveloped countries are now even more pervasive. To those who look no further, development seems to have been a stunning success. Yet look a little deeper, and it is like an elaborate movie set, carefully constructed in the midst of dystopian devastation.

Yes, hundreds of thousands of people are living extremely well, and millions are enjoying far higher levels of consumption than ever before. But billions have been displaced from the lands on which they once made a modest living to make way for mining operations, oil extraction, dams, agricultural estates, forestry plantations, resorts, golf courses, and myriad other development projects catering to the needs and wants of the few. The many live in squalid slums and struggle to survive as sweatshop workers, migrant agricultural laborers, street vendors, drug dealers, and sex workers.

The trees are gone from once-lush hillsides. Coral reefs once vibrant with life are underwater wastelands. The air is thick with pollutants. Cultures grounded in strong spiritual, family, and community values have given way to materialism and violence.

Politicians and the press display little awareness of life beyond the façade and even less understanding of the root causes of poverty and unemployment, inequality, violent crime, family and community breakdowns, and environmental collapse. Our leaders seem unable to move beyond blaming their political opponents and promoting the same old ineffectual solutions—accelerating economic growth through deregulation, cutting taxes, removing trade barriers, giving industry more incentives and subsidies, forcing welfare recipients to work, hiring more police, and building more jails.

I find it is often the people who live ordinary lives far removed from the corridors of power who have the clearest perception of what is really happening. Yet they are often reluctant to speak openly what they believe in their hearts to be true, because it is too frightening and differs too dramatically from what those with more impressive credentials and access to the media are saying. They feel isolated and helpless.

The questions nag: Are things really as bad as they seem to me? Why don't others see it? Am I stupid? Am I being intentionally misinformed? What can I do? What can anyone do?

I struggled for years with the same questions, at first with a similar sense of isolation, now with awareness that many millions of others are asking the same questions. I wrote *When Corporations Rule the World* as part of my own search for answers. A great many readers have told me that reading it opened their eyes and changed their lives. In most instances it helped them see with clarity and confidence what they suspected might be true and gave them the language to discuss it.

Getting the difficult and unpleasant truth on the table for discussion is a necessary first step toward action. Fear of the unknown can immobilize us, especially if we believe we are alone. Knowing we are not alone can help us face an increasingly terrifying reality with courage and empower us to act.

Let me begin by sharing a bit of the journey that led to my writing

When Corporations Rule the World and the decision to present this 20th anniversary edition with this updated prologue, along with an all-new introduction, an all-new conclusion, and an updated epilogue. I hope that this may help you approach this book as you would a conversation with a valued friend.

Roots of the Inquiry

I was born in 1937 into a conservative white upper-middle-class family in Longview, Washington, a small timber-industry town of some 25,000 people. Assuming that one day I would manage the family's retail music and appliance business, I had no particular interest in venturing beyond the borders of the United States. As a psychology major at Stanford University, I focused on musical aptitude testing and the uses of psychology to influence buying behavior. Then in 1959, during my senior year, a curious thing happened.

At that time a very conservative Young Republican, I was deeply fearful of the spread of communism and the threat it posed to the American way of life I held so dear. This fear drew me to take a course on modern revolutions taught by Robert North, a professor of political science. There I learned that poverty was fueling the communist revolutions I so feared.

In one of those rare, deeply life-changing moments, I made a decision. I would devote my life to countering this threat by bringing the knowledge of modern business management and entrepreneurship to those who had not yet benefited from it.

I prepared myself with an MBA in international business and a PhD in organizational theory from the Stanford Business School. Three years in Ethiopia setting up a business school with the help of my newlywed life partner, Frances Korten, provided my apprenticeship. I did my obligatory military service during the Vietnam War as a captain in the US Air Force, fulfilling staff assignments at the Special Air Warfare School, the Office of the Secretary of the Air Force, and the Office of the Secretary of Defense. I then signed up for what turned out to be a five-and-a-half-year tour on the faculty of the Harvard University Graduate School of Business.

For three of my Harvard Business School years I served as the Harvard adviser to the Nicaragua-based Central American Management Institute (INCAE), a graduate business school catering to the elite business families of Central American and Andean countries. After returning to Boston, I taught for two more years at the business school and then moved to the Harvard Institute for International Development and the Harvard School of Public Health.

At the beginning of 1978, Fran and I joined the Ford Foundation staff in the Philippines and remained in Southeast Asia for the next fourteen years. While Fran stayed with Ford, I moved on to spend eight years as a senior adviser with the US Agency for International Development (USAID), the official US foreign aid program.

I share this detail to establish the depth of my conservative establishment roots. The more interesting part of my story, however, has to do with my gradual awakening to a troubling truth: that conventional economic theory and practice is a leading cause of—not the solution to—poverty, exclusion, and environmental system collapse.

Personal Awakening

The Stanford course on modern revolutions awakened me to the reality of global poverty. In 1961, a summer in Indonesia immersed me in the heroic struggles, spiritual grounding, and generosity of people who live in desperate poverty. It was an aspect of the human experience I had not previously encountered.

While at INCAE in the early 1970s, I wrote a number of Harvard Business School–style management cases for a course I was teaching on the management of change. They were based on my Latin American experience. Many involved efforts by government, business, and voluntary agencies to improve the conditions of the urban and rural poor. They often carried a disturbing message: Externally imposed "development" was seriously disrupting human relationships and community life—often causing severe hardship for the very people it claimed to benefit.

By contrast, when people found the freedom and self-confidence to take control of their own economic lives, they generally fared far better. I became fascinated with the challenge of transforming development programs to support these kinds of self-led grassroots processes.

During our INCAE and Harvard years, Fran and I became involved in efforts to improve the management of family-planning programs. This brought us into contact with many local initiatives, including those of poor people who were trying to gain control of their lives in the face of economic policies that supported the expropriation of their resource base by those already better off.

When Fran and I left Harvard at the end of 1978 to join the Ford Foundation staff in Manila, Fran inherited a portfolio of grants that included a small grant to the Philippine National Irrigation Administration (NIA). It was intended to strengthen the NIA's ability to assist small farmer-owned-and-operated irrigation systems. This led to a long-term cooperation between the NIA and the Ford Foundation that ultimately transformed the NIA from an engineering-and-construction-centered organization that dictated to farmers to one that worked in partnership with farmer organizations and encouraged a substantial degree of local self-reliance.

Through our contact with a great many initiatives in Asia, we experienced the creative energies that people and communities can mobilize on their own behalf with modest support and encouragement from public authorities. We saw firsthand how foreign-funded development projects commonly overwhelm such efforts—even many projects that seek to embrace them.

We also learned how careful strategic grant making can "debureaucratize" large centralized public agencies and strengthen the control of local resources by local people. Aware of my writing and lectures on how this is accomplished, USAID invited me to help it apply these lessons to its programming in Asia as its regional adviser on development management based in Jakarta, Indonesia. I focused on this task for eight years, only to conclude that USAID was too big and bureaucratic itself to be effective as a catalyst in helping country development agencies become less bureaucratic.

These experiences left me with a deep conviction that real development cannot be purchased with foreign aid. Development depends on people's ability to gain control of, and effectively use, the real resources of their localities—land, water, labor, technology, and human ingenuity and motivation—to meet their needs. Yet most development interventions transfer control of local resources to large centralized public bureaucracies that are unaccountable to local people and unresponsive to their needs. The more money that flows through these central institutions, the more dependent people become, the less control they have over their own lives and resources, and the more rapidly the gap grows between those who hold central power and the local people and communities seeking to make a living using local resources.

I came to see a yawning gap between actions that increase economic growth and those that result in better lives for people. This difference raised a basic question: What would development look like if, instead of being focused on growth and money, it were truly people centered—making people both its purpose and its primary instrument? In 1984, I edited the anthology *People-Centered Development*. In 1986, I edited another anthology, *Community Management*. Both focused on getting resource control in the hands of people.

The more I saw development's presumed beneficiaries struggling to maintain their dignity and the quality of their lives in the face of the systemic attack by the development agencies and projects that were colonizing their resources, the more alienated I became from mainstream development thinking. In 1988, I left USAID but remained in Southeast Asia.

Having become disillusioned with official development agencies, I immersed myself in the world of nongovernmental organizations (NGOs) and soon found myself among NGO colleagues who were raising similar questions about the nature and process of development. I became a synthesizer and scribe of the collective insights emerging from an increasingly dynamic dialogue within the NGO community. It was a period of intense personal learning.

My next book, *Getting to the 21st Century: Voluntary Action and the Global Agenda*, published in 1990, focused on the threefold human crisis of deepening poverty, environmental destruction, and social disintegration. It traced the roots of the crisis to models that made growth the goal of development and treated people as mere means. It concluded that because the dominant institutions of modern society are creations of a growth-centered development vision, the leadership for change must come from voluntary citizen action.

Embracing this argument to recast my own commitments, I joined a number of colleagues to found the People-Centered Development Forum (PCDForum), a global citizen network engaged in articulating and advancing a people-centered vision of the future and redefining development practice in line with that vision. The PCDForum (now the Living Economies Forum) examined the role of national and global structures and institutions in stripping people and place-based communities of the ability to meet their own needs in responsible, sustainable ways.

This explains what some people may see as a paradox: although I talk of the need for local empowerment, much of my attention is focused on the transformation of global institutions. I am among those who seek to transform the global to empower the local.

A Ten-Day Reflection with Asian Colleagues

In November 1992, I traveled to Baguio, a Philippine mountain resort town, to meet with the leaders of several of Asia's leading NGOs. We engaged in a ten-day reflection on the Asian development experience and its implications for NGO strategies. We were concerned that Asia's much-touted economic success was confined to a few relatively small countries and dangerously superficial. Beneath the surface of dynamic competitive economies, we observed a deeper reality of impoverishment and a spreading disruption of the region's social and ecological foundations.

Our discussions turned to the need for a theory that would explain and provide guidance in addressing the deeper causes of the crisis. Without a theory, we were like a pilot without a compass.

Late one night, our discussions began to converge on two fundamental insights: First, we did not need an alternative theory of development as our guide. Rather, we needed a theory of sustainable societies that would apply to Northern and Southern countries alike. Second, the theory must go beyond the sterile formulations of mainstream economists and explain why human societies have chosen to so disrupt the natural self-organizing processes of living communities.

As we continued our discussion over the next few days, the pieces began to fall into place. The Western scientific vision of a mechanical universe has created a philosophical alienation from our inherently spiritual nature. This is reinforced in our daily lives by the increasing alignment of our institutions with the monetary values of the marketplace.

The more dominant that money becomes in our lives, the less sense we have of the spiritual bond that forms the foundation of vital human communities and binds us to the rest of Living Earth's community of life. The pursuit of spiritual fulfillment has been increasingly displaced by an all-consuming and increasingly self-destructive pursuit of money—a human artifact without substance or intrinsic value.

It seemed evident from our analysis that to reestablish a sustainable relationship to a living Earth, we must break free of the illusions of the world of money, rediscover spiritual meaning in our lives, and root our economic institutions in place and community. Consequently, we concluded that the task of people-centered development in its fullest sense must be the creation of life-centered societies in which the economy is but one of the instruments of good living—not the purpose of human existence. Because our leaders are trapped in the myths and the reward systems of the institutions they head, the leadership in this creative process of institutional and values re-creation must come from within civil society.

It was in so many ways an unremarkable insight. We had accomplished little more than to rediscover the ancient wisdom that a deep tension exists between our spiritual nature and our economic lives, and that healthy social and spiritual function depends on keeping the two in proper balance and perspective.

Nor was there anything new in recognizing the importance of civil society, which has always been—and will likely ever be—the driver of authentic democratic governance. Yet we deepened our personal insights into the practical relevance of these ideas to the crisis that imperils contemporary societies. I wrote *When Corporations Rule the World* to further develop and share these insights more broadly. It was an expression of my commitment to my Asian NGO friends and colleagues to help communicate their concerns and the lessons of their experience to a Northern audience—and in particular to expose the US role in driving the unfolding disaster.

The globally aware reader will note that *When Corporations Rule the World* has a strong focus on US corporations, choices, and consequences. European readers of the original edition frequently commented that what I described was distinctive to the United States. "Europe is different," they explained. Indeed, it was. It has since become ever less so. The US corporate agenda is a global agenda. The US experience is simply the leading edge. We in the United States are as the canaries in the mine shaft.

Returning Home

In the summer of 1992, shortly before the Baguio retreat, Fran and I left Southeast Asia to return permanently to the United States. We had announced our decision to friends and colleagues in our 1991 Christmas letter with the following explanation:

> We were drawn to these far-away regions in the early 1960s by a belief that they were the locus of the development problems to which we had decided as young university students to dedicate our careers. We began these careers challenged by a mission—to help share the lessons of America's success with the world—so that "they" could become more like "us."
>
> Development as we understood it thirty years ago, and as it is to this day vigorously promoted by the World Bank, the IMF [International Monetary Fund], the Bush administration, and most of the world's powerful economic institutions, isn't working for the majority of humanity. And the roots of the problem are not found among the poor of the "underdeveloped" world. They are found in the countries that set global standards for wasteful extravagance and dominate the global policies that are leading our world to social and ecological self-destruction.
>
> Now thirty years older and hopefully a good deal wiser, Fran and I have come to realize the extent to which America's "success" is one of the world's key problems. Indeed, the ultimate demonstration of this assertion is found in America itself.
>
> From our vantage point in Asia we have watched in horror as the same policies the United States has been advocating for the world have created a Third World within its own borders. This is revealed in its growing gap between rich and poor, dependence on foreign debt, deteriorating educational systems, rising infant mortality, economic dependence on the export of primary commodities—including the last remaining primary forests—indiscriminate dumping of toxic wastes, and the breakdown of families and communities.
>
> While we have been away from home, the powerful have consolidated the nation's wealth in their own hands and absolved themselves

of responsibility for their less fortunate neighbors. Labor unions have withered as American workers desperate to keep their jobs have been forced to compete with the even more desperate unemployed of Mexico, Bangladesh, and other Third World countries by negotiating for wage cuts with corporations that may still bear American names but honor no national allegiance.

We feel that our own education has been the primary product of our years abroad and that it is now time to return home to face up to our responsibilities to confront the problem at its geographical source. New York, a major center of economic power manifesting all the qualities of a contemporary Third World city—including wandering armies of the homeless juxtaposed with the extravagant lifestyles of the rich and famous, incapacitated government, and indiscriminate violence—seemed an appropriate choice. So we are moving to the belly of the beast, bringing the perspectives gained from our thirty years of learning about the causes of these conditions.

Only when we in the United States are prepared to assume responsibility for changing ourselves will others be able to fully reclaim the social and environmental spaces we have appropriated from them and recover their ability to meet their own needs within a just, democratic, and sustainable world of cooperative partnerships.

Birth of a Global Resistance

At the beginning of 1994, as I was writing *When Corporations Rule the World*, Jerry Mander, author, insightful social critic, and then head of the San Francisco–based Foundation for Deep Ecology, convened a small international gathering of some fifty NGO leaders to launch what became the International Forum on Globalization (IFG).

We were of many nationalities and came from widely varied backgrounds. We were all, however, engaged in resisting the use of World Bank and IMF structural adjustment programs and international trade agreements to consolidate global corporate power beyond the reach of democratic accountability. As we shared our experiences, we came to see a larger pattern of a global corporate agenda and its systemic implications. We also deepened our understanding of how sharply the real story of the North American Free Trade Agreement (NAFTA) and the World Trade Organization diverged from the story promoted to the public. *When Corporations Rule the World* draws extensively from what emerged as our shared analysis.

In November 1995, we held what proved to be a historic public teach-in on corporate globalization at the Riverside Church in New York City.

When Corporations Rule the World had launched just the month before. The IFG teach-in featured many of globalizing civil society's most influential, informed, and eloquent leaders and speakers, including Maude Barlow, Walden Bello, John Cavanagh, Victoria Tauli-Corpuz, Martin Khor, Sara Larraín, Vandana Shiva, Jerry Mander, Ralph Nader, Helena Norberg-Hodge, Jeremy Rifkin, Lori Wallach, and many others. I had the privilege of being among their number.

On a cold, wet November evening, the sanctuary filled to overflowing with 1,500 participants from all across the United States, Canada, Mexico, and beyond. Hundreds were turned away at the door for lack of space. It was a moment of public readiness to hear and address the truth that the corporate PR machine sought to obscure with false promises of growth, jobs, and prosperity for all. Our well-documented counterstory quickly spread through progressive networks around the world.

There followed countless teach-ins, conferences, and seminars on the issues of corporate globalization organized by civil society groups around the world. Dozens of books, articles, newsletters, and e-mail subscriber lists told the story: far from advancing universal democracy and prosperity, the true intention of "free" trade agreements is to consolidate corporate control of the world's resources, markets, labor, and technology for short-term profits.

On November 30, 1999, four years after the first IFG teach-in, trade representatives from all over the world met in Seattle, Washington, with representatives of the largest transnational corporations for a World Trade Organization (WTO) meeting. Their purpose was to craft global trade rules that would preempt the national laws of every member country. Some 50,000 union members, people of faith, environmentalists, youth, indigenous peoples, peace and human rights activists, feminists, small farmers, and others gathered in the streets of Seattle to express their opposition.

Seattle was only the tip of a very large iceberg. Simultaneous protests around the world brought hundreds of thousands of people to the streets. Seattle was not the first such protest, nor was it the largest, but it was the first to get intense global media coverage, and it succeeded in forcing the premature closure of the Seattle negotiations. That success inspired and emboldened a series of increasingly massive protests wherever the corporate oligarchy met to advance its agenda—until September 11, 2001.

When nineteen terrorists armed with box cutters brought down the New York City World Trade Towers—the symbolic world headquarters of corporate rule—they generated a flood of global sympathy for those who died and their bereaved families and turned Wall Street from villain to victim.

Within days of the attack, the US government declared perpetual war against terrorism, began rolling back civil liberties, and branded dissent as support for terrorists. Leaders of many other governments, glad for an excuse to limit dissent and buttress their own power, followed the US government's example. Around the world, voices of resistance against corporate globalization were briefly stunned into silence as the United States launched a major war in Afghanistan and talked of possible preemptive military action against Iraq, North Korea, Iran, Syria, and Libya—none of which had any connection to the 9/11 attack.

Influential political analysts debated the merits of an American empire. Documents circulated in which key administration officials openly advocated imposing a Pax Americana on the world through the unilateral application of US military power in the manner of the ancient Roman Empire.[1]

Instantly, the threat to freedom and democracy posed by trade agreements paled in comparative significance.

Outflanked, upstaged, and lacking a rallying focal point for public protests, the global resistance against the advance of corporate empire through deceptively labeled and surreptitiously negotiated free trade agreements lost its momentum, visibility, and focus. Contrary to appearance, however, the social energies it focused did not die; they scattered. As they scattered, they sparked countless new but less visible, less clearly connected initiatives, creating the foundation for a deep transformation of institutional power far beyond simply blocking the abuse of trade agreements that undermine democracy and deepen corporate rule.

For Every No There Must Be a Yes

Every successful social movement builds around a perceived gap between what is and what can be. Some participants focus on resisting and discrediting the stories and institutions that drive the status quo. Others focus on the stories and practices that build the new. Some address both. A key is to recognize that while resistance is essential to limit the damage, resistance alone is a losing strategy. For every no there must be a yes.

Shortly after the historic 1995 IFG teach-in, I joined with Sarah van Gelder and other colleagues to found YES! Magazine (http://yesmagazine .org), a nonprofit media organization dedicated to communicating powerful ideas and practical actions for transformational change. Our initial purpose was simply to keep alive the truth that there are deeply democratic, locally rooted alternatives to corporate rule and to a culture of individualism and materialism. Now as millions mobilize to make those alternatives a reality, we document and communicate the richness, variety, learning, and significance of their initiatives, reflect the varied emerging social movements back to themselves, and facilitate the articulation and communication of a shared vision of hope and possibility. Van Gelder serves as editor in chief. Fran Korten, my life partner, serves as publisher and executive director. I serve as board chair.

For some years I had sensed that a viable human economy must organize the way the rest of nature organizes. Yet mainstream biologists seemed to work only within the narrow "competition for survival" frame of neo-Darwinism used by market fundamentalists to legitimate their life-destroying theories. They seemed as out of touch with life's deeper processes as the economists who embrace market fundamentalism.

By chance, in 1996 I met Mae-Wan Ho and Elisabet Sahtouris, two leading advocates of the new biology. Both study living systems as self-organizing place-based cooperative communities. They observe that the evident competition within and between species is only one element of far more complex and fundamentally cooperative processes by which life organizes to maintain the conditions essential to its own existence. The underlying organizing principles of living communities in fact align to a remarkable extent with the principles of the community-based market economies envisioned by classical economists—of whom Adam Smith is the leading example.

I became an avid student of Ho, Sahtouris, and subsequently of Janine Benyus and Lynn Margulis. I explored the implications of their work for economic-system design in *The Post-Corporate World: Life after Capitalism*, which launched in 1999 at United Nations headquarters in New York City.

In the meantime, the IFG turned its primary attention from honing and documenting its critique of corporate rule to searching for a North-South consensus on an alternative governance framework for the global economy. We all shared a commitment to global justice and sustainability, but soon discovered some important and highly instructive differences in approach. Those of us from the geographical North were generally drawn to global solutions imposed by global institutions on national governments and local communities. Those from the geographical South noted that global solutions dictated by global institutions invariably favor the interests of the world's wealthiest people and most powerful nations.

Our Southern colleagues favored local initiatives based on local resources, needs, and cultural preferences. This view aligns with the organizing principles of healthy living systems. Eventually, we reached a consensus that the proper approach is a system of global institutions that support individual nations and communities in finding their distinctive path to justice and sustainability consistent with their resources, priorities, and values.

Under the skilled and heroic editorial leadership of John Cavanagh and Jerry Mander, we compiled and shared our conclusions in a report coauthored by twenty-one strong-minded intellectual activists of widely diverse backgrounds. The first edition of *Alternatives to Economic Globalization: A Better World Is Possible* was published in 2002. An updated and expanded edition was published in 2004. It continues to provide the best available institutional framework for a planetary system of local living economies.

In May 2001, Elisabet Sahtouris and I were invited by Social Venture Network, an alliance of extraordinary entrepreneurs at the authentic leading edge of the socially responsible business movement, to conduct a workshop exploring how living-system design principles might be applied to the design of a global system of community-based economies. That theme became the frame for SVN's fall 2001 conference. An after-conference workshop launched an initiative led by Judy Wicks and Laury Hammel, two visionary SVN leaders with a passionate commitment to the idea that the proper defining purpose of business is to serve life and community, to form the Business Alliance for Local Living Economies (BALLE), an alliance of local-economy initiatives throughout the United States and Canada. I served on the founding board through 2012.

Epic Challenge

In the summer of 2002, Fran and I were privileged to host our longtime friend and colleague Vandana Shiva at our Bainbridge home. We spent many hours with Shiva, a global living-economy activist extraordinaire from India, discussing the simultaneous collapse of the World Trade Center towers and the global resistance against corporate globalization.

Shiva noted that the mobilization of global civil society to thwart the misuse of trade agreements to circumvent democracy was based on the by then widely accepted critique of corporate globalization. Civil society, however, had no broadly accepted framework for addressing the larger and more visible threat to liberty and democracy: the forthright imposition of imperial rule by military force.

This conversation inspired *The Great Turning: From Empire to Earth Community*, which puts the corporate drive for global empire and the countervailing struggle for freedom in the deep historical context of a 5,000-year era of rule by institutions of imperial domination. Published in 2006, *The Great Turning* frames the challenge of carrying forward the long transition from imperial rule to a deeply democratic self-organizing Earth community.

In the fall of 2008, Wall Street financial markets crashed. Interlocking financial obligations created by complex derivatives threatened to bring down the entire global economy. Governments, and in particular the US government, had no choice but to bail out the institutions responsible for the crash. Failure to do so would risk a total financial collapse in which bank accounts would disappear and all economic activity would halt—leaving us without jobs, food, electricity, gasoline, and most other essentials of daily life.

It seemed that the resulting public anger made it an ideal moment to issue a public call for a serious economic restructuring. I quickly published articles in *Tikkun* and *YES!* magazines making the case that we should stop trying to fix a phantom-wealth Wall Street economy dedicated to expropriating real wealth it had no role in creating. Instead, we should create real-wealth Main Street economies populated by businesses that provide good jobs producing beneficial goods and services in response to community needs.

Steve Piersanti, the president and publisher of Berrett-Koehler Publishers, read the *YES!* article. Late in the evening of November 24, 2008, he sent me an e-mail suggesting I expand the article into a short book. Two months later, with the amazing support of the Berrett-Koehler staff, I launched *Agenda for a New Economy: From Phantom Wealth to Real Wealth,* with its call to shut down the Wall Street casino, from the pulpit of the historic Trinity Wall Street Church at a national theological conference. That pulpit looks right down Wall Street. Life rarely gets better than that moment.

As I began writing *Agenda for a New Economy,* John Cavanagh—a long-time friend, IFG colleague, and head of the Institute for Policy Studies in Washington, DC—and I agreed to form an informal alliance of visionary colleagues we called the New Economy Working Group (NEWGroup). Based at IPS, NEWGroup works to shape and advance a practical, leading-edge national new-economy policy agenda. Cavanagh and I serve as co-chairs. We launched an expanded and updated second edition of *Agenda for a New Economy: From Phantom Wealth to Real Wealth* in 2010 as a publication of the NEWGroup.

For the Lack of an Authentic Story

In March 2012, I was a guest at a small gathering of indigenous environmental leaders convened to discuss the then-upcoming debates of the

Rio+20 UN Conference on Sustainable Development. In the conference's preparatory meetings, corporatists (those who promote corporate rule) proposed that to save nature we must put a price on her.

These indigenous leaders recognized that this proposal would accelerate the monopolization by the richest among us of the resources essential to human life. Their position was clear and unbending. Earth is our Sacred Mother and she is not for sale. Her care is our sacred responsibility. Her fruits must be equitably and responsibly shared by all. A number of nonindigenous environmental and economic justice groups embraced the Living Earth–mother theme and joined with the indigenous groups to promote a legal recognition of the rights of nature.

I was struck by the contrast between the two frames. For Wall Street, Earth is simply a pool of salable commodities. To reduce its use, raise the price. They fail to mention that this limits its use to those best able to pay.

For indigenous peoples, Earth is a living being, a self-organizing community of life that maintains the conditions essential to life and provides sustained flows of nutrients, water, and energy that all its members—including humans—require. It is our sacred human duty to assure the health of her generative systems. Their health and productivity must never be compromised. The services these system provide are a common birthright of all and their fruits are rightfully shared.

I was also struck by how clearly these two contrasting stories defined the essential difference between a phantom-wealth economy and a real-wealth economy. The nature and implications of this contrast became the foundational theme of *Change the Story, Change the Future: A Living Economy for a Living Earth,* published in 2015 and launched in a series of events at Pasadena All Saints Episcopal Church.

Disclosure Statement

The issues discussed in these pages are inseparable from basic questions of values, so it is appropriate that I disclose the underlying political and spiritual values I bring to the exchange. With regard to political values, I identify as a progressive. Yet I retain a traditional conservative's deep distrust of large institutions and any concentration of unaccountable power.

I also continue to believe in the importance of the market and private ownership, but as envisioned by Adam Smith, in contrast to the ideological vision of market fundamentalists. As I often note, I believe private property is such a good thing that everyone should have some. And we must each manage our piece in trust to pass it on in better health to those who follow us.

I have no more love for big business than I have for big government.

Nor do I believe that the possession of great wealth bestows a right to great privilege or political voice.

I share the liberal's compassion for the disenfranchised, commitment to equity, and concern for the environment. I also believe that there are essential roles for government and limits to the rights of private property. I recognize that big government can be as unaccountable and destructive to societal values as can big business. And I believe that every individual shares a responsibility to and for the whole of life.

In short, I align with those who are defining a new human path grounded in a pragmatic commitment to life as humanity's defining value and who seek a new public culture and deeply democratic governing institutions that support an emerging vision of a thriving living earth community. We of such persuasion do not easily find our place along the conventional conservative–liberal spectrum of political preference.

I am often called an economist because I speak and write about the economy. I am quite uncomfortable with that label.

I first encountered economics in college when I chose it as my undergraduate major. I soon found it mechanistic, boring, and detached from reality, so I switched to the study of human behavior and organization. I've since come to realize that what most economists peddle as settled science is grounded in moral bankruptcy and intellectual fraud. This is strong language, but our ability to navigate our way to a viable and prosperous human future requires that we confront uncomfortable truths with open eyes and truthful voices.

Although this book takes a harshly critical look at the institution of the corporation and the system within which business functions, I have never been, and am not now, anti-business. My dad was a successful hometown businessman for whom I had great respect. He loved money, but he also taught me a basic truth that was foundational to his business practice: "If you are not in business to serve your community, you have no business being in business."

An efficient system of industry and commerce is essential to human well-being. As an MBA student, I believed that global corporations might offer an answer to the problems of poverty and human conflict. I have since concluded, however, that the systemic forces nurturing the growth and dominance of global corporations are at the heart of the current human dilemma. I now believe that to avoid collective catastrophe we must radically transform the underlying system of business to restore power to the small and local.

With regard to spiritual values, I was raised in the Protestant Christian faith but find wisdom in the teachings of all the world's great religions. I believe that each person has access to an inner spiritual wisdom and that our collective salvation as a species depends, in part, on tapping into this wisdom.

I believe that as we reawaken to our true nature as living beings, born of and nurtured by a living Earth born of a living universe, we may achieve the creative balance between market and community, science and religion, and money and spirit that is essential to the creation and maintenance of healthy human societies.

This Book

Part of our inability to come to terms with institutional systems failure stems from the fact that television reduces political discourse to sound bites and academia organizes intellectual inquiry into narrowly specialized disciplines. Consequently, we become accustomed to dealing with complex issues in bits and pieces.

Yet we live in a complex world in which nearly every aspect of our lives is connected in some way with every other aspect. When we limit ourselves to fragmented approaches to dealing with systemic problems, our solutions are certain to prove inadequate. If our species is to survive the crisis we have created for ourselves, we must develop a capacity for whole-systems thought and action.

When Corporations Rule the World presents an all-too-rare whole-systems perspective. In so doing it covers a broad territory with many elements. Each element is important. Even more important are the connections that allow us to see and understand the elements within a dynamic, whole-systems frame.

Whole-systems thinking calls us to be skeptical of simplistic solutions, to cultivate our ability to see connections between problems and events that conventional discourse ignores, and to find the courage to delve into subject matter outside our direct experience and expertise.

This book presents my synthesis. I am learning as you are learning. Exercise your own independent critical judgment. Construct your own synthesis. Always bear in mind that we are all participants in an act of creation. None of us can claim a monopoly on truth in our individual and collective search for an understanding of issues that in some instances are so complex they defy human understanding.

If you are among those who work in a large corporation, I urge you to step out of your corporate role and read *When Corporations Rule the World* from the perspective of your roles as a citizen and a parent concerned for the future of your children. This may make it easier and less painful to hear and assess the book's underlying message objectively and to consider its invitation to join the movement to transform a terminally destructive system.

I am aware that what I say here may be particularly difficult for economists. If you truly believe that the frame and theories of mainstream economics represent settled science, then I suggest you put this book aside and avoid the emotional stress of outrage that reading it may provoke.

If, however, you harbor doubts about economic theory as currently taught and practiced, read on. We have urgent need for economists of open, critical, and disciplined mind to join in developing a new economics grounded in the values, logic, and lessons of healthy living systems.

Whatever the path that brought you to his book, I urge you to read it actively and critically. Question. Challenge. Bring your own perspectives and insights to bear. Consider the implications for how you live your life, and engage your activism. Discuss it with friends. Find where you agree, where you disagree, and where you find the presentation incomplete. Share insights and explore new avenues together. Take the conversation to a new level. And act.

Although the general direction we must travel becomes clearer with each passing day, no one has yet been where we must go. If we seek a well-marked road, we will search in vain. To borrow from the title of a book of conversations between Myles Horton and Paulo Freire, two of the great social activists of our time, we set our sights on a destination beyond the distant horizon and then "we make the road by walking."

Capitalism and the Suicide Economy

Perhaps the greatest threat to freedom and democracy in the world today comes from the formation of unholy alliances between government and business. This is not a new phenomenon. It used to be called fascism. . . . The outward appearances of the democratic process are observed, but the powers of the state are diverted to the benefit of private interests.

—GEORGE SOROS, international financier

None are more hopelessly enslaved than those who falsely believe they are free.

—JOHANN WOLFGANG VON GOETHE

Twenty years ago, *When Corporations Rule the World* sounded a global alarm: The consolidation of power in a global economy ruled by corporations poses a growing threat to markets, democracy, humans, and life itself.

Unfortunately, subsequent events affirm all but extraneous details of the analysis. Corporate power is now more concentrated and operates ever further beyond human control. Its exercise is more reckless. Its political domination is more complete. Its consequences are more devastating. And system collapse is more certain and imminent.

All of this is now abundantly visible. People the world over have mobilized to resist and to build the foundations of a new life-serving economy in which money is a means, not an end.

As the devastation wrought by corporate rule accelerates, time grows ever shorter. Replacing the suicide economy we have with the living economy we must bring forth is imperative, and we must accomplish it within a blink of history's eye.

If we are to move beyond the current system's deep dysfunction, we must understand its cultural and institutional sources and how they contrast with the design principles by which healthy living communities self-organize. In 1995, the year *When Corporations Rule the World* launched, the news was filled with reports of eye-popping corporate executive compensation packages, corporate downsizing, and the outsourcing of good-paying jobs to countries distinguished by their low wages and weak labor and environmental protections.

It proved to be a moment of awakening to the depth and implications of an unfolding global corporate takeover with ever more brutal consequences for families, communities, democracy, liberty, Earth, and the livelihood of billions of people. People were looking for explanations and answers that *When Corporations Rule the World* provided. Translated into twenty languages, it sold more than 150,000 copies and became an international classic.

Those who seek alternatives to the current system continue to find it an invaluable resource. Hence this 20th anniversary edition. A re-edited and more readable version of the original text is preceded by an updated prologue sharing insights from my personal experience as a participant in the growing new-economy movement. This all-new introduction presents lessons from the experience of twenty more years of capitalism's broken promises. An all-new conclusion outlines high-leverage opportunities for breakthrough change, and an updated epilogue shares thoughts on our human nature and purpose as living beings born of and nurtured by a living Earth itself born of a living universe.

The Ultimate Tyranny

I seldom used the term *capitalism* in the original edition of *When Corporations Rule the World*. The casual reader might therefore miss that it is a book about the structure and dynamics of capitalism stripped of its relentlessly promoted PR façade as the global champion of human liberty, democracy, and the market economy. In its literal meaning *capitalism* means rule by capital, more specifically rule by the owners of capital for their exclusive private benefit—or simply rule by money.

There are more idealized definitions of capitalism, but I refer to the real capitalism—the kind we are living with. This capitalism is grounded in an elitist ideology of individualism supported by an institutional system devoted to the concentration and abuse of wealth for the exclusive benefit of a private ruling oligarchy. It is the capitalism that claims to champion democracy and markets even as it destroys them. The capitalism that claims to bring universal prosperity even while denying it to all but its most favored servants. The capitalism that destroys life to make money and organizes as a suicide economy that destroys the foundations of its own existence—and ours.

Though complex in the details of its implementation, capitalism concentrates wealth through an easily understood strategy grounded in a self-evident fact: our basic needs as humans, particularly the needs of our young, are such that we survive and thrive as a species only as members of functioning families and communities.

In traditional pre-money gift economies, the relationships that bind the community into a functioning unit are defined primarily by mutual caring and commitment. In a monetized market economy these relationships are defined primarily, even exclusively, by money at the expense of the mutual caring and commitment essential to individual happiness and healthy social function.

The implications of the difference are profound. In a gift economy our survival and well-being depend on the cultivation and exercise of our capacity for love and our sense of responsibility to and for the community of which we are a part. In the monetized market economy our survival and well-being depend on money—and therefore the institutions that control our access to money.

In the fully developed capitalist economy, this means we are reduced to dependence for our basic means of living on the corporations that the oligarchs create to leverage their own financial power with the savings of others in order to acquire and manage assets far beyond their own individual means. Programmed by its internal structures to value only money in service to the demands of distant and impersonal financial markets for ever-greater profits, the corporation behaves like a money-seeking robot systematically expropriating and destroying the real wealth of living communities to make money—phantom-wealth accounting tokens—unrelated to anything of real value.

We comply because the public culture cultivated by the corporate media, educational institutions, and even some religious institutions conditions us to equate money with wealth and the making of money with wealth creation. Thus, we accept the fiction that a growing gross domestic product (GDP) means that corporate rule is making us richer as a society—ignoring its destruction of the real wealth on which our health and well-being ultimately depend.

Billionaire financiers and the CEOs of global mega-corporations may appear to be in charge. They may believe they are in charge. They receive lavish rewards beyond the dreams of the most powerful of former kings and emperors.

They are, however, but well-compensated servants. The system is master. No one of them—indeed no group of them—has the power from within to turn the inherently unjust and destructive system from the service of money to the service of life. Those who presume they can—even though they may truly believe it—become party to a deception that diverts attention from the essential work of deep system change.

The greater our dependence on money, the greater the hold the ruling corporate robots have over our lives. They control both the creation and allocation of money and our access to food, water, housing, energy, transportation, education, health care, entertainment, recreation, and the other basics of a healthy, prosperous life. The more complete their control, the greater their ability to reduce the people who do the real work of producing real goods and services to ever more desperate subservience.

We more easily recognize tyrannies imposed by a highly visible police and military force. By contrast, capitalism's mechanisms of control are subtler and largely invisible. Those it enslaves, though they may live in desperation, may be unaware of the true nature and cause of their condition and even believe themselves to be free.

Promise versus Reality

When Corporations Rule the World first launched in 1995. Implementation of the North American Free Trade Agreement (NAFTA) began the year before. The agreement had won congressional approval based on assurances to the public that removing national borders as barriers to the free movement of goods and money would bring peace, prosperity, and good jobs to all. People were just beginning to question the credibility of these promises.

NAFTA is now old news, but it merits special attention here for three reasons:

1. It provides a powerful demonstration of the yawning gap between what capitalism promises and what it delivers.

2. It illustrates the process by which capitalism extends and deepens the corporate control of markets and resources to expropriate ever more of society's real wealth at the expense of working people, taxpayers—and the rest of nature.

3. It is the model for subsequent trade agreements, including the Trans-Pacific Partnership (TPP) and the Transatlantic Trade and Investment

Partnership (TTIP), that are crafted in highly secret negotiations dominated by corporate representatives. NAFTA gives us a window into what is at stake. Knowledge of its actual results prepares us to critically evaluate the false promises by which corporatists attempt to sell new agreements to a properly skeptical public.

As summed up in a report by Public Citizen's Global Trade Watch, NAFTA advocates promised the agreement would increase net US exports to both Canada and Mexico and create 170,000 new jobs in the United States in NAFTA's first two years. It would be a bonanza for US farmers, improve environmental standards throughout North America, lift Mexico to a first-world-level of economic prosperity and stability, and significantly reduce undocumented immigration from Mexico to the United States.[1] The promises proved false on every count.

The free trade agreements that corporations craft and vigorously promote have one purpose: to advance the consolidation of global corporate rule. These corporations have two agendas regarding jobs: Eliminate as many of them as possible. And push the wages and benefits for the remainder as far down as possible—except of course for top management compensation. Any benefits for people and the broader society are purely coincidental, as the results of NAFTA so clearly demonstrate.

In 1993, the year before NAFTA went into effect, the inflation adjusted pre-NAFTA net US trade deficit with Canada and Mexico was $27.1 billion. As NAFTA was implemented, that deficit steadily rose to $177 billion in 2013—a more than sixfold increase.[2] A study by the Economic Policy Institute estimates that by 2004 the agreement had eliminated roughly a million jobs in the United States.[3]

These are only the estimated losses from NAFTA job outsourcing to Mexico and Canada. Overall US job losses, especially quality manufacturing jobs, over the past twenty years to trade-driven job outsourcing to Mexico, China, and other low-wage countries number in the millions.[4] Few of those who lost their jobs have found new ones of comparable quality with comparable pay and benefits. The permanent loss of millions of jobs, combined with an increased inflow of migrant workers displaced by NAFTA from Mexico's rural sector, has put significant downward pressure on US wages and working conditions, undermined union bargaining power, and decimated the US middle class.

We might expect that the growing US trade deficit with Mexico and the massive outsourcing of US manufacturing to the maquiladoras on the Mexican side of the border would have been a boon to the Mexican economy. Quite the contrary, according to a November 24, 2013, *New York Times* article:

NAFTA has cut a path of destruction through Mexico. Since the agreement went into force in 1994, the country's annual per capita growth flat-lined to an average of just 1.2 percent—one of the lowest in the hemisphere. Its real wage has declined and unemployment is up. As jobs disappeared and wages sank, many of these rural Mexicans emigrated, swelling the ranks of the 12 million illegal immigrants living incognito and competing for low-wage jobs in the United States.[5]

In NAFTA's first four years an estimated 28,000 small and medium-sized Mexican businesses were destroyed. This included many retail, food processing, and light manufacturing firms displaced by US big-box corporate retailers selling goods imported from Asia.[6]

Overall the buying power of the average Mexican worker has fallen well below pre-NAFTA levels as prices for basic consumer goods have risen significantly faster than wage increases. And there has been a shift from jobs with benefits in the formal sector to informal sector self-employment in street vending.[7]

As for the promised prosperity of Mexican agriculture, this is where the NAFTA story is most tragic and telling. Most everyone, with the exception of giant global agribusiness corporations, has suffered a massive loss. Corn tortillas are the staple of the Mexican diet. Before NAFTA, millions of Mexican farmers made their living growing corn on small plots of land—*ejidos*—constitutionally guaranteed to them by Mexico's land-reform program and protected by tariffs from competition from highly subsidized US corn.

NAFTA eliminated Mexican government protections and guarantees for Mexican farmers, but not for US farmers. Cheap US corn flooded Mexico. The price paid to Mexican farmers dropped by 66 percent. Indebted farmers lost their land, which was bought up by foreign firms and consolidated into large plantations producing for export, much of it to the United States to compete with family farmers here. These imports combined with changes in US agricultural policy to hasten the loss of US family farms. On the Mexican side, according to a *New Republic* article, "1.1 million small farmers—and 1.4 million other Mexicans dependent upon the farm sector—were driven out of work between 1993 and 2005."[8]

As the prices received by Mexican corn farmers fell, the deregulated retail price of tortillas to the Mexican consumer rose by 279 percent in NAFTA's first ten years. This anomaly is explained by NAFTA investment rules that facilitated the consolidation of grain trading, milling, baking, and retail and allowed the few corporations that ended up in control of these activities to raise prices and reap handsome monopoly profits.[9]

The *New York Times* reports that "as a result, 20 million Mexicans live in 'food poverty.' Twenty-five percent of the population do not have access to basic food and one-fifth of Mexican children suffer from malnutrition."[10]

High unemployment facilitates the recruitment of displaced farmers into drug syndicates. Heavy border traffic facilitates the smuggling of both drugs from Mexico to the United States and guns from the United States to Mexico. The transnational industrial manufacturing corridors established in former rural areas to accommodate factories producing for export to the United States are seriously contaminated with toxic waste, with devastating health consequences for the workers and other inhabitants.

NAFTA also introduced unprecedented privileges and protections for foreign investors far beyond those available to domestic investors. These include the right to sue governments for regulations deemed to deprive them of expected profits. Claims are adjudicated by special tribunals each made up of three private sector attorneys unaccountable to any electorate and empowered to order unlimited public compensation of aggrieved investors.

The tribunal decisions are not subject to review by the judicial systems of any of the countries involved. Furthermore, according to the *New York Times*, the tribunals have the power to overturn the judgments of national courts—including decisions of the US Supreme Court. John D. Echeverria, now a professor at Vermont Law School, calls it "the biggest threat to United States judicial independence that no one has heard of and even fewer people understand."[11]

According to Public Citizen Trade Watch:

> Foreign firms have won more than $360 million taxpayer dollars thus far in investor-state cases brought under NAFTA. Of the 11 claims currently pending under NAFTA, demanding a total of more than $12.4 billion, all relate to environmental, energy, land use, financial, public health and transportation policies—not traditional trade issues.[12]

NAFTA of course is only one example of the corporate agenda that has been playing out over the past twenty years since the original launch of *When Corporations Rule the World*.

In the larger global scene, transnational corporations continue to grow in size and reach to further consolidate their monopoly control of technology, markets, media, finance, and natural resources. The growing ownership linkages among them seriously undermine market competition and increase systemic risk—the risk that a failure in one part of the system will trigger failures throughout.

Researchers at the Swiss Federal Institute of Technology in Zurich looked at ownership relationships among 43,060 transnational corporations (TNCs). The 2007 data reveal that only 737 holding companies have accumulated ownership control of 80 percent of the total value of all transnational corporations.

Among these 737 TNCs, the researchers identified a core group that, while relatively free from control by other corporations, have ownership control of other corporations that together hold 40 percent of the economic value of all TNCs. Three-quarters of the members of this core group are financial intermediaries.[13]

This is an extraordinary anti-market concentration of economic power in a world of 7 billion people and 196 countries. It is capitalism—rule by capital—in its full expression.

The financial sector, which itself produces nothing of value, accounts for an increasing share of GDP and corporate profits. Banks are now fewer and bigger. The banks that were too big to fail in the 2008 financial crash have experienced the greatest growth.

Frequent reports of massive criminal activity by the biggest banks—including fraud, insider trading, and the rigging of interest rates—have given them a public image akin to that of criminal syndicates (and have popularized the term *bankster*).

As financial markets have become more global, they have become more interconnected, lawless, unstable, and predatory. At the same time, corporations have shifted their financial assets to offshore banking and tax havens where they avoid financial and regulatory oversight.

As expected, we have seen a corresponding growth in tax evasion, money laundering, and illegal arms and drug trafficking.[14] A growing number of global corporations that maintain their headquarters in the United States pay little or no taxes, but expect the US government to provide them with subsidies, free access to public infrastructure, and global military and legal protection for their assets.

The consolidation of global corporate rule reduces local self-reliance and self-determination; drives a continued race to the bottom on wages, social safety nets, and labor and environmental standards; and increases systemic risk and instability. As the dynamics play out, the rich get richer and the rest struggle with unemployment, low wages, job insecurity, loss of social safety nets, and the health consequences of poor diets and toxic contamination.

Capitalism's Defining Purpose

Capitalism does not set out to impoverish the many and destroy nature. It has but one driving goal: to increase the financial assets of the world's richest people. The rest is unintended collateral damage. *Forbes* magazine, the self-appointed scorekeeper, exhaustively documents the extent of capitalism's success in its intended purpose.

The world in 1995 had 365 billionaires with a combined net worth of $892 billion. In 2014 there were 1,645 billionaires with an aggregate net worth of $6.4 trillion.[15] In 1995 Bill Gates ($12.9 billion) and Warren Buffett ($10.7 billion) were the richest people in the world.[16] In 2014, Gates was still number one at $76 billion, and Buffett was down to number 4 at $58.2 billion. It now takes a minimum of $31 billion in financial assets to make it onto the *Forbes* list of the world's twenty richest people.[17]

The most revealing results from what *Forbes* calls its Billionaire Scorecard relate to the global financial crash of 2008. The Forbes compilation for March 2008, prior to the crash, reported a then all-time record of 1,125 billionaires with a combined net worth of $4.4 trillion. The crash struck the world's billionaires a mighty blow as their numbers plummeted to 793 in 2009, sharing a total net worth of $2.4 trillion.

The billionaire set, however, was the primary beneficiary of the subsequent economic "recovery." Their $6.4 trillion 2014 record represented a 50 percent increase over their pre-crash 2008 record, up a trillion dollars from just 2013. (See table 1, The *Forbes* Billionaire Scorecard.)

The US economy has developed a consistent pattern since 1940. During every period of significant GDP growth, with the sole exception of 1991 to 2000 during the Clinton administration, the share of the gain that went to the bottom 90 percent of income earners *dropped* relative to the share that went to the top 10 percent.[18]

During first three years of recovery following the 2008 crash—2009 through 2012—the share of the gain from US GDP growth that went to the bottom 90 percent actually turned negative. Not only did the bottom 90 percent not benefit from the recovery, but a portion of their previous income was redistributed upward to the top 10 percent. By far the biggest takers were the top 1 percent, who captured 95 percent of the total gains.[19] The more recent data from *Forbes* on the billionaire set suggest that the basic pattern is global and worsened through 2013 and 2014.

This conclusion is also consistent with the Credit Suisse's *Global Wealth Report 2014*, which found that total global wealth grew by $20 trillion between mid-2013 and mid-2014 to reach a record $263 trillion. This is more than twice the estimated $117 trillion of total global wealth in 2000.[20] If that $263 trillion were shared equally among the world's 2014

Table 1 The *Forbes* Billionaire Scorecard

	1995	*2008*	*2009*	*2010*	*2011*	*2012*	*2013*	*2014*
Number of billionaires	365	1,125	793	1,011	1,210	1,226	1,426	1,645
Total net worth (in trillions)	$0.9	$4.4	$2.4	$3.6	$4.5	$4.6	$5.4	$6.4

Source: Forbes.com.

population of 7.2 billion people, it would come to $36,500 for every man, woman, and child.

Of course, the distribution is very far from equal. Individuals holding over $1 million in net worth, the world's richest 0.7 percent, hold 44 percent of the global wealth. The richest 10 percent hold 87 percent. The poorest 70 percent of the world's people, those with less than $10,000 in assets, share 3 percent.[21]

Credit Suisse expects aggregate personal wealth to continue to grow, from $263 trillion in 2014 to $369 trillion in 2019. The casual reader might conclude that the next five years will be a period of rapidly growing prosperity for all and miss the near certainty that most, if not all, of the forecast gain will go to the world's richest 10 percent and the bulk of that will go to the richest 1 percent. That reader will also most certainly miss a further implication of this brief note on the basis of the Credit Suisse calculations.

> Financial assets like equities increase in value when corporate profits rise, while new issuance of financial instruments also adds to the stock of financial wealth. Similarly, the value of real assets increases as a result of rises in the quantity and price of real estate.[22]

Assessments of wealth based solely on financial assets ignore a critical distinction between the world's pool of real-wealth assets—on which our health and well-being as living members of living societies depends—and the phantom-wealth financial assets that represent personal claims against the pool of real-wealth assets.

Properly defined, real wealth (real capital assets) consists of all the many things that are essential to produce our means of happy, joyful living. It includes all the many forms of human, natural, knowledge, and infrastructure capital.

Real wealth has a real presence and value in its own right. Money is an abstraction, a number, an accounting chit. Money's value resides exclusively in the things of real value for which it can be exchanged.[23]

Securities and real estate valuations fluctuate with market price, which may bear little or no relationship to the quantity and condition of the real-wealth assets involved. Think, for example, of stock and housing bubbles. Market price is determined by market scarcity relative to the demand created by people who have the ability to pay. It has no necessary relationship to the real worth or importance of whatever is being priced.

We can live without breathable air only for a few minutes, but since it is freely available, it has no market price. Therefore economists accord it no value in their calculations. We could arguably live quite comfortably without gold or diamonds, but the market gives them a high value.

Economists fail to recognize that destroying real capital to create phantom financial assets makes us poorer as a society, not richer. They treat the creation or inflation of financial assets as wealth creation even though it may be unrelated to the creation of anything of real value. This explains why economic studies such as the Credit Suisse study routinely report that wealth is growing even as families struggle to feed their children, wages stagnate or fall, a persistent lack of jobs drives millions of people out of the labor market entirely, and critical environmental systems collapse.

Failure to distinguish between real wealth and phantom wealth also explains why most economists missed the significance of the real estate bubble in the buildup to the 2008 financial crash. It explains why they failed to recognize that US Federal Reserve stimulus measures following the crash were simply inflating securities prices, not stimulating the real economy. It even explains why many economists seem unconcerned about growing concentrations of market-killing monopoly power. The use of monopoly power to create artificial scarcity raises the market price of monopolized assets and thereby grows phantom-wealth financial assets.

The Phantom-Wealth Machine

Real wealth includes land, fertile soils, clean air and water, our labor, ideas, technology, physical infrastructure, tools, and all the essentials of human living. The foundation of all real wealth is the living wealth of living people, communities, and Living Earth. A real-wealth living economy necessarily begins with the health of Living Earth.

In blissful ignorance, the scorekeepers of the capitalist suicide economy ignore this foundational truth and measure economic performance by the rate at which the economy transforms real living wealth into the phantom-wealth financial assets of the financial oligarchy. The capitalist's ultimate ideal is to grow these phantom assets rapidly and perpetually through financial gaming and the expropriation of real wealth without producing anything of value in return.[24]

For the first time in human history, capitalism has gone global. It imposes what is essentially a growing private tax on the entire global economy. It creates immense risk of a total system collapse—not only of the economy, but of Earth's living systems as well. And it lies beyond the ability of any government to counter.

The global corporate rule that drives this unfolding disaster is no accident of history. As described in chapter 10, in 1971 Lewis Powell Jr., soon to become a US Supreme Court justice, wrote a memo to the US Chamber of Commerce that called on US corporations to assert their political power in defense of the "free enterprise system." He spelled out a detailed plan to destroy unions and to reshape media, education, the law, and politics in accordance with the corporate interest. America's corporate leaders took up the challenge. Their efforts bore visible fruit with the 1980 election of Ronald Reagan to the US presidency.

Since 1980, the overall US economy has grown 145 percent. Median household income has grown 9 percent. The average income of the top 10 percent has grown 178 percent. Corporate profits after taxes have grown 239 percent.[25] These data reflect the remarkable success of the corporatists in achieving the goals that Powell outlined. It is not enough, however, to satisfy the corporatists' insatiable greed.

A 2013 McKinsey Global Institute report notes that since the 2008 financial crash, "growth in financial assets has stalled as banks and borrowers deleverage. Cross-border capital flows have fallen sharply, sending financial integration into reverse."[26]

The report's authors celebrate the growth of global financial assets from $56 trillion in 1990 to $206 trillion in 2007, a compound annual growth rate of 7.9 percent—roughly twice the rate of global economic growth in that period. They express concern, however, that following the 2008 financial crisis, the compound annual rate of growth in financial assets "slowed to an anemic 1.9 percent" and growth in "financial depth," defined as the ratio of financial assets to GDP, suffered a reversal.[27]

What Wall Street celebrates as growth in financial depth used to be called a financial bubble—the speculative inflation of financial assets above any real value by buyers of securities whose expectations of financial returns are unrelated to reality.

The economic journalist and historian William Greider described the nature and implications of such expectations in his 1997 book, *One World, Ready or Not: The Manic Logic of Global Capitalism.*

As capital owners and financial markets accumulate greater girth and a dominating influence, their search for higher returns becomes increasingly purified in purpose—detached from social concerns and abstracted from the practical realities of commerce. . . . Since returns on capital are rising faster than the productive output that must pay them, the process imposes greater and greater burdens on commerce and societies. . . . Across many centuries, this story of finance capital's capacity to become deranged in pursuit of higher returns has played out again and again in different forms of manias and crashes.[28]

Most of the growth in financial assets during recent decades is a product of Wall Street "financial engineering" to grow the phantom-wealth financial claims of the rich on the world's common pool of real wealth—rights to energy, land, water, knowledge, and other essentials of living. It is a form of legally sanctioned theft.

In *Capital in the Twenty-First Century* Thomas Piketty documented that when the rate of financial return is greater than the rate of GDP growth, the result is growing inequality. It is telling that this came as a profound and shocking revelation to most professional economists. Most economists, however, quickly recovered to reassure one another and the public that Piketty's research was flawed—ignoring the fact that his conclusion is logically self-evident.

In a proper economy, the financial services sector is a cost center to be minimized, not a profit center to be maximized. Its proper role is to steward and allocate society's savings among competing investment proposals from individuals and businesses engaged in the production of real goods and services. The less the sector's cost relative to the value of the real goods and services generated by its investments, the greater its efficiency and beneficial contribution to the economy. The greater its own slice of the economy and share of overall profits, the less its efficiency and the greater the private tax it imposes on society.

Capitalism has converted the financial services sector from a cost center to a combination profit center, Ponzi scheme, and casino. The sector devotes most of its talent and resources to gambling on complex financial instruments called derivatives. These are created from nothing; most serve no useful societal function, defy human understanding, and create a systemic risk that threatens the entire global economy. The legendary investor Warren Buffett famously called them weapons of mass destruction.[29]

According to the Bank for International Settlements, the global notional value of derivatives contracts has reached $710 trillion, 20 percent more than before the derivatives-driven financial crash of 2008. The Wall Street banks that were too big for the US government to allow to fail in 2008 are now collectively 37 percent larger than they were just before the crash.[30]

The sector evaluates its performance by how much it grows in size and profitability relative to the growth of the overall economy, that is, by the increase in the burden it imposes on the real-wealth economy of people, community, and the rest of nature. It seeks, and expects to capture, an ever-growing share of the real economic benefit created by people and the rest of nature while contributing ever less to society in return.

Because Wall Street's complex financial instruments defy human understanding, they also defy oversight, not only by regulators but even by the institutions' own managers. These instruments create dense webs of intricate relations among the world's biggest banks and other corporations, which creates an unacceptable risk that the failure of one might result in the failure of all. As a result, government is forced to step in to prevent the failure of any one of them when its bets go bad.

If all were to fail, most of the money in circulation, which consists mainly of numbers on computer hard drives, would suddenly disappear. Without money, our money-dependent economy would come to an abrupt stop. We would suddenly be without food, water, energy, communications, and most everything else we require for our daily living.

Confident that the government cannot allow them to fail, the big banks take inordinate risks secure in the knowledge that they will reap the profits if their bets pay off and others will pay the cost if they lose. It is the most lucrative and audacious extortion racket in all of human history.

With massive government bailouts, the financial institutions that created and profited from the excesses that nearly collapsed the global economy in 2008 quickly recovered to set new records for profits, share prices, and management bonuses. Meanwhile, the real economy continues to languish with high unemployment and depressed wages as the inequality gap continues to grow at an alarming pace. These trends come at a huge cost to the health of society and Living Earth.

The British epidemiologists Richard Wilkinson and Kate Pickett provide a thorough and compelling review of research demonstrating a strong relationship between wealth equality and virtually every indicator of physical, mental, and social health and happiness. In an egregiously unequal society, we all lose no matter how much money we may have.[31]

Capitalism's most critical collateral damage is its systematic destruction of Earth's living systems for onetime profits. The impacts are pervasive, interconnected, and in many instances—at least from any meaningful human perspective—permanent. To the extent that the news media draw our attention to the consequences, it is usually to discrete and generally localized examples. This focus on specific examples ignores the larger reality that Living Earth organizes as a living community of the whole to maintain the conditions essential to life.

Climate change is the one highly publicized environmental consequence of the capitalist suicide economy regularly addressed by the media as a systemic issue on a planetary scale. In 2014, the Intergovernmental Panel on Climate Change issued its strongest and most unequivocal report to date. It outlined the risks to virtually every environmental system essential to Earth's ability to support life. The results include increases in severe weather events and sea-level rise; ocean acidification; reductions in freshwater availability, fish stocks, and food production; the spread of vector-borne diseases; the displacement of people; and more civil conflict.[32]

Human health and well-being are only possible with a healthy Living Earth. In its annual *Living Planet Report,* the World Wildlife Federation uses three indicators to show how Earth's health is in serious decline:[33]

- The **Living Planet Index** is a measure of the size and diversity of vertebrate species populations, a proxy indicator for the overall health of Earth as a living community. It shows a decline of 52 percent between 1970 and 2010. Declines are greatest among freshwater species, an indication of the depletion and contamination of freshwater sources.

- The **Ecological Footprint** is a measure of the number of Earth-equivalent planets required to sustain indefinitely the demands that humans make on the rest of nature each year. By this calculation, we exceeded the limit of one Earth in 1970. In 2014, we consumed at a rate that would require 1.5 Earth-equivalent planets to sustain.

- The **Water Footprint** is a measure of human consumption of, and demand for, freshwater relative to available supplies. In 2014 more than a third of the world's population—about 2.7 billion people—were living in river basins that experience severe water scarcity for at least one month each year. The nature and degree of stress vary dramatically by country and region.

This is the real-wealth reality that capitalism ignores as it celebrates growth in the world's phantom-wealth assets.

The only credible explanation for the Wall Street phantom-wealth boom is the US Federal Reserve's huge infusion of money into the economy under its "quantitative easing" program. Trillions of dollars were released into the Wall Street casino by the Fed with a few computer keystrokes—a gift to financial speculators in the name of economic stimulus.[34] The resulting inflation of stock and real estate bubbles quickly drove Wall Street financial indexes, profits, share prices, and management bonuses to record highs.

Meanwhile growth in the gap between economic winners and economic losers grows ever more egregious. It is a chilling demonstration of the degree of separation between the fantasy world of phantom-wealth capitalism and the real world of living people.

The economists to whom we turn for expert guidance compile fantasy phantom-wealth statistics and tell us that we are getting richer. They go on to assure us that with more tax cuts, deregulation, the privatization of public assets, and free trade we can accelerate economic growth to create sufficient wealth to end poverty and to invent and deploy the technologies required either to heal nature or to end our dependence on her. How could they get it so wrong?

Priests of Idolatry

There are many reasons why we do not rise up in rebellion against a capitalist suicide economy so openly destructive of people and the rest of nature. Two stand out.

1. As noted previously, we have been reduced to a near-total dependence on the capitalist economy for our means of living. The truth of the consequence of this dependence, particularly in the absence of a clearly defined and credible alternative, is too terrifying to contemplate.

2. Economists sporting credentials from our most prestigious universities continue to assure us that the capitalist suicide economy is creating prosperity for all, that lapses in progress toward this goal can be remedied by faster growth, and that there is no alternative.

Economists claim their assessments are based on settled science. Yet the assumptions underlying their assessments are contradicted by both logic and real-world observation, as documented in more detail in chapter 5, "Assault of the Corporate Libertarians."

The Nobel Laureate economist Joseph Stiglitz suggests that economics as currently taught and practiced is less a science than it is "the West's prevailing religion."[35] Economists bear major responsibility for promoting what Pope Francis calls "the idolatry of money and the dictatorship of an impersonal economy lacking a truly human purpose."[36]

Economists with advanced degrees have become ordained priests who assure us our sins against life and one another will one day bring an eternal earthly paradise of effortless prosperity for all. Departments of economics have become religious seminaries in which novitiates are indoctrinated into the tenets of the faith. Corporate media serve as its missionary arm; the institutions of finance, its temples of worship.

The often-cited founders of modern economics such as Adam Smith, David Ricardo, Henry George, Thomas Malthus, and Karl Marx were political economists of great intellectual breadth and depth. In the tradition of Aristotle, they sought to understand how societies organize and manage their labor and natural endowments to meet their needs. The word *economics* comes from the Greek *oikonomia*, which means "household management" or "the management of household affairs."

As documented by the science historian Robert Nadeau in *Rebirth of the Sacred*,[37] a group of economists in the mid-1800s turned away from this grand tradition and began a quest to transform the study of economics into a rigorously mathematical scientific discipline. Physics was their model.[38] To this end, the founders of what came to be known as neoclassical economic theory took a badly conceived and soon-to-be outmoded mathematical model from physics and substituted economic variables for the physical variables.

Physicists were at the time developing the model in a failed attempt to account for the phenomena of heat, light, and electricity by positing the existence of a vague and ill-defined field of protean energy. After copying the equations of the theory as written down, but ultimately abandoned, by the physicists, the creators of neoclassical economic theory (William Stanley Jevons, Léon Walras, Francis Ysidro Edgeworth, and Vilfredo Pareto) substituted ill-defined economic variables for the ill-defined physical variables, reduced all values to financial values to facilitate quantification, stripped away any consideration of political power and interests, and declared economics a science.

Strangely enough, this claim is now widely accepted despite being utterly absurd. Subsequent generations of mainstream economists extended and revised this formalism. To this day economists insist that because their formalism excludes consideration of values and power, their theories are values-neutral—despite the fact that they establish money as society's defining value, assure growing inequality, promote destruction of Earth's capacity to support life, and advance coporate rule.[39]

As Nadeau elaborated in an e-mail exchange:

> One curious result was a theory of value premised on the assumption that the real value or "right price" of goods, commodities and services can only be determined by decisions made by economic actors and that all of these decisions can be reduced to and understood in terms of a

compulsion to maximize personal utility in the pursuit of selfish interests. Natural resources that could not be valued in these terms were presumed to have no economic value.[40]

In their quest to reduce all economic values to financial values, economists equated money with wealth, making money with creating wealth, and growth in the market price of an asset with growth in real value. They defined people as financial beings rather than living beings and ignored critical distinctions between the accumulated financial assets of individuals and the health and well-being of living communities. They forgot that the only legitimate purpose of an economy is to support households in making a living—not corporations in making a killing.

Money became the measure of well-being. The firm replaced the household as the defining unit of economic organization and analysis. Other streams of economic thought were dismissed as unscientific heresy. The once-rich, broad reality-based discipline of economics (management of the household to maximize the well-being of its members) was reduced to what we might best regard as a subdiscipline of finance (management of the financial assets of the corporation to maximize financial return).

After economists reduced all variables to financial variables based on market price, they reduced all capital assets (productive resources like land, labor, and technology) to financial assets, reasoning that since productive assets can be bought and sold in the market at the prevailing market price, money is an appropriate common metric.

Failing to distinguish between phantom-wealth money and the real-wealth capital that money can buy, economists call financial assets "financial capital"—or just capital—and treat money as the most valuable of resources and the ultimate economic constraint. They thus embrace what economists themselves call a fallacy of composition—inappropriately assuming that what is true for the individual is also true for the society.

For the individual in a "developed" society, a lack of money is generally the primary constraint on consumption—including most necessities of life. It is not, however, a significant constraint for any country with its own currency and a central bank that can create money in any quantity with a few computer keystrokes.

For a society that controls its own money supply, the critical constraints are its human capital (the health and skill of its workers), its social capital (the bonds of trust and caring essential to healthy community function), and its biosystem capital (the living systems essential to Earth's capacity to support life). The capitalist suicide economy depletes all three, including the most valuable and important of all: the biosystem capital that is the foundation of life itself.

> **It can be hard to tell the difference between an economics degree and a finance degree because they seem almost the same.**
> —Finance Degree Center blog post

Knowing nothing of life except for its commodity price, phantom-wealth economists fail to notice that depleting real capital to create financial capital makes society poorer, not richer. This lapse is an extraordinary embarrassment for a discipline that claims to be the queen of the social sciences. Any normally intelligent twelve-year-old is fully capable of understanding the distinction between a living forest or fishery and a system of financial accounts that exists only as electronic traces on a computer hard drive.

By referring to financial assets as "capital" and treating them as if they have intrinsic worth, economists sustain the deception that Wall Street is creating wealth rather than manipulating the financial system to accumulate unearned and unjust accounting claims against what remains of society's shrinking aggregate pool of real wealth.

Adopting the perspective of corporate finance, phantom-wealth economists align with the interests of Wall Street corporations, whose sole business purpose is making money. They advocate for public policies that grow corporate profits and diminish household well-being.

Phantom-wealth economists serve as the well-supported propaganda arm of capitalism and the suicide economy, defending a system of economic relationships that does not and cannot serve society and threatens human viability.

For these reasons, policy guidance from most professionally certified economists is not only likely to be useless from a societal perspective but actively destructive.

Our Power, Our Choice

In the prologue, I mentioned a ten-day retreat I attended in November 1992 with the leaders of some of Asia's most influential nongovernmental organizations (NGOs). It was a source of many foundational insights that have since shaped my work. One among them was the realization that money is just a number.

During the retreat, we discussed the cultural, social, and environmental devastation sweeping Asia in development's wake. An image came to mind from *The Blob*, a horror movie in which a transparent mass of protoplasm engulfs humans and animals, feeding on their flesh by dissolving and absorbing it. It seemed that as the money economy penetrated traditional communities, it consumed life to fatten its own featureless bulk.

I puzzled for months over that image. Eventually it hit me. Money is just a number with no meaning outside the human mind. It could not act with a willful drive to consume life. What we observed made no sense—until I realized that the source of the willful drive in this evil scenario is our human will. The system's motivating force is the systemic misdirection of our life energy.

Eventually I realized that this misdirection is the consequence of the illusion that money is wealth and the measure of our individual and societal worth and well-being. Focused on money, rather than on the life we want, we align our will and the power of our life energy with the cultural stories and financial and material rewards presented by the institutions of a global suicide economy.

The web in which we are entrapped is entirely of our own making. It is a web woven of illusion. We have made the illusion real and binding through the culture and institutions of capitalism. We are left dependent on global supply chains, harmful toxins, an automobile-dependent infrastructure, destabilizing carbon energy sources, and the pillage of nature's bounty at a rate far faster than nature can regenerate. The system is locked in place by political processes corrupted by money, a judicial system that prioritizes the rights of corporations over the rights of people and the rest of nature, and an educational system that presents as settled values-free science a discipline devoted to the idolatry of money.

As the gap between the promise and reality of capitalism grows ever wider, the illusion that lures us into submission grows ever more transparent to reveal the disturbing truth that in submitting to global corporate rule and mindless consumerism, we sacrifice the joys of living and risk humankind's future. In response, millions of people are acting to reclaim their lives and rebuild their communities. They sow the seeds of an emerging global social movement dedicated to democracy, a living economy, and Living Earth. I elaborate on the nature and significance of this movement and share my current thinking on strategic priorities in the all-new conclusion, "A Living Economy for Living Earth."

I learned as a student of business management that to correct a system failure, one must first understand its cause. We are dealing with a global-scale terminal system failure. Unless we understand the cultural and institutional sources of the failure, we can easily dissipate our energy treating its highly visible symptoms rather than eliminating its more daunting and less visible causes.

Many people find that *When Corporations Rule the World* continues to be a foundational source of that essential understanding. I now invite you to visit (or revisit) the re-edited original chapters as published back in 1995. Bear in mind that the re-edited chapters that follow—up to the all-new conclusion and updated epilogue—retain the book's original time frame, circa 1995.

PART I

Cowboys in a Spaceship

CHAPTER 1

From Hope to Crisis

People who celebrate technology say it has brought us an improved standard of living, which means greater speed, greater choice, greater leisure, and greater luxury. None of these benefits informs us about human satisfaction, happiness, security, or the ability to sustain life on earth.

—JERRY MANDER

The last half of the twentieth century has been perhaps the most remarkable period in human history. Scientifically we unlocked countless secrets of matter, space, and biology. We dominated Earth with our numbers, technology, and sophisticated organization. We traveled beyond our world to the moon and reached out to the stars. A mere fifty years ago, within the lifetime of my generation, many of the things we take for granted today as essential to a good and prosperous life were unavailable, nonexistent, or even unimagined. These include the jet airplane and global commercial air travel, computers, microwave ovens, electric typewriters, photocopying machines, television, clothes dryers, air-conditioning, freeways, shopping malls, fax machines, birth-control pills, artificial organs, suburbs, and chemical pesticides—to name only a few.

This same period saw the creation of the first consequential institutions of global governance: the United Nations, the International Monetary Fund, the World Bank, and the General Agreement on Tariffs and Trade (GATT). Western Europe was transformed from a continent of warring states into a peaceful and prosperous political and economic union. The superpower conflict between East and West, and its dark specter of nuclear Armageddon, already seems a distant historical memory, eclipsed by a rush of business deals, financial assistance, and scientific and cultural exchanges. There has been a dramatic spread of democracy to nations formerly ruled by authoritarian governments. We have conquered many once-devastating ill-nesses such as smallpox and polio. In just the past thirty years, we increased life expectancy in developing countries by more than a third, and cut their infant and under-five mortality rates by more than half.[1]

One of the most significant human commitments of the last half of the twentieth century has been to economic growth and trade expansion. We have been spectacularly successful in both. Global economic output expanded from $6.4 trillion in 1950 to $35.5 trillion in 1995 (constant 1997 dollars), a 5.5-fold increase. This means that, on average, we have added more to total global output in each of the past four decades than was added from the moment the first cave dweller carved out a stone axe up to the middle of the present century. During this same period, world trade soared from total exports of $0.4 trillion to $5 trillion (1997 dollars)—an 11.5-fold increase, and well over twice the rate of increase in total economic output.[2] More than a billion people now enjoy the abundance of affluence.

These are only a few of the extraordinary accomplishments of the last half-century. We have arrived at a time in history when we truly seem to have the knowledge, technology, and organizational capacity to accomplish bold goals, including the elimination of poverty, war, and disease. This should be a time filled with hope for a new millennium in which societies will be freed forever from the concerns of basic survival and security to pursue new frontiers of social, intellectual, and spiritual advancement.

A Threefold Human Crisis

The leaders and institutions that promised that growth and development would bring this golden age are not delivering. They assail us with won-drous new technological gadgets, such as airplane seats with individual television monitors, and an information highway that makes it possible to connect to the Internet while sunning ourselves on the beach. Yet the things that most of us really want—a secure means of livelihood, a decent place to live, healthy and uncontaminated food to eat, good education and health care for our children, a clean and vital natural environment—seem to slip further from the grasp of most of the world's people with each passing day.

Fewer and fewer people believe that they have a secure economic future. Family and community units and the security they once provided are disintegrating. The natural environment on which we depend for our material needs is under deepening stress. Confidence in our major institu-tions is evaporating, and we find a profound and growing suspicion among thoughtful people the world over that something has gone very wrong.

These conditions are becoming pervasive in almost every locality of the world and point to a global-scale failure of our institutions.

Even in the world's most affluent countries, high levels of unemployment, corporate downsizing, falling real wages, greater dependence on part-time and temporary jobs without benefits, and the weakening of unions are creating a growing sense of economic insecurity and shrinking the middle class. The employed find themselves working longer hours, holding multiple part-time jobs, and having less real income. Many among the young—especially of minority races—have little hope of ever finding jobs adequate to provide them with basic necessities, let alone financial security. The advanced degrees and technical skills of many of those who have seen their jobs disappear and their incomes and security plummet mock the idea that simply improving education and job training will eliminate unemployment.

In rich and poor countries, as competition for land and natural resources grows, those people who have supported themselves with small-scale farming, fishing, and other resource-based livelihoods find their resources are being expropriated to serve the few while they are left to fend for themselves. The economically weak find their neighborhoods becoming the favored sites for waste dumps or polluting smokestacks.

Small-scale producers—farmers and artisans—who once were the backbone of poor but stable communities are being uprooted and transformed into landless migrant laborers, separated from family and place. Hundreds of thousands of young children, many without families, make lives for themselves begging, stealing, scavenging, selling sex, and doing odd jobs on the streets of cities in Asia, Africa, and Latin America. There are an estimated 500,000 child prostitutes in Thailand, Sri Lanka, and the Philippines alone.[3] Millions migrate from their homes and families in search of opportunity and a means of survival. In addition to the 25 to 30 million people working outside their own countries as legal migrants, an estimated 20 to 40 million are undocumented migrant workers, economic refugees without legal rights and with little access to basic services. Some, especially women, are confined and subjected to outrageous forms of sexual, physical, and psychological abuse.[4]

The world is increasingly divided between those who enjoy opulent affluence and those who live in dehumanizing poverty, servitude, and economic insecurity. While top corporate managers, investment bankers, financial speculators, athletes, and celebrities bring down multimillion-dollar annual incomes, approximately 1.2 billion of the world's people struggle desperately to live on less than $1 a day. One need not go to some remote corner of Africa to experience the disparities. I see it daily within a block of my apartment in the heart of New York City. Shiny chauffeured stretch limousines with built-in bars and televisions discharge their elegantly coifed occupants at trendy, expensive restaurants while homeless beggars huddle on the sidewalk wrapped in thin blankets to ward off the cold.

Evidence of the resulting social stress is everywhere: in rising rates of crime, drug abuse, divorce, teenage suicide, and domestic violence; growing numbers of political, economic, and environmental refugees; and even the changing nature of organized armed conflict. Violent crime is increasing at alarming rates all around the world.[5]

The seemingly impossible dream of millions of young people in the United States—especially those of color—is simply to have a stable family and survive to adulthood. More than half of all children in the United States are being raised in single-parent families.[6] On an average day in the United States, 100,000 children carry guns with them to school, and forty of them are wounded or killed. Rare is the city, or even small town, in which people feel truly secure in their property and persons. Private security guards and systems have become a major growth industry around the world.

In developing countries, an estimated one-third of wives are physically battered. Of every 2,000 women in the world, one is a reported rape victim. The number of actual rape victims is obviously much higher. There may be as many as 9,000 dowry-related deaths of women in India each year.[7]

In the era of "peace" that began in 1945 with the end of World War II, more than 20 million people have died in armed conflicts. Only three of the eighty-two armed conflicts between 1989 and 1992 were between states. The remainder were wars in which the combatants were killing those of their own nationality. Ninety percent of war casualties at the beginning of the twentieth century were military combatants. As the century ended, 90 percent were civilians.[8]

The increase in the number of internal wars is a primary cause of an alarming increase in the number of refugees in the world. In 1960, the United Nations listed 1.4 million international refugees. By 1992, the number had grown to 18.2 million. And it was estimated that an additional 24 million people were displaced within the borders of their own countries.[9]

Environmentally, although there have been important gains in selected localities in reducing air pollution and cleaning up polluted rivers, the deeper reality is one of a growing ecological crisis. The ever-present threat of nuclear holocaust has been replaced by the threat of increasing exposure to potentially deadly ultraviolet rays as the protective ozone layer thins. The younger generation worries whether they may be turned into environmental refugees by climate changes that threaten to melt the polar icecaps, flood vast coastal areas, and turn fertile agricultural areas into deserts.

Even at present population levels, nearly a billion people go to bed hungry each night. Yet the soils on which we depend for food are being depleted faster than nature can regenerate them, and one by one the world's productive fisheries are collapsing from overuse. Water shortages have become pervasive, not simply from temporary droughts but also from depleted water tables and rivers taxed beyond their ability to regenerate. We hear of communities devastated by the exhaustion of their forests and fisheries and of people much like ourselves discovering that they and their children are being poisoned by chemical and radioactive contamination in the food they eat, the water they drink, and the earth on which they live and play.

As we wait for a technological miracle to resolve these apparent limits on continued economic expansion, as of 1999 some 77 million people were being added every year to the world's population. Each new member of the human family aspires to a secure and prosperous share of Earth's dwindling bounty. In 1950, the year I entered high school, the world population was 2.5 billion people. On October 12, 1999, world population officially reached 6 billion. The United Nations estimates that it will reach nearly 9 billion by 2050.[10] Bear in mind that demographers make their projections using mathematical models based only on assumptions about fertility rates. These models take no account of what Earth can sustain. Given the environmental and social stresses created by current population levels, it is likely that if we do not voluntarily limit our numbers, famine, disease, and social breakdown will do it for us.

Taken together, these manifestations of institutional systems failure constitute a threefold global crisis of deepening poverty, social disintegration, and environmental destruction. Most elements of the crisis share an important characteristic: its solution requires local action—household by household and community by community. This action can be taken only when local resources are in local hands. The most pressing unmet needs of the world's people are for food security, adequate shelter, clothing, health care, and education—the lack of which defines true deprivation. With rare exception, the basic resources and capacity to meet these needs are already found in nearly every country. The natural inclination of local people is usually to give these needs priority. If, however, control lies elsewhere, different priorities usually come into play.

Unfortunately, in our modern world, control seldom rests with local people. More often it resides either with central governmental bureaucracies or with distant corporations that lack both the capacity and the incentive to deal with local needs. The result is a crisis of confidence in our major institutions.

Loss of Institutional Legitimacy

Public-opinion polls reveal a growing sense of personal insecurity and loss of faith in major institutions all around the world. Particularly telling is the public attitude in the United States, the country that defines for many of the world's people their vision of prosperity, democracy, and high-tech consumerism. Here the polls tell us that the real dream of the vast majority of Americans is not for fast sports cars, fancy clothes, caviar, giant TV screens, and country estates, as the popular media might lead one to believe. Rather, it is for a decent and secure life[11]—which American institutions are failing to provide. The single greatest fear of Americans in 1994 was job loss.[12] Only 51 percent of nonmanagement employees in the United States felt that their jobs were secure—down from 75 percent ten years earlier. A similar drop occurred in the sense of job security among management employees.[13] Fifty-five percent of adult Americans no longer believed that one could build a better life for oneself and one's family by working hard and playing by the rules.[14] The US job market has subsequently improved, but the long-term trend is toward growing instability and insecurity.

The Louis Harris polling organization's annual index of confidence in the leaders of twelve major US institutions fell from a base level of 100 in 1966 to 39 in 1994. At the bottom of the list were the US Congress (8 percent of respondents expressed great confidence), the executive branch of government (12 percent), the press (13 percent), and major companies (19 percent). Meanwhile, the Louis Harris "alienation index"—which taps feelings of economic inequity, disdain from people with power, and powerlessness—rose from a low of 29 in 1966 to 67 in 1995. A Kettering Foundation report captured the mood of the American electorate: "Americans . . . describe the present political system as impervious to public direction, a system run by a professional political class and controlled by money, not votes."[15] International polls generally support similar results for other industrial countries.[16]

Confidence in our major institutions and their leaders has fallen so low as to put their legitimacy at risk—and for good reason. On the threshold of the golden age, these institutions are working for only a fortunate few. For the many, they are failing disastrously to fulfill the promise that once seemed within our reach.

CHAPTER 2

End of the Open Frontier

If current predictions of population growth prove accurate and patterns of human activity on the planet remain unchanged, science and technology may not be able to prevent either irreversible degradation of the environment or continued poverty for much of the world.

**—ROYAL SOCIETY OF LONDON
and US NATIONAL ACADEMY OF SCIENCES**

It is impossible for the world economy to grow its way out of poverty and environmental degradation. . . . As the economic subsystem grows it incorporates an even greater proportion of the total ecosystem into itself and must reach a limit at 100 percent, if not before.

—HERMAN DALY

What has gone wrong? Why is the dream that should be in our grasp turning into a nightmare? The fundamental nature of our problem was dramatically articulated in 1968 by Kenneth Boulding in his classic essay "The Economics of the Coming Spaceship Earth."[1] Boulding suggested that our problem results from acting like cowboys on a limitless open frontier when in truth we inhabit a living spaceship with a finely balanced life-support system.

Cowboys and Astronauts

How different are the lives of the cowboy and the astronaut! The cowboys of earlier frontier societies, such as the great American West, lived in a world of sparsely populated expanses blessed with seemingly inexhaustible material resources. Except for the objections of indigenous peoples who felt that they had a right to the lands on which they and their ancestors had lived for centuries, everything was free for the taking, to be used and discarded at will for Earth to absorb and the restless winds to scatter. The opportunities for those willing to work seemed limitless, and anyone who presumed that the gain of one must be the loss of another was dismissed as shortsighted and lacking vision. Each person was expected to compete in search of his or her fortune with the assumption that the gains of the individual would in the end be a gain for the community as well.

Astronauts live on spaceships hurtling through space with a human crew and a precious and limited supply of resources. Everything must be maintained in balance, recycled; nothing can be wasted. The measure of well-being is not how fast the crew is able to consume its limited stores but rather how effective the crew members are in maintaining their physical and mental health, their shared resource stocks, and the life-support system on which they all depend. What is thrown away is forever inaccessible. What is accumulated without recycling fouls the living space. Crew members function as a team in the interests of the whole. No one would think of engaging in nonessential consumption unless the basic needs of all were met and there was ample provision for the future.

Boulding's analogy conveys a basic truth: Modern societies are practicing cowboy economics in what has become a spaceship world. We still treat nature's bounty and waste-disposal services as free for the taking; we honor the strong and equate progress with never-ending increases in the rate of our consumption. As we surmise that ancient Egyptians measured themselves by the size of their pyramids, a future civilization may look back on our era and conclude that we measured our progress by the size of our garbage dumps. Living like cowboys in a spaceship world has tragic consequences:

- It overburdens the life-support system, resulting in its breakdown and a decrease in the level of human activity Earth can ultimately sustain.

- It creates intense competition between the more powerful and weaker members of the crew for a shrinking pool of life-support services. Some crew members consume wastefully, others are deprived of basic sustenance, social tensions mount, and the legitimacy of governance structures erodes—creating significant potential for social breakdown and violence.

To address the crisis, we must come to terms with a basic reality: we have passed over the historic threshold from an open frontier to a spaceship world. Our lives depend on the life-support systems of the natural world, and that world is now full. We must adjust ourselves to the principles of a life-centered spaceship economics.[2] On our current course, we are at once plundering Living Earth and tearing apart the fabric of nonmarket social relationships that are the foundation of human civilization, a direct consequence of our misperception of the human relationship to natural systems.

From Open Frontiers to a Full World

Throughout most of human history, the aggregate demand placed on Earth's ecosystem by human economic activities has been inconsequential compared with the enormous regenerative capacity of those systems, and we have not been forced to take the issue of resource limits seriously. When industrialization caused countries to exceed their national resource limits, they simply reached out to obtain what was needed from beyond their own borders, generally by colonizing the resources of nonindustrial people. Although the consequences were sometimes devastating for the colonized people, the added impact on Earth's ecosystem was scarcely noticed by the colonizers.

Thus, Europe's industrialization was built on the backs of its colonies in Africa, Asia, and Latin America. For the United States, this same need was met largely by colonizing its western frontiers at the expense of the Native Americans who inhabited them and by expanding its economic domain to embrace Latin America and the Philippines. Japan, a more recent colonizer, used a sophisticated combination of aid, foreign investment, and trade to colonize the resources of its neighbors in East and Southeast Asia. Asia's newly industrializing countries, South Korea and Taiwan, are now reaching out in a similar manner, as are Thailand and Malaysia.

When only a small portion of the world was industrialized, environmental frontiers were available for exploitation through settlement, trade, and traditional colonization. Similarly, frontier territories served as a social safety valve to absorb surplus population from industrial societies. Between 1850 and 1914, difficult economic conditions in Britain (average population of 32 million) prompted an outward migration of more than 9 million people, mainly to the United States.[3]

The era of colonizing open frontiers is now in its final stage. The most readily available frontiers have been exploited, and the competition for the few that remain in such remote locations as Irian Jaya, Indochina, Papua New Guinea, Siberia, and the Brazilian Amazon is intensifying.

It is relevant to our current inquiry to note that the out-migration from Britain in the late nineteenth and early twentieth centuries suggests that the commonly held idea—that colonialism benefited the people of the colonizing countries—is largely myth. The situation was more ambiguous and has much in common with the new corporate colonialism of economic globalization. For the most part, its benefits went to the moneyed classes,

Figure 2.1 Transition to a Full World

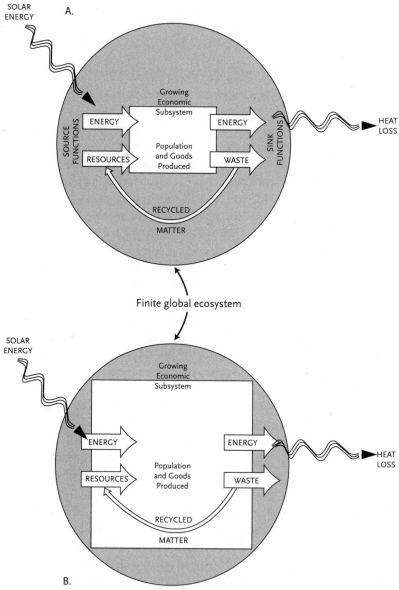

Source: Robert Goodland, Herman E. Daly, and Salah El Serafy, *Population, Technology and Lifestyle: The Transition to Sustainability* (Washington, DC: Island Press, 1992), 5.

not to the average citizen. A recent study of the British colonial experience by two American historians found that although wealthy investors profited from investments in the colonies, the middle class received only the tax bills that supported the vast military establishment required to maintain the empire. The study concluded, "Imperialism can best be viewed as a mechanism for transferring income from the middle to the upper classes."[4] Economic globalization is a modern form of the same imperial phenomenon, and it carries the same consequence.

The bottom line for our species is that because of population growth and the more than fivefold economic expansion since 1950, the environmental demands of our economic system now fill Earth's available environmental space. This has brought us to a historic transition point in the evolutionary development of our species—from living in a world of open frontiers to living in a full world—in a mere historical instant (see figure 2.1). We now have the option of adjusting ourselves to this new reality or destroying our ecological niche and suffering the consequences.

The first environmental limits that we have confronted, and possibly exceeded, are not the limits of renewable resources. They are environment's ability to absorb our wastes—referred to by ecologists as "sink functions." Evidence of our encounter with these limits is everywhere. Acid rain has damaged 31 million hectares of forest in Europe alone. At the global level, each year deserts encroach on another 6 million hectares of once-productive land. The area covered by tropical forest is reduced by 11 million hectares. There is a net loss of 26 billion tons of soil from oxidation and erosion. And 1.5 million hectares of prime agricultural land are abandoned due to salinization from irrigation projects.

Per capita grain production has been falling since 1984. Five percent of the ozone layer over North America, and probably globally, was lost between 1980 and 1990. And there has been a 2 percent increase in atmospheric carbon dioxide in the past one hundred years.[5]

There is now a vast literature and much debate assessing the data about whether a particular limit has been exceeded or will be passed within the next few years. Such exactness is far less important than coming to terms with the basic truth that we have no real option other than to re-create our economic institutions in line with the reality of a full world.

The countries that are consuming beyond their own environmental means control the rule-making process of the international economy. They adjust the rules to ensure their own ability to make up their national environmental deficits through imports—often without being mindful of the implications for the exporting countries.

El Salvador and Costa Rica . . . grow export crops such as bananas, coffee, and sugar on more than one fifth of their cropland. Export cattle ranches in Latin America and southern Africa have replaced rain forest and wildlife range. At the consumer end of the production line, Japan imports 70 percent of its corn, wheat, and barley, 95 percent of its soybeans, and more than 50 percent of its wood, much of it from the rapidly vanishing rain forests of Borneo. . . . [In the Netherlands] millions of pigs and cows are fattened on palm-kernel cake from deforested lands in Malaysia, cassava from deforested regions of Thailand, and soybeans from pesticide-dosed expanses in the south of Brazil in order to provide European consumers with their high-fat diet of meat and milk.[6]

The lands used by Southern countries to produce food for export are unavailable to the poor of those countries to grow the staples they require to meet their own basic needs. The people who are displaced to make way for export-oriented agriculture add to urban overcrowding or move to more fragile and less productive lands that quickly become overstressed. The grains that many Southern countries import from the North in exchange for their own food exports are often used primarily as feedstock to produce meat for upper-income urban consumers. The poor are double losers.

These dynamics are invisible to Northern consumers, who, if they do raise questions, are assured that this arrangement provides needed jobs and income for the poor of the South, allowing them to meet their food needs more cheaply than if they grew the basic grains themselves. It seems like a plausible theory, but in practice the only certain beneficiaries of this shift from food economy to trade dependence have been the transnational agribusiness corporations that control the global commodities trade.

Just as wealthy countries import resources when their demands exceed their own limits, they also export their surplus wastes when the volume exceeds their absorptive capacity. Indeed, waste-disposal practices reveal with particular clarity the relationship between power and the allocation of environmental costs. Polluting factories and waste-disposal sites are so consistently located in poor and minority neighborhoods or communities that we might use them as proxy indicators of the geographical distribution of political power.

Adding insult to injury, the rich commonly point to the miserable environmental conditions in which the poor are often forced to live as proof that the poor are less environmentally responsible than the wealthy. Such claims divert attention from two important realities: First, most environmental stress is a direct function of human consumption, and rich people unquestionably consume far more than do poor people. Second, poor people are far more likely to live next to waste dumps, polluting factories, and clear-cut forests than are wealthy people, but this doesn't mean that poor people's wastes are filling those dumps or that they are major consumers of the products produced in those factories or from those forests. Nor does it mean that they wouldn't prefer to live in more environmentally pristine settings. It simply means that wealthy people have the economic and political power to make sure that pollutants and wastes are dumped somewhere other than in their neighborhoods and to ensure that their neighborhoods remain pleasantly green and that polluting factories are located elsewhere. Poor people do not have this power. What we are seeing is a consequence of income inequality, not a difference in environmental awareness and concern. It can be corrected only by equalizing power.

Economic globalization has greatly expanded opportunities for the rich to pass their environmental burdens to the poor by exporting both wastes and polluting factories. This has been a particularly common practice among Japanese companies, with nearby Southeast Asia being a major recipient. The figures are striking. Japan has reduced its domestic aluminum smelting capacity from 1.2 million tons to 140,000 tons and now imports 90 percent of its aluminum.[7]

What this involves in human terms is suggested by a case study of the Philippine Associated Smelting and Refining Corporation. PASAR operates a Japanese-financed-and-constructed copper smelting plant in the Philippine province of Leyte to produce high-grade copper cathodes for shipment to Japan. The plant occupies 400 acres of land expropriated by the Philippine government from local residents at giveaway prices. Gas and wastewater emissions from the plant contain high concentrations of boron, arsenic, heavy metal, and sulfur compounds that have contaminated local water supplies, reduced fishing and rice yields, damaged the forests, and increased the occurrence of upper-respiratory diseases among local residents. Local people whose homes, livelihoods, and health have been sacrificed to PASAR now largely depend on the occasional part-time or contractual employment they are offered to do the plant's most dangerous and dirtiest jobs.

The company has prospered. The local economy has grown. The Japanese people have a supply of copper at no environmental cost to themselves. The local poor—the project's professed beneficiaries—have lost their means of livelihood and suffer impaired health. The Philippine government is repaying the foreign aid loan from Japan that financed the construction of supporting infrastructure for the plant. And Japanese are congratulating themselves for the cleanliness of their domestic environment and their generous assistance to the poor of the Philippines.[8]

There is nothing particularly special about this case, other than the fact that it has been documented. Thousands of similar stories illustrate the realities of corporate globalization. *The Economist,* an ardent globalization proponent, has argued that those who criticize such toxic dumping practices would deprive the poor of needed economic opportunities.[9]

Although an open trading system is sometimes advocated as necessary to make up for the environmental deficits of those who have too little, it more often works in exactly the opposite way—increasing the environmental deficits of those who have too little in order to provide additional environmental resources for those who already have more than their need. Furthermore, an open trading system makes it easier for the rich to keep the consequences of this transfer out of their own sight. The further out of sight those consequences are, the easier it is for those who hold power to ignore or rationalize them.

Consumption, Population, and Equity

We have endured far too many debates in which the representatives of rich countries condemn the population growth of the poor and refuse to discuss overconsumption and inequality, while the representatives of poor countries refuse to discuss population growth. In a full world, consumption, population, and equity are inseparably linked and must be dealt with holistically. Three studies illustrate these links.

The first is a study by William Rees, an urban planner at the University of British Columbia. Rees estimates that 4 to 6 hectares of land are required to maintain the consumption of the average person living in a high-income country, including the land that would be required to maintain current levels of energy consumption using renewable sources. In 1990, the total available ecologically productive land area (land capable of generating consequential biomass) in the world was estimated to be only 1.7 hectares per capita.[10] Rees estimates that the population of the Netherlands, for example, consumes an output equivalent of some 14 times as much productive land as is contained within its borders.[11] The deficits of the Netherlands and other industrial countries is covered up in part by drawing down their own natural resource stocks and in part through international trade that allows them to expropriate the resources of lower-income countries.

Among the industrial countries, per capita resource consumption is generally highest in the United States and Canada. However, since Europe and Japan have higher population densities, the case can be made that they are living even further beyond their own ecological means.

A study by Friends of the Earth Netherlands took such an analysis a step further, asking: What will be the allowable annual levels of the consumption of environmental resources and waste-absorption services for the average Dutch person in the year 2010 if (a) resource consumption levels are equal among all people living on Earth at that time and (b) the global level of resource consumption is sustainable? The results are sobering. The researchers found that in almost every area of consumption, the average person in the Netherlands is consuming far beyond his or her means and is thereby depriving people in poorer countries of the ability to meet their basic needs.[12]

Friends of the Earth USA applied the Dutch estimates to the United States and reached a similar conclusion.[13] For example, current annual per capita carbon dioxide emissions are 19.5 tons in the United States and 12 tons in the Netherlands. To meet suggested targets for the reduction of global warming, world per capita carbon dioxide emission levels from fossil fuel use must be brought down to 4 tons by 2010. If the burden of achieving this target were shared equitably, each person would be reduced in 2010 to consuming no more than one liter of carbon-based fuel per day. "A Dutch person will be given the choice of traveling 24 km (15.5 mi.) by car, 50 km (31 mi.) by bus, 65 km (40 mi.) by train or 10 km (6.2 mi.) by plane per day. A flight from Amsterdam to Rio de Janeiro can probably be undertaken only once every twenty years!"[14]

For those whose only transportation option is walking, such standards may seem luxurious. They are sobering indeed, however, for those of us accustomed to spending much of our lives in cars, planes, buses, and trains. It is even more sobering to note that our allowance of one liter of fossil fuel a day is our allowance not only for direct personal travel but for the fuels used to produce, transport, and market the items we consume as well—burdens we place on the environment but never see and tend to neglect.

A third study, presented at the annual meeting of the American Association for the Advancement of Science by Cornell University professor David Pimentel and his colleagues, asked similar questions but also looked at interactions among sectors and took population as a variable. For example, the study took into account that although we might cultivate more land, doing so would require more water. We could get more of our energy from the sun, but only by using more land. Each hectare of agricultural land could produce higher yields, but only by using more energy inputs.

The Cornell researchers also took into account that although we continue to bring new land under cultivation, 10 million hectares of productive arable land are already being abandoned each year due to severe degradation. These abandoned lands must be replaced simply to maintain existing food consumption levels. An additional 5 million hectares of new land must be put into production to feed the annual net addition to the world population, before making any dent in reducing existing malnutrition. Most of this new agricultural land comes from clearing forests.[15]

The Cornell research team concluded that Earth can sustain a population of 1 to 2 billion people consuming at a level roughly equivalent to the current per capita standard of Europe. To highlight the trade-off involved, they posed a fundamental question: "Does human society want 10 to 15 billion humans living in poverty and malnourishment or one to two billion living with abundant resources and a quality environment?"[16]

The calculations presented by all three studies are at best preliminary approximations based on controversial assumptions and the use of fragmented and often-unreliable data. They are, however, important to any realistic discussion of sustainability as they bring into focus the inescapable relationship in a full world between consumption, population, and equity and point to three important realities: First, if Earth's sustainable natural output were shared equally among its present population, the needs of all could be met. Second, it is a physical impossibility, even with the most optimistic assumptions about the potential of new technologies, for all the world's people to consume at levels even approximating those in North America, Europe, and Japan. Third, each doubling of world population reduces each individual's share of Living Earth's regenerative output by half.

If we take seriously the implications of studies such as those cited above, we have little real choice other than to give the highest priority to efforts to simultaneously end overconsumption, population growth, and inequality. They are inextricably linked, and no one, rich or poor, could possibly want the consequences that we will all bear if we do not achieve each of these outcomes in the very near future. It is of utmost importance that we develop adequate resource-use accounting systems, embodying concepts from the above-mentioned studies, to provide ourselves with adequate tools for monitoring progress toward bringing our lives into balance with Living Earth—household by household, locality by locality, and country by country. It is also essential that we break free of the myth that economic growth is the foundation of human progress.

CHAPTER 3

The Growth Illusion

To address poverty, economic growth is not an option: it is an imperative.

—MAHBUB UL HAQ,
former World Bank vice president

Economic growth provides the conditions in which protection of the environment can be best achieved.

—INTERNATIONAL CHAMBER OF COMMERCE

Perhaps no single idea is more deeply embedded in modern political culture than the belief that economic growth is the key to meeting most important human needs, including alleviating poverty and protecting the environment. Anyone who dares to speak of environmental limits to growth risks being dismissed out of hand as an anti-poor doomsayer. Thus most environmentalists call simply for "a different kind of growth," although it is seldom evident what kind that would be.

The Nobel laureate economist Jan Tinbergen and his distinguished colleague Roefie Hueting point out that there are two ways for an economy to grow, according to our current mode of reckoning. One is to increase the number of people employed. The other is to increase the labor productivity—the value of output per worker—of those already employed.

Historically, increases in labor productivity have been the most important source of growth. About 70 percent of this productivity growth has been in the 30 percent of economic activity accounted for by the petroleum, petrochemical, and metal industries; chemical-intensive agriculture; public utilities; road building and transportation; and mining—specifically the industries that are most rapidly drawing down natural capital, generating the bulk of our most toxic wastes, and consuming a substantial portion of our nonrenewable energy reserves.[1]

Furthermore, the more environmentally burdensome ways of meeting a given need are generally those that contribute most to the gross domestic product (GDP).[2] For example, driving a mile in a car contributes more to GDP than riding a mile on a bicycle. Turning on an air conditioner adds more than opening a window. Relying on processed packaged food adds more than using natural foods purchased in bulk in reusable containers. We might say that GDP, technically a measure of the rate at which money is flowing through the economy, might also be described as a measure of the rate at which we are turning resources into garbage.

We could expend a lot of effort on the probably unrealistic goal of making GDP go up indefinitely without creating more garbage. But why not instead concentrate on ending poverty, improving our quality of life, and achieving a balance with Living Earth? These are achievable goals—if we can free ourselves from the illusion that growth is the path to better living.

A Disillusioned Economist

In 1954, R. A. Butler, the British chancellor of the exchequer, spoke to a Conservative Party conference in which he pointed out that a 3 percent annual growth rate would double the national income per capita by 1980 and make every man and woman twice as rich as his or her father had been at the same age. The speech proved to be a turning point in British life. Previously, national goals had been set in terms of specific targets, such as building 300,000 houses a year or establishing a national health service. Henceforth, the primary goal would be economic growth. The ideological debate between the Left and the Right as to how a fixed pie would be distributed was largely defused. Attention centered on how to increase the size of the pie.

In 1989, British-born economist Richard Douthwaite set out to document the benefits of the subsequent doubling of Britain's per capita income. In his own words:

> Problems only arose when I attempted to identify what they [the benefits] were, especially as it quickly became apparent that almost every social indicator had worsened over the third of a century the experiment had taken. Chronic disease had increased, crime had gone up eightfold, unemployment had soared and many more marriages were ending in divorce. Almost frantically I looked for gains to set against these losses which, in most cases I felt, had to be blamed on growth.
>
> . . . Eventually . . . I gave up. The weight of evidence was overwhelming: the unquestioning quest for growth had been an unmitigated social

and environmental disaster. Almost all of the extra resources the process had created had been used to keep the system functioning in an increasingly inefficient way. The new wealth had been squandered on producing pallets and corrugated cardboard, non-returnable bottles and ring-pull drink cans. It had built airports, supertankers and heavy goods lorries, motorways, flyovers and car parks with many floors. It had enabled the banking, insurance, stock brokering, tax collecting and accountancy sector to expand from 493,000 to 2,475,000 employees during the thirty-three years. It had financed the recruitment of over three million people to the "reserve army of the unemployed." Very little was left for more positive achievements when all these had taken their share.[3]

We might apply a similar test to the more than fivefold increase in global output since 1950. The advocates of growth persistently maintain that economic growth is the key to ending poverty, stabilizing population, protecting the environment, and achieving social harmony. Yet during this same period, the number of people living in absolute poverty has kept pace with population growth: both have doubled. The ratio of the share of the world's income going to the richest 20 percent to that going to the bottom 20 percent poor has doubled. And indicators of social and environmental disintegration have risen sharply nearly everywhere. Although economic growth is not the sole cause of these problems, it certainly has not solved them.

The Limits of Growth

Few would dispute that there has been real and consequential human progress over the past several centuries and that advances in technology and the consequent productivity increases have resulted in real gains in human well-being. At the same time, as this chapter elaborates, there is little basis for assuming that economic growth, as we currently define and measure it, results in automatic increases in human welfare. As the British economist Paul Ekins points out, it is possible to conclude that a particular instance of growth has been a good thing only by:

- showing that the growth has taken place through the production of goods and services that are inherently valuable and beneficial;
- demonstrating that these goods and services have been distributed widely throughout the society; and
- proving that these benefits outweigh many detrimental effects of the growth process on other parts of society.[4]

Our measures of GDP make no such distinctions. Indeed, a major portion of what shows up as growth in GDP is a result of:

- shifting activities from the nonmoney social economy of household and community to the money economy, with the consequent erosion of social capital;
- depleting natural resource stocks such as forests, fisheries, and oil and mineral reserves at far above their recovery rates; and
- counting as income the costs of defending ourselves against the consequences of growth, such as disposing of waste, cleaning up toxic dumps and oil spills, providing health care for victims of environmentally caused illnesses, rebuilding after floods resulting from human activities such as deforestation, and financing pollution-control devices.

Standard financial accounting deducts from income an allowance for the depreciation of capital assets. The economic accounting systems by which economic growth is measured make no comparable adjustment for the depletion of social and natural capital. Indeed, economic accounting counts many costs of economic growth as economic gains, even though they clearly reduce rather than increase our well-being. The results are sometimes ludicrous. For example, the costs of cleaning up the Exxon *Valdez* oil spill on the Alaska coast (and the costs of repairing damage from the terrorist bombing of the World Trade Center in New York) counted as a net contribution to economic output. According to this distorted logic, disasters that are tragic for the people and the environment are beneficial to society.

In their book *For the Common Good*, Herman Daly and John Cobb Jr. reconstruct the national income accounts for the United States from 1960 to 1986, counting only those increases in output that relate to improvements in well-being and adjusting downward for the depletion of human and environmental resources. The result is an index of real economic welfare rather than simply aggregate output. Their index reveals that, on average, individual welfare in the United States peaked in 1969, then remained on a plateau and fell during the early and mid-1980s. Yet from 1969 to 1986, GNP per person went up by 35 percent, and fossil fuel consumption increased by around 17 percent. The main consequence of this growth has been that most of us are now working harder to maintain a declining quality of life.[5]

Often, how the economic pie is allocated is more important to our well-being than its absolute size. United Nations Development Programme (UNDP) studies show that it is not necessary to have particularly high economic output for a country to meet the basic needs of its people. In fact, some countries with relatively modest economic output do better in this regard than other countries with much higher GDP. Saudi Arabia's literacy rate is lower than Sri Lanka's despite the fact that its per capita income is fifteen times higher. Brazil's child mortality rate is four times that of Jamaica, even though its per capita income is twice as high.[6]

Obviously, some minimum level of economic output is essential to meet basic needs, and this required level is probably a good deal higher than the current output of the world's poorest countries. However, for most of the world's people, the question of whether their basic needs are met depends less on the absolute level of per capita income than on how productive output is allocated. If the priority is to provide people with a good diet, shelter, clothing, clean water, health care, basic transport, education, and other essentials of good living, then it is within the means of most countries to do so within existing levels of productive output. In many instances it would require little more than reallocating the resources now devoted to military purposes.

Clean water and proper sanitation are perhaps the most important contributors to good health and long life. Experience in places such as the state of Kerala in India prove that such necessities can be provided at quite modest income levels. By contrast, countries with high income levels are experiencing increases in rates of cancer, respiratory illnesses, stress and cardiovascular disorders, and birth defects, as well as falling sperm counts. A growing body of evidence links all these phenomena to the by-products of economic growth—air and water pollution, chemical additives and pesticide residues in food, high noise levels, and increased exposure to electromagnetic radiation.[7]

Suburbanization, greater dependence on the automobile for mobility, and an increased use of television for entertainment are associated with economic growth. Each has reduced the normal human contacts and inter-actions that used to be a regular part of village and urban life as people met on paths and sidewalks, created family and community entertainment, and congregated in local shops and coffee stalls.

Rapid economic growth in low-income countries brings modern air-ports, television, express highways, and air-conditioned shopping malls with sophisticated consumer electronics and fashion labels for the fortunate few. It rarely improves living conditions for the many. This kind of growth requires gearing the economy toward exports to earn foreign exchange to buy the things that wealthy people desire. Thus the lands of the poor are appropriated for export crops. The former tillers of these lands then find themselves subsisting in urban slums on starvation wages paid by sweatshops producing items for export. Families are broken up, the social fabric is strained to the breaking point, and violence becomes endemic. Those whom growth has favored then need still more foreign exchange to import arms to protect themselves from the rage of the excluded.

Growth and the Poor

Any mention of the need to end growth elicits protests that doing so would condemn the poor to perpetual deprivation. Ironically, the argument that the well-being of the poor depends on economic growth comes mainly from professional development workers, economists, financiers, corporation heads, and others who have no problem putting food on their tables. When the poor speak for themselves, they more often talk of secure rights to the land and waters on which they live and from which they obtain their livelihood. They seek decent jobs that pay a living wage. They want health care and education for their children. In a world in which all things come to those with money, they may also say, "We need money." Rarely, if ever, do they say, "We must have economic growth." Growth is a rich man's game.

It is all too common for poor people's deprivation to increase during periods of rapid economic expansion and decrease during periods of economic contraction. The reason is simple: the policies that favor economic expansion commonly shift income and assets to those who own property at the expense of those who labor for their livelihood. Although growth does not necessarily cause poverty, the policies advanced in its name often do.[8] Consider, for example, the following policy outcomes typically associated with economic growth:

- Depleting natural resources often provides financial gains for the economically powerful at the expense of people whose livelihood base is disrupted.
- Shifting activities from the social (nonmoney) economy to the money economy increases the dependence of the working classes on money and thereby on those who own assets, provide professional services, and control access to jobs and the creation and allocation of money.
- Shifting the control of agricultural lands, forests, and fisheries from those engaged in creating subsistence livelihoods to property owners engaged in investing for profit adds to measured economic output, redistributes the ownership of these assets to the capital-owning classes, expands the pool of low-cost wage labor, and pushes wages downward.

For centuries, the indigenous Igorot ("people of the mountains") of Benguet province, Philippines, have engaged in small-scale "pocket mining" of the rich gold veins found on their ancestral lands. The men dug small, round caves into the mountain. Women and children hammered the gold-bearing rocks into nuggets the size of corn kernels.[9] The lands of the Igorot are now dominated by huge open-pit mines operated by the Benguet Corporation—owned in approximately equal shares by wealthy Filipinos, the Philippine government, and US investors—to produce gold for export. Dozens of bulldozers, cranes, and trucks cut deep gashes into the mountain, stripping away the trees and topsoil and dumping enormous piles of rocky waste into the riverbeds. The local people tell visitors how, with their water sources destroyed, they can no longer grow rice and bananas and must go to the other side of the mountain for water to drink and bathe in. Their traditional mining grounds are threatened, and their rights ignored.[10]

Instead of using water to separate the gold from the rock, as the Igorot do, the mining company uses toxic chemicals, including cyanide compounds, and flushes them down the river, poisoning the water and killing the cattle that drink it. Downstream, rice farmers in the affected area of Pangasinan province are losing an estimated 250 million pesos a year as the mine tailings cover their irrigated fields and cause sharp declines in yields, resulting in a net population exodus. Farther down the river, fisherfolk in the gulf report substantial reductions in their catch as tailings smother the coral reefs. It's good for growth. Benguet and the other major mining companies involved earn combined net profits of 1.1 billion pesos a year—a massive resource transfer from the poor to the rich.[11] Countless such stories are told wherever mining companies operate.

The poor suffer similar consequences when timber companies move in to strip their forests bare, usually without regard for the rights of local people. As a young peasant woman in a remote community of San Fernando in the southern Philippine province of Bukidnon explained to visitors, "Without trees there is no food and without food, no life." An old man explained that before the logging trucks came to his village, "There was plenty of fish, plenty of corn, and plenty of rice."

People went on to describe how their rivers have changed shape, turned muddier, shallower. During the monsoons, the river now overflows its banks and swallows adjacent fertile fields in formerly flood-free areas. Creeks that once nourished the fields during the dry season have disappeared; landslides have become common during the rainy season. The rat population, which previously found food in the forests and was kept in check by forest predators, now ravages farmers' fields at night. In a once-prosperous community, more than four out of five children suffer some degree of malnutrition.[12]

In the name of promoting economic growth, such devastation is often heavily supported by public subsidies. For each ton of mine tailings they produce, the typical Philippine mining company earns 96.73 pesos and pays 0.5 peso in taxes.[13] In the United States, the government gives away mining rights to federal lands for $12 a hectare or less. Adding insult to injury, miners are able to take a tax deduction of 5 to 22 percent of their gross income as a "depletion allowance" to compensate them for the depletion of these federal lands. In Japan, the government offers loans, subsidies, and tax incentives for domestic mineral exploration and development.[14] Infrastructure costs associated with mining and timber extraction by Japanese companies in Southern countries are commonly funded by loans disbursed under the Japanese foreign aid program to be repaid by the host country with public funds.

As opportunities for industrial employment have declined in high-income countries, economists have looked to the service economy to pick up the slack. Little note is taken of the fact that much of the service economy expansion results from colonizing the social economies of households and communities.

These social economies once productively engaged more than half the working hours of the adult population, mostly women, in meeting many of the basic needs of families and carrying out the countless neighborly functions essential to the maintenance of healthy, caring communities. Indeed, there was a time when social economies engaged both women and men in carrying out most of the productive and reproductive activities through which people met their basic needs for food, shelter, clothing, childcare, health care, care of the elderly, housekeeping, education, physical security, and entertainment. Social economies are by nature local, nonwaged, nonmonetized, and nonmarket. They are energized more by love than by money.

As productive and reproductive functions such as childcare, health care, food preparation, entertainment, and physical security are transferred from the social economy to the market economy, they show up as additions to economic output and thus contributions to economic growth—though the transfer may do nothing to improve the quantity and quality of the services provided. This shift also increases the demand for economic overhead functions, which are counted as additions to economic output although they are actually an enormous source of economic inefficiency.

Consider that when family and community members worked directly with and for one another, there were no tax collectors, managers, government regulators, accountants, lawyers, stockbrokers, bankers, middlemen, advertising account executives, marketing specialists, investment brokers, or freight haulers collecting their share of the output of those who did the actual productive work. The full value of the goods and services produced was shared and exchanged within the family and the community, among those who actually created the value.[15] The result was an extraordinarily efficient use of resources to meet real needs.

Many people find that the market economy's overhead costs have become so high that, even with two wage earners and longer work hours, they cannot adequately meet needs that they once met quite satisfactorily on their own. Parents—often a single, impoverished female parent—are left with little time, energy, or encouragement to do more than function as income earners and night guardians.

The modern urban home has become little more than a place to sleep and watch television. Few people find time to participate in the vast array of community activities and services that once made neighborhoods more than a physical address. The dense fabric of relationships based on long-term sharing and cooperation that social economies once maintained comes unraveled. High rates of deprivation, depression, divorce, teenage pregnancy, violence, alcoholism, drug abuse, crime, and suicide are among the more evident consequences in both high- and low-income countries.[16]

Because such shifts have given women new opportunities, they are often hailed as a victory for women's equality. Yet rather than promoting new partnerships that involve men more fully in family and community as women expand their participation in the workplace, the change has more often simply increased the burden on women. This has placed heavy stresses on family relationships and left communities dependent on paid professional staff to perform functions parents once provided for their children and neighbors once provided for one another.

Many children grow up in commercial day-care centers or are left at home or in the streets without any adult supervision. Many women who started working to expand their options now find themselves tied to poorly compensated and unfulfilling jobs on which their families have become dependent.

Economists applaud the economic growth that results from creating new highly paid professional classes and new opportunities for the health care, social services, and security services industries to deal with the resulting family and community breakdown. The net costs to societies—and especially to the poor, for whom the money economy provides inadequate opportunities—are ignored.

The displacement of the poor from the lands on which they live and obtain their livelihood has been a long historical process. Time after time the consequence has been economic growth for the strong and deprivation for the weak. Economists estimate that between 1750 and 1950, Britain's per capita income roughly doubled, but the quality of life for the majority of people steadily declined. Before 1750, travelers to the British country-side reported little evidence of deprivation. For the most part, people had adequate food, shelter, and clothing, and the countryside had a prosperous appearance. Most farming was done on open fields, with families holding the rights to farm small, scattered strips of land. Even those without such rights were able to provide for themselves from the common lands, which provided grazing for their animals, rabbits to eat, and wood for their fires. A few industrious souls managed to consolidate larger properties through exchange, rental, and purchase and to hedge or wall them off from the rest—a process commonly referred to as enclosure, but this was a slow and cumbersome process.[17]

Then landed interests chose to speed up the process through the intro-duction of legislation that made enclosure a requirement. As enclosure progressed, the poor were increasingly deprived of access to the lands from which they once derived their living. With no other source of livelihood, they were forced to work as laborers for the larger farmers. The resulting surge in the labor pool depressed wages and increased the profits of the larger landowners. The introduction of land taxes forced many smaller farmers to sell the bits of land they held.

The result was a major consolidation of landholdings and a continuing flow of labor from the countryside to the city to supply the factories of the Industrial Revolution with workers—many of them women and young children—who were willing to accept employment in factories that "were viler than prisons. . . . So appalling were these conditions that British fac-tory employees in the early nineteenth century were probably worse off than the slaves on American plantations."[18]

In contrast to their experience during this early period of "economic expansion," conditions for ordinary people in Britain improved from 1914, the year World War I began, through the end of World War II, including the years between the wars, when there was no overall growth in Britain's national income. As explained by Douthwaite, the wars made it politically necessary to control the forces of capitalism. The government introduced heavy taxes on top incomes and controlled wages.

Although government held wage increases below the level of inflation, more people were employed, and their work was steady. As a consequence, the real purchasing power of most wage-earner households improved. Fur-thermore, when the government sanctioned wage increases, it frequently authorized the same absolute increase for everyone. Thus the raises for unskilled workers were proportionally higher than for skilled workers. The overall result was a massive shift toward equity.[19]

Following World War I, a reduction of the workweek from fifty-four hours to forty-six or forty-eight hours to absorb the influx of returning military personnel kept unemployment low and wages high. Those without jobs were protected by the national employment insurance scheme introduced in 1911. Paid for by the substantial taxes on high incomes, it systematically transferred income from wealthier taxpayers to those most in need.

World War II resulted in much the same consequence for the poor. The benefit came not from the growth in output that accompanied the war effort but from a combination of high demand for labor, the erosion of wage differentials, government control of profits, and the implementation of a highly progressive tax structure. Income equality increased dramatically, and the enforced saving that resulted from rationing left an enormous pent-up demand following the war, easing the transition to a peacetime economy.

Similar patterns were experienced in the United States. The imperatives of the depression of the 1930s and World War II galvanized political action behind measures that resulted in a significant redistribution of income and built the strong middle class that came to be seen as the hallmark of America's economic strength and prosperity.

The resulting structure of relative equity and shared economic prosperity remained more or less intact until the 1970s, when a combination of economic competition from East Asia, labor unrest, inflation, and a rebellious youth culture mobilized conservative forces to reassert themselves. An all-out political attack on labor unions, social safety nets, market regulation, and trade barriers realigned the institutional forces of American society behind big-money interests. In the 1970s and 1980s, the percentage of working Americans whose wages placed them below the poverty line increased sharply, and the society become increasingly polarized between haves and have-nots with respect to employment opportunities and earnings.[20]

Those who call for expanding the economic pie as the answer to poverty overlook an important reality. Whether or not a person has access to the resources required for survival depends less on absolute income than on relative income. In a free-market economy, each individual is in competition for access to inherently limited environmental space, and the person with the most money invariably wins.

As we have seen above, economic growth often raises the incomes of the wealthy faster than those of the poor. Even if all incomes were to increase at the same rate, the consequence would be much the same—the absolute gap between rich and poor would increase. It is simple arithmetic. Take the uniform annual 3 percent global increase in per capita income that the Brundtland Commission on the Environment and Development proposed as the answer to global poverty and environmental problems. That would translate into a first-year annual per capita increase (in US dollars) "of $633 for the United States; $3.60 for Ethiopia; $5.40 for Bangladesh; $7.50 for Nigeria; $10.80 for China and $10.50 for India. By the end of ten years, such growth will have raised Ethiopia's per capita income by $41—hardly sufficient to dent poverty there—while that of the United States will have risen by $7,257."[21] The per capita increase in purchasing power in the global marketplace for the average American would thus be 177 times that of the average Ethiopian.

Without concurrent redistribution, an expanding pie brings far greater benefit to the already wealthy than to the poor, increases the absolute gap between rich and poor, and further increases the power advantage of the former over the latter. This advantage becomes a life-and-death issue in a resource-scarce world in which the rich and poor are locked in mortal competition for a depleting resource base.

If the prophets of illusion who promote growth as the answer to poverty are really concerned with the plight of the poor, let them advocate measures that directly increase the ability of the poor to meet their basic needs—not tax breaks for the rich.

Growth in the Name of Development

Many development economists believe that moving a country on the path to industrialization requires that labor be forced off the farm and into the cities so that agriculture can be modernized and an urban industrial labor pool can be created. The parallels to the enclosure process in Britain are striking. Costa Rica provides a particularly egregious contemporary example of how it works.

Before the International Monetary Fund (IMF) and the World Bank restructured Costa Rica's economic policies in the name of easing its foreign-debt problems, Costa Rica was widely known as one of the most stable, peaceful, prosperous, and equitable of Southern countries. It had a strong base of small farmers and few of the large landholdings characteristic of other Latin American societies.

The policies imposed by the IMF and the World Bank shifted the economic incentives away from small farms producing foods that Costa Ricans eat toward large estates producing for export. As a consequence, thousands of small farmers have been displaced, their lands have been consolidated into large ranches and agricultural estates producing for export, and Costa Rica's income gap is becoming more like that of the other Latin American countries.

An increase in crime and violence has required sharp increases in public expenditures on police and public security. The country now depends on imports to meet basic food requirements, and the foreign debt that structural adjustment was supposed to reduce has doubled. Outrageous as the consequences of their policies have been, the IMF and the World Bank point to Costa Rica as a structural adjustment success story because economic growth has increased and the country is now able to meet its growing debt-service payments.[22]

In Brazil, the conversion of agriculture from smallholders producing food for domestic consumption to capital-intensive production for export displaced 28.4 million people between 1960 and 1980—a number greater than the entire population of Argentina.[23] In India, large-scale development projects have displaced 20 million people over a forty-year period.[24] In 1989, then current World Bank projects were displacing 1.5 million people, and projects in preparation threatened another 1.5 million. Bank staffers were unable to point to a single bank-funded project in which the displaced people had been relocated and rehabilitated to a standard of living comparable to what they enjoyed before displacement.[25]

A conference on Asian development sponsored by Asian nongovernmental organizations working at the grass roots on environmental and poverty issues revealed an aspect of Asia's development experience that the gushing reports in World Bank documents and business periodicals never mention:

> In Thailand, ten million rural people face eviction from the land they live on to make way for commercial tree farms. Ground water is depleted and mangroves are continually destroyed by export-oriented shrimp farms. Tribal people struggle for recognition of ancestral land rights in the forests of Eastern Malaysia and Indonesia. In the Philippines, the government's land reform program is systematically eroded by the conversion of prime agricultural lands into industrial estates and other non-agricultural uses—even as the country needs to spend its scarce foreign exchange on rice imports. Agricultural chemicals and toxic industrial wastes, including those brought to the region by foreign corporations and agencies under the guise of international assistance, continue to poison us. Dams and geothermal projects displace people and destroy agricultural and forest lands to meet the energy demands of

export-oriented industries. Slum dwellers are evicted to make way for industries and shopping centers that benefit others. Destructive fishing practices, commonly supported by corporate interests serving foreign markets, deprive our fisherfolk of their livelihoods and threaten the regenerative capacities of our oceans.[26]

Urban development plans in Bangkok, Thailand, call for the eviction of 300,000 people for highways and other urban development projects. Low-income families that resist find their water and electricity cut off. Further resistance is likely to result in the arson or bulldozing of their homes.[27] A million Mexican families were displaced from their farms as a consequence of the North American Free Trade Agreement. The engine of economic growth has proved far more effective in creating development refugees than in fulfilling its promise to end human deprivation in the world's low-income countries.

If our concern is with sustainable human well-being for all people, then we must penetrate the economic myths embedded in our culture by the prophets of illusion, free ourselves of our obsession with growth, and dramatically restructure economic relationships to focus on two priorities:

1. Bring human uses of the environment into balance with the regenerative capacities of the ecosystem.

2. Give priority in the allocation of available natural capital to ensuring that all people have the opportunity to fulfill their physical needs adequately and to pursue their full social, cultural, intellectual, and spiritual development.

Among the barriers to accomplishing this transformation is the powerful coalition of political interests aligned behind an institutional agenda that is taking us in a quite different direction. These are the corporate interests that benefit when societies make the pursuit of economic growth the organizing principle of public policy.

PART II

Contest for Sovereignty

CHAPTER 4

Rise of Corporate Power in America

Chartered privileges are a burden, under which the people of Britain, and other European nations, groan in misery.

—THOMAS EARLE, pamphleteer, 1823

Today's business corporation is an artificial creation, shielding owners and managers while preserving corporate privilege and existence. Artificial or not, corporations have won more rights under law than people have—rights which government has protected with armed force.

—RICHARD L. GROSSMAN and **FRANK T. ADAMS**

The fact that the interests of corporations and people of wealth are closely intertwined tends to obscure the significance of the corporation as an institution in its own right. On the more positive side, the corporate charter is a social innovation that allows for the aggregation of financial resources in the service of a public purpose. On the negative side, it allows one or more individuals to leverage massive economic and political resources behind narrowly focused private agendas while protecting themselves from legal liability for the public consequences.

Less widely recognized is the tendency of individual corporations, as they grow in size and power, to develop their own institutional agendas aligned with imperatives inherent in their nature and structure that are not wholly under the control even of the people who own and manage them. These agendas center on increasing their own profits and protecting themselves from the uncertainty of the market. They arise from a combination of market competition, the demands of financial markets, and efforts by individuals within them to advance their careers and increase their personal income.

Large corporations commonly join forces to advance shared political and economic agendas. In the United States, they have been engaged for more than 150 years in restructuring the rules and institutions of governance to suit their interests. Some readers may feel uneasy with my anthropomorphizing the corporation, but I do so advisedly, because once created, corporations tend to take on a life of their own beyond the intentions of their human participants.

Corporations have emerged as the dominant governance institutions on Earth, with the largest among them reaching into virtually every country of the world and exceeding most governments in size and power. Increasingly, it is the corporate interest rather than the human interest that defines the policy agendas of states and international bodies.

Instruments of Colonial Extraction

It is instructive to recall that the modern corporation is a direct descendant of the great merchant companies of fifteenth- and sixteenth-century England and Holland. These were limited-liability joint-stock companies to which the Crown granted charters that conferred on them the power to act as virtual states in dealing with vast foreign territories.

For example, in 1602 the Dutch Crown chartered the United East India Company, giving it a monopoly over Dutch trade in the lands and waters between the Cape of Good Hope at the southern tip of Africa and the Strait of Magellan at the tip of South America. Its charter vested it with sovereign powers to conclude treaties and alliances, maintain armed forces, conquer territory, and build forts. It subsequently defeated the British fleet and established sovereignty over the East Indies (now Indonesia) after displacing the Portuguese.[1] Early on it acquired large tracts of land in eastern Indonesia through a system of loans to cultivators that led to their eventual dispossession. It prohibited the growing of cloves on lands not in Dutch hands. Unable to produce sufficient food to sustain themselves on the remaining infertile land of their islands, the local people were obliged to buy rice from the company at inflated prices, eventually ruining the local economy and reducing the population to poverty.[2]

The British East India Company was the primary instrument of Britain's colonization of India, a country it ruled until 1784 much as if it were a private estate. The company continued to administer India under British supervision until 1858, when the British government assumed direct control.[3]

In the early 1800s, the British East India Company established a thriving business exporting tea from China and paying for its purchases with illegal opium. China responded to the resulting social and economic disruption by confiscating the opium warehoused in Canton by British merchants. This precipitated the Opium War of 1839 to 1842—which Britain won. As tribute, the British pressed a settlement on China that included the payment of a large indemnity to Britain, granted Britain free access to five Chinese ports for trade, and secured the right of British citizens accused of crimes in China to be tried by British courts.[4] This settlement was a precursor to modern "free trade" agreements imposed by powerful Northern nations on weaker Southern nations.

British Crown corporations also played an important role in the colonization of North America. The London Company founded the Virginia colony and for a time ruled it as company property. The Massachusetts Bay Company held rights to trade and colonization in the New England region. The Hudson's Bay Company, which was founded to establish British control over the fur trade in the Hudson's Bay watershed area of North America, was an important player in the British colonization of what is now Canada.

The corporate charter represented a grant from the Crown that limited an investor's liability for losses of the corporation to the amount of his or her investment in it—a right not extended to individual citizens. Each charter set forth the specific rights and obligations of a particular corporation, including the share of profits that would go to the Crown in return for the special privileges extended. Such charters were bestowed at the pleasure of the Crown and could be withdrawn at any time. Not surprisingly, the history of corporate-government relations since that day has been one of continuing pressure by corporate interests to expand corporate rights and to limit corporate obligations.

Holding Corporations at Bay

Much of America's history has been shaped by a long and continuing struggle for sovereignty between people and corporations. Although there have been similar struggles in other Western democracies, the US experience assumes special importance because of the dominant role the United States has had in shaping the institutions of the world economy since the end of World War I. This global role became increasingly self-conscious and assertive when the United States emerged from World War II as the world's most powerful nation.

Even as its economic power declined compared with that of Japan and Europe, the United States remained the dominant player in shaping international institutions such as the United Nations, the International Monetary Fund, the World Bank, and the World Trade Organization. As we shall see in following chapters, corporate interests have figured prominently in how the United States has defined its national interest in relation to these and other global institutions. Thus the history of corporate power in the United States, which was born of a revolution against the abusive power of the British kings and the chartered corporations used by the Crown to maintain control over colonial economies,[5] is of more than purely national significance.

The English Parliament, which during the seventeenth and eighteenth centuries was made up of wealthy landowners, merchants, and manufacturers, passed many laws intended to protect and extend their private monopoly interests. One set of laws, for example, required that all goods exported to the colonies from Europe or Asia first pass through England. Similarly, specified products imported from the colonies also had to be sent first to England. The Navigation Acts required that all goods shipped to or from the colonies be carried on English or colonial ships manned by English or colonial crews. Furthermore, although they had the necessary raw materials, the colonists were forbidden to produce their own caps, hats, and woolen and iron goods. Raw materials were shipped from the colonies to England for manufacture, and the finished products were returned to the colonies.[6]

These practices were strongly condemned by Adam Smith in *The Wealth of Nations*. Smith saw corporations, much as he saw governments, as instruments for suppressing the beneficial competitive forces of the market. His condemnation of corporations was uncompromising. He specifically mentioned them twelve times in his classic thesis, and not once did he attribute any favorable quality to them. Typical is his observation that "it is to prevent this reduction of price, and consequently of wages and profit, by restraining that free competition which would most certainly occasion it, that all corporations, and the greater part of corporation law, have been established."[7]

The publication of *The Wealth of Nations* and the signing of the US Declaration of Independence both occurred in 1776. Each was, in its way, a revolutionary manifesto challenging the abusive control of markets to capture unearned profits and inhibit local enterprise. Smith and the American colonists shared a deep suspicion of both state and corporate power. The US Constitution instituted the separation of governmental powers to create a system of checks and balances that was carefully crafted to limit opportunities for the abuse of state power. It makes no mention of corporations, which suggests that those who framed it did not foresee or intend that corporations would have a consequential role in the affairs of the new nation.

In the young American republic, there was little sense that corporations were either inevitable or necessary. Family farms and businesses were the mainstay of the economy, much in the spirit of Adam Smith's ideal, although neighborhood shops, cooperatives, and worker-owned enterprises were also common. This was consistent with a prevailing belief in the importance of keeping investment and production decisions local and democratic.[8]

The corporations that were chartered were kept under watchful citizen and governmental control. The power to issue corporate charters was retained by the individual states, rather than being given to the federal government, so that it would remain as close as possible to citizen control. Many provisions were included in corporate charters and related laws that limited use of the corporate vehicle to amass excessive personal power.[9]

The early charters were limited to a fixed number of years and required that the corporation be dissolved if the charter were not renewed. Generally, the corporate charter set limits on the corporation's borrowing, ownership of land, and sometimes even its profits. Members of the corporation were liable in their personal capacities for all debts incurred by the corporation during their period of membership. Large and small investors had equal voting rights, and interlocking directorates were outlawed. Furthermore, a corporation was limited to conducting only those business activities specifically authorized in its charter. Charters often included revocation clauses. State legislators maintained the sovereign right to withdraw the charter of any corporation that in their judgment failed to serve the public interest, and they kept close watch on corporate affairs. By 1800, only some two hundred corporate charters had been granted by the states.[10]

In the nineteenth century an active legal struggle emerged between corporations and civil society regarding the right of the people, through their state governments, to revoke or amend corporate charters. Action by state legislators to amend, revoke, or simply fail to renew corporate charters was fairly common throughout the first half of the century. However, this right came under attack in 1819 when New Hampshire attempted to revoke the charter issued to Dartmouth College by King George III before US independence. The Supreme Court overruled the revocation on the ground that the charter contained no reservation or revocation clause.

Outraged citizens, who saw this decision as an attack on state sovereignty, insisted that a distinction be made between a corporation and the property rights of an individual. They argued that corporations were created not by birth but by the pleasure of state legislatures to serve a public good. Corporations were therefore public, not private, bodies, and elected state legislators thereby had an absolute legal right to amend or repeal their charters at will. The public outcry led to a significant strengthening of the legal powers of the states to oversee corporate affairs.[11]

As late as 1855, in *Dodge v. Woolsey*, the Supreme Court affirmed that the Constitution confers no inalienable rights on a corporation, ruling that the people of the states have not

> released their power over the artificial bodies which originate under the legislation of their representatives. . . . Combinations of classes in society . . . united by the bond of a corporate spirit . . . unquestionably desire limitations upon the sovereignty of the people. . . . But the framers of the Constitution were imbued with no desire to call into existence such combinations.[12]

Spoils of the Civil War

The US Civil War (1861–65) marked a turning point for corporate rights. Violent anti-draft riots rocked the cities and left the political system in disarray. The huge profits pouring in from military procurement contracts allowed industrial interests to take advantage of the disorder and rampant political corruption to virtually buy legislation that gave them massive grants of money and land to expand the western railway system. The greater its profits, the tighter the emergent industrial class was able to solidify its hold on government to obtain further benefits.[13] Seeing what was unfolding, President Abraham Lincoln observed just before his death:

> Corporations have been enthroned. . . . An era of corruption in high places will follow and the money power will endeavor to prolong its reign by working on the prejudices of the people . . . until wealth is aggregated in a few hands . . . and the Republic is destroyed.[14]

The nation was divided against itself by the war; the government was weakened by the assassination of Lincoln and the subsequent election of the alcoholic war hero Ulysses S. Grant as president. The nation was in disarray. Millions of Americans were rendered jobless in the subsequent depression, and a tainted presidential election in 1876 was settled through secret negotiations.[15] Corruption and insider deal making ran rampant. President Rutherford B. Hayes, the eventual winner of those corporate-dominated negotiations, subsequently complained, "This is a government of the people, by the people, and for the people no longer. It is a government of corporations, by corporations, and for corporations."[16] In his classic work, *The Robber Barons,* Matthew Josephson wrote that during the 1880s and 1890s, "The halls of legislation were transformed into a mart where the price of votes was haggled over, and laws, made to order, were bought and sold."[17]

These were the days of men such as John D. Rockefeller, J. P. Morgan, Andrew Carnegie, James Mellon, Cornelius Vanderbilt, Philip Armour, and Jay Gould. Wealth begot wealth as corporations took advantage of the disarray to buy tariff, banking, railroad, labor, and public lands legislation that would further enrich them.[18] Citizen groups committed to maintaining corporate accountability continued to battle corporate abuse at the state level, and corporate charters continued to be revoked both by courts and state legislatures.[19]

Gradually, however, corporations gained sufficient control over key state legislative bodies to virtually rewrite the laws governing their own creation. Legislators in New Jersey and Delaware took the lead in watering down citizens' rights to intervene in corporate affairs. They limited the liability of corporate owners and managers and issued charters in perpetuity. Corporations soon had the right to operate in any fashion not explicitly prohibited by law.[20]

A conservative court system that was consistently responsive to the appeals and arguments of corporate lawyers steadily chipped away at the restraints a wary citizenry had carefully placed on corporate powers. Step by step, the court system set new precedents that made the protection of corporations and corporate property a centerpiece of constitutional law. These precedents eliminated the use of juries to decide fault and assess damages in cases involving corporate-caused harm and took away the right of states to oversee corporate rates of return and prices. Judges sympathetic to corporate interests ruled that workers were responsible for causing their own injuries on the job, limited the liability of corporations for damages they might cause, and declared wage and hours laws unconstitutional. They interpreted the common good to mean maximum production, no matter what was produced or who it harmed.[21] These were important concerns to an industrial sector in which, from 1888 to 1908, industrial accidents killed 700,000 American workers—roughly a hundred a day.[22]

In 1886, in a stunning victory for the proponents of corporate sovereignty, the chief justice of the United States declared in *Santa Clara County v. Southern Pacific Railroad* that a private corporation is a natural person under the US Constitution—although, as noted above, the Constitution makes no mention of corporations. Subsequent court decisions interpreted this to mean that corporations are entitled to the full protection of the

Bill of Rights, including the right to free speech and other constitutional protections extended to individuals.[23]

Thus corporations came to claim the full rights enjoyed by individual citizens while being exempted from many of the responsibilities and liabilities of citizenship. In being guaranteed the same right to free speech as individual citizens, they achieved, in the words of Paul Hawken, "precisely what the Bill of Rights was intended to prevent: domination of public thought and discourse."[24] The subsequent claim by corporations that they have the same right as any individual to influence the government in their own interest pits the individual citizen against the vast financial and communications resources of the corporation and mocks the constitutional intent that all citizens have an equal voice in the political debates surrounding important issues.

These were days of violence and social instability brought on by the excesses of capitalism that Karl Marx described to powerful political effect. Working conditions were appalling, and wages scarcely covered subsistence. Child labor was widespread. By one estimate, 11 million of the 12.5 million families in America in 1890 subsisted on an average of $380 a year and had to take in boarders to survive.[25] Both organized and wildcat strikes were common, as was industrial sabotage. Employers used every means at their disposal to break strikes, including private security forces and federal and state military troops. Violence evoked violence, and many died in the industrial wars of this era.

These conditions gave impetus to a growing labor movement. Between 1897 and 1904, union membership rose from 447,000 to 2,073,000.[26] Unions provided fertile ground for the thriving socialist movement that was taking root in America and called for the socialization and democratic control of the means of production, natural resources, and patents. These were times of open class warfare, with zealous new recruits joining the army of the dispossessed in growing numbers, ready to fight and sacrifice for the cause. Socialists who sought to organize labor along class lines vied for primacy with more conventional unionists who preferred to organize along craft or industrial lines.[27]

These movements united ethnic groups. An emergence of black pride and culture began to unify blacks. The women's movement took hold, with women forming their own labor unions, leading strikes, and assuming active roles in populist and socialist movements.[28] In 1920, female suffrage (the right to vote) was guaranteed by a constitutional amendment.

In the end, the conditions of chaos and violence that characterized the period of explosive free-market industrial expansion were not conducive to the interests of either industrialists or labor. Competitive battles between the most powerful industrialists were cutting into profits. There was considerable fear among industrialists of the growing political power of socialist and other popular movements, which threatened to bring fundamental change that might eliminate their privileged position.

This set the stage for consolidation and compromise, which transformed social and institutional relationships among the corporate barons. Industrialists merged their individual empires to consolidate their power and limit competition among them. Formerly bitter rivals, J. P. Morgan and John D. Rockefeller joined forces in 1901 to amalgamate 112 corporate directorates, combining $22.2 billion in assets under the Northern Securities Corporation of New Jersey. This massive sum was equivalent to twice the total assessed value of all property in thirteen states in the southern United States. The result:

> The heart of the American economy had been put under one roof, from banking and steel to railroads, urban transit, communications, the merchant marine, insurance, electric utilities, rubber, paper, sugar refining, and assorted other mainstays of the industrial infrastructure.[29]

Eventually, major industrialists came to realize that by providing better wages, benefits, and working conditions, they could undercut the appeal of socialism and at the same time win greater worker loyalty and motivation. There was a parallel interest in regularizing loosely organized, craft-based production processes to take greater advantage of the methods of industrial engineering and mass production. This meant organizing around more highly structured, rule-driven production processes that demanded worker stability and discipline.

Big business came to see advantages in working with large moderate (nonsocialist) labor unions that negotiated uniform wages and standards throughout an industry and enforced worker discipline according to agreed-upon rules. These arrangements increased stability and predictability within the system without ultimately challenging the power of the industrialists or the market system.[30]

These reforms took place against a backdrop of continuing struggle. A pro-business judicial system that consistently ruled against labor interests prompted the labor movement to become increasingly political, resulting in labor's development of a legislative agenda and an alliance with the Democratic Party. Reform legislation at local, state, and national levels began to set new social standards and reshape the context of labor relations. Particularly important to labor was the Clayton Antitrust Act, which banned court injunctions against striking workers.[31]

Even so, during the Roaring Twenties, corporate monopolies were allowed to flourish within a loosely regulated national economy. A stock market fueled by borrowed money seemed to be a limitless engine of wealth creation. With faith in the free market and the power of big business at its peak, an ebullient President Herbert Hoover proclaimed, "We shall soon with the help of God be within sight of the day when poverty will be banished from the nation." Irving Fisher, perhaps the leading US economist of the day, announced that the problem of the business cycle had been solved and that the country had settled on a high plateau of endless prosperity.[32]

It was evident that the average American family was better fed, better dressed, and blessed with more of life's amenities than any average family in history.[33] This reality masked the enormous underlying inequality of an America in which just 1 percent of families controlled 59 percent of the wealth.[34] In October 1929, only a few months after Fisher announced the end of business cycles, the highly leveraged financial system came crashing down. Financial fortunes evaporated almost overnight. It took World War II to provide the impetus for a new social contract between government, business, and labor based on Keynesian economic principles that set the global economic system back on the track of prosperity.

The Ascendance and Reversal of Pluralism

By the time Franklin D. Roosevelt became president in 1933, business excesses of the 1920s, the Depression, and the resulting plight of farmers, laborers, the elderly, blacks, women, and others had produced a wave of political and cultural radicalism throughout the United States. Roosevelt feared that without dramatic action, this radicalism might overwhelm the entire structure of government. He set about to save the system by pushing through an epic agenda of social and regulatory reforms. Congress's passage of his National Industrial Recovery Act (NIRA) was key, as it gave government a mandate to play a more active role in achieving an economic recovery that market forces alone seemed unable to manage.

On May 27, 1935, the Supreme Court voided the NIRA and ruled that states could not set minimum wage standards. This decision continued a century-old pattern of Supreme Court defense of business and corporate rights over civil or human rights. The Supreme Court's action on NIRA and the minimum wage radicalized a furious Roosevelt, motivating his commitment to a sweeping reform of American institutions. He set about to break up the business trusts, strengthen the regulation of business and financial markets, and push through legislation providing stronger guarantees for worker rights. Programs of public employment were started, and a social safety net was put into place.

Roosevelt attacked the Supreme Court with a vengeance and tried to expand its membership with new appointments of his choice. His attempt to "pack" the court failed, but his charges had a distinct impact on the justices themselves, and the majority became more supportive of progressive initiatives. In the end, Roosevelt's long period in office allowed him to appoint justices to fill seven of the court's nine seats, setting the court on a liberal course that lasted until the 1970s, when the Republican president Richard Nixon began to re-create the court in its earlier pro-business image.[35]

World War II brought the government into an even more central and politically accepted role in managing economic affairs. The government placed controls on consumption, coordinated industrial output, and decided how national resources would be allocated in support of the war effort. A combination of a highly progressive tax system put in place to finance the war effort, full employment at good wages, and a strong social safety net brought about a massive shift in wealth distribution in the direction of greater equity. In 1929, there were 20,000 millionaires in the United States and 2 billionaires. By 1944 there were only 13,000 millionaires and no billionaires. The share of total wealth held by the top 0.5 percent of US households fell from a high of 32.4 percent in 1929 to 19.3 in 1949.[36] It was a great victory for the expanding middle class and for those among the working classes who rose to join its ranks.

Pluralism flourished into the 1960s, a period of cultural rebellion in the United States. A new generation, the flower children, vocally challenged basic assumptions about lifestyles, the military-industrial complex, foreign military intervention, the exploitation of the environment, the rights and roles of women, civil rights, equity, and poverty. The US corporate establishment was badly shaken by the apparent threat to its values and interests. Perhaps most threatening of all was that the young were dropping out of the consumer culture. This generation was rebelling not so much against poverty and the deprivations of exploitation as against the excesses of affluence. This rejection of materialism by a new generation of Americans in some ways presented a more fundamental threat to the system than had earlier generations of angry workers seeking a living wage and safe working conditions.

The names of consumer activist Ralph Nader and environmentalist Rachel Carson became household words. Liberal Democrats had firm control of Congress and were passing important legislation that extended the scope of governmental regulation to strengthen environmental protection and product and worker safety. The government was aggressively pursuing antitrust cases to break up monopolies and keep markets competitive.

Abroad, US corporations were under attack on two fronts. Japan and Asia's newly industrializing countries (NICs)—Taiwan, South Korea, Singapore, and Hong Kong—had become enormously successful in penetrating US markets. At the same time, US corporations were being prevented from fully penetrating Southern economies, including those of the NICs, by aggressive government support of domestic industries, protectionism, and foreign investment restrictions. US corporations felt these Southern government policies put them at an unfair disadvantage. With high taxes on corporations and investor incomes and rigorous enforcement of environmental and labor standards at home, US corporations felt doubly handicapped in global competition. US corporations cried foul and demanded the creation of "a level playing field."[37]

It was a critical historical moment, and the corporate establishment rallied to protect its interests, as will be examined in more detail in Part III. The election of Ronald Reagan as president in 1980 ushered in a concerted and highly successful effort to roll back the clock on the social and economic reforms that had created the broad-based prosperity that made America the envy of the world in order to enhance the global power and profits of US corporations.

In his insightful book *Dark Victory*, the Philippine economist Walden Bello provides a global South perspective on the Reagan agenda:

> [A] highly ideological Republican regime in Washington . . . abandoned the grand strategy of "containment liberalism" abroad and the New Deal modus vivendi at home. Aside from defeating communism, Reaganism in practice was guided by three other strategic concerns. The first was the re-subordination of the [geographical] South within a U.S.-dominated global economy. The second was the rolling back of the challenge to U.S. economic interests from the NICs, or "newly industrializing countries," and from Japan. The third was the dismantling of the New Deal's "social contract" between big capital, big labor and big government which both Washington and Wall Street saw as the key constraints on corporate America's ability to compete against both the NICs and Japan.[38]

The international debt crisis of 1982 provided an opportunity to address the threat of prospective NICs. The US-dominated World Bank and International Monetary Fund moved to restructure the economies of debt-burdened Southern countries to open them to penetration by foreign corporations. The structural adjustment policies imposed by these institutions rolled back government involvement in economic life in support of domestic entrepreneurs, eliminated barriers to imports from the North, lifted restrictions on foreign investment, and integrated Southern economies more tightly into the Northern-dominated world economy. Trade policy was the weapon of choice for imposing similar reforms on the NICs.[39]

The full political resources of corporate America were mobilized to regain its control of the political agenda and the court system. High on the political agenda were domestic reforms intended to improve the global competitiveness of the United States by getting government "off the back" of business. Taxes on the rich were radically reduced and restraints on corporate mergers and acquisitions removed. Enforcement of environmental and labor standards was weakened. The government sided with aggressive US corporations seeking to make themselves more globally competitive by breaking the power of unions, reducing wages and benefits, downsizing corporate workforces, and shifting manufacturing operations abroad to benefit from cheap labor and lax regulation.[40]

As these measures took hold in the United States, unemployment became a chronic problem, and labor unions lost members and political clout. Wages began to decline, as did the incomes of the poorest households. A fortunate few profited handsomely. The earnings of big investors, top managers, entertainers, star athletes, and investment brokers skyrocketed. The number of billionaires in the United States increased from 1 in 1978 to 120 in 1994.[41] Lending abuses by a deregulated savings and loan industry left US taxpayers with a bill for $500 billion to clean up the mess. These were hard times for ordinary citizens. Greed had a field day.

As the Reagan initiatives took hold abroad, backed by similar conservative revivals in other Western nations, the same patterns emerged in most of the other Western countries as well as the indebted countries of the South. Inequality increased within and between countries. Unemployment rose to alarming levels, and many social indicators that had shown steady improvement over the previous three decades stagnated or in some instances began to decline. Many of the indebted Southern countries fell even further into international debt. The number of billionaires in the world increased from 145 in 1987 to 358 in 1994.[42]

The Reagan administration had pledged to arrest the US decline. However, it made a number of strategic policy blunders that strengthened US military might and economic growth in the short term, but seriously weakened the US position in the global economy over the longer term. First, massive deficit spending on the military contributed to making the United States the world's leading international debtor country. The main holder of that debt was Japan, the major competitor of the United States.

Second, by denying any government role in economic planning and priority setting, the Reagan administration left the economic future of the United States entirely in the hands of corporations that were being pressed by the capital markets to focus only on short-term profits. Third, by allowing corporations to pursue their anti-labor strategy, the United States squandered its key resource in the competitive global marketplace—its human capital.[43] Overall, however, the strategy has worked brilliantly for the largest corporations, their top managers, and their wealthiest share-holders—at the expense of Earth and most of its people.

This was not the result of a formal conspiracy. Major shifts in national policy do not come about as a consequence of corporate and political elites gathering in a conference room to define a grand strategy to consolidate their personal power. They are far too independent minded and represent too broad a range of conflicting interests. As Bello observes:

> What usually occurs is a much more complex social process in which ideology mediates between interests and policy. An ideology is a belief-system—a set of theories, beliefs and myths with some internal coherence—that seeks to universalize the interests of one social sector to the whole community. In market ideology, for instance, freeing market forces from state restraints is said to work to the good not only of business, but also to that of the whole community.
>
> Transmitted through social institutions such as universities, corporations, churches or parties, an ideology is internalized by large numbers of people, but especially by members of the social groups whose interests it principally expresses. An ideology thus informs the actions of many individuals and groups, but it becomes a significant force only when certain conditions coincide. . . . Market ideology became a dominant force only when a political elite which espoused it ascended to state power on the back of an increasingly conservative middle-class social base, at the same time that the corporate establishment was deserting the liberal Keynesian consensus in its favor, because of the changed circumstances of international economic competition.[44]

A Question of Governance

Interwoven into the political discourse about free markets and free trade is a persistent message: the advance of free markets is the advance of democracy. Advocates of the free market would have us believe that an unregulated market is a more efficient and responsive mechanism for political expression than the ballot, because business is more efficient and more responsive to people's preferences than are uncaring politicians and inefficient bureaucrats. The logic is simple: In the marketplace, people express their priorities directly and precisely by how they spend their consumer dollars. A vote for one among the available political candidates is by comparison a blunt instrument for expressing choice. Therefore the market is the most effective and democratic way to define the public interest.

Given the growing distrust of government, it is a compelling message, and it embodies an important truth: markets and politics are both about governance, power, and the allocation of society's resources. It is also a misleading message that masks an important political reality. In a political democracy, each person gets one vote. In the market, one dollar is one vote, and you get as many votes as you have dollars. No dollar, no vote. Markets are inherently biased in favor of people of wealth.

Equally important, markets have a strong bias in favor of very large corporations, which command more massive financial resources than even the wealthiest individuals. As markets become freer and more global, the power to govern increasingly passes from national governments to global corporations, and the interests of those corporations diverge ever further from the broader human interest—assertions documented in detail in Parts III and IV.

People, even the greediest and most ruthless, are living beings with needs and values beyond money. We need air to breathe, water to drink, and food to eat. Most of us have families. Nearly all of us find inspiration in things of beauty, such as a natural landscape or a newborn baby. Our bodies are flesh, and real blood runs through our veins.

Behind its carefully crafted public relations image and the many fine, ethical people it may employ, the body of a corporation is its corporate charter, a legal document, and money is its blood. At its core it is an alien entity with one goal: to reproduce money to nourish and replicate itself. Individuals are dispensable. The corporation owes only one true allegiance: to the financial markets, which are more totally creatures of money than even the corporation itself.

The problem is deeply embedded in the structure and rules by which corporations are compelled to operate. The marvel of the corporation as a social innovation is that it can bring together hundreds of thousands of people within a single structure and compel them to act in accordance with a corporate purpose that is not necessarily their own. Those who revolt or fail to comply are expelled and replaced by others who are more compliant.[45]

As the Washington journalist William Greider writes in *Who Will Tell the People?*:

[The corporations'] . . . tremendous financial resources, the diversity of their interests, the squads of talented professionals—all these assets and some others are now relentlessly focused on the politics of governing.

This new institutional reality is the centerpiece in the breakdown of contemporary democracy. Corporations exist to pursue their own profit maximization, not the collective aspirations of the society. They are commanded by a hierarchy of managers, not the collective aspirations of the society.[46]

Human societies have long faced the question whether the power to rule will reside only with the rich or be shared by all. We now face a different and even more ominous question, which—to the extent that its implications are fully understood—should unite rich and poor alike in a common cause. Will the power to rule reside with people, no matter their financial circumstance, or will it reside with the artificial persona of the corporation?

During this critical historical moment, in which our species faces the fundamental challenge of rediscovering the purpose and unity of life, we must decide whether the power to govern will be in the hands of living people or will reside with corporate entities driven by a different agenda. To regain control of our future and bring human societies into balance with Earth, we must reclaim the power we have yielded to these artificial entities. One important step will be to free ourselves from the ideological illusions and policies that free corporations from human accountability.

CHAPTER 5

Assault of the Corporate Libertarians

If there were an Economist's Creed, it would surely contain the affirmation, "I believe in the Principle of Comparative Advantage." And "I believe in free trade."

—**PAUL KRUGMAN**, economist

The difference between a system dominated by General Motors and Exxon and one based upon the individual landholding farmer and small business person of an earlier day in American history may very well be greater—in the real life experience of the average person—than the difference between a system based upon large private bureaucracies in the United States and public bureaucracies in socialist nations.

—**GAR ALPEROVITZ**, political economist

In the quest for economic growth, free-market ideology has been embraced around the world with a near-religious fervor. Money is its sole measure of value, and its practice advances policies that are deepening social and environmental disintegration everywhere. The economics profession serves as its priesthood. It champions values that demean the human spirit. It assumes an imaginary world divorced from reality. And it reshapes our institutions of governance in ways that make our most urgent problems more difficult to resolve. Yet to question its doctrine has become heresy, invoking risk of professional censure and damage to one's career in most institutions of business, government, and academia. In the words of the Australian sociologist Michael Pusey, it has reduced economics to "an ideological shield against intelligent introspection and civic responsibility,"[1] and infused the study of economics in most universities with a strong element of ideological indoctrination.

The Sanctification of Greed

The beliefs espoused by free-market ideologues are familiar to anyone conversant with the language of contemporary economic discourse:

- Sustained *economic growth,* as measured by gross national product, is the path to human progress.
- *Free markets,* unrestrained by governments, generally result in the most efficient and socially optimal allocation of resources.
- *Economic globalization,* achieved by removing barriers to the free flow of goods and money anywhere in the world, spurs competition, increases economic efficiency, creates jobs, lowers consumer prices, increases consumer choice, increases economic growth, and is generally beneficial to almost everyone.
- *Privatization,* which moves functions and assets from governments to the private sector, improves efficiency, lowers prices, and increases responsiveness to consumer preferences.
- The primary responsibility of government is to provide the infrastructure necessary to advance commerce and enforce the rule of law with respect to *property rights and contracts.*

These beliefs are based on a number of explicit, underlying assumptions embedded in the theories of neoliberal economics:

- Humans are motivated by self-interest, which is expressed primarily through the quest for financial gain.
- The action that yields the greatest financial return to the individual or firm also yields the most benefit to society.
- Competitive behavior is more rational for the individual than cooperative behavior and ultimately more beneficial for society.
- Human progress and improvements in well-being are best measured by increases in the aggregate market value of economic output.

To put it in harsher language, these ideological doctrines assume that:

- People are by nature motivated primarily by greed.
- The drive to acquire is the highest expression of what it means to be human.

- The relentless pursuit of greed and acquisition leads to socially optimal outcomes.
- The interests of human societies are best served by encouraging, honoring, and rewarding the above values.

A number of valid ideas and insights about markets have become twisted into an extremist ideology that raises the baser aspects of human nature to a self-justifying ideal. Although this ideology denigrates the most basic human values and ideals, it has become so deeply embedded within the values, institutions, and popular culture of contemporary society that we accept it almost without question. This pervasive ideology plays a critical role in shaping nearly every aspect of public policy. It plays to the declining economic fortunes of the majority and to well-founded public distrust of big government in order to build a populist political constituency for agendas with decidedly nonpopulist consequences.

Reminiscent of twentieth-century Marxist ideologues, advocates of this extremist ideology seek to cut off debate by proclaiming the inevitability of the historical forces advancing their cause. They tell us that a globalized free market that leaves resource allocation decisions in the hands of giant corporations is inevitable, and we had best concentrate on learning how to adapt to the new rules of the game. They warn that those who hold back and fail to get on board will be swept aside; the rewards will go only to those who acquiesce.

The extremist quality of their position is revealed in the stark choices they pose between a "free" market unencumbered by governmental restraint or a centrally planned, state-controlled economy based on the former Soviet model. They countenance no middle ground, such as a market that functions within a framework of democratically determined rules.

Similarly, they divide the world into two groups: "free" traders who would remove all economic borders to allow goods and money to flow unimpeded by public oversight; and isolationists who would build impenetrable walls around countries, cutting off all trade and exchange with others. Again, in defiance of history and logic they recognize no middle ground, such as the possibility that governments might establish appropriate rules to assure that cross-border exchanges are fair and balanced to the mutual benefit of people on both sides.

In its various guises, this ideology is known by different names—neoclassical, neoliberal, or libertarian economics; neoliberalism, market capitalism, market fundamentalism, or market liberalism. Some economists make hair-splitting distinctions among them. For present purposes, I use the terms interchangeably. In Australia and New Zealand, Michael Pusey's book *Economic Rationalism in Canberra* has popularized the term *economic rationalism* and injected it into the public debate.[2] Latin Americans commonly use the term *neoliberalism*. In the United States it sometimes goes by *neoclassical*. Mostly in the United States it goes without a generally recognized name. Unnamed, it goes undebated, and its underlying assumptions remain unexamined.

The more descriptive label for those of this ideological persuasion, however, is *corporate libertarianism,* because whatever they call themselves, the "free"-market, "free"-trade policies they advocate do not free trade, markets, or people. Rather they free global corporations to plan and organize the world's economic affairs to the benefit of their bottom line, without regard to public consequences.

The Corporate Libertarian Alliance

Three major constituencies have joined in a powerful political alliance to advance the ideological agenda of corporate libertarianism with a dogmatic fervor normally associated with religious crusades.

Neoliberal economists: Most mainstream economists align with the neoliberal school of economic rationalism. Rationalism is defined as "the doctrine that knowledge comes wholly from pure reason, without aid from the senses."[3] This is the underlying doctrine of contemporary mainstream economics, which builds its economic models deductively from first principles, without reference to the real world. This commitment to rationalism has given economics its standing as the only truly objective, value-free social science—and led it to conclusions that often defy both common sense and observable reality. Most of the profession embraces two first principles as fundamental articles of faith: One is that individuals are motivated solely by self-interest. The other is that individual choice based on the unrestrained pursuit of self-interest leads to socially optimal outcomes. It is immediately evident to most anyone without advanced training in economics that both principles are demonstrably false.

Neoliberal economists generally treat corporations the same as individual people and presume that maximizing the freedom of corporations is the same as maximizing the freedom of real people—ignoring the reality that the corporate charter is a vehicle for creating massive concentrations of authoritarian power, and that more freedom for corporations inevitably means less freedom for most people. Through this distorting bit of intellectual sleight of hand, neoliberal economists provide corporate libertarianism with a patina of intellectual legitimacy. In return, corporate interests provide neoliberal economists with generous funding and a powerful political constituency.

Property rights advocates: Ardent property rights advocates, sometimes called "market liberals," commonly present themselves as libertarians dedicated to the defense of individual rights and freedom. While true libertarians seek to defend individual freedom against intrusion from coercive institutions of any kind, market liberals are mostly concerned with protecting the rights of property from public accountability. This highly elitist ideology in effect apportions rights to people in proportion to the property they own. According to Roger Pilon of the Cato Institute, a libertarian think tank in Washington, DC, market liberals believe that "rights and property are inextricably connected. . . . Broadly understood . . . property is the foundation of all our natural rights. Exercising those rights, consistent with the rights of others, we may pursue happiness in any way we wish." In the exercise of these rights individuals form voluntary associations with others through the mechanism of the contract.[4] In the eyes of a market liberal, the only responsibility attached to the rights of property are to respect the same rights of others, obey the law, and honor contractual agreements. Those without property have no rights that the market liberal is bound to respect.

Like the neoliberal economists, market liberals make little distinction between individuals and corporations. Corporations are presumed to have the same right as an individual to use their property in any way that suits their self-interest. Market liberals give corporate libertarianism its cast of moral legitimacy. In return, corporate interests give leading proponents of market liberalism, such as the Cato Institute, the same financial support and political leverage they give to the neoliberal economists.

Members of the corporate class: Corporations and members of the corporate class—such as corporate managers, lawyers, consultants, public relations specialists, financial brokers, and wealthy investors—constitute the third pillar of the corporate libertarian alliance. Some are drawn to corporate libertarianism purely by financial self-interest or because they are paid to do so, others by moral conviction. Although few members of the corporate class have a serious interest in the fine points of academic theories or moral philosophy, they find a natural common cause with those who provide an intellectual and ethical case for freeing corporations from the restraining hand of government and absolving them of moral responsibility for the social and environmental consequences of their actions. Furthermore, they have the financial resources at their disposal to handsomely reward those who legitimate their power.

This combination of economic theory, moral philosophy, and elite political interest makes for a powerful alliance. Yet in many ways it has served even its own members poorly, as its corrupting influence has not been limited to the broader society. It has led neoliberal economists to seriously debase the integrity and social utility of economics by reducing it to a system of ideological indoctrination that violates its own theoretical foundations and is deeply at odds with reality. It has similarly engaged libertarians in a cause that violates their own commitment to individual freedom, as corporations infringe on the property rights of real people and use their growing power to suppress the individual freedoms of all but society's wealthiest members. The enormous political success of the alliance in shielding corporations from public accountability has created a monster that even the members of the corporate class no longer control and is creating a world that they would scarcely wish to bequeath to their children.

The contemporary corporation increasingly exists as an entity apart— even from the people who work for it. Every member of the corporate class, no matter how powerful his or her position within the corporation, has become expendable, as many top executives have learned. As corporations gain in autonomous institutional power and become more detached from people and place, the human interest and the corporate interest increasingly diverge. It is like being invaded by alien beings intent on colonizing Earth, reducing us to serfs, and then eliminating those of us they don't need.

The Betrayal of Adam Smith and David Ricardo

It is ironic that corporate libertarians regularly pay homage to Adam Smith as their intellectual patron saint, since it is obvious to even the most casual reader of his epic work *The Wealth of Nations* that Smith would have vigorously opposed most of their claims and policy positions. For example, corporate libertarians fervently oppose any restraint on corporate size or power. Smith, on the other hand, opposed any form of economic concentration on the ground that it distorts the market's natural ability to establish a price that provides a fair return on land, labor, and capital; to produce a satisfactory outcome for both buyers and sellers; and to optimally allocate society's resources.

Through trade agreements, corporate libertarians press governments to provide absolute protection for the intellectual property rights of corporations. Smith was strongly opposed to trade secrets as contrary to market principles,[5] and he would have vigorously opposed governments enforcing a person or corporation's claim to the right to monopolize a lifesaving drug or device and to charge whatever the market would bear.

Corporate libertarians maintain that the market turns unrestrained greed into socially optimal outcomes. Smith would be outraged by those who attribute this idea to him. He was talking about small farmers and artisans trying to get the best price for their products to provide for themselves and their families. That is self-interest, not greed. Greed is a high-paid corporate executive firing 10,000 employees and then rewarding himself with a multimillion-dollar bonus for having saved the company so much money. Greed is what the economic system being constructed by the corporate libertarians encourages and rewards.

Smith strongly disliked both governments and corporations. He viewed government primarily as an instrument for extracting taxes to subsidize elites and intervening in the market to protect corporate monopolies. In his words, "Civil government, so far as it is instituted for the security of property, is in reality instituted for the defense of the rich against the poor, or of those who have some property against those who have none at all."[6] Smith never suggested that government should not intervene to set and enforce minimum social, health, worker safety, and environmental standards in the common interest or to protect the poor and nature from the rich. Given that most governments of his day were monarchies, the possibility probably never occurred to him.

The theory of market economics, in contrast to free-market ideology, specifies a number of basic conditions needed for a market to set prices efficiently in the public interest. The greater the deviation from these conditions, the less socially efficient the market system becomes. Most basic is the condition that markets must be competitive. I recall the professor in my elementary economics course using the example of small wheat farmers selling to small grain millers to illustrate the idea of perfect market competition. Today, four companies—ConAgra, ADM Milling, Cargill, and Pillsbury—mill nearly 60 percent of all flour produced in the United States, and two of them—ConAgra and Cargill—control 50 percent of grain exports.[7]

In the real world of unregulated markets, successful players get larger and, in many instances, use the resulting economic power to drive out or buy out weaker players to gain control of even larger shares of the market. In other instances, "competitors" collude through cartels or strategic alliances to increase their profits by setting market prices above the level of optimal efficiency. The larger and more collusive individual market players become, the greater their ability to use their monopoly power to manipulate prices, the more difficult it is for newcomers and small independent firms to survive, and the more political power the biggest firms wield to demand concessions from governments that allow them to externalize even more of their costs to the community.

Given this reality, one might expect the neoliberal economists who claim Smith's tradition as their own to be outspoken in arguing for the need to restrict mergers and acquisitions and break up monopolistic firms to restore market competition. More often, they argue exactly the opposite position—that to "compete" in today's global markets, firms must merge into larger combinations. In other words, they use a theory that assumes small firms to advocate policies that favor large firms.

Market theory also specifies that for a market to allocate efficiently, the full costs of each product must be borne by the producer and be included in the selling price. Economists call it cost internalization. Externalizing some part of a product's cost to others not a party to the transaction is a form of subsidy that encourages excessive production and use of the product at the expense of others.

When, for example, a forest products corporation is allowed to clear-cut government lands at giveaway prices, it lowers the cost of timber products, thus encouraging their wasteful use and discouraging their recycling. It also becomes difficult for more responsible producers to compete. While profitable for the company and a bargain for consumers, the public is forced, without its consent, to bear a host of costs relating to watershed destruction, loss of natural habitat and recreational areas, global warming, and diminished future timber production.

The consequences are similar when a chemical corporation dumps wastes without adequate treatment, thus passing the resulting costs of air, water, and soil pollution to the community in the form of health costs, genetic deformities, discomfort, lost working days, a need to buy bottled water, and the cost of cleaning up contamination. If the users of the resulting chemical products were required to pay the full cost of their production and use, there would be a lot less chemical contamination in our environment, our food and water would be cleaner, there would be fewer cancers and genetic deformities, and we would have more frogs and songbirds. If the full cost of producing and driving cars were passed on to the consumer, we would all benefit from a dramatic reduction in urban sprawl, traffic congestion, the paving over of productive lands, pollution, global warming, and depletion of finite petroleum reserves.

If the full costs were indeed included in the market price, it would be a serious blow to GDP. It would be a significant boon to life.

There is good reason why cost internalization is one of the most basic principles of market theory. Yet in the name of market freedom, corporate libertarians actively advocate eliminating government regulation and point to the private cost savings for consumers while ignoring the social and environmental consequences for the broader society. Indeed, in the name of being internationally competitive, corporate libertarians urge nations and communities to increase market-distorting subsidies—including resource giveaways, low-wage labor, lax environmental regulation, and tax breaks—to attract the jobs of footloose corporations. An unregulated market invariably encourages the externalization of costs because the resulting public costs become private gains. In the end it seems that corporate libertarians are more interested in increasing corporate profits than in defending market principles.

The larger the corporation and the "freer" the market, the greater is its ability to force others to bear its costs and thereby subsidize its profits. Some call this theft. Economists call it "economies of scale."

Neva Goodwin, a heterodox economist, the head of the Global Development and Environment Institute at Tufts University, and an advocate of cost internalization, puts it bluntly: "Power is largely what externalities are about. What's the point of having power, if you can't use it to externalize your costs—to make them fall on someone else?"[8]

Corporate libertarians tirelessly inform us of the benefits of trade based on the theories of Adam Smith and David Ricardo. What they don't mention is that the benefits that trade theory predicts assume the local or national ownership of capital by persons directly engaged in its management. Indeed, these same conditions are fundamental to Smith's famous assertion in *The Wealth of Nations* that the invisible hand of the market translates the pursuit of self-interest into a public benefit. Note that the following is the only mention of the famous invisible hand in the entire 1,000 pages of *The Wealth of Nations:*

> By preferring the support of domestic to that of foreign industry, he [the entrepreneur] intends only his own security, and by directing that industry in such a manner as its produce may be of the greatest value, he intends only his own gain, and his is in this, as in many other cases, led by an invisible hand to promote an end which was no part of his intention.[9]

Smith assumed a natural preference on the part of the entrepreneur to invest at home where he could keep a close eye on his holdings. Of course, this was long before jet travel, telephones, fax machines, and the Internet. Because local investment provides local employment and produces local goods for local consumption using local resources, the entrepreneur's natural inclination contributes to the vitality of the local economy. And because the owner and the enterprise are both local, they are more readily held to local standards. Even on pure business logic, Smith firmly opposed the absentee ownership of companies.

The directors of such companies, however, being the managers rather of other people's money than of their own, it cannot well be expected, that they should watch over it with the same anxious vigilance with which the partners in a private copartnery frequently watch over their own. . . . Negligence and profusion, therefore, must always prevail, more or less in the management of the affairs of such a company.[10]

Smith believed the efficient market is composed of small owner-managed enterprises located in the communities where the owners reside. Such owners normally share in the community's values and have a personal stake in the future of both the community and the enterprise. In the global corporate economy, footloose money moves across national borders at the speed of light, society's assets are entrusted to massive corporations lacking any local or national allegiance, and management is removed from real owners by layers of investment institutions and holding companies.

We find similar contradictions when we look at David Ricardo's theory of comparative advantage, which corporate libertarians regularly invoke as proof of their argument that unrestrained free trade advances the public good. This theory, originally articulated by Ricardo in 1817, provides an elegant demonstration that, *under certain conditions,* trade between two countries works to the benefit of the people of both. Three conditions, among others, are fundamental to this outcome: capital must not be allowed to cross national borders from a high-wage to a low-wage country, trade between the participating countries must be balanced, and each country must have full employment.

When these conditions are met, investment in each country will tend to flow toward those activities in which each has a comparative advantage based on differences in their natural endowments. To use Ricardo's example, because of difference in climate it may be relatively more efficient to produce wine in Portugal and woolen goods in England. In the event of open trade between the two, the hapless vintner in England who finds himself unable to compete with imported Portuguese wines will covert his wine fields to pasture lands for sheep and his winery to a woolens mill employing the same people.

In Ricardo's time, most trade involved either basic commodities or the exchange of finished national goods produced by national enterprises. Today, products are commonly assembled using components and services produced in many different countries. Global corporations, rather than national economies, are likely to be the coordinating units, with the result that roughly a third of the $3.3 trillion in goods and services traded internationally in 1990 consisted of transactions within a single firm.[11] A growing portion of international trade is intra-industry, meaning that countries are exchanging the same product—as when the United States and Japan sell automobiles to each other—making it difficult to argue that natural comparative advantage is involved and rendering trade theory irrelevant in assessing the consequent costs and benefits.

In the pursuit of free trade, corporate libertarians actively promote the removal of restrictions on the transfer of factories across borders and the free international movement of money, belittle trade balances as irrelevant, and look to unemployment as a beneficial brake on inflation—in each instance disregarding essential conditions of the trade theory they invoke to support their cause.

In truth, the "trade agreements" advocated by corporate libertarians are not about trade; they are about economic integration. Although the theory of comparative advantage applies to balanced trade between otherwise independent national economies, a very different theory—the theory of downward leveling—applies when national economies are integrated.

When capital is confined within the national borders of trading partners, it must flow to those industries in which its home country has a comparative advantage. When the economies are merged, capital flows to whatever locality offers the maximum opportunity to externalize costs through cash subsidies, tax breaks, substandard pay and working conditions, and lax environmental standards. Income is thus shifted from workers to investors, and costs are shifted from investors to the community.[12] It seems a common practice for corporate libertarians to justify their actions based on theories that apply only in the world that by their actions they seek to dismantle.

Neva Goodwin suggests that neoclassical economists have invited this distortion and misuse of economic theory by drawing narrow boundaries around their field that exclude most political and institutional reality. She characterizes the neoclassical school of economics as the political economy of Adam Smith minus the political and institutional analysis of Karl Marx:

> The classical political economy of Adam Smith was a much broader, more humane subject than the economics that is taught in universities today. . . . For at least a century it has been virtually taboo to talk about economic power in the capitalist context; that was a communist [Marxist] idea. The concept of class was similarly banned from discussion.[13]

Adam Smith was as acutely aware of issues of power and class as he was of the dynamics of competitive markets. However, the neoclassical economists and the neo-Marxist economists bifurcated his holistic perspective on the political economy, one taking those portions of the analysis that favored the owners of property, and the other taking those that favored the sellers of labor. Thus, the neoclassical economists left out Smith's considerations of the destructive role of power and class, and the neo-Marxists left out the beneficial functions of the market. Both schools of thought advanced extremist social experiments on a massive scale that embodied a partial vision of society, with disastrous consequences.

Economic Demagoguery

On the evening of December 1, 1994, a lame-duck session of the US Senate approved by a margin of seventy-six to twenty-four the Uruguay-round agreement of the General Agreement on Tariffs and Trade (GATT) that created the World Trade Organization. Responding to their corporate financial sponsors, a broad coalition of Republican and Democratic senators supported the measure in defiance of widespread and growing opposition among those Americans familiar with the agreement and its threat to jobs, the environment, and democracy. The strong and unequivocal backing of the agreement by President Bill Clinton and Vice President Al Gore deepened the chasm between them and their core labor and environmental constituencies.

C-SPAN, a cable television news channel, held a telephone call-in session following the vote. Doug Harbrecht, the trade editor of *Business Week*, was the guest resource person. As caller after caller phoned in to express outrage at the politicians who voted for the agreement in support of big-money interests and total disregard of the popular will, Harbrecht commented that the pro-GATT position represented impeccable economics but bad politics.

As did many of his colleagues, Harbrecht mistook free-market ideology for good economics. The global economic integration advanced through GATT and the World Trade Organization is at odds with the most basic principles of market economics and puts in place an economic system designed to self-destruct at an enormous cost to human societies. This can scarcely be considered the practice of "impeccable" economics.

How can neoliberal economists advocate economic integration if it advances conditions that are at odds with those required for efficient market function? An important part of the answer is found in their legendary ability to assume away reality.

This ability has been immortalized in an apocryphal story about three scientists—a physicist, a chemist, and an economist—marooned on a desert island. They've salvaged a can of beans from the wreck of their ship, but unfortunately, they have no evident means of opening it. They agree that with so much scientific brainpower among them, they can surely complete this simple task.

The physicist points to a nearby palm tree and suggests that she will climb the tree and drop the can on a rock below at the proper angle to pop it open. The chemist points out that the beans will be spilled on the ground and suggests that they might use salt water to create a chemical reaction that will rust away the top. Then the economist says, "You are both making this simple task too complicated. First, we will assume a can opener." Like this economist, when the real world diverges from the conditions necessary to support their preferred policy options, economic rationalists are prone to solve the conflict by assuming the conditions that support their recommendations.

Take the case of the obvious reality that the human economy is embedded in and dependent on the natural environment. As far back as 1798, Thomas Robert Malthus suggested that environmental limits might make population growth a problem for the future of humanity. Neoliberal economists have dealt with this inconvenience by adopting an analytical model that assumes economies consist of isolated, wholly self-contained, circular flows of exchange values (labor, capital, and goods) between firms and households, without reference to the environment. In other words, they avoid the problem of environmental limits by creating a model that assumes the environment doesn't exist. They then conclude from this model that the economy does not depend on the environment and dismiss those who challenge the possibility of infinite growth on a finite Earth with the stinging epithet "Neo-Malthusian!"

A belief in the possibility of unlimited growth is the very foundation of the ideological doctrine of corporate libertarianism, because to accept the reality of physical limits is to accept the need to limit greed and acquisition in favor of economic justice and sufficiency. This would require a fundamental reorientation of economic priorities to focus on equity rather than growth.

The propensity of the neoliberal economists to choose their assumptions to fit their conclusions is revealed with particular clarity in the computer simulations they use to demonstrate the economic benefits of lowering trade barriers. During the public debates on the North American Free Trade Agreement (NAFTA), proponents of the agreement aggressively brandished the results of computer simulations, known as general equilibrium models, as proof that NAFTA would create large numbers of new jobs for each of the participating NAFTA countries: Canada, Mexico, and the United States.[14]

The economist James Stanford examined the models used to generate these projections and found that each one incorporated assumptions from classical trade theory sharply at odds with economic reality. To illustrate the contradictions, he related the following hypothetical discussion between an autoworker in the midwestern United States and one of the pro-NAFTA economic modelers. The worker related to the modeler her fears that:

> If NAFTA is approved, Ford will surely move its Taurus plant to Mexico, where it can hire workers for a tenth of my pay with no independent union, and export cars back to the United States. With the labor market already depressed in this part of the country I don't see any prospect of finding a job at comparable pay.

The economic modeler, looking surprised, assures her that he is an expert on the subject of trade and that her fears are entirely unfounded:

> Don't worry. I've constructed a computer simulation that shows you will actually benefit from the trade agreement because of the new jobs NAFTA will create in America. Here's how it works. In my model I assume *capital is immobile*. Therefore, Ford cannot move its plant to Mexico. Nor would it want to, because I assume *unit labor costs are the same in both countries* and in my model *Americans have a clear preference for U.S.-made products*, even if they are more expensive.
>
> My model also assumes *full employment* and specifies that *anything imported to the US from Mexico must be balanced by American exports*, so new export industries will necessarily spring up here to replace any industries that might be displaced by Mexican imports. Since you earn above-average wages at Ford, you obviously possess valuable skills. With full employment you will certainly find another job very shortly in one of these new export industries, probably with higher pay than your current job. So NAFTA will be great for you.

A worker confronted with such an explanation might conclude that the economic modeler had just arrived from an alien planet with little knowledge of affairs on Earth. Although the discussion is hypothetical, the "Just assume a can opener" assumptions articulated by the economist (italicized for ease of identification) are not. Each of them is built into one or more of the economic models that trade experts used to prove that the United States would realize employment gains from NAFTA.

In comparing the models and their results, Stanford found a direct relationship between unrealistic assumptions and favorable job projections—the less realistic the assumptions, the more optimistic the projections. The more realistic models predicted either negative or negligible economic consequences for at least one of the partners.[15]

Those who use these models to press their case make no mention of the underlying assumptions. The misrepresentations are so flagrant and persistent that one sometimes suspects an intent to misinform the public.

For example, during the NAFTA debates, the unabashedly pro-free-trade *New York Times* took the unusual step of presenting a trade economics primer on its front page. The primer provided a textbook explanation of the theory of comparative advantage to bolster its editorial position in support of the NAFTA legislation. No mention was made, however, of the underlying assumptions of the theory, let alone of how those assumptions diverge from reality. Letters submitted by me and others to the editor of the *New York Times* pointing out the omission were not published.

Those who engage in such distortion lend legitimacy to flawed economic policies that advantage the greediest among us to the disadvantage of the rest.

The Moral Justification of Injustice

The moral philosophers of market liberalism perpetrate similar distortions by neglecting the distinction between the rights of property and the rights of people. Indeed, they equate the freedom and rights of individuals with market freedom and property rights. The freedom of the market is the freedom of those with money. When rights are a function of property rather than personhood, only those with property have rights.

It is a basic premise of democracy that each individual has equal rights before the law and an equal voice in political affairs—one person, one vote. We can rightfully look to the market as a democratic arbiter of rights and preferences only to the extent that money and property are equitably distributed. Although a market can allocate efficiently with less than complete equality, when 358 billionaires enjoy a combined net worth of $760 billion—equal to the net worth of the poorest 2.5 billion of the world's people—the market is neither just nor efficient and it loses all legitimacy as a democratic institution.[16]

Publications such as *Fortune, Business Week, Forbes,* the *Wall Street Journal,* and *The Economist*—all ardent advocates of corporate libertarianism—rarely if ever praise an economy for its progress toward eliminating poverty or achieving greater equity. Rather, they regularly evaluate the performance of economies by the number of millionaires and billionaires they produce, the competence of managers by the cool dispassion with which they fire thousands of employees, the success of individuals by how many millions of dollars they acquire in a year, and the success of companies by the global reach of their power and their ability to dominate global markets.

Take for example, the cover story of the July 5, 1993, issue of *Forbes*, trumpeting the extraordinary accomplishments of the free market under the banner "Meet the World's Newest Billionaires":

> As disillusion with socialism and other forms of statist economics spreads, private, personal initiative is being released to seek its destiny. Wealth, naturally, follows. The two big openings for free enterprise in this decade have come in Latin America and the Far East. Not surprisingly, the biggest clusters of new billionaires on our list have risen from the ferment of these two regions. Eleven new Mexican billionaires in two years, seven more ethnic Chinese.[17]

Taking a slightly more populist view, *Business Week* presented a special report titled "A Millionaire a Minute" in its November 29, 1993, issue. It included this breathless account of what the free market has accomplished in Asia:

> Wealth. To most Asians just one generation ago, it meant moving to the U.S.—or selling natural resources to Japan. But now, East Asia is generating its own wealth on a speed and scale that probably is without historical precedent. The number of non-Japanese Asian multimillionaires is expected to double to 800,000 by 1996. . . . East Asia will surpass Japan in purchasing power within a decade. And with savings increasing $550 billion annually it is becoming the world's biggest source of liquid capital. "In Asia," says Olarn Chaipravat, chief executive of Siam Commercial Bank, "money is everywhere." . . . There are new markets for everything from Mercedes Benz cars to Motorola mobile phones to Fidelity mutual funds. . . . To find the nearest precedent, you need to rewind U.S. history 100 years to the days before strong unions, securities watchdogs and antitrust laws.[18]

Such stories do not simply glorify the pursuit of greed, they perversely elevate it to the level of a religious mission. Never mind that although a few Asians have made vast fortunes and a tiny minority of Asians have risen to the overconsumer class, the suffering of the 675 million Asians who live in absolute poverty continues unabated. In a special 1994 issue, "21st Century Capitalism," *Business Week* confirmed that market economics have serious class issues and that the corporate libertarians are clear as to whose class interests they are advancing:

> The death throes of communism clearly gave birth to the new era, leaving most nations with only one choice—to join . . . the market economy. . . .

Almost 150 years following the publication of the *Communist Manifesto*, and more than half a century after the rise of totalitarianism, the bourgeoisie has won.[19]

It seems the corporate libertarians are a good deal more concerned with making money for the rich than with meeting human needs. Even the oft-cited claim of neoliberal economics to "value-free objectivity" supports this bias, as it rests on the questionable premise that a decision is objective and value-free if it is based solely on financial return—specifically financial return to money. Never mind that this means financial return to those who have money, assuring that the benefits flow ultimately to those who have money rather than those who do not.

Seldom has this been more starkly highlighted than in a widely publicized staff memo written by Lawrence Summers (the US secretary of the treasury in the final years of the Clinton administration) in his capacity as chief economist of the World Bank. Summers argued that it is economically most efficient for the rich countries to dispose of their toxic waste in poor countries, because poor people have both shorter life spans and less earning potential than wealthy people.[20] In a subsequent commentary on the Summers memo, *The Economist* took this obscenity even further, stating that it is a moral duty of the rich countries to export their pollution to poor countries because this provides poor people with economic opportunities of which they would otherwise be deprived.[21]

In a further twist of moral logic, corporate libertarians argue that it is the moral duty of the rich to help the poor by consuming more. In international affairs this translates into an appeal for rich countries to increase their consumption of exports from poor countries—a convenient rationalization for colonizing more of the world's resources to support more consumption by those least in need.[22] The possibility that the productive resources of low-income countries might better be used by their own people to produce the things they need to improve their own lives is never considered.

If corporate libertarians had a serious allegiance to market principles and human rights, they would be calling for policies aimed at achieving the conditions under which markets function in a democratic fashion in the public interest. They would be calling for an end to corporate welfare, the breakup of corporate monopolies, the equitable distribution of property ownership, the internalization of social and environmental costs, local ownership, a living wage for working people, rooted capital, and a progressive tax system. Corporate libertarianism is not about creating the conditions that market theory argues will optimize the public interest, because its real concern is with private, not public, interests.

Millions of thoughtful, intelligent people who are properly suspicious of big government, believe in honest and hard work, have deep religious values, and are committed to family and community are being deceived by the false information and distorted intellectual and moral logic repeated constantly in the corporate media. They are being won over to a political agenda that runs counter to both their values and their interests.

Those who work within our major corporate, academic, political, governmental, and other institutions find the culture and reward systems so strongly aligned with the corporate libertarian ideology that they dare not speak out in opposition for fear of jeopardizing their jobs and their careers. We must break through the veil of illusion and misrepresentation that is holding us in a self-destructive cultural trance and get on with the work of re-creating our economic systems in service to people and living Earth.

CHAPTER 6

The Decline of
Democratic Pluralism

What an astounding thing it is to watch a civilization destroy itself
because it is unable to re-examine the validity under totally new circumstances of an economic ideology.

—SIR JAMES GOLDSMITH

From the results, one can easily see that the whole point of privatization is neither economic efficiency nor improved services to the consumer but simply to transfer wealth from the public purse—which
could redistribute it to even out social inequalities—to private hands.

—SUSAN GEORGE

The champions of corporate libertarianism gleefully greeted the
disintegration of the Soviet empire in 1989 as a victory of the free market
and a mandate to press forward their cause. Francis Fukuyama proclaimed
that the long path of human evolution was reaching its ultimate conclusion:
a universal global consumer society. He called it the end of history.[1]

The governments and corporations of the West quickly reached out
to urge Eastern Europe and the countries of the former Soviet Union
to embrace the lessons of Western success by opening their borders and freeing their economies. Armies of Western experts were fielded to help these
and other "transition states" write laws that would prepare the way for
Western corporations to penetrate their economies.

Simultaneously, the industrial West intensified its effort to create a unified global economy through the General Agreement on Tariffs and Trade

(GATT), establish a powerful World Trade Organization (WTO), and create regional markets through such initiatives as the North American Free Trade Agreement (NAFTA), the Maastricht Treaty (the European Union), and the Asia-Pacific Economic Cooperation (APEC). Anxious to please powerful corporate interests and lacking other viable ideas, US president Bill Clinton embraced economic globalization as both his jobs program and his foreign policy.

Marxist socialism died an ignoble death. However, it is no more accurate to attribute the West's economic and political triumph to the unfettered marketplace than it is to blame the USSR's failure on an activist state. Contrary to the boastful claims of corporate libertarians, the West did not prosper in the post–World War II period by rejecting the state in favor of the market. Rather, it prospered by rejecting extremist ideologies of both Right and Left in favor of democratic pluralism: a system of governance based on a pragmatic, institutional balance among the forces of government, market, and civil society.

Driven by the imperatives of depression and war, America emerged from World War II with government, market, and civil society working together in a healthier, more dynamic, and more creative balance than at any time since the pre–Civil War years. A relatively egalitarian income distribution created an enormous mass market, which in turn drove aggressive industrial expansion. America certainly was far from socialist, but neither was it truly capitalist. We might more accurately call it pluralist. This is the America that readily withstood the challenges posed by the Soviet empire to emerge as the Cold War victor. The America of democratic pluralism and equality defeated communism, not "free"-market America.

Although the specifics differed, similar patterns of democratic pluralism prevailed in most of the Western industrial democracies. Some moved more toward the public ownership and management of nationalized industries than others but within a pluralistic framework in which both market and government were strong players.

In contrast, the Soviet system embraced an ideological extremism so strongly statist that the market and the private ownership of property were virtually eliminated. The same ideology resulted in eliminating the civic sector's essential public oversight role. This left only a hegemonic and unaccountable state. Lacking the pluralistic balance and civic accountability afforded by the civic and market sectors, the Soviet economy was both unresponsive to popular needs and inefficient in its use of resources. The consequent suffering of the Soviet people was not the consequence of an activist state. It was the consequence of an extremist ideology that excluded everything except the state.

The West is now on a similar extremist ideological path; the difference is that we are captive to detached and unaccountable corporations rather than to a detached and unaccountable state. It is ironic that the closer the corporate libertarians move us toward their ideological ideal of laissez-faire capitalism, the less responsive the economy becomes to the real needs of people and Earth. Ironically, the reasons for the failure are virtually identical to the reasons the Marxist economies failed:

- Both lead to the concentration of economic power in unaccountable centralized institutions—the state in the case of Marxism, and the transnational corporation in the case of capitalism.

- Both create economic systems that destroy the living systems of Earth in the name of economic progress.

- Both produce a disempowering dependence on mega-institutions that erodes the social capital on which the efficient function of markets, governments, and society depends.

- Both take a narrow economistic view of human needs that undermines the sense of spiritual connection to Earth and to the community of life essential to maintaining the moral fabric of society.

An economic system can remain viable only as long as society has mechanisms to counter the concentration and abuse of both state and market power and the erosion of the natural, social, and moral capital that such abuses commonly exacerbate. Democratic pluralism isn't a perfect answer to the governance problem, but it seems to be the best we have discovered in our imperfect world.

Maintaining Competitive Markets

Although business often complains that government interferes unduly with its affairs, most calls for freeing the market ignore a basic reality: the efficient function of a market economy depends on a strong government. This need is well established in contemporary market economic theory and has been demonstrated in practice. In their exhaustive critique of neoliberal economics titled *For the Common Good*, Herman E. Daly and John Cobb Jr. list the conditions on which the market depends for its efficient function yet cannot provide for itself.[2]

Fair competition: By its nature, competition creates winners and losers. Winners become more powerful as they grow. Losers disappear. The bigger the winners, the more difficult it is for new entrants to gain a foothold and the more monopolistic the market becomes. Even children who play the family board game Monopoly know how it works. As the game progresses, Monopoly players acquire property on which they charge one another rent. Those who get property early in the game eventually drive the less fortunate bankrupt. The game officially ends when all players have gone bankrupt save one. Astute players know that anyone who arrives late and joins the game after others have acquired initial properties doesn't stand a chance. Most players drop out after one player gains substantial advantage as there is no prospect of a clever or lucky player coming from behind to win a surprise victory. Interest is restored only when assets are redistributed and a new game is started.

Real-world monopoly is much the same, except that the larger players have the additional advantage of being able to use their financial power to influence legislators to rewrite the rules of the game to give themselves even more advantage. The result is an inexorable tendency toward monopoly that can be restrained only by government action, backed by a politically aware citizenry, to regularly break up concentrations of economic power.

Moral capital: Free market ideology assumes that each person acts to maximize his or her individual self-interest in response to market forces that turn such behavior to maximum benefit for all. In the real world, markets often reward greedy, dishonest, and immoral behavior, with highly detrimental consequences for society. A market in which participants are driven purely by greed and a desire to obtain a momentary competitive advantage by any means—a market without trust, cooperation, compassion, and individual integrity—is not just an unpleasant place to work and do business. It is also highly inefficient, as it incurs inordinate costs for lawyers, security guards, auditors, investigators, prosecutors, courts, and regulators and in the end often produces disastrous consequences. Neither a society nor a market economy can function efficiently without a moral foundation.

Public goods: Many investments and services that are essential to the public good—such as investments in basic scientific research, public security and justice, public education, roads, and national defense—are not supplied by the market because once they have been produced, they are freely available for anyone to use. Even most corporate libertarians recognize a role for government in providing such public goods, at least those essential for the profitable function of private business. The actual work may be done by private contractors, but the bills must be paid by governments out of tax revenue.

Full-cost pricing: It is a fundamental principle of market theory that the market allocates resources efficiently only when sellers and buyers bear the full cost of the products they produce, purchase, and consume. Rarely, if ever, will full costs be internalized in an unregulated market, because competitive pressures make it necessary to externalize costs whenever possible. A producer that successfully externalizes social and environmental costs extracts a greater profit and attracts more investors, or offers a lower price and captures a greater market share at the expense of more responsible competitors, or both. It is wonderful when a company discovers inherent economic advantages in reducing its waste and paying its workers a fair wage, but experience shows that there is nothing inherent in the workings of the market to ensure that social and environmental costs will be internalized without active governmental intervention.

A just distribution: In a market system there is a strong tendency, especially during periods of economic expansion, for the owners of capital to increase their wealth and incomes while the incomes of those who sell their labor lag or decline. A market in which economic power is unjustly distributed will allocate resources to producing luxuries for those with money while depriving those with no money of even the most basic necessities of life. Justice, market efficiency, and institutional legitimacy all depend on constant intervention by government to continuously redistribute income to maintain the equitable distribution of wealth that markets require for a just and efficient allocation of resources to meet the needs of all.

Ecological sustainability: As the human economy grows to fill its ecological space, limiting the scale of the economic subsystem to maintain an optimal balance with nature becomes necessary for species survival. Carbon dioxide emissions must be maintained below absorption levels. Fishery harvests must be held to sustainable levels. Unfortunately, the unregulated market is blind to countless such constraints. Government must set the limits and ensure that appropriate signals are sent to the market. Even proposed "market solutions" to environmental problems, such as tradable pollution permits, depend on government intervention to set the limits, issue permits, and monitor compliance.

The market produces socially optimal outcomes only when government and civil society are empowered to act to maintain these six conditions of market efficiency. A market freed from governmental restraint is inherently unsustainable because it erodes its own institutional, social, and environmental foundations.

The Corrosive Effects of Globalization

Market mechanisms are essential to modern societies. However, for the market to serve the public good, business must recognize the essential roles of government and civil society in maintaining the conditions on which the economic and social efficiency of markets depends, even though this may reduce corporate profits, limit the freedom of corporate action, and increase the price of some consumer goods. The payoffs for society include good jobs that pay a living wage and protect the health and safety of workers and the community, a clean environment, economic stability, job security, and strong and secure families and communities.

There will also be cases of government inefficiency, just as there are cases of corporate inefficiency. It is appropriate to reduce the costs of such inefficiency both to taxpayers and to business. It is also appropriate to ensure that increases in consumer prices do not make it more difficult for people of modest incomes to meet their basic needs. However, we should not be concerned when governmental intervention in the public interest makes it more costly to consume things that we may not really need, reduces excessive corporate profits, and gives corporations fewer freedoms than people.

To play its essential role in relation to the market, a government must have jurisdiction over the economy within the borders of its territory. It must be able to set the rules for the domestic economy without having to prove to foreign governments and corporations that such rules are not barriers to international trade and investment. A government must be able to assess taxes and regulate the affairs of corporations that conduct business within its jurisdiction without being subject to corporate threats to sue for lost profits, withhold critical technologies, or transfer jobs to a foreign facility. For government to fulfill its essential market function, economic boundaries must coincide with political boundaries. If they do not, as in a global economy with open borders, government becomes impotent and democracy becomes a hollow façade.

Domestic economies that favor locally owned businesses need not exclude imported goods and outside investors. Where a community finds true benefits in foreign trade and investment, it should surely welcome them. But people have both the right and the need to be in control of their own economic lives through their own enterprises and the rules they set for themselves through their own democratically elected governments. If they wish to place economic speed bumps on their borders to create an advantage for local investment, they have every moral right to do so. Such a strategy worked for the Western nations during the post–World War II economic boom and resulted in the broad domestic sharing of economic benefits.

Sweden offers an instructive case study of what democratic pluralism can accomplish and what happens when it is eroded by globalization.

The Case of Sweden

Sweden is known among the Western industrial countries for its success in achieving prosperity and equity through mixing elements of both capitalist and socialist models within a strong framework of democratic pluralism.

Few realize that industrialization came a hundred years later to Sweden than to England. Until the years following World War II, Sweden remained an extremely poor country. In the countryside, many people lived on small farms that, given the poor soil and climate, barely provided them with a living. Some died in famines or emigrated. Many others, even well into this century, lived in serf-like conditions on large estates. Illiteracy was widespread. In the late 1940s, it was still common for a family to live in an apartment consisting of one room plus a kitchen (toilet facilities were shared with other families). Even the Swedish royal house was relatively poor by the standards of most of its European cousins.[3]

Sweden's modern success was a creation of the Swedish Social Democratic Party, which melded and sustained a national consensus that kept it in power for forty-four years, from 1932 to 1976.[4] The Social Democrats built Sweden's elaborate social welfare system. Their wage policies brought working people into the middle class and created a greater degree of wage equity—including equity between the wages of women and men—than in any other Western country.[5] The Social Democrats place a high priority on maintaining full employment. To encourage Swedish transnational firms such as Volvo, Electrolux, Saab, and Ericsson to concentrate their operations in Sweden, the applicable effective tax rate was much lower for profits generated in Sweden than for those generated abroad.[6]

An alliance between the major Swedish industrial corporations and organized labor served as the party's political base and supported the centralized and peaceful negotiation of wages and working conditions by national unions and employers' organizations. This alignment produced significant benefits for both big labor and big capital.

The arrangement, however, had important structural flaws that eventually destabilized it. One was a tax system that subsidized larger firms that were expanding and investing at the expense of small-scale and family firms. This led to an increasing concentration and monopolization of ownership of the Swedish economy. Although wage policies stressed equality within the working class, the gap between the working class and those who controlled capital grew substantially. At the time, this gap was considered the price of maintaining the industrialists' commitment to the coalition. In the end, it brought about the coalition's destruction.[7]

When the first shock of rising oil prices hit in 1973–74, the resulting economic slowdown brought a fiscal crisis and triggered popular resistance to higher taxes. During this same period, Sweden was opening its economic borders and becoming a more active player in the international economy. This loosened the bonds that tied capital to local labor and weakened national labor movements.

In the early stages of globalization, the outward expansion of Swedish firms generated new employment at home, and the objectives of the two sides of the alliance did not significantly conflict. But once Sweden's transnationals began to define their own interests as global rather than national, the alliance between blue-collar workers and the owners of capital began to disintegrate. By this time, Sweden's highly educated white-collar workers outnumbered blue-collar workers, and the younger generation was taking the welfare state for granted, further weakening the political base of Sweden's Social Democrats.[8]

The growing contradiction between government support for the global expansion of Swedish transnationals and the need to create employment and rising real wages at home could no longer be sustained. In 1976, the Social Democrats lost the election to a three-party, center-right coalition government.

When the Social Democrats returned to power in 1982, they were a chastened party intent on promoting policies that would allow Sweden's industrialists sufficient profit margins on domestic investment to keep them "believing in Sweden," a phrase coined by P. G. Gyllenhammar, the chairman of Volvo. Maintaining a belief in Sweden meant increasing the share of the national product going to profits compared with wages so that Sweden's industrialists would find it worthwhile to invest at home. This was accepted as the price of maintaining full employment at a time when unemployment elsewhere in Europe was running at 8 to 9 percent or higher.[9]

The resulting policies pushed corporate profits to previously unimaginable levels. With so much more money in their pockets than could be absorbed by productive investments, Swedish investors turned to speculation, driving up the prices of real estate, art, stamps, and other speculative goods. To stop the upward spiral, the government loosened monetary controls so that the excess funds could spill over into Europe. Money flowed out at such a rate that it helped push real estate prices in London and Brussels to record highs. As the speculative bubble fed on itself, the quick profits offered by speculation drained funds away from productive investments within Sweden. When the bubble in Swedish real estate finally burst, the Swedish banking system lost $18 billion in uncollectible loans. The bill was picked up by the state and passed on to the Swedish taxpayers.[10]

During this period, Sweden's major industrialists played an active role in dismantling the "Swedish model" constructed by the Social Democratic alliance. The Swedish Employers' Federation rejected centralized wage bargaining, which had been one of the model's cornerstones, and allied itself with the Conservative Party. It also bankrolled think tanks espousing a corporate libertarian economic ideology and conducted a major public relations effort praising individualism and the free market while denouncing the Social Democratic state as oppressive and inept.[11] This weakened the political apparatus of the state and its ability to define long-term policies.

In 1983, Volvo's Gyllenhammar stepped in to fill the void by forming the European Round Table of Industrialists, made up of the heads of the leading European transnationals, including Fiat, Nestlé, Philips, Olivetti, Renault, and Siemens. The purpose was to define long-term policies for the state and to serve as an international lobby to press for their implementation.[12]

By the end of 1992, the richest 2 percent of Swedish households owned 62 percent of the value of the shares traded on the Stockholm stock exchange and 23 percent of all wealth in the country. While the average Swedish household grew poorer from 1978 to 1988, the richest 450 households doubled their assets.[13] Unemployment had been below 3 percent when the Social Democrats were first voted out of office.[14] It rose to 5 percent in 1992 and was projected to reach 7 percent, even though another 7 percent of the workforce was already engaged in countercyclical retraining programs and public employment projects.

From the beginning, the Swedish model contained the seeds of its own destruction. It built a powerful financial elite whose interests were far removed from those of the majority middle class. It bred a sense of welfare complacency among the Swedish people and failed to instill in the younger generation an awareness of democracy's need to be continually re-created through constant citizen vigilance and political activism. And its prosperity had been built on the unsustainable exploitation of Sweden's natural resources of timber, iron ore, and hydroelectric power.

As the elites gained more financial power, they were able to pyramid their claims on the resources of society without making a corresponding productive contribution. As the economic borders were opened, the jobs of those who depended on earning wages for doing productive work became hostage to those who controlled capital. The more the government, in its desperation to keep jobs at home, gave in to the demands of the financial elite, the greater the amount of money that passed into their hands, the greater their power to dictate public policy in their own interest, and the greater the stresses on the social fabric. The parallels to the US experience examined in Part III are striking.

The Swedish experience reveals a lesson of fundamental importance: democratic pluralism cannot long survive extreme inequality.

The Need for Creative Balance

Communism established the hegemony of the state. Capitalism establishes the hegemony of financial markets and the corporation. A healthy society is built on the balanced interaction of three distinct yet interlinked sectors of activity: civic, governmental, and economic. All are human creations and a given individual may participate in all three, yet the integrity of the whole depends on clearly distinguishing their roles and their legitimate sources of power.

Civic: Less formally institutionalized than the other three sectors, the civic sector affords the greatest creative freedom to the individual to act from a sense of inner spiritual connection to life and community. The distinctive role of the civic sector is to generate, maintain, and renew the sense of meaning and the symbols of cultural identity that are the foundation of the coherence and integrity of a healthy society. An active civic sector is the conscience of the society, the source of its cultural vitality and renewal, and an essential counter to the concentration and abuse of power by governmental and economic institutions.[15]

Governmental: Government is the sector to which the civic sector freely, but reluctantly, gives the authority to use coercive power in the public interest, including the power to confiscate property and to deprive a person of physical liberty and even life. By the exercise of this authority government carries out such essential functions as maintaining public order and national security, collecting taxes, and reallocating society's resources to maintain equity and meet other public needs. Government's distinctive competence is in reallocating wealth, not in creating it. Its power must be continually checked by an active civil society.

Economic: The distinctive competence of a proper economic sector is in creating wealth through the production of beneficial goods and services, not in redistributing it. Market economies respond to consumer demand. Markets are, however, ill equipped to set society's larger priorities and maintain an equitable distribution of wealth. Markets have no mechanism for preventing the unscrupulous from selling guns, drugs, and tobacco products to children, creating environmental damage, and endangering workers, or for insuring the accuracy of product labels. They cannot maintain public streets, run schools for poor children, or mandate recycling. Nor do they distinguish between profits earned from the efficient production of goods and unearned profits gained by speculating, exercising monopoly power, externalizing costs, expropriating common property resources, or creating artificial demand for unnecessary and even harmful products. In each instance there is a need for democratically elected governments to establish the boundaries of market behavior acceptable to the society.

Democratic pluralism melds the forces of the market, government, and civil society to maintain a dynamic balance among the often-competing societal needs for essential order and equity, the efficient production of goods and services, the accountability of power, the protection of human freedom, and continuing institutional innovation. This balance finds expression in the regulated market, not the free market, and in trade policies that link national economies to one another within a framework of rules that maintains domestic competition and favors domestic enterprises that employ local workers, meet local standards, pay local taxes, and function within a robust system of democratic governance.

In a healthy society the civic sector is appropriately considered to be the first sector, as it is the arena of citizenship, individual expression, and democratic participation. At the same time, the health of the society depends on the vitality of all three sectors. Without the institutions of government and the economy, the society will be lawless and impoverished. Since government is the body through which citizens establish and maintain the rules for all sectors, it is appropriately considered the second sector. The role of the economic sector is to serve society's needs as defined by people through their purchases, their choice of work, and the rules and priorities determined democratically through their participation in government. It is therefore properly subordinate to both the civic and governmental sectors and is appropriately designated the third sector.

Playing by Different Rules

Contrary to popular myth, capitalist economies and market economies operate by different rules to serve different ends. The institutions of a capitalist economy are designed to concentrate control of the means of production in the hands of the few to the exclusion of the many. A capitalist economy is characterized by concentrations of monopoly power, financial speculation, absentee ownership, deregulation, public subsidies, the externalization of costs, and central economic planning by mega-corporations.

By contrast the institutions of a market economy, as envisioned by Adam Smith and described by market theory, are intended to facilitate the self-organizing processes by which people engage in the production and exchange of goods and services to create an adequate and satisfying livelihood for themselves and their families. A true market economy features human-scale enterprises, honest money, rooted local ownership, and a framework of democratically chosen rules intended to maintain the conditions of efficient market function—including equity and cost internalization. It is a natural companion to democracy and a pluralistic society.

The publicly traded limited-liability corporation is capitalism's institutional form of choice because it allows the virtually unlimited concentration of power for the purpose of pursuing private gain with minimal public accountability or legal liability. Actual shareholders, the real owners, rarely have any role in corporate affairs and bear no personal liability beyond the value of their investments. Directors and officers are protected from financial liability for acts of negligence or commission by the corporation's massive legal resources and company-paid insurance policies. The same criminal act that would result in a stiff prison sentence, or even execution, if committed by an individual brings a corporation only a fine—usually inconsequential in relation to corporate assets and likely less than what it gained by committing the infraction.[16] The prosecution of corporate executives for illegal corporate acts is extremely rare. It is with good reason that the economist William M. Dugger characterizes the corporation as "organized irresponsibility."[17]

Unlike real people, who are eventually rendered equal by the grave, corporations are able to grow and reproduce themselves without limit, "living" and amassing power indefinitely. Eventually, that power evolves beyond the ability of any mere human to control, and the corporation becomes an autonomous entity unto itself, using its power to "create its own culture, using the lens of career to focus corporate culture on profit, size, and power."[18] Those who serve the corporate interest are well rewarded and derive substantial personal power from their position. But in the end, they are only employees who serve the institution at its pleasure.

Few real persons can begin to match the political resources that a large corporation is able to amass in its behalf. Corporations may lack the right to vote, but that is a minor inconvenience, given their ability to mobilize hundreds of thousands of votes from among their workers, suppliers, dealers, customers, and the public, and to package millions of dollars in political contributions.

Left to their devices, corporations colonize markets and defeat the very mechanisms that theory tells us make the market work in the public interest. The publicly traded limited-liability corporation may be the favored institution of capitalism, but it is not a market institution. To the contrary, it is aggressively *anti*-market, because it works tirelessly to erode the essential conditions of the market's social efficiency.

It is fully appropriate, therefore, that citizens view corporations with the same skepticism as did the early American settlers, granting corporate charters judiciously only to serve well-defined public purposes, setting clear rules for corporate function, holding corporations fully accountable for their actions, and barring them from political participation of any kind.

The owners and managers of corporations have the full rights of any citizen—in their capacity as citizens—to participate in defining public goals and policies. However, corporations are not people. They are alien to the ways of life, blind to the complex nonmaterial needs of human societies, and have no proper role in the political processes by which real people define the public interest and set standards for corporate conduct.

A corporate charter represents a privilege—not a right—that is granted by a government subject to the will of its people in return for the acceptance of corresponding obligations. It is up to the people who make up the electorate—not the fictitious persona of the corporation—to define these privileges and obligations. We are learning through harsh experience that the survival of democracy depends on holding firm to this principle.

Democratic pluralism faces a paradox. During times of change, societies need to mobilize the full creative potential of their citizens in a way that can be achieved only under democratic pluralism. Yet it is in such stressful times that democratic pluralism seems least adequate and most susceptible to the certainty offered by the simplistic appeals of ideological demagogues. Instead of offering direction, democratic pluralism calls on people to find their own direction with a view to the good of the whole. Instead of certainty, it nurtures variety to the point of apparent chaos.

These are its weakness, but also its genius. Democratic pluralism provides a framework within which each citizen can bring to bear their full creative powers toward finding innovative solutions to shared problems—in the context of family, community, and nation. Gradually, through a diffuse and chaotic social learning process, the lessons from countless innovations are distilled into changes in local, national, and ultimately global institutions and policies. As the Ecological Revolution unfolds, we need that creative power now as never before.

CHAPTER 7

Illusions of the Cloud Minders

This troubled planet is a place of the most violent contrasts. Those that receive the rewards are totally separated from those who shoulder the burdens. It is not a wise leadership.

—**SPOCK**, "The Cloud Minders," *Star Trek*

With the information technologies already available, I can sit on the beach of my Florida home with a laptop computer and a cellular telephone and monitor the video cameras installed throughout my manufacturing company in Ohio to ensure that my people are on the job and doing their work properly.

—**Interview with company owner on US National Public Radio, August 31, 1994**

"The Cloud Minders," episode 74 of the popular science fiction television series *Star Trek*, took place on the planet Ardana. First aired on February 28, 1969, it depicted a planet whose rulers devoted their lives to the arts in a beautiful and peaceful city, Stratos, suspended high above the planet's desolate surface. Down below, the inhabitants of the planet's surface, the Troglytes, worked in misery and violence in the planet's mines to earn the interplanetary exchange credits used to import from other planets the luxuries the rulers enjoyed on Stratos. In this modern allegory, an entire planet had been colonized by rulers who successfully detached and isolated themselves from the people and the localities of the planet's surface on whose toil their luxuries depended.

The imagery of this *Star Trek* episode has stuck vividly in my mind. How like Ardana is our own world, where the truly rich and powerful work in beautifully appointed executive suites in tall office towers; travel to meetings by limousine and helicopter; jet between continents high above the clouds, pampered with the finest wines by an attentive crew; and live in protected estates, affluent suburbs, and penthouse suites amid art, beauty, and a protected environment. They are as insulated from the lives of the ordinary people of Earth as those who lived on Stratos were insulated from the lives of the Troglytes. They too are living in a world of illusion, draining the world of its resources and so isolated from reality that they know not what they do, nor how else to live.

The Magic Market

The isolation of the rich and powerful is exemplified by the annual gathering of the directors of the World Bank and the International Monetary Fund (IMF). The following is an account by the journalist Graham Hancock from one such meeting:

> I had come [to Washington, DC] simply to attend the joint annual meeting of the Boards of Governors of the World Bank and the International Monetary Fund, two institutions that play a central role in mobilizing and disbursing funds for impoverished developing countries. . . . The total cost of the 700 social events laid on for delegates during that single week was estimated at $10 million. . . . A single formal dinner catered by Ridgewells cost $200 per person. Guests began with crab cakes, caviar and creme fraîche, smoked salmon and mini Beef Wellingtons. The fish course was lobster with corn rounds followed by citrus sorbet. The entrée was duck with lime sauce, served with artichoke bottoms filled with baby carrots. A hearts of palm salad was also offered accompanied by sage cheese soufflés with a port wine dressing. Dessert was a German chocolate turnip sauced with raspberry coulis, ice-cream bonbons and flaming coffee royale. . . . Washington limousine companies were doing a roaring trade.[1]

At the same meeting that favored its delegates with $10 million worth of lavish meals and social events, Barber Conable, the former US congressman and then recently appointed president of the World Bank, presented the following charge to the 10,000 men and women present:

> Our institution is mighty in resources and in experience but its labours will count for nothing if it cannot look at our world through the eyes of the most underprivileged, if we cannot share their hopes and their fears. We are here to serve their needs, to help them realize their strength, their potential, their aspirations. . . . Collective action against global poverty is the common purpose that brings us together today. Let us therefore rededicate ourselves to the pursuit of that great good.[2]

If the delegates had indeed made an effort to look at their world through the eyes of the most underprivileged, they might well have lost their appetite. Take, for example, this simple interview with a sharecropper's child in nearby Selma, Alabama, by Raymond Wheeler of CBS TV:

"Do you eat breakfast before school?"

"Sometimes, sir. Sometimes I have peas."

"And when you get to school, do you eat?"

"No, sir."

"Isn't there any food there?"

"Yes, sir."

"Why don't you have it?"

"I don't have the 35 cents."

"What do you do while the other children eat lunch?"

"I just sits there on the side" [his voice breaking].

"How do you feel when you see the other children eating?"

"I feel ashamed" [crying]. [3]

Far from encouraging delegates to see the world through the eyes of the poor, the organizers of World Bank–IMF meetings take great care to shield them from the specter of poverty.

The World Bank and IMF are leading proponents of economic rationalism and free-market, export-led growth strategies. They have for years been lauding South Korea, Taiwan, Singapore, and Hong Kong as examples of success. Thus when the directors met in Bangkok, Thailand, in October 1991, it was natural that the meeting served as a celebration of the recent "success" story of free-market, export-led growth in Thailand.

No expense or inconvenience was spared by Thailand's government to impress on the delegates that Thailand had arrived as a full member of the elite club of newly industrialized nations (NICs). To ensure the desired impression, a shiny new convention complex was rushed to completion in downtown Bangkok to host the conference. Two hundred families were evicted from their homes to widen roads to and from the site.[4] A nearby squatter settlement was leveled so that the delegates would not be troubled by unpleasant views of Bangkok's poverty. Schools and government offices were closed to limit traffic congestion and help clear the air of emissions so that the delegates might rush with the least inconvenience, free of respiratory distress in their air-conditioned cars, between elegant cocktail parties and official dinners along routes chosen—and walled off, where necessary—to avoid disconcerting views of Bangkok's slums. English-speaking engineers, doctors, and lawyers were pressed into service as drivers of the delegates; nurses and teachers waited tables in the conference restaurants to ensure that instructions were understood and that no need of a visiting dignitary would go unmet.

Such cosmetic measures could only partially hide the reality that Bangkok, a once-beautiful city, has been ravaged by the consequences of its development "success." Amid shining shopping malls, high-rise office buildings, and luxury hotels, filth and squalor abound. Three hundred thousand new vehicles are added to Bangkok's monumental traffic jams each year, slowing traffic to an average of less than ten kilometers (about six miles) per hour. On more than two hundred days a year, air pollution in Bangkok exceeds maximum World Health Organization safety limits, and emissions are increasing by 14 percent a year.[5]

The World Bank–IMF meeting in Thailand was a fitting metaphor for the illusion within which the world's power holders live. The illusion is maintained in part through the construction of a life of luxury set apart in enclaves, and in part by self-justifying belief systems, such as corporate libertarianism, and by the adulation of wealth and the wealthy by the business press and a plethora of economic researchers and consultants. Most of all, it is maintained by the dysfunctions of an economic system that lavishes rich rewards on power holders for decisions that place terrible burdens on the rest of humanity.

Growing the Great Divide

The gap that separates the world's rich and poor, both within and between countries, is unconscionable and growing. In 1992, the United Nations Development Programme (UNDP) dramatized the inequity by representing the world's income distribution with a graph in the shape of a champagne glass.[6]

As shown in figure 7.1, the 20 percent of the world's people who live in the world's wealthiest countries receive 82.7 percent of the world's income; only 1.4 percent of the world's income goes to the 20 percent who live in the world's poorest countries. In 1950, about the time the commitment was made to globalize the development process, the average income of the 20 percent of people living in the wealthiest countries was about thirty times that of the 20 percent living in the poorest countries. By 1989, this ratio had doubled to sixty times.

Based on national averages, these figures represent disparities among countries and substantially understate the disparity among people. For example, all Americans are placed in the world's top income category, including the homeless, the rural poor, and the urban slum dwellers. When the UNDP estimated the global distribution based on individual incomes rather than on national averages, the average income of the top 20 percent was 150 times that of the lowest 20 percent.

Even this figure masks the extreme inequity revealed when the incomes of the top 20 percent are desegregated. Although global data are not available, data from the United States illustrate the point. In 1989, the top 20 percent of American households had an average income of $109,424 a year.[7] However, those households in the 80th to 90th percentiles received, on average, a relatively modest $65,900. Those in the top 1 percent averaged $559,795—receiving as a group more total income than the bottom 40 percent of all Americans.[8]

Yet even this is mere pocket change to Wall Street investment brokers such as the infamous Michael Milken, who in one year took home a cool half-billion dollars for his labors selling junk bonds on Wall Street, and to the chief executive officers (CEOs) of America's major corporations and the top-earning celebrities. In 1992, Thomas F. Frist Jr., CEO of Hospital Corporation of America, led the pack of overpaid American executives with $127 million, nearly 780,000 times the average $163 per capita income of the poorest 20 percent of the world's people! The 1992 average take of the CEOs of the 1,000 largest corporations surveyed by *Business Week* was $3.8 million—up 42 percent from the previous year. Furthermore, the gap between the pay of top executives and the pay of those who work for them is growing rapidly.[9] In 1960, the average CEO of a major company received 40 times the compensation of the average worker. In 1992, he (there were only two women among *Business Week*'s top 1,000 CEOs) received 157 times as much.[10]

These well-paid executives are, however, only pretenders to wealth compared with the wealth of those who live by the earnings of their investment portfolios. *Forbes*'s "four hundred richest people in America" enjoyed an increase in their combined net worth of $92 billion between 1982 and 1993, bringing them to a total of $328 billion[11]—more than the combined 1991 gross national products (GNPs) shared by a billion people living in India, Bangladesh, Sri Lanka, and Nepal.[12]

Eager to assure its wealthy readers that their good fortune was not at the expense of others, *Forbes* prefaced its inventory of the wealthiest Americans with the following caveat:

Aha! Then the redistributionists are right. The rich have gotten richer. Yes and no. The truly rich may have gotten richer, but there's no evidence

Figure 7.1 Global Income Distribution

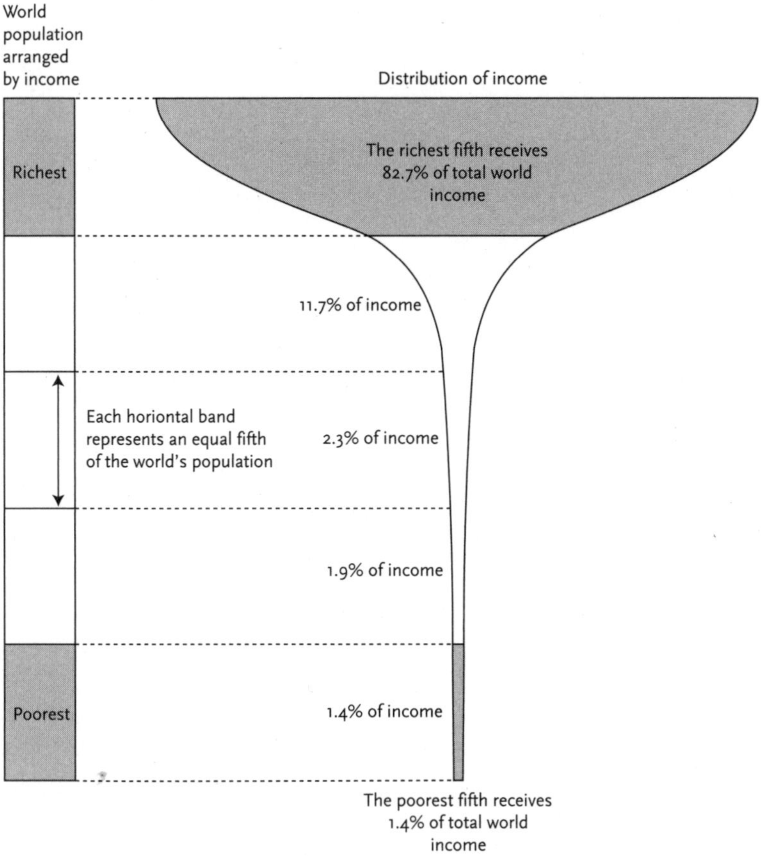

World
population
arranged
by income

Distribution of income

Richest

The richest fifth receives
82.7% of total world
income

11.7% of income

Each horiontal band
represents an equal fifth
of the world's population

2.3% of income

1.9% of income

Poorest

1.4% of income

The poorest fifth receives
1.4% of total world
income

Source: United Nations Development Programme, *Human Development Report 1992*
(New York: Oxford University Press, 1992).

that their proportionate share of the nation's wealth has grown. The price
of admission to the Forbes Four Hundred has increased approximately
as much as the stock market, as measured by the Dow Jones index. The
tremendous increase in the stock market—which has rubbed off nicely
on the super rich—rubs off on every pension holder and shareholder in
America as well. . . .

Weep not for the rich. But don't get the dumb idea that they have
gotten rich off the rest of us.[13]

Surely there were some widows and pensioners of modest means among the beneficiaries of the stock market gains. However, the protestation of *Forbes* (a publication of and for the Stratos dwellers) that equity has been maintained is but one manifestation of the isolation of the Stratos dwellers and their belief that their world is the world. The four hundred richest Americans may not have increased their share of total stock wealth, but apart from stocks owned by pension funds, 83.1 percent of the stock market wealth owned by American households is owned by the wealthiest 10 percent. Moreover, 37.4 percent of stock wealth is owned by the richest 0.5 percent.[14]

From 1977 to 1989, the average real income of the top 1 percent of US families increased by 78 percent, whereas that of the bottom 20 percent decreased by 10.4 percent.[15] Thus the poorest among us became not only relatively poorer but also absolutely poorer. What these figures don't tell us is that these absolute decreases occurred in spite of the fact that those who were employed in 1989 were working longer hours than they had in 1977, and far more families had two people working full time as more women entered the workforce. For many US families among the bottom 60 percent, even longer hours and an extra breadwinner were not enough to make up for the decline in wages.

The simple truth that the *Forbes* editors and other Stratos dwellers are prone to ignore is that each time a major corporation announces a cutback of thousands of jobs, the Stratos families get richer and the incomes of the thousands of workers whose jobs have been eliminated decline. It is part of an ongoing process of shifting wealth and economic power from those who are engaged in the production of real value to those who already have large amounts of money and believe it is their right to see those amounts grow without limit, regardless of their own needs or productive contribution.

Is it possible for those who sip from the lip of the champagne glass to truly appreciate the lot of the vast mass of humanity that shares only the meager dregs that settle into the stem? If they were to acknowledge that their own abundance is the cause of the plight of those so deprived, could any person bear the terrible moral burden? There is substantial incentive to avoid facing such moral contradictions by maintaining the reassuring cultural illusions of Stratos.

A Different World

Forbes prefaced its 1993 listing of the four hundred richest people in America with an article on the struggle of the very rich to make ends meet in today's economy. In one year's time, the price of a one-kilo tin of beluga malossol caviar had increased by 28 percent to $1,408. A Sikorsky S-780 helicopter with full executive options had increased 8 percent to $7 million. And a suitable night's hotel lodging in New York was up 15 percent to $750.[16] Theirs is a different world.

When Henry Kissinger, long one of the most influential players in US foreign policy circles, takes his dog, Amelia, with him on his morning constitutional, a bodyguard follows behind to handle the scooper duties. When Kissinger goes on vacation, Amelia rides by limousine to Mrs. Peepers' kennel in rural Maryland, where she stays as a houseguest in a private room.[17] Many Americans were amused when the press caught George H. W. Bush gazing in wonder at a grocery checkout scanner and realized that he was one of the last people in the United States to encounter this addition to the checkout routine.

When Alexander Trotman assumed the post of chairman, president, and CEO of Ford Motor Company in 1993, he was responsible for making more than 3 million vehicles a year. Yet he did not own a car of his own and had never bought one from a dealer. Ford, as is common practice in the auto industry, provides all its top executives with new cars—ensuring that they always have cars that are in perfect working order without ever having the experience of negotiating with a dealer and hassling with registration, insurance, repairs, and maintenance.[18]

In 1989, Lone Star Industries took a $271 million loss. Its CEO, James E. Stewart, ordered layoffs, sold off $400 million of corporate assets, eliminated the dividend to stockholders, and told his managers to fly coach. Yet he maintained a $2.9 million expense account for himself and continued to commute in the corporate jet between his home in Florida and the company headquarters in Stamford, Connecticut. As CEO of RJR Nabisco, F. Ross Johnson built a palatial hangar in Atlanta to house the corporation's ten planes and twenty-six corporate pilots. Next door he built a three-story VIP lounge complete with inlaid mahogany walls, Italian marble floors, and an atrium with a Japanese garden.[19] Ivan Boesky, the global financier, was known to order eight entrées from the menu at the exclusive Cafe des Artistes, sample each, and then decide which he would eat.[20]

In June 1991, I attended the annual conference of the American Forum for Global Education in Hartford, Connecticut. Ed Pratt, the chairman and CEO of Pfizer Inc., a drug and medical products producer with annual worldwide sales of $7 billion, was an opening speaker. He received an award for his contributions to global education and shared his insights on educational needs with several hundred American educators, telling them that the education of young Americans must focus on giving them the greatest competitive edge in the new global economy. In his view, there was no time for unnecessary frills—such as studying foreign languages. He reported that in his travels around Pfizer's world operations, he found that everyone with whom there was any need to talk already spoke English. So he advised that the classroom hours that children in other countries spend learning English be devoted to teaching American students science and economics.

Nike, a major footwear company, refers to itself as a "network firm." This means that it employs 8,000 people in management, design, sales, and promotion and leaves production in the hands of some 75,000 workers hired by independent contractors. Most of the outsourced production takes place in Indonesia, where a pair of Nikes that sells in the United States or Europe for $73 to $135 is produced for about $5.60 by girls and young women paid as little as fifteen cents an hour. The workers are housed in company barracks, there are no unions, overtime is often mandatory, and if there is a strike, the military may be called to break it up. The $20 million that basketball star Michael Jordan reportedly received in 1992 for promoting Nike shoes exceeded the entire annual payroll of the Indonesian factories that made them.[21]

When asked about the conditions at plants where Nikes are produced, John Woodman, Nike's general manager in Indonesia, gave a classic Stratos-dweller response. Although he knew that there had been labor problems in the six Indonesian factories making Nike shoes, he had no idea what they had been about. Furthermore he said, "I don't know that I need to know. It's not within our scope to investigate."[22]

The Nike case is a striking example of the distortions of an economic system that shifts rewards away from those who produce real value to those whose primary function is to create marketing illusions to persuade consumers to buy products they do not need at inflated prices. It is little wonder that many managers, like the Nike manager who avoided contact with Indonesian workers, prefer to avoid talking to too many people outside the elite circles.

It seems fitting that in 1993 the winner in the annual executive compensation package sweepstakes was master illusionist Michael Eisner, chairman of the Walt Disney Company, a corporation dedicated to the creation of fantasy worlds. Eisner's compensation package of $203.1 million equaled 68 percent of the company's total profits of $299.8 million for that year—surely ample enough to create a few personal illusions of his own.[23]

This is the cloud world in which the architects of the global economic order live. For themselves and their corporations, local markets become too confining. No amount of wealth and power is enough. They must constantly push new frontiers, build new empires, and colonize new markets. There is good reason to conclude that people who are so isolated from the daily reality of those they rule are ill prepared to define the public interest.

Redefining North and South

Great wealth and the embrace of a world of illusion are not found only in "wealthy" countries. The *Forbes* 1993 directory of the world's wealthiest people listed eighty-eight billionaires from low- and middle-income countries, up from sixty-two only a year earlier. Mexico headed the list with twenty-four billionaires in 1993, up from thirteen in 1992.[24]

Consider the Philippines, a poor economic performer by the standards of East and Southeast Asia. Its per capita GNP is $730, and an estimated 60 percent of its people lack an adequate income to provide even a minimum healthy diet for themselves and their families. *Forbes* listed two Philippine billionaires in 1992 and five in 1993.

From 1988 to 1992, I worked from an office located on the eleventh floor of a high-rise building in Makati, the commercial and financial center of Manila, the capital city of the Philippines. From my window I looked out on three of Manila's five-star hotels and a number of high-rise bank buildings. Almost any time of the day I could see one or more private helicopters ferrying Manila's business elites to and from the tops of these high-rise buildings far above the cars stalled in Manila's legendary traffic jams and the lines of carless commuters waiting amid thick diesel fumes for public transportation. On the other side of Manila, thousands of less fortunate Filipinos had built their shacks of scavenged materials on top of Smokey Mountain, a steaming garbage dump, and made their living picking through the stinking mountain of garbage for bottles, bits of plastic, and other salable items.

Hundreds of thousands of Filipinos go abroad each year in a desperate search for work to sustain themselves and their families. Many of the women arrive in Japan to work as "entertainers" or take jobs as household servants in the Middle East. They commonly find themselves working under conditions of virtual slavery and sexual exploitation. The Philippine government considers its overseas workers to be an essential source of foreign exchange earnings to pay for, among other things, imports to stock the country's luxurious air-conditioned mega-malls with advanced consumer electronics and designer fashions and to service the country's $32 billion foreign debt.

In an earlier day, when economies were defined by national borders and even by individual localities, rich and poor alike who lived within the borders of a nation or a town generally shared a sense of national and community interest. No matter how great the conflict among them might be, their destinies intertwined. Industrialists had a stake in the educational system that produced their workers and in the physical infrastructure of transportation and other public facilities on which their productive enterprises depended. No matter how begrudgingly, they accepted the obligation to pay taxes to help support essential social and physical infrastructures.

In recent years, one of the demographic realities of the United States has been an increasing geographical segregation by income. Those in the upper income brackets have been clustering in affluent suburban communities organized as independent political jurisdictions, where they share facilities only with members of their own affluent class. Thus, they are able to finance good schools and other public services without the need to pay additional taxes to contribute toward providing similar facilities for lower-income families. Low-income families thus become similarly clustered in low-income jurisdictions that have a far greater need for social services than the wealthier clusters but lack the tax base to finance them.[25]

The consequences of this separation by political jurisdiction were exacerbated in the United States during the 1980s when the federal government began shifting greater responsibility to local jurisdictions for funding social services. In 1978, when federal transfers to local government peaked, almost 27 percent of state and local funding came from federal grants. By 1988, federal funding had fallen to 17 percent. This was all part of a larger effort by the Reagan administration to dismantle the income-redistribution mechanisms that earlier administrations had put into place during America's era of democratic pluralism. Robert Reich refers to it as the secession by the privileged few from the rest of America. The result has been a growing gap in the quality of education and other public services enjoyed by rich and poor; a deepening of the class divide, commonly exacerbated by racial lines; and an increasing isolation of the wealthy in their worlds of illusion.[26]

Of the many countries I have visited, Pakistan most starkly exemplifies the experience of elites living in enclaves detached from local roots. The country's three modern cities—Karachi, Lahore, and Islamabad—feature enclaves of five-star hotels, modern shopping malls, and posh residential areas within a poor and feudalistic countryside governed by local lords who support private armies with profits from a thriving drug and arms trade and who are inclined to kill any central government official who dares to enter. Health and education indicators for Pakistan's rural areas are comparable to those for the most deprived African nations.

On two of my visits to Pakistan, I was the guest of some of the country's most successful businessmen. Widely traveled graduates of the best British and American universities, they spoke and moved with the confidence, gracious demeanor, and sense of hospitality typical of cosmopolitan aristocrats who are fully at ease with their money and position. My hosts regularly traveled the world to supervise their widespread business interests, moving easily among the global business elites and feeling as much at home in New York or London as in Karachi, Lahore, or Islamabad.

Particularly striking, however, was the extent to which—in contrast to their knowledge of and interest in the rest of the world—they had little knowledge of or interest in what was happening in their own country beyond the borders of their enclave cities. It was as though the rest of Pakistan were an inconsequential foreign country not worthy of notice or mention. They were almost completely detached from any sense of national interest. What I failed to realize at the time was that this phenomenon was not an aberration of underdevelopment so much as the cutting edge of a global social and political trend—a melding of the world's financial elites into a stateless community in the clouds, detached from the world in which the vast majority of ordinary mortals live.

We have long thought of the world as divided into rich and poor countries. As economic globalization progresses, we find growing islands of great wealth in poor countries and growing seas of poverty in rich countries. The North and South distinction is now most meaningfully used to acknowledge the reality of a world divided by class lines more than by geography.

A Self-Destructing System

The global economic system is rewarding corporations and their executives with generous profits and benefits packages for contracting out their production to sweatshops paying substandard wages, for clear-cutting primal forests, for introducing labor-saving technologies that displace tens of thousands of employees, for dumping toxic wastes, and for shaping political agendas to advance corporate interests over human interests.

The system shields those who take such actions from the costs of their decisions, which are borne by the system's weaker members—the displaced workers who no longer have jobs, the replacement workers who are paid too little to feed their families, the forest dwellers whose homes have been destroyed, the poor who live next to the toxic dumps, and the unorganized taxpayers who pick up the bills. The consequence of delinking benefits from their costs is that the system is telling the world's most powerful decision makers that their decisions are creating new benefits, when in fact they are simply shifting more of the Earth's available wealth to themselves at the expense of people and the rest of nature.

Systems theorists, who concern themselves with understanding the dynamics of complex, self-regulating systems, would say that the economic system is providing these decision makers with positive feedback, rewarding them for decisions that upset the system's dynamic equilibrium and cause the system to oscillate out of control, risking eventual collapse. Stable systems depend on negative feedback signals that provide incentives to correct errant behavior and move the system back toward equilibrium.

The genius of Adam Smith's concept of a market economy is that although he never used the cybernetic terminology of systems theorists, he was one of the first to recognize the basic principles of a complex, self-regulating human system. Implicitly, he applied those principles to create an idealized model of a self-regulating economic system that would efficiently allocate society's resources to produce those things that people most want without the intervention of a powerful central ruler. It was a brilliant intellectual achievement and had enormous appeal to intellectuals who were attracted to elegant theories, to populists who had a deep distrust of powerful rulers—and to propertied elites who found in it a moral justification for greed.

Unfortunately, the economic rationalists who are Smith's intellectual descendants took a narrower and more mechanistic view of economic systems and embraced market freedom as an ideology, without Smith's focus on the conditions required to maintain the market's self-regulating balance. Ideologues make poor system designers because they are oriented to simplistic prescriptions rather than to the creation of balanced, self-regulating systems.

As resulting social tensions mount and the system's failures become more evident, established political alignments become increasingly strained. Capitalizing on a growing sense of public uncertainty and fear, political demagogues and opportunists are having a field day. In the United States, they attack big government and environmentalists while calling for tax cuts, government downsizing, the restoration of family values and make-it-or-perish individual responsibility, the elimination of restrictions on natural resource exploitation, increased defense expenditures, a tougher stand on crime, market deregulation, and free trade.

Posing as conservatives committed to protecting ordinary people from the abuses of big government, they play simultaneously to the self-reliant, who distrust government; to the economically burdened, who seek tax relief; to workers in resource-based industries, who fear environmental restrictions; and to corporate interests, which are eager for greater freedom to increase profits by externalizing costs.

The proposals offered to attract these varied constituencies are rife with contradictions. Few will contribute to restoring the values of family, community, and self-reliance. To the contrary, they allow the world's largest corporations the freedom to colonize still more of the world's markets and resources to the benefit of the already rich, further shift tax burdens from those best able to pay to those least able to pay, and enlarge the police powers of the state to stem the resulting social unrest.

The terms of the political debate must be redefined to focus clearly on the real issue: the contest for power between the big and central and the small and local—between corporations and ordinary people. The time is ripe for a realignment of political alliances, which is likely to come into full flower only when the true populists realize that their enemy is not only big government but also the giant corporations that owe no allegiance to place, people, or human interest.

Economic globalization is the foundation on which the empires of the new corporate colonialism are being built. The corporate libertarians tell us that the process of economic globalization is advancing in response to immutable historical forces and that we have no choice but to adapt and learn to compete with our neighbors. It is a disingenuous claim that belies the well-organized, generously funded, and purposeful efforts by the cloud minders to dismantle national economies and build the institutions of a global economy organized by and for the benefit of the world's largest, most monopolistic corporations. In Part III we examine their vision and how they have gone about realizing it.

PART III

Corporate Colonialism

CHAPTER 8

Dreaming of Global Empires

The world economy has become more integrated. But to travel is not the same as to arrive. Full integration will be reached only when there is free movement of goods, services, capital and labour and when governments treat firms equally, regardless of their nationality.

—*THE ECONOMIST*

The men who run the global corporations are the first in history with the organization, technology, money, and ideology to make a credible try at managing the world as an integrated economic unit. . . . What they are demanding in essence is the right to transcend the nation-state, and in the process, transform it.

—**RICHARD J. BARNET** and **RONALD E. MULLER**

The past two decades have seen the most rapid and sweeping institutional transformation in human history. It is a conscious and intentional transformation in search of a new world economic order in which business has no nationality and knows no borders. It is driven by global dreams of vast corporate empires, compliant governments, a globalized consumer monoculture, and a universal ideological commitment to corporate libertarianism. To counter the economic, social, and environmental devastation being wrought nearly everywhere by the realization of this corporate colonial vision, we must learn to recognize its message and the methods of its propagation.

The Vision

One of the most respected and articulate visionaries of the new economic order is Akio Morita, the founder and chairman of Sony Corporation. The

June 1993 *Atlantic Monthly* carried an open letter from Morita to the heads of state who were then preparing for the 1993 G-7 Summit in Tokyo. He called on them to find

> the means of lowering all economic barriers between North America, Europe, and Japan—trade, investment, legal, and so forth—in order to begin creating the nucleus of a new world economic order that would include a harmonized world business system with agreed rules and procedures that transcend national boundaries.[1]

Morita went on to make clear that, in his view, it is time for all local interests, including local cultures and other symbols of local identity, to give way to the larger good that the free-market system makes possible. In his ideal world,

> Japanese rice farmers would not be able to keep their market closed, nor would Japanese keiretsu be allowed to exclude foreign suppliers from their production systems or imported goods from retail shelves. But neither would Americans be able to deal with perceived unfairness through methods such as unilateral tariffs. And Europeans would not be able to sit in unilateral judgment on what is or isn't a "European" car.
>
> Over time we should seek to create an environment in which the movement of goods, services, capital, technology, and people throughout North America, Europe, and Japan is truly free and unfettered.[2]

Within such a world order, complaints about restrictions on foreign access to markets would be quickly investigated and resolved by a supranational arbitration panel that would "propose specific remedies to facilitate foreign entry in areas found to be unfair or insufficiently open."[3] Governmental efforts to maintain market competition through antitrust regulations would be tempered by an acceptance of the needs of companies that are "sharing research and development, carrying out joint manufacturing, or forming various kinds of beneficial partnerships and alliances." Governments would coordinate exchange rates to reduce arbitrary risks from currency fluctuations incurred by global corporations as they move goods and capital freely around the world to wherever offers the greatest return.[4]

The underlying message is clear. Local people, acting through their governments, should no longer have the right to govern their own economies in the local interest. Government should respond instead to the needs of the global corporation. Morita's words echo those of George Ball, America's undersecretary of state for economic affairs, who in 1967 said to the British National Committee of the International Chamber of Commerce:

The political boundaries of nation-states are too narrow and constricted to define the scope and activities of modern business. . . . By and large, those companies that have achieved a global vision of their operations tend to opt for a world in which not only goods but all the factors of production can shift with maximum freedom.[5]

In the July 15, 1991, issue of its official newsletter, the International Monetary Fund drew on a study by DeAnne Julius, the chief economist of Shell International Petroleum Company, to stress the importance of trade agreements that would assure capital the same freedom of movement as goods. It proposed three principles:

- Foreign companies should have complete freedom of choice as to whether they participate in a local market by importing goods or by establishing a local production facility.

- Foreign firms should be governed by the same laws and be accorded the same rights in a country as domestic firms.

- Foreign firms should be allowed to undertake any activity in a country that is legally permissible for domestic firms to undertake.

Carla Hills, the US trade representative under the Bush administration, expressed her commitment to this goal: "We want corporations to be able to make investments overseas without being required to take a local partner, or export a given percentage of their output, to use local parts, or to meet any of a dozen other restrictions."[6] It is a view widely shared in corporate circles. An international survey of business executives conducted by the *Harvard Business Review* in 1990 found that some 12,000 respondents from twenty-five countries agreed by a substantial margin that there should be free trade between nations and the least possible protection for domestic enterprise. By a similar margin, they rejected the idea that businesses should be committed to their home country or face barriers to moving facilities to another part of the world.[7]

The corporate empire builders are rapidly making their dream a reality. From 1965 to 1992, the percentage of world economic output traded between countries rose from just under 9 percent to just under 19 percent.[8] Overall, trade has been expanding at roughly twice the rate of growth in economic output. From 1983 to 1990, worldwide foreign investment grew four times faster than world output and three times faster than world trade, leading *The Economist* to conclude that foreign investment is the area "where the most rapid progress has been made since 1980."[9] Given that as much as 70 percent of world trade is controlled by just five hundred corporations,[10] and a mere 1 percent of all transnationals own half the total stock of foreign direct investment,[11] it seems that *The Economist* measures progress by the rate at which a few transnational corporations are consolidating their hold on the global economy.

Corporations beyond National Interests

It has become a matter of pride and principle for corporate executives to proclaim that their firms have grown beyond any national interest. Typical is the statement of Charles Exley Jr., CEO of National Cash Register, who proudly told the *New York Times*, "National Cash Register is not a US corporation. It is a world corporation that happens to be headquartered in the United States."[12] According to C. Michael Armstrong, former chair in charge at IBM World Trade Corporation, "IBM, to some degree, has successfully lost its American identity."[13]

Such statements are not mere posturing. IBM Japan employs 18,000 Japanese workers and is one of Japan's major computer exporters, including to the United States.[14] In 1993, General Motors Corporation of the United States announced an agreement with Toyota Motor Corporation of Japan under which General Motors would produce up to 20,000 cars a year in the United States for sale in Japan under the Toyota brand name.[15]

In truth, the question of the national origin of the content of a product has become so complex that it is nearly impossible to determine with certainty. It is not evident that even the companies in question know, or particularly care about, the percentage distribution of the national origin of their products' content. In a 1990 cover story, *Business Week* noted:

> Though few companies are totally untethered from their home countries, the trend toward a form of "stateless" corporation is unmistakable. The European, American, and Japanese giants heading in this direction are learning how to juggle multiple identities and multiple loyalties. . . . These world corporations are developing chameleon-like abilities to resemble insiders no matter where they operate. At the same time, they move factories and labs "around the world without particular reference to national borders," says Unisys Corp. Chairman W. Michael Blumenthal.[16]

In other words, in their day-to-day operations, the allegiance of the world's largest corporations is purely to their own bottom line—without regard to any national or local interest.

During the transition phase from national to transnational, many corporations styled themselves as "multinational," which meant they took on many national identities, maintaining relatively autonomous production and sales facilities in individual countries, establishing local roots and presenting themselves in each locality as a good local citizen. Globalized operations might be linked to one another, but they were as well deeply integrated into the individual local economies in which they operated. During this phase, many did function to some extent as local citizens.

As structural adjustment programs and free trade agreements rendered national economic borders increasingly irrelevant, most corporations that operate internationally became self-consciously transnational. This commonly involved building their operations around globally integrated supplier networks. For example, when Otis Elevator set about to create an advanced elevator system, it contracted out the design of the motor drives to Japan, the door system to France, the electronics to Germany, and small-gear components to Spain. System integration was handled from the United States.[17] The goal was to eliminate considerations of nationality in an effort to maximize the economies of centralized global procurement.[18]

Although a transnational corporation may choose to claim local citizenship when that posture suits its purpose, local commitments are temporary. Only when asking its "home government" for special tax breaks, subsidies, or governmental representation in negotiations that bear on its global marketing and investment interests is a transnational corporation likely to wrap itself in a national flag and profess its deep commitment to strengthening "national" competitiveness.

The Economist has suggested that the appropriate strategy for those who own the rights to products or processes in a fully globalized economy is not to produce anything. Instead, they should simply license rights to these products and processes for an amount sufficient to yield the same profits they would have made if they had produced the products locally or for export.[19] In other worlds, those who hold monopoly control of patented technologies should not be expected to produce anything—they should simply collect the profits. This is a far cry from Adam Smith's ideal of a competitive market economy in which the returns go to small producers.

The more protected individual markets are, the more a global firm is forced to function in a multinational mode, producing locally in each setting to achieve access to that market and integrating itself into the local economy. As local settings are opened to the global economy, it becomes possible, and highly profitable, for a firm to take advantage of the differences between localities with regard to wages, market potential, employment standards, taxes, environmental regulations, local facilities, and human resources. This means arranging its global operations to produce products where costs are lowest, sell them in more affluent markets, and shift the resulting profits to where tax rates are least burdensome. The ability to shift production from one country to another weakens the bargaining power of any given locality and shifts the balance of power from the local human interest to the global corporate interest.

The more readily a firm is able to move capital, goods, technology, and personnel freely among localities in search of such advantage, the greater the competitive pressure on localities to subsidize investors by absorbing their social, environmental, and other production costs. The larger and more open the markets, the greater the profit opportunity for firms that are sufficiently large and nimble to capitalize on the differences—and the greater the larger firms' competitive advantage over smaller local firms that remain rooted in a particular community and play by its rules.

A recent study of multinational enterprises (MNEs) by the Office of Technology Assessment of the US Congress observed:

> Because they span national borders, many MNEs are less concerned with advancing national goals than with pursuing objectives internal to the firm—principally growth, profits, proprietary technology, strategic alliances, return on investment, and market power. . . . The U.S. economy (or any other, for that matter) cannot remain competitive unless MNEs that sell and conduct business in America also contribute to its research and technology base, employment, manufacturing capabilities, and capital resources. . . .
>
> The interests of all nations ought to be fairly straightforward—quality jobs, a rising standard of living, technological and industrial development, ensured rights of workers and consumers, and a high-quality environment at home and globally. . . . As compared to nations, the interests of MNEs are far more situation-oriented and linked to opportunity.[20]

In general, Japanese corporations have been oriented toward a Japanese national interest. American corporations have taken the lead in rejecting national interest in favor of a more narrowly defined corporate interest. European firms tend to fall somewhere in between. The clear trend is toward a corporate interest delinked from any national interest.

Governments in the Service of Consumerism

Kenichi Ohmae, managing director of McKinsey & Company Japan, is another respected guru of the new economic order. In his widely read book *The Borderless World*, Ohmae tells national governments that clinging to their traditional roles as managers of national economies is futile, because national economies no longer exist.

For example, when governments attempt to use traditional interest rate and money supply instruments to stimulate a nonexistent national economy, the jobs that result may well be created in other countries that experience a resulting increase in demand for their exports. If a government raises interest rates to control inflation, foreign funds will gush in from abroad and render the policy meaningless.[21]

Globalization has rendered many of the political roles of government obsolete as well. Companies with globalized operations routinely and effortlessly sidestep governmental restrictions based on old assumptions about national economies and foreign policy. For example, Honda circumvents restrictions on importing Japanese cars into Taiwan, South Korea, and Israel by shipping Honda vehicles to these countries from its US plant in Ohio.

When Japan opened bidding on new telecommunications facilities to US manufacturers, Canada's Northern Telecom moved many of its production facilities to the United States so that it could win Japanese contracts as a US company. When President Ronald Reagan ordered economic sanctions against Libya in January 1986, Brown & Root, a Houston engineering concern, simply shifted a $100 million contract for work on Libya's Great Man-Made River project to its British subsidiary.[22]

The appropriate response for the bureaucrats, in Ohmae's view, is to yield to the inevitable—accept the reality that government is obsolete, get out of the way, and let goods and money flow freely in response to market forces:

> Multinational companies are truly the servants of demanding consumers around the world. . . . When governments are slow to grasp the fact that their role has changed from protecting their people and their natural resource base from outside economic threats to ensuring that their people have the widest range of choice among the best and the cheapest goods and services from around the world—when, that is, governments still think and act like the saber-rattling mercantilist ruling powers of centuries past—they discourage investment and impoverish their people. Worse, they commit their people to isolation from an emerging world economy, which, in turn effectively dooms them to a downward spiral of frustrated hopes and industrial stagnation. . . . [As] recent events in Eastern Europe have shown, the people—as consumers and as citizens—will no longer tolerate this antiquated role of government.[23]

Ohmae counsels governments to actively join global corporations in assuring consumers that they should not be concerned about where a product is produced. He supports his argument by pointing out that production costs are typically only about 25 percent of the end-user price; the major contribution to a product's price comes increasingly from marketing and support functions. "Such functions as distribution, warehousing, financing, retail marketing, systems integration, and services are all legitimate parts of the business system and can create as many, and often more jobs than simply manufacturing operations."[24] In effect, Ohmae is arguing that a country can meet its employment needs by concentrating on marketing and consuming goods that are produced elsewhere.

The United States has already largely embraced Ohmae's vision as the organizing principle of its economy. Foreign producers now supply 30 percent of the goods, other than oil, sold in the US domestic market—up from 15 percent at the beginning of the 1980s.[25] Meanwhile, the United States became the world's leading international debtor nation, while suffering rising unemployment and falling wages.

If people were indeed only consumers, there might be merit to Ohmae's argument. But people have other roles and values that lead to real and legitimate concerns about such matters as where a good is produced and what rules will govern local economic affairs. The human interest and the corporate interest differ.

Community versus Corporate Interests

The global economy has created a dynamic in which competition among localities has become as real as competition among firms. Moore County, South Carolina, won a competitiveness bid in the 1960s and 1970s when it lured a number of large manufacturers from the unionized industrial regions of the northeastern United States with promises of tax breaks, lax environmental regulations, and compliant labor. Proctor Silex was one of the companies attracted. Later, when Proctor Silex expanded its local plant, Moore County floated a $5.5 million municipal bond to finance necessary sewer and water hookups—even though nearby residents were living without running water and other basic public services. Then in 1990, the company decided that Mexico offered more competitive terms and moved again. It left behind 800 unemployed Moore County workers, drums of buried toxic waste, and the public debts the county had incurred to finance public facilities in the company's behalf.[26]

Americans need go no farther than the Mexican border to get an idea of what it now takes to be globally competitive. Maquiladoras are assembly plants in the free trade zone on the Mexican side of the border that ship most or all of their production to the United States. The zone has become a powerful magnet, attracting many US companies, including General Electric, Ford, General Motors, GTE Sylvania, RCA, Westinghouse, and Honeywell, that are seeking low-cost locations in which to produce for the US market.[27] Growth has been explosive, from 620 maquiladora plants employing 119,550 workers in 1980 to 2,200 factories employing more than 500,000 Mexican workers in 1992. Many feature the most modern high-productivity equipment and technology. Although the productivity of Mexican workers who work in modern plants is comparable to that of US workers, the average hourly wage in maquiladora factories is just $1.64, compared with an average manufacturing wage of $16.17 in the United States.

To maintain the kinds of conditions transnational corporations prefer, the Mexican government has denied workers the right to form independent labor unions and has held wage increases far below productivity increases. In the summer of 1992, more than 14,000 Mexican workers at a Volkswagen plant turned down a contract negotiated by their government-dominated labor union. The company fired them all, and a Mexican court upheld the company's action. In 1987, in the midst of a bitter two-month strike in Mexico, Ford Motor Company tore up its union contract, fired 3,400 workers, and cut wages by 45 percent. When the workers rallied around dissident labor leaders, gunmen hired by the official government-dominated union shot workers at random in the factory.

Loose enforcement of environmental regulations is another attraction. An investigative team from the US General Accounting Office reported to Congress that all six newly opened US plants it inspected in Mexico were operating without the required environmental licenses. Other studies have found evidence of massive toxic dumping in the maquiladora zones, polluting rivers, groundwater, and soil, and causing severe health problems among workers and deformities among babies born to young women working in the zone.

Since investors are exempted from property taxes on their factories, public infrastructure—roads, water, housing, and sewage lines—is grossly inadequate. The workers live in shantytowns that stretch for miles. The dwellings are constructed of scrap materials and have no sewer systems; most have no running water. Worker families commonly store water in discarded barrels whose markings show that they once contained toxic chemicals.

According to Professor Gueramina Valdes Villalva of the Colegio de la Frontera Norte in Juarez:

> We have begun to see more fourteen-year-olds in the plants. Because of the intensive work it entails, there is a constant burnout. If they've been here three or four years, workers lose efficiency. They begin to have problems with eyesight. They begin to have allergies and kidney problems. They are less productive.[28]

Mexican workers, including children, are heroes of the new economic order in the eyes of corporate libertarians—sacrificing their health, lives, and future on the altar of global competition.

Not all global corporations locate in Mexico. In 1993, South Carolina was again being praised by business publications for its aggressive efforts to win the favor of international investors. Its major coup was a successful bid for a new BMW auto plant. BMW had spent three years assessing offers from 250 localities in ten countries before deciding to place its $400 million facility in South Carolina. According to *Business Week*, company officials were attracted by the temperate climate, year-round golf, and the availability of a number of mansions at affordable prices. They also liked the region's cheap labor, low taxes, and limited union activity.

When BMW indicated that it favored a 1,000-acre tract on which a large number of middle-class homes were already located, the state spent $36.6 million to buy the 140 properties and leased the site back to the company at $1 a year. The state also picked up the costs of recruiting, screening, and training workers for the new plant and raised an additional $2.8 million from private sources to send newly hired engineers for training in Germany. The total cost to the South Carolina taxpayers for these and other subsidies to attract BMW will be $130 million over thirty years.[29]

This is an all-too-typical example of how taxpayers are subsidizing the production costs of major global companies. In 1957, corporations in the United States provided 45 percent of local property tax revenues. By 1987, their share had dropped to about 16 percent.[30] A 1994 study by the Progressive Policy Institute of the Democratic Leadership Conference identified what it considered to be unjustified subsidies and tax benefits extended to corporations in the United States amounting to $111 billion over five years.[31] The trend is clear. The largest corporations are paying less tax and receiving more subsidies.

This is the globally competitive market at work, forcing localities to absorb private costs to increase private profits. The game of global competition is rigged. It pits companies against people in a contest that the people almost always lose.

A serious reading of the financial press and the treatises of the architects of globalization suggests that the ideal world of the global dreamers can be characterized as one in which:

- the world's money, technology, and markets are controlled and managed by gigantic global corporations;

- a common consumer culture unifies all people in a shared quest for material gratification;

- there is perfect global competition among workers and localities to offer their services to investors at the most advantageous terms;
- corporations are free to act solely on the basis of profitability without regard to national or local consequences;
- relationships, both individual and corporate, are defined entirely by the market; and
- there are no loyalties to place and community.

Embellished by promises of limitless and effortless affluence, the vision of a global economy has an entrancing appeal. Beneath its beguiling surface, however, we find a modern form of enchantment, a siren song created by the skilled image makers of Madison Avenue, enticing societies to weaken communities to free the market, eliminate the livelihoods of workers to create fortunes for capitalists, and destroy life to increase unneeded and often-unsatisfying consumption. Contrary to what the corporate libertarians would have us believe, the seductive melodies that beckon us are not produced by inexorable historical forces beyond human influence. They come from the well-rehearsed human voices of Stratos dwellers calling out to us from their city in the clouds across a great gap that most of humanity can never cross.

CHAPTER 9

Building Elite Consensus

The foreign policies of nation-states, particularly economic and monetary policies, have always been a highly elitist matter. Policy options are proposed, reviewed, and executed within the context of a broad bipartisan consensus that is painstakingly managed by very small circles of public and private elites. . . . Where necessary, a consensus is engineered on issues which must get congressional/parliamentary approval, but wherever possible executive agreements between governments are used to avoid the democratic process altogether.

—PETER THOMPSON

Strong growth in the poorer parts of the world will be needed to sustain enough growth in the West to maintain adequate levels of employment and to enable Western governments to deal with their pressing social problems.

—FELIX ROHATYN

It is helpful to understand how the corporate globalization agenda has been crafted and carried forward largely outside the public discourse. It is not a matter of a small elite group meeting in secret to craft a master plan for taking over the world. It works much more like any other networking or shared culture-building process out of which alliances among individuals and groups emerge and evolve. There is no conspiracy, though in practical terms, the consequences are much as if there were.

In this chapter, we take a brief look at each of three major forums that have served the consensus-building process in support of economic globalization: the Council on Foreign Relations, the Bilderberg Group, and the Trilateral Commission. They are not the only organizations important to this process. But they are distinctive in their effectiveness in bringing together key individuals from government, business, the media, and academia to create a consensus that aligns our most powerful institutions with the economic globalization agenda.

Visions of American Hegemony

The roots of the current drive toward economic globalization go back to the trauma of the depression that preceded World War II. America's policy elites were deeply concerned about ensuring that nothing similar would ever recur. There were two prevailing ideas as to how this might be accomplished. One would have required major reforms of the US economy, including strong governmental intervention in the market. The other depended on ensuring the domestic American economy sufficient access to foreign markets and raw materials to sustain the continuous expansion required to maintain full employment without market reforms. The latter was by far the more popular alternative among those in power, including a small elite group of foreign policy planners associated with the Council on Foreign Relations.

A meeting ground for powerful members of the US corporate and foreign policy establishments, the Council on Foreign Relations styles itself as a forum for the airing of opposing views—an incubator of leaders and ideas. Its activities are organized around dinner meetings and study programs for its members—often involving influential world figures or foreign policy thinkers—in settings that are conducive to candid, off-the-record discussion. It similarly styles its influential *Foreign Affairs* journal as a forum for the open debate of significant foreign policy issues.[1]

The portion of the Council's history that is of particular interest to our present inquiry began on September 12, 1939, less than two weeks after the outbreak of World War II. On that day, Walter Mallory, executive director of the Council, and Hamilton Armstrong, the editor of *Foreign Affairs,* met in Washington with George Messersmith, assistant secretary of state and a member of the Council. They outlined a long-range planning project to be carried out by the Council in close collaboration with the State Department on long-term problems of the war and plans for peace. Several war and peace study groups composed of foreign policy experts would produce confidential expert recommendations for President Franklin D. Roosevelt,[2] who, during his tenure as governor of New York, had lived in a town house next door to the Council's headquarters. Relations between Roosevelt and the Council continued to be close. At that point in history, the State Department lacked the funds and personnel to undertake such studies, so its leadership accepted the Council's proposal. By the end of the war, the partnership had produced 682 confidential memoranda for the government, with funding provided in part from the Rockefeller Foundation.[3]

The planners anticipated that the defeat of Germany and Japan and the wartime devastation of Europe would leave the United States in an undisputed position to dominate the postwar economy. They believed the more open that economy was to trade and foreign investment, the more readily the United States would be able to dominate it. Working from that logic, the plans produced by the State Department–Council planning groups placed a substantial emphasis on creating an institutional framework for an open global economy.[4]

In April 1941, a confidential memo from the Council's Economic and Financial Group provided the government with the following suggestion on how to frame the public presentation of US objectives for propaganda purposes during the war:

> If war aims are stated which seem to be concerned solely with Anglo-American imperialism, they will offer little to people in the rest of the world, and will be vulnerable to Nazi counter promises. Such aims would also strengthen the most reactionary elements in the United States and the British Empire. The interests of other peoples should be stressed, not only those of Europe, but also of Asia, Africa, and Latin America. This would have a better propaganda effect.[5]

Memorandum E-B34, issued by the Council to the president and the State Department on July 24, 1941, outlined the concept of a "Grand Area." This was the area of the world that the United States would need to dominate economically and militarily to ensure materials for its industries with the "fewest possible stresses."[6] The minimum necessary Grand Area would consist of most of the non-German world. Its preferred scope would consist of the Western Hemisphere, the United Kingdom, the remainder of the British Commonwealth and Empire, the Dutch East Indies, China, and Japan. The concept outlined in the memo involved working for economic integration within the largest available core area and then expanding outward to weave other areas into the core, as circumstances allowed.

This same memorandum called for the creation of worldwide financial institutions to stabilize currencies and facilitate programs of capital investment in the development of backward and underdeveloped regions.[7] This recommendation aligned with similar proposals being put forward by Harry White at the US Department of Treasury that led to establishment of the International Monetary Fund (IMF), to be responsible for keeping currencies stable and liquid to facilitate trade, and the International Bank for Reconstruction and Development (IBRD), commonly known as the World Bank, to facilitate capital investments in "backward and underdeveloped" regions and open them for development.[8]

The subsequent US initiative on behalf of economic globalization worked from two basic premises. First, in order to maintain the existing capitalist economic system, the United States must have access to the resources and markets of much of the world so that it could create a sufficient export surplus to maintain full employment at home. Second, by spreading the US economic model throughout the world within a globalized economy, the world would become united in peace and prosperity. Apparently, little note was taken of the evident contradiction that if maintaining the prosperity of a US-style economy required gaining control of most of the world's resources and markets, it would be impossible for other countries to replicate the US experience. Nor is it evident that much thought was given to the contradiction of financing industrial exports to low-income countries with international development loans that could be repaid by these countries only if they developed export surpluses with the countries that had initially extended the loans.

If such questions were raised, they were quickly pushed into the background by the urgency of the war effort and the powerful interests the vision served. Furthermore, much as the US foreign policy planners anticipated, the United States was in the driver's seat immediately following World War II. America's foreign policy elites were gripped by a sense of America's newfound power and responsibility in the world. A bit of hubris was perhaps inevitable.

The North Atlantic Alliance

Europe's emergence from the ashes of war, the decision to form a European political and economic union, and the West's confrontation with the communist empire of the Soviet Union created an imperative to expand the earlier hegemonic US vision to embrace the idea of a North Atlantic community that would provide the leadership in a Western-dominated global system. This created an obvious need for mechanisms through which the policies of the North Atlantic countries might be coordinated. The formal mechanisms, such as the North Atlantic Treaty Organization (NATO), formed in 1949, and the Organisation for Economic Co-operation and Development (OECD), established in 1961, are well known.

Less known is a powerful but unofficial group with no acknowledged membership, generally referred to as the Bilderberg Group, named for the Hotel de Bilderberg of Oosterbeek, Holland, at which a group of North American and European leaders first met in May 1954. Subsequent

Bilderberg Group meetings and the relationships they nurtured played a significant role in advancing the European Union and shaping a consensus among leaders of the Atlantic nations.[9] Participants include heads of state, other leading politicians, key industrialists and financiers, and an assortment of intellectuals, trade unionists, diplomats, and influential representatives of the press with demonstrated sympathy for establishment views. One Bilderberg Group insider observed that "today there are very few figures among governments on both sides of the Atlantic who have not attended at least one of these meetings."[10]

US president Dwight D. Eisenhower regularly sent Gabriel Hauge, his White House domestic policy chief and former director and treasurer of the Council on Foreign Relations, as his personal representative to Bilderberg meetings. President John F. Kennedy appointed Bilderberg alumni to virtually every senior position in his State Department—Secretary of State Dean Rusk, Undersecretary of State George W. Ball, George McGhee, Walt Rostow, McGeorge Bundy, and Arthur Dean.[11]

Józef Retinger, the permanent secretary of Bilderberg until his death in 1960 and a leading proponent of European unification, explained that the Bilderberg meetings provided freedom in discussing difficult issues that more official forums could not provide:

> Even if a participant is a member of a government, a leader of a political party, an official of an international organization or of a commercial concern, he does not commit his government, his party or his organization by anything he may say. . . . Bilderberg does not make policy. Its aim is to reduce differences of opinion and resolve conflicting trends and to further understanding, if not agreement, by hearing and considering various points of view and trying to find a common approach to major problems. Direct action has therefore never been contemplated, the object being to draw the attention of people in responsible positions to Bilderberg's findings.[12]

Trilateralism

The subsequent emergence of Japan as a third economic force within the orbit of the West led to the idea of a trilateral alliance that would merge the economic interests of three regional partners: North America (the United States and Canada), Western Europe, and Japan. This idea became a frequent topic of discussion at Bilderberg meetings. It was decided to create a new forum that included the Japanese and had a more formal structure than Bilderberg.

In 1973, the Trilateral Commission was formed by David Rockefeller, chairman of Chase Manhattan Bank, and Zbigniew Brzezinski, who served as the commission's director and coordinator until 1977, when he became national security adviser to US president Jimmy Carter.[13] The Trilateral Commission describes itself as follows:

> The Commission's members are about 325 distinguished citizens, with a variety of leadership responsibilities from these three regions. When the first triennium of the Trilateral Commission was launched in 1973, the most immediate purpose was to draw together—at a time of considerable friction among governments—the highest level unofficial group possible to look together at the common problems facing our three areas. At a deeper level, there was a sense that the United States was no longer in such a singular leadership position as it had been in earlier post–World War II years, and that a more shared form of leadership—including Europe and Japan in particular—would be needed for the international system to navigate successfully the major challenges of the coming years. These purposes continue to inform the Commission's work.[14]

In contrast to Bilderberg, which is known for its secrecy, the Trilateral Commission is a more transparent organization that readily distributes its membership and publication lists to anyone who calls its publicly listed phone number, and its publications are available for sale to the public. Whereas Bilderberg includes many heads of state, other top government officials, and royalty, members of the Trilateral Commission who assume high-level administrative positions in government resign from the Commission for the period of their tenure.[15]

The collective power of the Commission's members is impressive. They include the heads of four of the world's five largest nonbanking transnational corporations (Itochu, Sumitomo, Mitsubishi, and Mitsui & Co.); top officials of five of the world's six largest international banks (Sumitomo, Fuji, Sakura, Sanwa, and Mitsubishi); and heads of major media organizations (Japan Times, Le Point, Times Mirror, the Washington Post Company, CNN, and Time Warner).

Presidents Jimmy Carter, George H. W. Bush, and Bill Clinton were all members of the Trilateral Commission, as was Thomas Foley, former Speaker of the US House of Representatives. Many key members of the Carter administration were both Bilderbergers and Trilateral Commission members, including Vice President Walter Mondale, Secretary of State Cyrus Vance, National Security Adviser Brzezinski, and Treasury Secretary W. Michael Blumenthal.[16] Former members of the Trilateral Commission who went on to hold key positions under the Clinton administration include Warren Christopher, secretary of state; Bruce Babbitt, secretary of the interior; Henry Cisneros, secretary of housing and urban development; Alan Greenspan, chairman of the US Federal Reserve System; Joseph Nye Jr., chairman of the National Intelligence Council, Central Intelligence Agency; Donna E. Shalala, secretary of health and human services; Clifton Wharton Jr., deputy secretary of state; and Peter Tarnoff, undersecretary of state for political affairs.[17]

Although the Commission publishes its own position papers, its views are conveyed through many outlets not necessarily associated with it. The trilateralist vision of Sony chairman Akio Morita that was published in *The Atlantic Monthly* and discussed in the previous chapter is an example. At the time he published the article, Morita was the Japanese chairman of the Trilateral Commission.

It is important to note that the Council on Foreign Relations, the Bilderberg, and the Trilateral Commission bring together heads of competing corporations and leaders of competing national political parties for closed-door discussions and consensus-building processes that the public never sees. Although the participants may believe that they represent a broad spectrum of intersectoral and even international perspectives, in truth it is a closed and exclusive process limited to elite Stratos dwellers. Participants are predominantly male, wealthy, from Northern industrial countries, and, except for the Japanese on the Trilateral Commission, Caucasian. Other voices are excluded.

The resulting narrowness of perspective is evident in the publications of the Trilateral Commission. They are written by seasoned and thoughtful professionals, and a diversity of views is presented. Yet they all accept without question the ideological premises of corporate libertarianism. The benefits of economic integration and a harmonization of the tax, regulatory, and other policies of the trilateral countries—and ultimately of all countries—are assumed as an article of faith. The debate centers on how, not whether.

No note is taken of the fact that harmonizing standards—which necessarily means setting standards—can be accomplished only through international negotiations, which by their nature must be carried out in secret by the administrative branches of governments. Thus, in the absence of an elected international parliament, a call to harmonize standards is a call to take decisions regarding the standards by which businesses will operate out of the hands of democratically elected national legislative bodies and pass them to the unelected bureaucrats who work with corporate representatives to draft agreements without public representation or knowledge.

Such a situation lends itself especially well to cozy insider deal making, especially when the representatives of governments and corporations have already developed close personal relationships through such organizations as the Council on Foreign Relations, the Bilderberg, and the Trilateral Commission. For example, Carla Hills, who as US trade representative under President George H. W. Bush played a key role in negotiating the General Agreement on Tariffs and Trade (GATT), which established the new World Trade Organization, was a member of the Trilateral Commission.

The fact that Bush and Clinton were both members of the Trilateral Commission makes it easy to understand why there was such a seamless transition from the Republican Bush administration to the Democratic Clinton administration with regard to the US commitment to pass the North American Free Trade Agreement (NAFTA) and GATT. Clinton's leadership in advancing what many progressives thought to be a Bush agenda on these agreements won him high marks from his colleagues on the Trilateral Commission but seriously alienated major elements of his core constituency, who had looked to him to provide a less corporatist view of the trade agenda. On this most fundamental of issues, the electoral system gave the voters only the illusion of choice.

The policy actions being advanced by the elite consensus constitute an increasingly effective attack on the institutions of democracy, the very purpose of which is to prevent a small inside elite from capturing control of the instruments of governance. Their dominance of the policy debate largely precludes any discussion of alternatives to prevailing assumptions.

Corporate globalization is neither in the human interest nor inevitable. It is axiomatic that political power aligns with economic power. The larger and more global the corporation, the greater its political power. The greater the political power of corporations and those aligned with them, the less the political power of the people and the less meaningful democracy becomes. There is an alternative: to localize economies, disperse economic power, and bring democracy closer to the people. However, networks and alliances made up exclusively of Stratos dwellers are unlikely to articulate any alternatives that strengthen the power of the Troglytes on whose compliant labor their power and privilege depend. To the contrary, as we shall see in the next chapter, the Stratos dwellers are mobilizing the full resources of the world's largest corporations behind an effort to place themselves as far as possible beyond the reach of democratic accountability.

CHAPTER 10

Buying Out Democracy

Funds generated by business (by which I mean profits, funds in business foundations and contributions from individual businessmen) must rush by multimillions to the aid of liberty . . . to funnel desperately needed funds to scholars, social scientists, writers, and journalists who understand the relationship between political and economic liberty.

—WILLIAM SIMON,
former secretary of the US Treasury Department

Before NAFTA we thought corporations could only buy Southern governments. Now we see they also buy Northern governments.

—IGNACIO PEÓN ESCALANTE,
Mexican Action Network on Free Trade

US corporations entered the 1970s besieged by a rebellious anti-consumerist youth culture, a mushrooming environmental and product safety movement, and a serious economic challenge from Asia. Not only was their dream of global hegemony in tatters, but they even risked losing control of their own home turf. In response, they mobilized their collective political resources to regain control of the political and cultural agenda.

Their methods included a combination of sophisticated marketing techniques, old-fashioned vote buying, funding for ideologically aligned intellectuals, legal action, and many of the same grassroots mobilization techniques that environmental and consumer activists had used against the corporations during the 1960s and 1970s. Their campaigns were well funded, professionally organized, and sophisticated. The major goals were deregulation, economic globalization, and the limitation of corporate liability—in short, the enlargement of corporate rights and the reduction of corporate responsibilities. And their campaign continues in full force.

Mobilizing Corporate Political Resources

In 1971, the US Chamber of Commerce sought the advice of Virginia attorney and future Supreme Court justice Lewis Powell about the problems facing the business community. Powell produced a memorandum, "Attack on American Free Enterprise System," that warned of an assault by environmentalists, consumer activists, and others who "propagandize against the system, seeking insidiously and constantly to sabotage it." He argued that it was time "for the wisdom, ingenuity, and resources of American business to be marshaled against those who would destroy it."[1] This set the stage for an organized effort by a powerful coalition of business groups and ideologically compatible foundations to align the US political and legal system with their ideological vision.

Among Powell's recommendations was a proposal that the business community organize and fund a legal center to promote the general interests of business in the nation's courts. This led to the formation of the Pacific Legal Foundation (PLF) in 1973. Housed in the Sacramento Chamber of Commerce building, it was the first of a number of corporate-sponsored "public interest" law firms dedicated to promoting the interests of their sponsoring corporations.[2] The PLF specialized in defending business interests against "clean air and water legislation, the closing of federal wilderness areas to oil and gas exploration, workers' rights, and corporate taxation." Some 80 percent of its income was from corporations or corporate foundations.[3]

In a 1980 speech, PLF's managing attorney, Raymond Momboisse, turned reality on its head by attacking environmentalists for their "selfish, self-centered motivation . . . ; their ability to conceal their true aims in lofty sounding motives of public interest; their indifference to the injury they inflict on the masses of mankind; their ability to manipulate the law and the media; and, most of all, their power to inflict monumental harm on society."[4]

Business interests funded the establishment of law and economics programs in leading law schools to support scholarly research advancing the premise that the unregulated marketplace produces the most efficient—and thereby the most just—society. Business funded all-expenses-paid seminars at prestigious universities such as George Mason and Yale to introduce sitting judges to these economic principles and their application to jurisprudence.[5]

Before the 1970s, business interests were represented by old-fashioned corporate lobbying organizations with straightforward names: Beer Institute, National Coal Association, Chamber of Commerce, or American Petroleum Institute. As aggressive public interest groups succeeded in mobilizing broad-based citizen pressures on Congress, business decided that another approach was needed.

Corporations began to create their own "citizen" organizations with names and images that were carefully constructed to mask their corporate and sponsorship and their true purpose. The National Wetlands Coalition, which features the logo of a duck flying blissfully over a swamp, was sponsored by oil and gas companies and real estate developers to fight for the easing of restrictions on the conversion of wetlands into drilling sites and shopping malls. The corporate-sponsored Consumer Alert fights government regulations of product safety. Keep America Beautiful attempts to give its sponsors, the bottling industry, a green image by funding anti-litter campaigns, while those same sponsors actively fight mandatory recycling legislation. The strategy is to convince the public that litter is the responsibility of consumers—not the packaging industry.[6]

The views of these and similar industry-sponsored groups—thirty-six of them are documented in the book *Masks of Deception: Corporate Front Groups in America*—are regularly reported in the corporate press as the views of citizen advocates. The sole reason for their existence is to convince the public that the corporate interest *is* the public interest and that labor, health, and the environment are "special" interests. The top funders of such groups include Dow Chemical, Exxon, Chevron USA, Mobil, DuPont, Ford, Philip Morris, Pfizer, Anheuser-Busch, Monsanto, Procter & Gamble, Phillips Petroleum, AT&T, and Arco.[7]

Business interests funded the formation of conservative think tanks such as the Heritage Foundation and revived lethargic pro-establishment think tanks such as the American Enterprise Institute, which experienced a tenfold increase in its budget.[8] In 1978, the Institute for Educational Affairs was formed to match corporate funders with sympathetic scholars producing research studies supporting corporate views on economic freedom.[9]

In 1970, only a handful of the Fortune 500 companies had public affairs offices in Washington; by 1980, more than 80 percent did. In 1974, labor unions accounted for half of all political action committee (PAC) money. By 1980, the unions accounted for less than a fourth of this funding.[10] With the inauguration of President Ronald Reagan in 1981, the ideological alliance of corporate libertarians consolidated its control over the instruments of power.

Although many of those involved in these campaigns truly believe that they are acting in the public interest, what we are seeing is a frontal assault on democratic pluralism to advance the ideological agenda of corporate libertarianism. Though advanced in the name of freedom and democracy, this massive abuse of corporate power mocks both.

Building Business Lobbies

Business roundtables are national associations of the chief executive officers (CEOs) of the largest transnational corporations. Whereas more inclusive business organizations such as national chambers of commerce and national associations of manufacturers include both large and small firms representing many different interests and perspectives, the members of business roundtables are all large transnational corporations firmly aligned with the economic globalization agenda.

The first Business Roundtable was formed in the United States in 1972. Its 200 members include the heads of forty-two of the fifty largest Fortune 500 US industrial corporations, seven of the eight largest US commercial banks, seven of the ten largest US insurance companies, five of the seven largest US retailers, seven of the eight largest US transportation companies, and nine of the eleven largest US utilities.

In this forum, the CEO of the DuPont chemical company sits with the CEOs of his three major rivals: Dow, Occidental Petroleum, and Monsanto. The head of General Motors sits with the heads of Ford and Chrysler—and so on with each major industry. In this forum, the heads of the world's largest US-based corporations put aside their competitive differences to frame a common corporate political agenda for America. The US Business Roundtable describes itself as

> an association of chief executive officers who examine public issues that affect the economy and develop positions which seek to reflect sound economic and social principles. Established in 1972, the Roundtable was founded in the belief that business executives should take an increased role in the continuing debates about public policy.
>
> The Roundtable believes that the basic interests of business closely parallel the interests of the American people, who are directly involved as consumers, employees, investors and suppliers. . . . Member selection reflects the goal of having representation varied by category of business and by geographic location. Thus, the members, some 200 chief executive officers of companies in all fields, can present a cross section of thinking on national issues.[11]

The Business Roundtable, surely one of America's most exclusive and least diverse membership organizations, has an unusually narrow notion of what constitutes a "cross section" of thinking on national issues. With few, if any, exceptions, its membership is limited to white males over fifty years of age whose annual compensation averages more than 170 times the US per capita gross national product.[12] Its members head corporations that disavow a commitment to national interests and stand to gain substantially from economic globalization. Once positions are defined, the Roundtable organizes aggressive campaigns to gain their political acceptance, including personal visits by its member CEOs to individual senators and representatives.

The Roundtable took an especially active role in campaigning for the North American Free Trade Agreement (NAFTA). Recognizing that the public might see free trade as a special-interest issue if touted by an exclusive club of the country's 200 largest transnationals, the Roundtable created a front organization, USA*NAFTA, that enrolled some 2,300 US corporations and associations as members.

Although USA*NAFTA claimed to represent a broad constituency, every one of its state captains was a corporate member of the Business Roundtable. All but four Roundtable members enjoyed privileged access to the NAFTA negotiation process through representation on advisory committees to the US trade representative. Roundtable members bombarded Americans with assurances through editorials, op-ed pieces, news releases, and radio and television commentaries that NAFTA would provide them with high-paying jobs, stop immigration from Mexico, and raise environmental standards.

Nine of the USA*NAFTA state captains (Allied Signal, AT&T, General Electric, General Motors, Phelps Dodge, United Technologies, IBM, ITT, and TRW) were among the US corporations that, according to the Interhemispheric Resource Center, had already shipped up to 180,000 jobs to Mexico during the twelve years prior to the passage of NAFTA. Some among the NAFTA captains were corporations that had been cited for violating worker rights in Mexico and for failing to comply with worker safety standards. Many were leading polluters in the United States and had exported to or produced in Mexico products that were banned in the United States.[13]

Democracy for Hire

Washington, DC's major growth industry consists of for-profit public relations firms and business-sponsored policy institutes engaged in producing facts, opinion pieces, expert analyses, opinion polls, and direct-mail and telephone solicitation to create "citizen" advocacy and public-image-building campaigns on demand for corporate clients. William Greider calls it "democracy for hire."[14] Burson-Marsteller—the world's largest public relations firm, with net 1992 billings of $204 million—worked for

Exxon during the Exxon *Valdez* oil spill and for Union Carbide during the Bhopal disaster. The top fifty public relations firms billed over $1.7 billion in 1991.[15]

In the United States, the 170,000 public relations employees engaged in manipulating news, public opinion, and public policy to serve the interests of paying clients now outnumber actual news reporters by about 40,000—and the gap is growing. These firms will organize citizen letter-writing campaigns, provide paid operatives posing as "housewives" to present corporate views in public meetings, and place favorable news items and op-ed pieces in the press.

A 1990 study found that almost 40 percent of the news content in a typical US newspaper originates from public relations press releases, story memos, and suggestions. According to the *Columbia Journalism* Review, more than half of the *Wall Street Journal*'s news stories are based solely on press releases.[16] The distinction between advertising space and news space grows less distinct with each passing day.

While the Republicans have long been known as the party of money, the Democratic Party was historically the party of the people, with strong representation of working-class and minority interests. The Democrats once depended heavily on their strong grassroots political organization—on people more than money—to deliver the votes on Election Day. These structures in turn forced politicians to maintain some contact with the grass roots and ensured a degree of local accountability. Ties to the party were strong.

With the growing role of television in American life and the decline in the US labor movement, costly television-based media campaigns have become increasingly central in deciding election outcomes. As a consequence, the grassroots organization that was once the foundation of the Democratic Party structure has disintegrated, causing it to lose its populist moorings and leaving those who once constituted its political base feeling unrepresented.

With the breakdown of this structure, those who run for office under the Democratic Party banner have become increasingly dependent on developing their own fund-raising organizations. This has left them more vulnerable to the influence of moneyed interests and greatly strengthened the hand of big business in setting policy agendas of both parties. The scholar-journalist William Greider maintains that the policy direction of the Democratic Party is now set largely by six Washington law firms that specialize in selling political influence to moneyed clients and in raising money for Democratic politicians. Working closely with Republicans as well, these firms are in the business of brokering power to whoever will pay their fees.[17] This is the sorry state of American democracy.

The Republican Party has responded most handily to the new circumstances, expertly adapting sophisticated techniques of mass marketing to the task of winning elections. With these techniques, it has accomplished the improbable task of exploiting the alienation of powerless citizens to build a populist political base in support of an elitist agenda. As elaborated by Greider in *Who Will Tell the People:*

> As men of commerce, Republicans naturally understood marketing better than Democrats, and they applied what they knew about selling products to politics with none of the awkward hesitation that inhibited old-style politicians. As a result, voters are now viewed as a passive assembly of "consumers," a mass audience of potential buyers. Research discovers through scientific sampling what it is these consumers know or think and, more important, what they feel, even when they do not know their own "feelings." A campaign strategy is then designed to connect the candidate with these consumer attitudes. Advertising images are created that will elicit positive responses and make the sale.[18]

American democracy isn't for sale only to America's transnational corporations. The Mexican government spent upwards of $25 million and hired many of the leading Washington lobbyists to support its campaign for NAFTA. In the late 1980s, Japanese corporations were spending an estimated $100 million a year on political lobbying in the United States and another $300 million building a nationwide grassroots political network to influence public opinion.

Together, the Japanese government and Japanese companies employed ninety-two Washington law, public relations, and lobbying firms on their behalf. This compared with fifty-five for Canada, forty-two for Britain, and seven for the Netherlands. The purpose is to rewrite US laws in favor of foreign corporations—and they often succeed.[19]

Corporate libertarianism—an ideology whose claims and promises are as false and self-serving as the claims of cigarette companies that nicotine is nonaddictive and cigarette smoke poses no health hazard—has become the dominant philosophy of our political culture and of our most powerful institutions. This is the accomplishment of a persistent campaign that uses the most sophisticated techniques yet developed by the masters of mass marketing and media manipulation. It is one element of a larger campaign to globalize markets and to embed corporate libertarianism and consumerism as defining values of a homogenized global culture.

CHAPTER 11

Marketing the World

Whoever has the power to project a vision of the good life and make it prevail has the most decisive power of all. . . . American business, after 1890, acquired such power and . . . in league with key institutions, began the transformation of American society into a society preoccupied with consumption, with comfort and bodily well-being, with luxury, spending, and acquisition, with more goods this year than last, more next year than this.

—WILLIAM LEACH

Corporate executives dream of a global market made up of people with homogenized tastes and needs. . . . Logos on bottles, boxes, and labels are global banners, instantly recognizable by millions who could not tell you the color of the U.N. flag.

—RICHARD J. BARNET and JOHN CAVANAGH

In modern societies, television has arguably become our most important institution of cultural reproduction. Our schools are probably the second most important. Television has already been wholly colonized by corporate interests, which are now laying claim to our schools. The goal is not simply to sell products and strengthen the consumer culture. It is also to create a political culture that equates the corporate interest with the human interest in the public mind. In the words of Paul Hawken, "Our minds are being addressed by addictive media serving corporate sponsors whose purpose is to rearrange reality so that viewers forget the world around them."[1]

The rearrangement of reality begins with the claim that in a market economy, the consumer decides and the market responds. In a world of small buyers and sellers, this may have been true. No individual seller could expect to create a new culture conducive to buying his or her product. This is not our current reality. Present-day corporations have no reservations about reshaping the values of whole societies to create a homogenized culture of indulgence. As corporate demand has grown for supporting services in advertising, graphics, media, creative production, consumer research, marketing education, and countless others, whole industries have emerged to help corporations create insatiable desires for the things they sell and cultivate political values aligned with the corporate interest.

First America, Then the World

There was a day when the prevailing American culture was the mass marketer's worst nightmare. Frugality and thrift were central to the famed "Puritan ethic" that the early settlers brought with them to America. The Puritans believed in hard work, participation in community, temperate living, and devotion to a spiritual life. Their basic rule of living was that one should not desire more material things than could be used effectively. They taught their children, "Use it up, wear it out, make do, or do without."[2]

The Quakers also had a strong influence on early America and, although more tolerant and egalitarian, shared with the Puritans the values of hard work and frugality as important to one's spiritual development. Ralph Waldo Emerson and Henry David Thoreau, both important early American writers, viewed simplicity as a path to experiencing the divine.[3]

The consumer culture emerged largely as a consequence of concerted efforts by the retailing giants of the late nineteenth and early twentieth centuries to create an ever-growing demand for the goods they offered for sale. The American historian William Leach has documented in *Land of Desire: Merchants, Power, and the Rise of a New American Culture* how they successfully turned a spiritually oriented culture of frugality and thrift into a material culture of self-indulgence. Leach finds the claim that the market simply responds to consumer desires to be nothing more than a self-serving fabrication of those who make their living manipulating reality to persuade consumers to buy what corporations find it profitable to sell:

> Indeed, the culture of consumer capitalism may have been among the most nonconsensual public cultures ever created, and it was nonconsensual for two reasons. First, it was not produced by "the people" but by commercial groups in cooperation with other elites comfortable with and committed to making profits and to accumulating capital on an ever-ascending scale. Second, it was nonconsensual because, in its mere day-to-day conduct (but not in any conspiratorial way), it raised to the fore only one vision of the good life and pushed out all others. In this way, it diminished American public life, denying the American people

access to insight into other ways of organizing and conceiving life, insight that might have endowed their consent to the dominant culture (if such consent were to be given at all) with real democracy.[4]

The populist cultures that grew out of the hearts and aspirations of ordinary people in America stressed the democratization of property and the virtues of a republic based on independent families owning their own land and tools, producing for themselves much of what they consumed, and participating in communities of sharing. Theirs was the model of a strong social economy, supplemented by involvement in the money economy at the margin of their lives.

The shift from a social economy of household and community production to a primarily monetized economy took place in America in the mid-1800s, a period in which the large corporations came into ascendance. As late as 1870, however, the average number of workers in a given firm was still fewer than ten. Markets remained predominantly local or regional, and most businesses were individually owned and managed. They were a bit larger than Adam Smith's market ideal, but still consistent with the underlying principles.

Large corporations became increasingly skillful in creating desire for their products. Eventually, marketing was born as a management specialty, and the early business schools began offering courses to meet the demand for trained practitioners. As more people became dependent on wage employment in the factories, governments gained a stake in promoting consumerism as a way of maintaining employment.

Business became skilled in using colors, glass, and light to create exciting images of a this-world paradise conveyed by elegant models and fashion shows. Museums offered displays depicting the excitement of the new culture. Gradually, the individual was surrounded by messages reinforcing the culture of desire. Advertisements, department store show windows, electric signs, fashion shows, the sumptuous environments of the leading hotels, and billboards all conveyed artfully crafted images of the good life. Credit programs made it seem effortless to buy that life. According to Leach:

> The United States was the first country in the world to have an economy devoted to mass production and it was the first to create the mass consumer institutions and the mass consumer enticements that rose up in tandem to market and sell the mass-produced goods. More effectively and pervasively than any other nation, America . . . forged a unique bond among different institutions that served to realize business aims.[5]

Today, television is the primary medium through which corporations shape the culture and behavior of Americans. The statistics are chilling.[6]

The average American child between the ages of two and five watches three and a half hours of television a day; the average adult, nearly five hours. Only work and sleep occupy more of the average adult's life, with television effectively replacing community and family life, cultural pursuits, and reading. At this rate, the average American adult is seeing approximately 21,000 commercials a year, most of which carry an identical message: "Buy something—do it now!"

The hundred largest corporations in America pay for roughly 75 percent of commercial television time and 50 percent of public television time. With a half minute of prime-time network advertising selling for between $200,000 and $300,000, only the largest corporations can afford it. Although there may be no overt control over program content, television producers are hired to produce television programming that advertisers will buy and necessarily have these corporations and their views of proper programming content constantly in mind.

Jerry Mander explains why television is a nearly ideal communications medium for serving the corporate purpose:

> By its ability to implant identical images into the minds of millions of people, TV can homogenize perspectives, knowledge, tastes, and desires, to make them resemble the tastes and interests of the people who transmit the imagery. In our world, the transmitters of the images are corporations whose ideal of life is technologically oriented, commodity oriented, materialistic, and hostile to nature. And satellite communications is the mechanism by which television is delivered into parts of the planet that have, until recently, been spared this assault.[7]

As global corporations reach out to the four corners of the earth, they bring with them not only established products and brand names but also their favored media and the sophisticated marketing methods by which they colonize every culture they touch.

The Economist reported that in 1989, global corporate spending for advertising totaled more than $240 billion. Another $380 billion was spent on packaging, design, and other point-of-sale promotions. Together, these expenditures amounted to $120 for every single person in the world.[8] Although the bulk of this corporate expenditure is directed toward creating demand for specific products, it also contributes to creating a generalized global consumer culture and to making a connection in the public mind between corporate interests—in particular the interests of large corporations—and the public interest.

Overall, corporations are spending well over half as much per capita to create corporation-friendly consumers as the $207 per capita ($33 for

Southern countries) the world spends on public education.[9] Furthermore, growth in advertising expenditures far outpaces increases in education spending. Advertising expenditures have multiplied nearly sevenfold since 1950—one-third faster than the world economy.[10]

The One World of MTV Knows—"Coke Is Best"

In his *Atlantic Monthly* article in praise of economic integration, Akio Morita identified distinctive local cultures as a trade barrier.[11] The need to respect local tastes and cultural differences as a condition of gaining consumer acceptance greatly complicates global marketing campaigns. The dream of corporate marketers is a globalized consumer culture united around brand-name loyalties that will allow a company to sell its products with the same advertising copy in Bangkok as in Paris or New York. It is happening.

In the words of Roberto C. Goizueta, chairman of the Coca-Cola Company, "People around the world are today connected by brand-name consumer products as much as by anything else."[12] Coca-Cola's success in making itself a global symbol has served as an inspiration for corporate executives everywhere.

Few media provide greater potential for realizing this advertisers' dream than MTV, the rock music television channel. Its near-universal appeal to teenagers and preteens around the world makes it an ideal instrument for the globalization of the consumer culture. By 1993, MTV's popular rock-and-roll programming, with its kaleidoscope of brief, disconnected images, was available on a daily basis to 210 million households in seventy-one countries.

According to Richard J. Barnet and John Cavanagh, the MTV entertainment network, which specializes in pop videos and serves as a continuous commercial for a wide array of commercial products, "may be the most influential educator of young people on five continents." They continue:

> The performances and the ads merge to create a mood of longing—for someone to love, for something to happen, for an end to loneliness, and for things to buy—a record, a ticket to a rock concert, a T-shirt, a Thunderbird. The advertising is all the more effective because it is not acknowledged as such. . . . All across the planet, people are using the same electronic devices to watch or to listen to the same commercially produced songs and stories.[13]

Sarah Ferguson believes that the commercialization of youth culture, especially the music that was once a primary instrument of expressive rebellion for adolescents, keeps youth from owning even their own rebellion and actively inhibits the development of a counterculture. She writes, "The loop taken by a new musical style from the underground to the mainstream is now so compressed that there's no moment of freedom and chaos when a counterculture can take root."[14]

Among the most aggressive efforts to universalize the consumer culture is that of the Avon beauty products company. On August 2, 1994, the show *TV Nation* documented the campaign by Avon to win new customers among dirt-poor *campesinas* in the Amazon basin of Brazil, where 70,000 saleswomen take the Avon message to every rural doorstep. Ademar Serodio, the president of Avon Brazil, explained, "Instead of asking people to buy more from us, we start discovering people who never bought from us before."

As revealed in footage of saleswomen making door-to-door house calls in the remote village of Santarem, many of these new customers are thin, aging, wrinkled women living with their barefoot children in shacks with dirt floors. Most people in Santarem don't read or write, and the average household income is $3 per day.

Hundreds of Avon saleswomen were fielded in Santarem to follow up on TV advertising showing romantic scenes of sensuous, young, light-skinned women with dashingly handsome young men. They tell the aged women, broken by years of childbearing and toil in the sun, that they can be beautiful if they use Avon products. A major promotion centers on a skin-renewal product called Renew—costing $40 a jar—which works by burning off the top layer of the user's skin. A TV ad uses special effects to create the image of a woman peeling away years of aging from her face to appear magically younger. According to Rosa Alegria, communications director for Avon Brazil, "Women do everything to buy it. They stop buying other things like clothes, like shoes. If they feel good with their skin, they prefer to stop buying clothes and buy something that is on the television. People think it is a real miracle."[15]

Corporations in the Classroom

Corporations are now moving aggressively to colonize the second major institution of cultural reproduction: schools. According to Consumers Union, 20 million US schoolchildren used some form of corporate-sponsored teaching materials in their classrooms in 1990. Some of these are straightforward promotions of junk food, clothing, and personal-care items. For example, the National Potato Board joined forces with Lifetime Learning Systems to present Count Your Chips, a math-oriented program celebrating the potato chip for National Potato Lovers' Month. Nutra-Sweet, a sugar substitute, sponsored a "total health" program.[16]

Corporations have also been aggressive in getting their junk food into school vending machines and school lunch programs. Trade shows and journals aimed at school food-service workers are full of appeals such as: "Bring Taco Bell products to your school!" "Pizza Hut makes school lunch fun." Coca-Cola launched a lobbying attack on proposed legislation to ban the sale of soft drinks and other items of "minimal nutritional value" in public schools.

Randall W. Donaldson, a spokesman for Coca-Cola in Atlanta, said: "Our strategy is ubiquity. We want to put soft drinks within arms' reach of desire. We strive to make soft drinks widely available, and schools are one channel we want to make them available in."[17]

Other messages seek to indoctrinate young minds in the beliefs and values of corporate libertarianism. Thus Mobil Corporation, which is well known for buying op-ed space in the *New York Times* to promote its view of the public interest, offered a curriculum module produced by the Learning Enrichment Corporation for classroom use that claimed to help students evaluate the North American Free Trade Agreement (NAFTA), mainly by touting its benefits.

Faced with the inevitability of an environmentally aware public, corporations have responded by painting themselves green and seeking to define the problem and its solutions in ways that support corporate objectives. Another Mobil contribution to public education is a video prepared for classroom use that touts plastic as the best waste to put in landfills. An Exxon module titled "Energy Cube" omits discussion of fuel efficiency, alternatives to fossil fuels, and global warming. Indeed, it attempts to equate gasoline with solar energy in students' minds by explaining that its "energy value comes from solar energy stored in its organic chemical bonds."

Mobil and other corporations actively support the National Council on Economic Education, whose mission is to promote the teaching of economics in elementary and high schools. A paid Mobil op-ed piece in the *New York Times* lamented the fact that high school seniors were able to give correct answers to only 35 percent of questions on a national economic literacy survey. Obviously, Mobil has its own idea of what a correct answer is. The op-ed piece noted:

When it comes to domestic issues, it helps to understand the impact that raising or cutting taxes will have on job security and your standard of living. And when it comes to environmental policy and regulations, it's necessary to comprehend basic economic principles such as supply and demand, cost versus benefit and a company's need for profits.[18]

General Motors mailed a video "I Need the Earth and the Earth Needs Me" to every public, private, and parochial elementary school in the country. Against a backdrop of happy children swimming in sparkling waters and running in picturesque landscapes, the GM video promotes such activities as planting trees and recycling. There is no mention of mass transit or the need to redesign cities to reduce transportation needs. GM recommends forming car pools and recycling used motor oil. All the statements made in the video and the accompanying teacher's guide are accurate. Yet the overall picture is misleading because it omits critical facts and ideas.

Channel One, an advertiser-sponsored school television program, beams its news and ads for candy bars, fast food, and sneakers directly into the classroom for twelve minutes a day in more than 12,000 schools. In exchange for a satellite dish and video equipment for each classroom, the school must agree that Channel One will be shown on at least 90 percent of school days to 90 percent of the children. Teachers are not allowed to interrupt the show or turn it off. A survey found that most students thought that since Channel One was shown in school, the products advertised on it must be good for them.[19]

Mark Evans, a senior vice president of Scholastic, presented the following challenge to business in an essay in *Advertising Age:*

> More and more companies see educational marketing as the most compelling, memorable and cost-effective way to build share of mind and market into the 21st century. . . . [A Gillette program introducing teenagers to its safety razors is] . . . building brand and product loyalties through classroom-centered, peer-powered lifestyle patterning. . . . Can you devise promotions that take students from the aisles in school rooms to the aisles in supermarkets?[20]

If not, presumably Scholastic, one of the leading US producers of school curriculum materials, stands ready to help.

Other corporations are proposing to operate public schools on a for-profit basis. The possibilities for profiting by turning classrooms into new mass media outlets for corporate marketing, image building, and ideological molding pitched to young and malleable minds are staggering—and frightening.

The World of 1984

Corporations spend money on advertising, lobbying, advocacy, and public relations, whether in schools or the mass media, to manipulate our minds and emotions to advance their interests using whatever methods will elicit the desired consumer response. Paul Hawken describes their methods:

Soft-focus shots of deer in virgin forests are used as totemic proof of a paper company's commitment to the future even as they continue to clear-cut and fight congressional renewal of the Endangered Species Act. Native Americans look approvingly over a littered wildflower meadow being cleaned up by children using plastic bags advertised as biodegradable which in fact are not. (Mobil Oil was sued and chastised by attorneys general in several states for this ad.) Simpson Paper introduces a line of "recycled" paper with fractional amounts of post-consumer waste under the names of Thoreau, Whitman, and Leopold. British nuclear power companies announce that nuclear energy is green energy since it does not pollute the air.[21]

Tobacco companies spend millions to convince the public that there is no scientific basis for claims that smoking is harmful to their health; auto manufacturers fight emissions standards; gun manufacturers fight gun controls; chemical companies illegally dump their toxic wastes; and drug companies engage in monopoly pricing. It happens every day. For all the corporate claims to the contrary, *Business Week* itself said it well: "Modern multinationals are not social institutions. They will play governments off one another, shift pricing to minimize taxes, seek to sway opinion, export jobs, or withhold technology to maintain a competitive edge."[22]

Corporate efforts to shape our culture and our politics through the control of television bring to mind George Orwell's *1984* and his images of an authoritarian society ruled by ever-present television monitors that manipulate citizens' perceptions of the world. Our reality is more subtle and the techniques more sophisticated than Orwell anticipated. And the strings are pulled by corporations rather than governments. We are ruled by an oppressive market, not an oppressive state.

The techniques have an elegant simplicity. They center on manipulating the cultural symbols in which our individual identities and values are anchored. Before mass media, these symbols were collective creations of people relating to one another and expressing their inner feelings through artistic media. They represented our collective sense of who we are. The more time we spend immersed in the corporate-controlled-and-packaged world of television, the less time we have for the direct human exchanges through which cultural identity and values were traditionally expressed, reinforced, and updated. Increasingly, those who control the mass media control the core culture.

The architects of the corporate global vision seek a world in which universalized symbols created and owned by the world's most powerful corporations replace the distinctive cultural symbols that link people to particular places, values, and human communities. Our cultural symbols provide an important source of identity and meaning; they affirm our worth, our place in society. They arouse our loyalty to, and sense of responsibility for, the health and well-being of our community and its distinctive ecosystem. When the control of our cultural symbols passes to corporations, we are essentially yielding to them the power to define who we are. Instead of being Americans, Norwegians, Egyptians, Filipinos, or Mexicans, we become simply members of the "Pepsi generation," detached from place and any meaning other than those a corporation finds it profitable to confer on us. Market tyranny may be more subtle than state tyranny, but it is no less effective in enslaving the many to the interests of the few.

CHAPTER 12

Adjusting the Poor

They no longer use bullets and ropes. They use the World Bank and the IMF.

—JESSE JACKSON

To attract companies like yours . . . we have felled mountains, razed jungles, filled swamps, moved rivers, relocated towns . . . all to make it easier for you and your business to do business here.

—Philippine government ad in *Fortune*

In the flurry of global institution building that followed World War II, the spotlight of public attention was focused on the United Nations, which was to include all countries, each with an equal voice—at least in its General Assembly. Delegates to the UN are public figures, and debates are open to public view and often heated. Yet the General Assembly has little real power. The real ability to act is limited to and vested in the Security Council, in which each of the major powers maintains the right of veto. Judging from its governance structures, it must be concluded that the more representative UN was created primarily to occupy the public eye and function as a forum for debate.

In contrast, three other multilateral institutions were created with relatively little fanfare to operate with real authority outside the public eye— the International Bank for Reconstruction and Development (commonly known as the World Bank), the International Monetary Fund (IMF), and the General Agreement on Tariffs and Trade (GATT), now the World Trade Organization (WTO). These three agencies are commonly referred to as the Bretton Woods institutions, in tribute to a meeting of the representatives of forty-four nations who gathered in Bretton Woods,

New Hampshire, July 1–22, 1944, to reach agreement on an institutional framework for the post–World War II global economy.

The public purpose of what became known as the Bretton Woods system was to unite the world in a web of economic prosperity and interdependence that would preclude nations from taking up arms. Another purpose in the eyes of its architects was to create an open world economy unified under US leadership that would ensure unchallenged US access to the world's markets and raw materials.[1] Two of the Bretton Woods institutions—the IMF and the World Bank—were actually created at the Bretton Woods meeting. The GATT was created at a subsequent international meeting.

Although formally designated as "special agencies" of the UN, the Bretton Woods institutions function autonomously from it. Their governance and administrative processes are secret, carefully shielded from public scrutiny and democratic debate. Indeed, the internal operating processes of the World Bank are so secretive that access to many of its most important documents relating to country plans, strategies, and priorities is denied to even its own governing executive directors. In the World Bank and the IMF, the big national powers have both veto power over certain decisions and voting shares in proportion to their shares of the subscribed capital—ensuring their ability to set and control the agenda.[2]

In this chapter, we examine how, in playing out their roles, the World Bank and the IMF have worked in concert to deepen the dependence of low-income countries on the global system and then to open their economies to corporate colonization. In the following chapter, we look at how the GATT and its successor, the World Trade Organization (WTO), are being used by the world's largest corporations to consolidate their power and place themselves beyond public accountability.

Creating a Demand for Debt

The primary original purpose of the World Bank was to finance European reconstruction. However, there was very little demand from the European countries for World Bank loans. What Europe needed was rapidly dispersing grants or concessional loans for balance-of-payment support and imports to temporarily meet basic needs while its own economies were being rebuilt. The US Marshall Plan provided this type of assistance; the World Bank did not. By 1953—nine years after its establishment—total World Bank lending was only $1.75 billion, of which only $497 million was for European reconstruction. That amount paled in comparison to the $41.3 billion transferred to Europe under the Marshall Plan.[3]

The World Bank's annual report for 1947–48 acknowledged that the lack of demand for its loans was not limited to Europe. As the Bank began to look to the low-income countries for customers, it ran into a similar problem. Countries were not presenting the Bank with acceptable projects.

Two problems were identified. The first was the borrowers' lack of technical and planning skills to prepare loan proposals.[4] The second problem, meticulously documented by Robin Broad in her study of the World Bank and the IMF in the Philippines, was more basic: the business elites who regularly rotated in and out of key government positions were split between economic nationalists and transnationalists.

The economic nationalist group comprised those businesspeople who were engaged primarily in serving the local market. They naturally favored avoiding international economic entanglements and sought to protect national markets and resources from the uncertainties of the international economy.[5] Most were wary of international lenders and spurned the Bank's overtures. In the Bank's early days, control over economic policy in most low-income countries was firmly in the hands of economic nationalists.

Transnationalists were more closely aligned with the Bank's ideology and were inclined to be more receptive to moves that drew the national economy into the global orbit. They were the Bank's natural allies.[6] Transnationalists were found among two groups. The first was made up of businesspeople who had links with transnational banks and corporations through joint ventures, licensing agreements, marketing arrangements, and other connections that aligned their interests with policies that allow the free international flow of goods and capital. The second group comprised the highly educated technical bureaucrats who had studied economics, often abroad, and interacted on a regular basis with foreign or multilateral institutions.[7]

The development debates of the day centered on a key question: where would newly industrializing countries find the market demand to drive the growth of their economies, particularly their industrial sectors? The leading protagonists in the debate recognized only two possibilities: either concentrating industrialization on providing locally produced substitutes for those goods that the country currently imported (import-substitution strategies) or building domestic industry primarily to serve foreign export markets (export-led strategies).

The former strategy, advocated by the Argentine economist Raúl Prebisch and the UN Economic Commission for Latin America (ECLA), was oriented toward self-reliance and ran directly counter to the mandates of the Bank and the IMF to open domestic economies to the expansion of foreign trade and investment.[8] Import substitution reduced the requirement for imports and thus the need for foreign exchange. The strategy was anathema to a bank that existed primarily to make foreign currency loans to increase the purchase of goods and services from the Northern industrial countries. Economic nationalists were inclined to favor an import-substitution strategy, whereas transnationalists were more likely to favor an export-led strategy.

In the 1950s, the Bank pursued a strategy designed to address both barriers. It gave priority to "institution building" projects aimed at creating autonomous governmental agencies that would be regular World Bank borrowers. Generally, World Bank staff sought to ensure that these agencies were relatively autonomous from their governments and would be staffed primarily by transnational technocrats with strong professional, as well as financial, ties to the Bank. In 1956, the Bank created the Economic Development Institute. It initially offered seminars to senior government officials from borrowing countries to imbue them with the Bank's point of view on the theory and practice of development. It also provided technical training for personnel from the newly created agencies in the Bank's procedures and methods for loan preparation and implementation.[9]

The World Bank's claim that it simply responds to the needs and requests of borrowing countries is as false as the claim by corporate libertarians that the market simply responds to consumer demand. The Bank did what the big retail outlets did in the late 1800s when faced with a frugal culture that failed to produce sufficient customers. It set about to reshape values and institutions in ways that would create customers for its product. And much like the corporations that chose this course, the Bank gave scant attention to the larger consequences of actions taken to justify its own existence and advance the power agenda of its sponsors.

Once its demand-creation strategy was in place, the World Bank set about to increase its leverage over the policies of its more important client countries by establishing donor coordination groups under its direction on a country-by-country basis. For example, the Bank had flooded India with loans in the 1950s in an unsuccessful effort to build enough leverage to win India away from a policy of import substitution and active government intervention in the economy. Still, its advice went unheeded by India's powerful nationalist finance minister. The Bank changed its tactics, formed a donor group, and promised substantial increases in aid if India moved toward more free-market, export-oriented policies. By 1971, the Bank chaired sixteen such donor groups.[10] This opened a new era of cooperation among donors under the leadership of the World Bank and increased its policy leverage.[11]

When the Bill Collector Calls

In 1943, Wilbert Ward, a vice president of National City Bank of New York, raised a prophetic question about the proposal to establish the World Bank:

> If you are going to set up a bank you should set up an organization to finance transactions that will in the end liquidate themselves. Otherwise it is not a bank. . . . Where can we loan thirty to fifty billion around the world with any prospects of its being repaid?[12]

To this day, this question has never been satisfactorily answered. The standard response of World Bank economists is that World Bank loans will be repaid out of returns from the economic growth they stimulate. Of course that is only true if the growth is generating foreign exchange from exports or foreign investment. The reality is that most borrowing countries have been able to service existing international debts only by increasing their international borrowing. The more they borrow, the more they become dependent on international borrowing and the more their attention is focused not on their own development but on obtaining loans. It becomes like a drug addiction.

In the 1970s, price increases by the Organization of the Petroleum Exporting Countries (OPEC) placed oil-importing low-income countries in a critical foreign exchange position. At the same time, commercial banks were awash in petrodollars deposited by the OPEC countries and were looking for places to lend these dollars profitably. There seemed to be an ideal fit between the needs of the banks and the needs of low-income countries.

By this time, the World Bank's client countries had become accustomed to supplementing their export-based foreign exchange earnings with borrowing, and the line between foreign borrowing for self-liquidating investments and borrowing for current consumption had become badly blurred. Given the low real interest rates prevailing at the time the OPEC money was being recycled through the system, the offers being made by the commercial banks seemed like a potential bonanza, and countries borrowed with abandon. Few on either side of the lending-borrowing frenzy seemed to notice that the whole scheme was a house of cards, dependent on borrowing ever more to cover debt service on former loans while still yielding net inflows.

Lending from the World Bank and its sister regional banks was a fairly orderly process until the late 1970s, when the rise in oil prices effected by OPEC members caused the foreign debts of Southern countries to skyrocket. From 1970 to 1980, the long-term external debt of low-income countries increased from $21 billion to $110 billion. That of middle-income countries rose from $40 billion to $317 billion.[13] As real interest rates soared, it became evident that the borrowing countries were so seriously overextended that default was imminent, potentially leading to a collapse of the whole system. The World Bank and the IMF, acting as overseers of the global financial system, stepped in—much as court-appointed receivers in bankruptcy cases—to set the terms of financial settlements between virtually bankrupt countries and the international lenders.

In their capacity as international receivers, the World Bank and the IMF imposed packages of policy prescriptions on indebted nations under the rubric of "structural adjustment." Each structural adjustment package called for sweeping economic policy reforms intended to channel more of the adjusted country's resources and productive activity toward debt repayment, to privatize public assets and services, and to further open national economies to the global economy. Restrictions and tariffs on both imports and exports were reduced, and subsidies were offered to attract foreign investors.

Some of the reforms, such as a reduction of subsidies to domestic oligarchs, were long overdue. However, others provided new subsidies for exporters and foreign investors. Government spending on social services for the poor was reduced in order to free more funds for loan repayment. In adjusted countries in Africa and Latin America, aggregate governmental spending per person on social services declined between 1980 and 1987, while the share of the total budget devoted to interest payments increased. The share of all other budget categories—including defense—decreased. In Latin America, the portion of government budgets allocated to interest payments increased from 9 percent to 19.3 percent. In Africa, it rose from 7.7 percent to 12.5 percent.[14]

There were two underlying purposes for these reforms. The first was to ensure that loans from both the commercial and the multilateral banks were repaid. There was a strong emphasis on policies to strengthen exports and attract foreign investment in order to generate foreign exchange for this purpose. The second purpose was to advance the integration of domestic economies into the global economy. Import barriers were reduced or removed, based on the argument that this was necessary to improve access to materials used by export-oriented industries and to create competitive pressures to increase the efficiency of domestic firms so that they might, in turn, compete successfully in global markets.

The World Bank and the IMF proclaimed their structural adjustment programs to be a resounding success and declared the debt crisis resolved. They pointed to the fact that many of the adjusted countries subsequently experienced higher growth rates, expanded their export sectors, increased the total value of their exports, attracted new foreign investment, and became current on their debt repayments. Yet international debts and trade deficits increased and social conditions deteriorated.

The adjusted countries were pushed into a downward spiral. To attract foreign investors, they suppressed union organizing to hold down wages, benefits, and labor standards. They gave special tax breaks and subsidies to foreign corporations and cut corners on environmental regulations. The fact that dozens of countries sought simultaneously to increase foreign exchange earnings by increasing the export of natural resources and agricultural commodities drove down the prices of their export goods in international markets, and created pressures to extract and export even more to maintain foreign exchange earnings.

Falling prices for export commodities, profit repatriation by foreign investors, and increased demand for manufactured imports stimulated by the reduction of tariff barriers resulted in continuing trade deficits for most countries. From 1980 (the beginning of the World Bank–IMF decade of structural adjustment) to 1992, the aggregate trade deficit of low-income countries increased from $6.5 billion to $34.7 billion. The Bank and the IMF responded with more loans to cover the growing trade deficits as a reward for carrying out structural adjustment. As a result, the international indebtedness of low-income countries increased from $134 billion in 1980 to $473 billion in 1992. Annual interest payments on this debt increased from $6.4 billion to $18.3 billion.[15] Rather than increasing their self-reliance, the world's low-income countries, under the guidance of the World Bank and the IMF, mortgage yet more of their future to the international system each year.

Calling it guidance may be too polite. In their roles as international debt collectors, the World Bank and the IMF have become increasingly intrusive in dictating the public policies of indebted countries and undermining progress toward democratic governance and public accountability. As Jonathan Cahn argues in the *Harvard Human Rights Journal*:

> The World Bank must be regarded as a governance institution, exercising power through its financial leverage to legislate entire legal regimens and even to alter the constitutional structure of borrowing nations. Bank-approved consultants often rewrite a country's trade policy, fiscal policies, civil service requirements, labor laws, health care arrangements,

environmental regulations, energy policy, resettlement requirements, procurement rules, and budgetary policy.[16]

In its governmental role, the World Bank—a global bureaucracy—is making decisions for people to whom it is not accountable that would normally be the responsibility of elected legislative bodies. The very process of the borrowing that created the indebtedness that gave the World Bank and the IMF the power to dictate the policies of borrowing countries represented an egregious assault on the principles of democratic accountability.

Loan agreements, whether with the World Bank, the IMF, other official lending institutions, or commercial banks, are routinely negotiated in secret between banking officials and a handful of government officials—who in many instances are themselves unelected and unaccountable to the people on whose behalf they are obligating the national treasury to foreign lenders. Even in democracies, the borrowing procedures generally bypass the normal appropriation processes of democratically elected legislative bodies.

Thus, governmental agencies are able to increase their own budgets without legislative approval, even though the legislative body will have to come up with the revenue to cover repayment. Foreign loans also enable governments to increase expenditures without the need to raise taxes—a feature that is especially popular with wealthy decision makers. The same officials who approve the loans often benefit directly through participation in contracts and "commissions" from grateful contractors. The system creates a powerful incentive to overborrow.

In effect, those officials who sign foreign loan agreements are obligating the people of a country to financial obligations completely outside any process of public review and consent. This becomes especially egregious when, as has happened to millions of people in World Bank client countries, the loan-funded projects displace the poor from homes and lands, pollute their waters, cut down their forests, and destroy their fisheries. Then, adding insult to injury, when the bills come due, the poor are told that their social services and wages must be cut to repay the country's loan obligations.

The Corporate Connection

Although it seeks to create an image of serving the poor and their borrowing governments, the World Bank is primarily a creature of the transnational financial system. The Bank's direct financial links to the transnational corporate sector on both the borrowing and the lending ends of its operation have received far too little attention.

Technically, the Bank is owned by its member governments, which contribute its paid-in capital; this was only $10.5 billion, as of 1993. In addition, member governments have pledged $155 billion that can be called by the Bank if needed to meet its financial obligations. The paid-in capital and the pledges are not actually loaned out. They secure the Bank's extensive borrowing operations in the international financial markets, where it raises the funds that are then re-lent to governments at more favorable rates than they could obtain by borrowing directly.

Although the Bank lends to governments, its projects normally involve large procurement contracts with transnational construction firms, large consulting firms, and procurement contractors. These firms are one of the Bank's most powerful political constituencies.

The area of Bank operations that is watched most closely by the Bank's executive directors—representatives of its shareholder governments—is the procurement process. Each director wants to ensure that the countries he or she represents are getting at least their fair share of procurement contracts. The US Treasury Department is quite up front in its appeals to the corporate interest in supporting funding replenishments for the Bank. Treasury officials point out that for every $1 the US government contributes to the World Bank, more than $2 comes back to US exporters in procurement contracts. As Treasury Secretary Lloyd Bentsen assured Congress in 1994, "The dollars we have sent abroad through the development banks come back home in increased US exports and more US jobs."[17]

The sole function of one arm of the World Bank, the International Finance Corporation, is to make government-guaranteed loans on favorable terms to private investors whose projects are too risky to qualify for commercial bank financing. It accounts for 10 to 12 percent of total World Bank lending.[18] The potentials for abuse are even greater than with the Bank's core lending programs. To date, the Bank has kept the International Finance Corporation so far out of the public eye that it is seldom mentioned, even by Bank critics. However, given its own ideological belief in free-market forces, it seems difficult for the Bank to justify a major operation devoted to using publicly guaranteed funds to finance large private ventures that are so risky that commercial banks will not fund them.

If the Poor Mattered

When the formation of the World Bank was proposed, Republican senator Robert Taft emerged as a formidable opponent. His argument, made in 1945, reveals a significant insight into why foreign aid based on large financial flows is a deeply flawed idea:

> I think we overestimate the value of American money and American aid to other nations. No people can make over another people. Every nation

must solve its own problems, and whatever we do can only be of slight assistance to help it over its most severe problems. . . . A nation that comes to rely on gifts and loans from others is too likely to postpone the essential, tough measures necessary for its own salvation.[19]

Taft maintained that the major beneficiaries would be Wall Street investment bankers: "It is almost a subsidy to the business of investment bankers, and will also undoubtedly increase the business to be done by the larger banks."[20] Subsequent events have substantially affirmed Taft's argument.

We may infer from the programs and policies of the World Bank and the IMF that they favor a world in which all goods for domestic consumption are imported from abroad and paid for with money borrowed from foreign banks. All domestic productive assets and natural resources are owned by foreign corporations and devoted to export production to repay the foreign loans. And all public services are operated by foreign corporations on a for-profit basis. It makes no sense if the goal is help the poor. It makes perfect sense if the goal is to increase the power and profits of global corporations.

Properly understood, development is a process by which people increase their human, institutional, and technical capacities to produce the goods and services needed to achieve sustainable improvements in their quality of life using the resources available to them. Many of us call such a process people-centered development, not only because it benefits people but also because it is centered in people. It is especially important to involve the poor and excluded, thus allowing them to meet their own needs through their own productive efforts.[21] A small amount of help from abroad can be very useful in a people-centered development process, but too much foreign funding can prevent real development and even break down the existing capabilities of a people to sustain themselves.

Debates about import-substitution versus export-led development rarely acknowledge the people-centered alternative. Both start from the top, focusing on the production of more of the things that people who are already well-off want to buy. The poor and their needs have no presence in either frame.

When a country seeks to replace imports with domestic production, it usually means producing at home more of the goods that those who are relatively well-off buy from abroad. When a country seeks to increase its exports, it generally means gearing domestic productive capability to producing things for relatively well-off foreigners.

In theory, either strategy will produce more jobs for poor people so that they can participate in the money economy. But usually the jobs these strategies provide are too few and too poorly compensated to eliminate poverty. Either strategy can, and in all too many instances does, displace local production of the things that poor people use in order to produce more of the things that wealthier people want—even depriving the poor of their basic means of livelihood, such as when the lands of small farmers are taken over by estates producing for export.

Let's reduce the problem to its basics. Poverty—generally defined as a lack of adequate money—is not the issue. The deprivations associated with a lack of money are the problem: the lack of access to adequate food, clothing, shelter, and other essentials of a decent life. The people-centered alternative focuses on policies that create opportunities for people who are experiencing deprivation to produce the things that they need to have a better life.

This is, in many respects, what Japan, Korea, and Taiwan did. Each made significant investments to achieve a high level of adult literacy and basic education, carried out radical land reform to create a thriving rural economy based on small farm production, and supported the development of rural industries that produced things needed by small farm families. These became the foundation of larger industries. The development of these countries was equity led, not export led—contrary to the historical revisionism of corporate libertarians. Only after these countries had developed broad-based domestic economies did they become major exporters in the international economy.

From the standpoint of transnational corporate capital and the World Bank, a people-centered development strategy presents a major problem. Since it creates very little demand for imports, it also creates little demand for foreign loans. Furthermore, it favors local ownership of assets and thus provides few investment opportunities for transnational corporations.

During a visit to South Africa in January 1992, I used a hypothetical example to illustrate this point. By the time of my visit, the era of apartheid had come to an end, and the country was preparing for a transition to black rule. I was struck by the strict demarcation of living space that isolated the black population in remote townships. Although this was not a surprise, the lack of evidence of economic activity in the townships was. There were neither modern commercial centers nor the myriad shops, stalls, and street vendors that are ubiquitous in poor neighborhoods in most of the world. It was then that I realized the full extent to which the economy had been designed to ensure that blacks remained wholly dependent on the white urban economy. Developing black entrepreneurship seemed an obvious and necessary goal toward the creation of a fully integrated society.

The World Bank was especially aggressive among the foreign aid donors pouring into the country with offers of assistance. One of the few bless-ings of apartheid was that because of the resulting international sanctions, South Africa had accumulated very little foreign debt. With its abundant resources, it was, from an international banker's perspective, an "underbor-rowed" country. The World Bank was thus drawn to South Africa like a bear to honey. Among other projects, the Bank was proposing a large loan for housing in the black townships. Everyone agreed that housing was a critical need. The question was how that need might best be met. Consider three hypothetical options:

Option 1: The World Bank provides a major foreign exchange loan for housing. The proceeds are used to import foreign building materials and construction equipment and to hire foreign contractors to build completed housing tracts. South African blacks will have new houses within a fairly brief time. Apart from temporary employment, however, few if any new local capacities will be developed, and there will be little impact on the local economy, until it comes time to generate the foreign exchange to repay the loan. Then the country will need to boost its exports, a task that will justify measures favoring the white firms that are in a position to reach out to export markets. Others will face austerity, particularly the poor blacks whose public services will be cut back.

Option 2: The World Bank provides a major loan for housing. The foreign exchange proceeds from the loan are exchanged for South African rand at South Africa's Central Bank, and the rand are used to contract large white-owned domestic corporations to build the housing, using local labor and domestically produced building materials. The black communi-ties get their housing and some temporary employment, the white economy gets a major boost, and the country gets a onetime temporary injection of foreign exchange that may be used to import luxury goods or arms for the military or to transfer financial assets of white South Africans to foreign accounts. The dependence of the black economy on the white economy remains intact. The international economic dependence of South Africa increases. The loan must be repaid in foreign exchange, with consequences the same as those in option 1.

Option 3: South Africa graciously thanks the Bank for its visit, declines the offer, and puts it on the next plane back to Washington. Local funds are mobilized from the existing excess liquidity of the domestic banking system to finance black housing. Programs are put in place to provide train-ing for black South Africans in a variety of entrepreneurial and technical skills. Incentives and support are provided to encourage the formation of small black firms to produce doorframes, bricks, and basic plumbing and electrical fixtures and to provide construction contracting services. Because the technologies and materials involved in low-income housing are quite basic and are readily available in South Africa, there is virtually nothing for which foreign exchange is needed. So there is no legitimate reason to incur foreign debt. With this option, the black population gets its housing plus new skills, new economic power, new sources of livelihood, and a start toward a thriving black-controlled economy. A system is in place to build and maintain housing as required. The white economy would also benefit, as it would necessarily be the source of some of the materials and services. There would be no new foreign debt to repay.

Of the three options, only the third creates new black capabilities and economic power and strengthens economic self-reliance. It is the only option that can be considered truly developmental. The greater the involvement of foreign aid agencies, especially the World Bank or a regional development bank, the less likely it becomes that option 3 will be chosen, because it gives the foreign funder little, if any, role.

Of course, South Africa is something of a special case in the extent of its domestic resources and technical capabilities. There is, however, scarcely any country in the world that does not have the resources and technology needed to provide its people with their basic needs in food, clothing, shelter, education, and health care—if these are national priorities.

Foreign aid, even grant aid, becomes actively anti-developmental when the proceeds are used to build a dependence on imported technology and experts, encourage import-dependent consumer lifestyles, fund waste and corruption, displace domestically produced products with imports, and drive millions of people from the lands and waters on which they depend for their livelihood. All of these are common outcomes of World Bank projects and structural adjustment programs.

In addition, there is evidence that most Bank projects are failures, even by the Bank's own narrowly defined economic criteria. In 1992, an internal World Bank study team headed by Willi Wapenhans published a report, "Effective Implementation: Key to Development Impact." It concluded that 38 percent of Bank-funded projects completed in 1991 were failures at the time of completion.[22]

Earlier, the Bank's Operations Evaluation Department had conducted four- to ten-year follow-up evaluations on projects that the Bank had rated as successful at the time of completion. The study found that twelve of twenty-five projects rated as successful when completed eventually turned out to be failures.[23] If only half of the 62 percent of projects rated successful at completion in 1991 eventually achieved their projected returns, then less than a third of all Bank projects will have provided sufficient economic return to justify the original investment.

However, failures or not, the loan must be repaid in scarce foreign exchange. The Bank bears no liability for its own errors.

If measured by contributions to improving the lives of people or strengthening the institutions of democratic governance, the World Bank and the IMF have been disastrous failures, imposing an enormous burden on the world's poor and seriously impeding their development. In terms of fulfilling the mandates set for them by their original architects—advancing economic globalization under the domination of the economically powerful—they both have been resounding successes. In addition, the IMF was highly successful in averting, at least temporarily, a global financial crisis created by the unpayable debts of low-income countries on terms favorable to the Northern commercial banks.

Together, the World Bank and the IMF have helped build powerful political constituencies aligned with corporate libertarianism, weakened the democratic accountability of Southern governments, usurped the functions of democratically elected officials, and removed most consequential legal and institutional barriers to the recolonization of Southern economies by transnational corporations. They have arguably done more harm to more people than any other pair of nonmilitary institutions in human history.

We now turn to the third institution in the Bretton Woods triumvirate—the GATT-WTO—to examine its role in creating and enforcing a transnational corporate bill of rights.

CHAPTER 13

Guaranteeing Corporate Rights

Cosmopolitan globalism weakens national boundaries and the power of national and subnational communities, while strengthening the relative power of transnational corporations.

—HERMAN E. DALY

In the corporate economies of the contemporary West, the market is a passive institution. The active institution is the corporation . . . an inherently narrow and short-sighted organization. . . . The corporation has evolved to serve the interests of whoever controls it, at the expense of whoever does not.

—WILLIAM M. DUGGER

The framework for a post–World War II economy, which had been worked out largely between the United States and Britain, called for the creation of three multilateral institutions: the World Bank, the International Monetary Fund (IMF), and an international trade organization. The latter organization was stillborn because of concerns in the US Congress that its powers would infringe on US sovereignty. The General Agreement on Tariffs and Trade (GATT) served in its stead, with a somewhat ambiguous status, as the body through which multilateral trade agreements were fashioned and enforced.

It was not until January 1, 1995, that the triumvirate was finally completed. A new global organization, the World Trade Organization (WTO), was quietly born during the Uruguay round of GATT. It was a landmark triumph for corporate libertarianism. A trade body with an independent legal identity and a staff similar to those of the World Bank and the IMF is now in place, with a mandate to press forward and eliminate barriers to the free movement of goods and money. The needs of the world's largest corporations are now represented by a global body with legislative and judicial powers that is committed to ensuring their rights against the intrusions of democratic governments and the people to whom those governments are accountable. What the World Bank and the IMF had accomplished in institutionalizing the doctrines of corporate libertarianism in low-income countries, the WTO has a mandate and enforcement powers to carry forward in the industrial countries.

The World's Highest Judicial and Legislative Body

The key provision in the 2,000-page agreement creating the WTO is buried in paragraph 4 of Article XVI: "Each member shall ensure the conformity of its laws, regulations and administrative procedures with its obligations as provided in the annexed Agreements." The "annexed Agreements" include all the substantive multilateral agreements relating to trade in goods and services and intellectual property rights. This provision allows a WTO member country to challenge any law of another member country that it believes deprives it of benefits it expected to receive from the new trade rules. This includes virtually any law that requires imported goods to meet local or national health, safety, labor, or environmental standards that exceed WTO-accepted international standards. Unless the government against which the complaint is lodged can prove to the WTO panel that a number of restrictive provisions have been satisfied, it must bring its own laws into line with the lower international standard or be subject to perpetual fines or trade sanctions.

The WTO's goal is to "harmonize" international standards. Regulations requiring that imported products meet local standards on such matters as recycling, use of carcinogenic food additives, auto safety, toxic substances, labeling, and meat inspection are all subject to challenge. The offending country must prove that a purely scientific justification exists for its standards. The fact that its citizens simply do not want to be exposed to the higher level of risk associated with the lower WTO standards isn't acceptable.

Conservation measures that restrict the export of a country's own resources—such as forestry products, minerals, and fish products—can be ruled unfair trade practices, as can requirements that locally harvested timber or other resources be processed locally to provide local employment. Cases may also be brought against countries that attempt to give preferential treatment to local over foreign investors or that fail to protect the intellectual property rights (patents and copyrights) of foreign companies. Local interests are no longer a valid basis for local laws under the new

WTO regime. The interests of international trade, which are primarily the interests of transnational corporations, take priority.

Challenges may also be brought against the laws of state and local governments located within the jurisdiction of a member country, even though these governments are not signatories to the new agreement. The national government under whose jurisdiction they fall becomes obligated to take all reasonable measures to ensure the compliance of these state or local administrations. Such "reasonable measures" include preemptive legislation, litigation, and withdrawal of financial support.

The fact that local laws are subject to challenge under the WTO does not necessarily mean that they will be. However, there are numerous cases in which these same types of laws were successfully challenged under the previous, less stringent, GATT rules. Even before the GATT-WTO was ratified, the United States, Canada, the European Community, and Japan had each compiled extensive lists of one another's laws that they intended to target for challenge once the agreement was in place.

Although the GATT-WTO is an agreement among countries, and challenges are brought by one country against another, the impetus for a challenge normally comes from a transnational corporation that believes itself to be disadvantaged by a particular law. That corporation looks for a government that can be encouraged to bring a challenge. It need not be the government of its country of incorporation; a challenge can be brought by the government of any country that can make a reasonable case that its economic interest is being harmed. For example, a US company growing fruit in Mexico for export to California might use a pesticide that leaves a toxic residue on the fruit. If the toxicity level complied with the international standard but was greater than the level accepted by the state of California, the corporation might persuade the Mexican government to bring a case against the California standard under WTO. California would have no right to appeal an unfavorable WTO decision in either California or the US courts.

Elsewhere in the world, tobacco companies have repeatedly used trade agreements to fight health reforms intended to reduce harm from cigarette smoking. When Taiwan was working on a law that would ban cigarette sales in vending machines, restrict public smoking areas, prohibit all forms of tobacco advertising and promotion, and fund a public education campaign to encourage people to give up smoking, the US trade representative responded to complaints from transnational tobacco companies by threatening to call for trade sanctions against Taiwan—even though these laws would affect domestic Taiwanese tobacco companies and US imports equally. After bans on foreign tobacco companies were repealed in Korea as a result of similar pressure, the percentage of male teenage smokers rose from 1.6 percent to 8.7 percent of the male teen population.[1]

When a challenge to a national or local law is brought before the WTO, the contending parties present their cases in a secret hearing before a panel of three trade experts, generally lawyers who have made a career of representing corporate clients on trade issues. There is no provision for the presentation of alternative perspectives, such as amicus briefs from nongovernmental organizations, unless a given panel chooses to solicit them. Documents presented to the panels are secret, except that a government may choose to release its own documents. The identification of the panelists who supported a position or conclusion is explicitly forbidden. The burden of proof is on the defendant to prove that the law in question is not a restriction of trade as defined by the WTO.

When a panel decides that a domestic law violates WTO rules, it may recommend that the offending country change its law. It becomes, in effect, the world's highest court. Countries that fail to make the recommended change within a prescribed period face financial penalties, trade sanctions, or both.

Under the proposed rules, the recommendations of the review panel are automatically adopted by the WTO sixty days after the presentation unless there is a unanimous vote of WTO members to reject them. This means that more than a hundred countries, including the country that won the decision, must vote against a panel decision to overturn it—rendering the appeals process meaningless.

As was GATT, the WTO is a trade organization, and its mandate is to eliminate barriers to international trade and investment. The national representatives who vote in its councils are specialized trade representatives whose primary mandate is to open other markets to exports from their own countries. Responsibilities for maintaining foreign exchange balances; full employment; health, safety, and environmental standards and for protecting the democratic right of citizens fall under the jurisdiction of other bureaucracies. It may reasonably be anticipated that the WTO will follow the pattern of GATT in giving trade goals precedence over all other public policy concerns.

The WTO has legislative as well as judicial powers. GATT allows the WTO to change certain trade rules by a two-thirds vote of WTO member representatives. The new rules become binding on all members. The WTO becomes, in effect, an unelected global parliament of trade lawyers with the power to amend its own charter without referral to national legislative bodies.

Because economic activities have assumed such a large role in modern societies, control of economic rules is one of the most important powers in the world today. Under the WTO, these rules will be set by a group of unelected trade representatives as the world's most powerful legislative body. WTO tribunals will become the world's highest court to which the judgments and authority of all other courts will be subordinated.

Governance in the Corporate Interest

The world's major transnational corporations have had a highly influential insider role in GATT negotiations and are similarly active in the WTO. They are especially well represented in the US delegation, which has had a pivotal role in shaping the GATT and WTO agreements. The key to this corporate access is the US Trade Act of 1974, which provides for a system of trade advisory committees to bring a public perspective to US trade negotiations.[2] The trade committees are supposed to conform to the Federal Advisory Committee Act of 1972, which sets guidelines for the membership of all such federal advisory committees. These include a requirement that public representation must be "fairly balanced in terms of points of view represented and the functions to be performed by the advisory committee." Advisory committee processes are also required to be open to public scrutiny.

The US trade representative's office has chosen to define this requirement to mean only that the advisory committee membership must represent the business community with regard to "balance among sectors, product lines, between small and large firms, among geographical areas, and among demographic groups."[3] A study by Public Citizen's Congress Watch released in December 1991 found that of 111 members of the three main trade advisory committees, only 2 represented labor unions. An approved seat for an environmental advocacy organization had not been filled, and there were no consumer representatives. The trade panels rarely announced their meetings to the public and never allowed the public to attend.

The corporate interest, however, was well represented. The study found that 92 members of the three committees represented individual companies, and 16 represented trade industry associations, 10 of them from the chemical industry. Members of the Advisory Committee for Trade Policy and Negotiations, the most important of the panels, included such corporate giants as IBM, AT&T, Bethlehem Steel, Time Warner, 3M, Corning,

BankAmerica, American Express, Scott Paper, Dow Chemical, Boeing, Eastman Kodak, Mobil, Amoco, Pfizer, Hewlett-Packard, Weyerhaeuser, and General Motors—all of which were also members of the US Business Roundtable. Of the corporate members all but General Motors were represented either by the chairman of the board or the president in most instances, whichever of these officers functioned as CEO. According to Public Citizen's Congress Watch:

> Advisory committees are so intertwined with governmental trade negotiators that panel members require security clearances. One of the perks of membership is a special reading room filled with classified documents available for perusal by nongovernmental advisors. To enable trade advisors' opinions regarding the current GATT talks to reach negotiators more quickly, a database has been established that instantly puts an advisory committee member's words at the negotiators' fingertips. Government sponsors of the trade advisory system take enormous trouble to keep trade advisors fully informed of every twist and turn in the negotiating process. Despite their enormous influence, the corporate trade counselors work in near total obscurity.[4]

A 1989 Department of Commerce document described the involvement of advisory committee members in the 1979 Tokyo round of GATT:

> The advisory members spent long hours in Washington consulting directly with negotiators on key issues and reviewing the actual texts of proposed agreements. For the most part, government negotiators followed the advice of the advisory committee. . . . Whenever advice was not followed, the government informed the committees of the reasons it was not possible to utilize their recommendations.[5]

Of the 92 corporations represented on the three trade advisory panels, 27 companies or their affiliates had been assessed fines by the US Environmental Protection Agency (EPA) totaling more than $12.1 million between 1980 and 1990 for failure to comply with existing environmental regulations. Five—DuPont, Monsanto, 3M, General Motors, and Eastman Kodak—made the EPA's top ten list of hazardous waste dischargers. Twenty-nine of the member companies or their affiliates had collectively contributed more than $800,000 in a failed attempt to defeat California's Safe Drinking Water and Toxics Enforcement Act, a statewide initiative to require accurate labeling on potentially cancer-causing products and to limit toxic discharges into drinking water. Twenty-nine had put up over $2.1 million in a successful bid to defeat another California initiative called Big Green, which, among other provisions, would have set tighter standards for the discharge of toxic chemicals.[6]

Clayton Yeutter, in his capacity as US secretary of agriculture under George Bush, stated publicly that one of his main goals was to use GATT to overturn strict local and state food safety regulations. He rationalized, "If the rest of the world can agree on what the standard ought to be on a given product, maybe the US or EC will have to admit that they are wrong when their standards differ."[7]

The WTO uses the global health and safety standards for food set by the Codex Alimentarius Commission, or Codex. Codex is an intergovernmental body established in 1963 and run jointly by the UN Food and Agriculture Organization (FAO) and the World Health Organization (WHO) to establish international standards on pesticide residues, additives, veterinary drug residues, and labeling. Critics of Codex observe that it is heavily influenced by industry and has tended to harmonize standards downward. For example, a Greenpeace USA study found that Codex safety levels for at least eight widely used pesticides were lower than current US standards by as much as a factor of twenty-five.[8] The Codex standards allow DDT residues up to fifty times those permitted under US law.[9]

Governmental delegations to Codex routinely include nongovernmental representatives, but they are chosen almost exclusively from industry. One hundred forty of the world's largest transnational food and agrochemical companies participated in Codex meetings held between 1989 and 1991. Of a total of 2,587 individual participants, only 26 came from public interest groups.[10] Nestlé, the world's largest food company, had 38 representatives. A Nestlé spokesperson explained, "It seems to me that governments are more likely to find qualified people in companies than among the self-appointed ayatollahs of the food sector."[11]

Protecting Intellectual Property Monopolies

Many of the GATT-WTO provisions have been promoted as necessary to ensure the efficient functioning of competitive markets. Yet the GATT-WTO does nothing to limit the ability of transnational corporations to use their economic power to drive competitors out of the market by unfair means; absorb competitors through mergers and acquisitions; or form strategic alliances with competitors to share technology, production facilities, and markets. Indeed, one of the few areas in which the GATT-WTO calls for strengthening government regulations and standards is in its agreement on intellectual property rights: patents, copyrights, and trademarks. Here the call is for a strong assertion of governmental regulatory authority to protect corporate monopoly rights to information and technology.

Particularly ominous is the effort to use the GATT-WTO to privatize the rights to genetic materials, including seeds and natural medicinals, through patenting. US companies have aggressively pursued patent protection for seeds and genetic materials in the United States, persuading the US government to extend patent protection to all genetically engineered organisms, from microorganisms to plants and animals, excluding only genetically engineered humans.

By patenting the processes by which genes are inserted into a species of seeds, a few companies have effectively obtained monopoly rights over genetic research on an entire species and on any useful products of that research. These companies have been pressing hard to turn such patents into worldwide monopolies under the GATT-WTO. In 1992, Agracetus, a subsidiary of W. R. Grace, was granted a US patent on all genetically engineered, or "transgenic," cotton varieties and had applications pending for similar patents in other countries accounting for 60 percent of the world's cotton crop, including crops in India, China, Brazil, and the European Union. In March 1994, it received a European patent on all transgenic soybeans and had a similar patent pending in the United States.

Through the ages, farmers have saved seed from one harvest to plant their next crop. Under existing US patent law, a farmer who saves and replants the offspring of a patented seed violates patent law.[12] The corporate move to create global monopolies over seeds and other life-forms through patents has been the subject of massive demonstrations by farmers in India, who realized that under GATT-WTO agreements, they could be prohibited from growing their own seed stocks without paying a royalty to a transnational corporation.[13]

The industry view of what is right and proper with regard to people's rights to their means of subsistence has been clearly expressed by Hans Leenders, secretary general of the industry association of corporate seed houses and breeders:

> Even though it has been a tradition in most countries that a farmer can save seed from his own crop, it is under the changing circumstances not equitable that a farmer can use this seed and grow a commercial crop out of it without payment of a royalty. . . . The seed industry will have to fight hard for a better kind of protection.[14]

Measures extending patent protection over genetic materials are promoted on the ground that they will speed the advance of agricultural research and improve global food security. Critics argue that such patents stifle research by preventing the use of genetic materials and techniques by any researcher not working under specific license granted by the patent holder.

Vandana Shiva, a leader of the Southern opposition to the patenting of life-forms, says, "This is just another way of stating that global monopoly over agriculture and food systems should be handed over as a right to multinational corporations."[15] What we are seeing is a blatant effort by a few corporations to establish monopoly control over the common biological heritage of Living Earth.[16]

A review of the accomplishments of the three Bretton Woods institutions brings their actual functions into sharp focus. The World Bank has served as an export-financing facility for large Northern-based corporations. The IMF has served as the debt collector for Northern-based financial institutions. The GATT has served to create and enforce a corporate bill of rights protecting the world's largest corporations against intrusion in their affairs by people, communities, and democratically elected governments.

The World Bank and the IMF celebrated their fiftieth anniversary in 1994. Citizen organizations from around the world marked the event by organizing a global campaign around the theme "Fifty Years Is Enough." Fifty years of Bretton Woods has indeed been far more than enough. The world's people and environment can scarcely afford more.

World War II did not end the global domination of the weak by strong states. It simply cloaked colonialism in a less obvious, more beguiling form. The new corporate colonialism is no more a consequence of immutable historical forces than was the old state colonialism. It is a consequence of conscious choices based on the pursuit of elite interest.

This elite interest has been closely aligned with the corporate interest in advancing deregulation and economic globalization. As a consequence, the largest transnational corporations and the global financial system have assumed increasing power over the conduct of human affairs in the pursuit of interests increasingly at odds with the human interest.

It is not possible to have healthy, equitable, and democratic societies when political and economic power is concentrated in a few gigantic corporations able to dictate public priorities. We have created a system that is now beyond the control even of those who created it and whom it richly rewards for serving its ends. In Part IV, we examine the nature and dynamics of this system.

A Rogue Financial System

CHAPTER 14

The Money Game

In this new market . . . billions can flow in or out of an economy in seconds. So powerful has this force of money become that some observers now see the hot-money set becoming a sort of shadow world government—one that is irretrievably eroding the concept of the sovereign powers of a nation state.

—BUSINESS WEEK

Each day, half a million to a million people arise as dawn reaches their part of the world, turn on their computers, and leave the real world of people, things, and nature to immerse themselves in playing the world's most lucrative computer game: the money game.[1] Online, they enter a cyberspace fantasy world constructed of numbers that represent money and complex rules by which the money can be converted into a seemingly infinite variety of forms, each with its own distinctive risks and reproductive qualities. Through their interactions, the players engage in competitive transactions aimed at acquiring the money that other players hold. Players can also pyramid the amount of money in play by borrowing from one another and bidding up prices. They can also purchase a great variety of exotic financial instruments that allow them to leverage their own funds without actually borrowing. It is played like a game. But the consequences are real.

The story of economic globalization is only partly a tale of the fantasy world of Stratos dwellers and the dreams of global empire builders. Another story of impersonal forces is at play, deeply embedded in our institutional systems: a tale of money and how its evolution as an institution is transforming human societies in ways that no one intended toward ends that are inimical to the human interest. It is a tale of the pernicious side of the market's invisible hand, of the tendency of an unrestrained market to reorient itself away from the efficient production of wealth to the extraction and concentration of wealth. It is a tragic tale of how good and thoughtful people have become trapped in serving, even creating, a system devoted to the unrestrained pursuit of greed, producing outcomes they neither seek nor condone.

Although the consequences are global, our primary focus here, as in previous chapters, is predominantly on the United States because, since World War II, the United States has had the dominant role in shaping the global economy and its institutions. Thus, there has been a tendency for the strengths and dysfunctions of the global system to be revealed first in the United States and then to spread throughout the world.

Delinking Money from Value

To understand what has happened to the global financial system, we must begin with an understanding of the nature of money. Money is one of humanity's most important inventions, created to meet an important need.

The earliest market transactions were based on the direct exchange of things of equal value, which meant that a transaction could occur only when two individuals met who each possessed an item they were willing to trade for an item possessed by the other. The useful expansion of commerce was greatly constrained. This constraint was partially relieved when people began to use certain objects that had their own intrinsic value as a medium of exchange—decorative shells, blocks of salt, bits of precious metals, or precious stones.

Eventually, metal coins provided standard units of exchange based on the amount of precious metal, generally silver or gold, they contained. Later the idea emerged that it was more convenient to keep the precious metal in a vault and issue paper money that could be exchanged for the metal on demand. In a sense, the paper bill was originally the equivalent of a receipt showing that the bearer owned an amount of precious metal, but the paper receipt was more convenient and transportable.

Each of these innovations was, however, a step toward delinking money from things of real value. An additional step was taken at the historic 1944 Bretton Woods conference that created the World Bank and the International Monetary Fund. The countries represented at this meeting agreed to create a new global financial system in which each participating government guaranteed to exchange its own currency on demand for US dollars at a fixed rate.

The US government, in turn, guaranteed to exchange dollars on demand for gold at a rate of $35 per ounce. This effectively placed all the world's currencies on the gold standard, backed by the US gold stored at Fort Knox. Many governments thus came to accept US dollars as gold deposit certificates and chose to hold their international foreign exchange reserves in dollars rather than gold.

This system worked reasonably well for more than twenty years, until it became widely evident that the United States was creating far more dollars to finance its massive military and commercial expansion around the world than it could back with its gold. If all the countries that were holding dollars decided to redeem them for gold, the available supply would be quickly exhausted, and a great many of those who had placed their faith in the integrity of the dollar would be left holding nothing but worthless pieces of paper.

To preclude this eventuality, President Richard Nixon declared on August 15, 1971, that the United States would no longer redeem dollars on demand for gold. The dollar was no longer anything other than a piece of high-grade paper with a number and some intricate artwork issued by the US government. The world's currencies were no longer linked to anything of value except the shared expectation that others would accept them in exchange for real goods and services.

Once computers came into widespread use, the next step was relatively obvious: eliminate the paper and simply store the numbers in computers. Although coins and paper money continue to circulate, more and more of the world's monetary transactions involve direct electronic transfers between computers. Money has become almost a pure abstraction delinked from anything of real value. Four developments are basic to this transformation of the financial system:

1. The United States financed its global expansion with dollars, many of which now show up on the balance sheets of foreign banks and foreign branches of US banks. These dollars are not subject to the regulations and reserve requirements of the US Federal Reserve system.

2. Computerization and globalization melded the world's financial markets into a single global system in which an individual at a computer terminal can maintain constant contact with price movements in all major markets and execute trades instantaneously in any or all of them. A computer can be programmed to do the same without human intervention, automatically executing transactions involving billions of dollars in fractions of a second.

3. Investment decisions that were once made by many individuals are now concentrated in the hands of a relatively small number of professional investment managers. The pool of investment funds controlled by mutual funds doubled in three years to total $2 trillion at the end of June 1994, as individual investors placed their savings in professionally managed investment pools rather than buying and holding individual stocks.[2] Meanwhile, there has been a massive consolidation of the banking

industry—more than 500 US banks merged or closed between September 1992 and September 1993 alone[3]—concentrating the control of huge pools of funds within the major international "money center" banks. Pension funds, now estimated to total $4 trillion in assets, are managed mostly by the trust departments of these giant banks, adding enormously to their financial power. Pension funds alone account for the holdings of about a third of all corporate equities and about 40 percent of corporate bonds.[4]

4. Investment horizons have shortened dramatically. The managers of these investment pools compete for investors' funds based on the returns they are able to generate. Mutual fund results are published daily in the world's leading newspapers, and countless services compare fund performance monthly and yearly. Individual investors have the ability to switch money among mutual funds with the push of a button on a phone or their computer mouse, based on these results. For the mutual fund manager, the short term is a day or less and the long term is perhaps a month. Pension fund managers have a slightly longer evaluation cycle.

Individual savings have become consolidated in vast investment pools managed by professionals under enormous competitive pressures to yield nearly instant financial gains. The time frames involved are far too short for a productive investment to mature, the amount of money to be "invested" far exceeds the number of productive investment opportunities available, and the returns the market has come to expect exceed what most productive investments are able to yield even over a period of years. Consequently, the financial markets have largely abandoned productive investment in favor of extractive investment and are operating on autopilot without regard to human consequences.

The financial system increasingly functions as a world apart at a scale that dwarfs the productive sector of the global economy, which itself functions increasingly at the mercy of the massive waves of money that the money-game players move around the world with split-second abandon.

Joel Kurtzman, formerly the business editor of the *New York Times* and subsequently editor of the *Harvard Business Review*, estimated that for every $1 circulating in the productive world economy, $20 to $50 circulates in the economy of pure finance, although no one knows the ratios for sure. In the international currency markets alone, some $800 billion to $1 trillion changes hands each day,[5] far in excess of the $20 billion to $25 billion required to cover daily trade in goods and services. According to Kurtzman:

Most of the $800 billion in currency that is traded . . . goes for very short-term speculative investments—from a few hours to a few days to a maximum of a few weeks. . . . That money is mostly involved in nothing more than making money. . . . It is money enough to purchase outright the nine biggest corporations in Japan—overvalued though they are—including Nippon Telegraph & Telephone, Japan's seven largest banks, and Toyota Motors. . . . It goes for options trading, stock speculation, and trade in interest rates. It also goes for short-term financial arbitrage transactions where an investor buys a product such as bonds or currencies on one exchange in the hopes of selling it at a profit on another exchange, sometimes simultaneously by using electronics.[6]

This money is not associated with any real value. Yet the money managers who carry out the millions of high-speed, short-term transactions stake their reputations and careers on making that money grow at a rate greater than the prevailing rate of interest. This growth depends on the system's ability to endlessly increase the market value of the financial assets being traded, irrespective of what happens to the output of real goods and services. As this growth occurs, the financial or buying power of those who control the inflated assets expands, compared with the buying power of other members of society who are actually creating value but whose real and relative compensation is declining.[7]

The Great Money Machine

There are two common ways to create money without creating value. One is by creating debt. Another is by bidding up asset values. The global financial system is adept at using both of these devices to create money delinked from the creation of value.

DEBT

The way in which the banking system creates money by pyramiding debt is familiar to anyone who has taken an elementary economics course. In the United States it begins when the Federal Reserve buys government bonds in the open market. Say the Fed buys a $1,000 bond from Person A, who deposits the check in his account with Bank M. The Federal Reserve then credits the reserve account of Bank M with $1,000 to cover the purchase. As Bank M is only required to maintain a reserve of, say, 10 percent of deposits, it is thus able to loan $900 against this reserve to Person B, which Person B deposits in her account in Bank N.

Now Person A has a cash asset of $1,000 in Bank M, and Person B has a cash asset of $900 in Bank N. Keeping a 10 percent reserve, Bank N is able to loan $810 to Person C, who deposits it in Bank O, which then loans $729 to Person D, and so on. The original purchase of $1,000 bond by the Fed ultimately allows the banking system to generate $9,000 in new deposits by issuing $9,000 in new loans—money created without a single thing of value having necessarily been produced.

The total of $1,000 in new money interjected into the banking system by the Federal Reserve is thus pyramided into $10,000 in new money, of which $9,000 is in loans on which the banks involved expect to receive the going rate of interest, let us say 8 percent. This means that the banking system expects to obtain a minimum annual interest return of $720 on $9,000 that has been created simply by entering an amount in the account of a borrower and crediting themselves with a corresponding asset in the amount of the outstanding loan. Now you know why banking is such a good business.

In this instance, we have used the classic textbook example of how banks create money, assuming an average 10 percent reserve requirement—the actual varies from zero to 14 percent depending on the size of the bank and the nature of the account—that must be retained on deposit with the US Federal Reserve system.[8] Without such a reserve requirement, the banking system could, in theory, create money without limit.

As the United States has spent beyond its means abroad, a growing portion of the total supply of dollars circulating in the world has accumulated in the accounts of foreign banks or foreign branches of US banks. Known as Eurodollars, they are not subject to the reserve requirement of the US Federal Reserve. If banks hold accounts where governments do not impose a reserve requirement, these banks can loan out the full amount of these deposits, should they choose to do so, giving the global banking system the capacity to endlessly expand the supply of dollars.

As the global financial system has expanded, many kinds of financial institutions other than banks have become involved in large-scale lending operations. Each contributes to the money-creation process in ways identical to the banking system, but often with less stringent controls and reserve requirements than those placed on banks within the United States.

ASSET VALUES

The price of a stock or a tangible asset such as land or a piece of art is determined by the market's demand for it. In an economy awash with money and investors looking for quick returns, that demand is substantially influenced by speculators' expectations that other speculators will continue to push up the price. Nicholas F. Brady, who served as US treasury secretary under President George H. W. Bush, observed, "If the assets were gold or oil, this phenomenon would be called inflation. In stocks, it is called wealth creation."[9] The process tends to feed on itself. As the price of an asset rises, more spectators are drawn to the action and the price continues to increase, attracting still more speculators—until the bubble bursts, as when the crash of the overinflated Mexican stock market caused the 1995 peso crisis.

Vast changes in the buying power of people who own such assets can occur within a very short time, with no change whatever in the underlying value of the asset or in society's ability to produce real goods and services. We are so conditioned to the idea that changes in buying power are related to changes in real wealth that it is easy to overlook the fact that this relationship is often simply an illusion. Consider the following excerpt from Joel Kurtzman's book *The Death of Money*, describing what happened on October 19, 1987, when the New York Stock Exchange's Dow Jones Industrial Average fell by 22.6 percent in one day:

> If measured from the height of the bull market in August 1987, investors lost a little over $1 trillion on the New York Stock Exchange in a little more than two months. That loss was equal to an eighth of the value of everything that is manmade in the United States, including all homes, factories, office buildings, roads, and improved real estate. It is a loss of such enormous magnitude that it boggles the mind. One trillion dollars could feed the entire world for two years, raise the Third World from abject poverty to the middle class. It could purchase one thousand nuclear aircraft carriers.[10]

Those who invested in the stock market did indeed lose individual buying power. Yet the homes, factories, office buildings, roads, and improved real estate to which Kurtzman refers did not change in any way. In fact, this $1 trillion could not have fed the world for even five minutes, for the simple reason that people can't eat money. They eat food, and the collapse of stock market values did not itself increase or decrease the world's actual supply of food by so much as a single grain of rice. Only the prices at which shares in particular companies could be bought and sold changed. There was no change in the productive capacity of any of those companies or even in the cash available in their own bank accounts.

Furthermore, although stock values represent the potential purchasing power of individual investors, they do not accurately reflect the aggregate buying power of all the investors in the market for the simple reason that you can't buy much with a stock certificate. You cannot, for example, give one to the checkout clerk at your local grocery store for your purchase. You first have to convert the stock to cash by selling it.

Now, although any individual can sell a stock certificate at the prevailing price and spend the money to buy groceries, if everyone decided to convert their stocks into money to buy groceries at the same time, much the same thing would happen as did on October 19, 1987. The aggregate value of their stock holdings would deflate like a punctured balloon. The "money"—the buying power—would instantly evaporate. What we are dealing with is market speculation that creates an illusion of wealth. It conveys real power on those who hold it, but only as long as the balloon remains inflated.

The whole nature of trading these vast sums in the world's financial markets is changing dramatically. The trend is toward replacing financial analysts and traders with theoretical mathematicians, "quants," who deal in sophisticated probability analysis and chaos theory to structure portfolios on the basis of equations. Since humans cannot make the calculations and decisions with the optimal speed required by the new portfolio management strategies, trading in the world's financial markets is being done directly by computers, based on abstractions that have nothing to do with the business itself. According to Kurtzman:

> These computer programs are not trading stocks, at least in the old sense, because they have no regard for the company that issues the equity. And they are not trading bonds per se because the programs couldn't care less if they are lending money to Washington, London, or Paris. They are not trading currencies, either, since the currencies the programs buy and sell are simply monies to be turned over in order to gain a certain rate of return. And they are not trading futures products. The futures markets are only convenient places to shop. The computers are simply . . . trading mathematically precise descriptions of financial products (stocks, currencies, bonds, options, futures). Which exact product fits the descriptions hardly matters as long as all the parameters are in line with the description contained in the computer program. For stocks, any one will do if its volatility, price, exchange rules, yield, and beta [risk coefficient] fit the computer's description. The computer hardly cares if the stock is IBM or Disney or MCI. The computer does not care whether the company makes nuclear bombs, reactors, or medicine. It does not care whether it has plants in North Carolina or South Africa.[11]

The decisions of the financial system are increasingly being made by computers on the basis of esoteric mathematical formulas with the sole objective of replicating money as a pure abstraction. This is a long way from the invisible hand of the market Adam Smith had in mind when *The Wealth of Nations* was published in 1776, but it is the reality of a world ruled by "free market" forces in the 1990s. The global financial system has become a parasitic predator that lives off the flesh of its host—the productive economy.

CHAPTER 15

Predatory Finance

You can't make any money like this. The dollar is moving sideways, the movement is too narrow. . . . Anyone speculating or trading in the dollar or any other currency can't make money or lose money. You can't do anything. It's been a horror.

—**CARMINE ROTONDO**, foreign exchange trader at Security Pacific Bank

One of the ideological premises of corporate libertarianism is that investment is by nature productive in the sense that it increases the size of the economic pie, adds to the net well-being of society, and therefore is of potential benefit to everyone. In a healthy economy, most investment is productive. The global economy is not, however, a healthy economy. In all too many instances, it rewards extractive investors who do not create wealth but simply extract and concentrate existing wealth. The extractive investor's gain is at the expense of other individuals or the society at large.

In the worst case, an extractive investment actually decreases the overall wealth of the society, even though it may yield a handsome return to an individual. This occurs when an investor acquires control of a productive asset or resource—such as land, timber, or even a corporation—from a group that is maintaining the asset's productive potential, then liquidates it for immediate profit. The investor is extracting value, not creating it. In some instances, such as an ancient forest, the asset may be irreplaceable. An investment that simply creates money or buying power, such as through the inflation of land or stock values, without creating anything of corresponding value, is also a form of extractive investment. The investor creates nothing, yet his or her share of a society's buying power is increased.

Speculation is another form of extractive investment. The financial speculator is engaged in little more than a sophisticated form of gambling—betting on the rise and fall of selected prices. When a speculator wins, he or she is simply capturing claims to wealth created by others. When a large speculator funded with borrowed money loses, the survival of major financial institutions may be placed at risk, resulting in demands for a public bailout to save the financial system from collapse. In either instance, the public loses. Rarely does a speculator's activity contribute to the wealth or well-being of society.

Although there may be some merit to speculators' claims that their activities increase market stability and liquidity, these claims have a hollow ring in increasingly volatile, globalized financial markets in which speculative financial movements are a major source of instability and economic disruption. Whatever contribution speculators may make to increasing financial market liquidity, it comes at a substantial cost in terms of the profits and fees they extract. Costs of the additional risks and economic distortions created by a sophisticated class of financial instruments known as derivatives far exceed any possible benefit to society.

The derivatives contracts that are currently a hot topic in the financial press involve bets on movements of stock prices, currency prices, interest rates, and even entire stock market indices. Futures contracts on interest rates didn't exist until the late 1970s. Outstanding contracts on interest rates now total more than half the gross national product of the United States.[1] The total value of outstanding derivatives contracts was estimated to be about $12 trillion in mid-1994, with growth projected to $18 trillion by 1999.[2] In 1993, *The Economist* estimated the value of the world's total stock of productive fixed capital to be around $20 trillion.[3]

What makes derivatives particularly risky is that they are commonly purchased on margin, meaning that the buyer initially puts up only a small deposit against the potential financial exposure. The largest players may not be required to put up any money at all, even though their potential financial exposure may run into hundreds of millions of dollars.[4]

The more sophisticated derivatives are highly complex and are often not well understood, even by those who deal in them. In the words of *Fortune:*

> When they are employed wisely, derivatives make the world simpler, because they give their buyers an ability to manage and transfer risk. But in the hands of speculators, bumblers, and unscrupulous peddlers, they are a powerful leveraged mechanism for creating risk.[5]

Creating Uncertainty and Risk

For global corporations engaged in producing and trading real goods and services, the sometimes considerable swings in the exchange relationships among different currencies can be a serious problem, possibly playing a larger role in determining profit or loss than productive efficiency or market share. Speculators, by contrast, thrive on volatility, as it is their source of extractive gain through:

1. *Arbitraging* temporary price differences for the same or similar commodities or financial instruments in two markets. The arbitrager makes a simultaneous purchase in the market where the price is lower and a corresponding sale in the market where the price is higher. The margins are narrow, but the action is essentially riskless, and when large sums of money are involved, the strategy can be quite profitable. The key is to act before anyone else notices the same opportunity. Speed is so important that one firm spent $35 million to buy a supercomputer simply to gain a two-second advantage in arbitraging stock futures in Tokyo.[6]

2. *Speculating* on price changes in commodities, currency exchange rates, interest rates, and financial instruments such as stocks, bonds, and various derivative products. Speculation involves betting on short-term price fluctuations. These bets can involve significant risks, especially if they are leveraged with borrowed money.

3. *Insuring* others against the risks of future price changes. Those who sell derivatives contracts promote them as a form of risk insurance, as when a farmer locks in a price for a crop through a futures contract. However, the more complex derivatives have more to do with gambling than with insuring against risk.

There would be little opportunity for speculative profit in a stable financial market. In most instances, the extractive investor is taking advantage of price fluctuations to claim a portion of the value created by productive investors and by people doing real work—a private tax levied on the productive output of others. It is difficult to see, for example, how arbitraging electronically linked markets to reduce a two-millisecond price differential serves any public purpose. The greater the volatility of financial markets, the greater the opportunity for these forms of extraction.

The riskier and more destabilizing forms of extractive investments have received a major boost from the formation of a new breed of mutual funds—called hedge funds—that specialize in high-risk, short-term speculation and require a minimum initial investment of $1 million. The biggest of these, Quantum Fund headed by George Soros, controls more than $11 billion of investor money. Since aggressive hedge funds may leverage investor money to borrow $25 or more for every investor dollar, this would give a fund with $10 billion in equity potential control over as much as $250 billion. Many of the largest hedge funds produced a return of more than 50 percent for their shareholders in 1993. The downside risks are also substantial, however. One small hedge fund lost $600 million in two months in the mortgage markets and went out of business.[7]

The fact that hedge funds are generally highly leveraged greatly increases both the potential gains and the risks. It also ties up banking system funds in activities that are of questionable benefit to society when the credit needs of homebuyers, farmers, and productive businesses go unmet.

The claim that speculators increase price stability by moving markets more quickly toward their equilibrium was recently debunked by George Soros himself in testimony before the Banking Committee of the US House of Representatives. Soros told the committee that when a speculator bets that a price will rise and it falls instead, he is forced to protect himself by selling, which accelerates the price drop and increases market volatility. Soros, however, told the committee that price volatility is not a problem unless everyone rushes to sell at the same time and a "discontinuity" is created, meaning there are no buyers. In that case, those with positions in the market are unable to bail out and may suffer "catastrophic losses."[8] His testimony clearly revealed the perspective of the professional speculator, for whom volatility is a source of profits. If he were involved in productive forms of investment, he would surely have had a more critical view of price volatility.

Soros speaks from experience when he claims that speculators can shape the directions of market prices and create instability. He has developed such a legendary reputation as a shaper of financial markets that a *New York Times* article, "When Soros Speaks, World Markets Listen" credited him with being able to increase the price of his investments simply by revealing that he has made them. After placing bets against the German mark, he published a letter in the *Times* (London) saying, "I expect the mark to fall against all major currencies." According to the *New York Times*, it immediately did just that "as traders in the United States and Europe agreed that it was a Soros market."[9] On November 5, 1993, the *New York Times* business pages included the story, "Rumors of Buying by Soros Send Gold Prices Surging."

In September 1992, Soros sold $10 billion worth of British pounds in a bet against the success of British prime minister John Major's effort to maintain the pound's value.[10] In so doing, he was credited with a major role in forcing a devaluation of the pound that contributed to breaking up the system of fixed exchange rates that governments were trying to put into place in the European Union. Fixed exchange rates are anathema for speculators because they eliminate the volatility on which speculators depend. For his role in protecting the opportunity for speculative profits, Soros extracted an estimated $1 billion from the financial system for his investment funds.[11]

The resulting gyrations in the money markets caused the British pound to fall 41 percent against the Japanese yen over eleven months. These are the kinds of volatility that speculators consider a source of opportunity.[12]

There is a substantial and growing basis for the conclusion of Felix Rohatyn, a senior partner with Lazard Frères & Co., that

> in many cases hedge funds, and speculative activity in general, may now be more responsible for foreign exchange and interest-rate movements than interventions by the central banks.
>
> ... Derivatives ... create a chain of risks linking financial institutions and corporations throughout the world; any weakness or break in that chain (such as the failure of a large institution heavily invested in derivatives) could create a problem of serious proportions for the international financial system.[13]

The fact that many major corporations, banks, and even local governments have become active players in the derivatives market as a means of boosting their profits began to attract the attention of the business press in 1994. The risks can be substantial, yet the institutions that have been major players generally do not disclose their financial exposure in derivatives in their public financial statements, preferring to treat them as "off-balance-sheet" transactions. This makes it impossible for investors and the public to properly assess the real risks involved.

The truth becomes known only as major losses are reported, as when Procter & Gamble announced a $102 million derivatives loss after interest rates rose more sharply than anticipated,[14] or when bad real estate loans required a federal bailout of the Bank of New England. The bank's balance sheet showed about $33 billion in total assets. Regulators, however, found that it had off-balance-sheet commitments of $36 billion in various derivatives instruments.[15] The PaineWebber Group announced in July 1994 that it would spend $268 million to bail out one of its money market funds, which had been marketed as a safe and secure investment, when it came up short on a derivatives speculation. In 1994, BankAmerica and Piper Jaffray Companies took similar actions.[16]

The most publicized derivatives shock of 1994 came in December, when California's Orange County announced that its investment fund of $7.4 billion in public monies from 187 school districts, transportation authorities, and cities faced losses of $1.5 billion. It had borrowed $14 billion to invest in interest-sensitive derivatives and lost its bet when interest rates rose. As a result, Orange County faced a severe cutback in public services, including its schools, and the possibility of sharp tax increases.[17]

The news broke on February 25, 1995, that a twenty-eight-year-old trader in the Singapore office of Barings Bank had, over roughly four weeks, bet $29 billion of the firm's money on derivatives tied to Japanese Nikkei stock-index futures and Japanese interest rates—and ran up losses of $1.3 billion. The loss wiped out the venerable 233-year-old bank's $900 million in capital and forced it into bankruptcy.[18] In the first four hours of trading following the announcement, the Tokyo Nikkei index fell by 4.6 percent.[19] That the actions of a single low-level trader could single-handedly destroy a venerable multibillion-dollar bank with reckless unmonitored trades is indicative of a system dangerously out of control.

Profiting from Volatility

The financial resources that private speculators bring into play in the world's money markets mock governmental efforts to manage interest and exchange rates to maintain economic stability and growth. Allan Meltzer, one of the world's leading authorities on central banks and monetary policy, estimated that if the world's central bankers agreed among themselves on a coordinated commitment to protect a currency from a speculative attack, they might at best be able to muster $14 billion a day, a mere drop in the bucket compared with the more than $800 billion that currency speculators trade daily.[20]

The US dollar fell by approximately 10 percent against both the Japanese yen and the German mark during the first half of 1994. On June 24, 1994, the US Federal Reserve and sixteen other central banks mobilized a coordinated intervention and bought an estimated 3 to 5 billion US dollars to slow the fall. The market scarcely noticed.

We have reached a point at which such interventions do little to decrease volatility. They simply transfer taxpayer dollars into the hands of speculators.

The onset of the Mexican peso crisis in December 1994 gave new insight into how costly the financial system dysfunctions have become. Although little discussed by the financial press, the backdrop to Mexico's financial crisis was very different from the picture of an economic miracle that had been presented to the public by big business and the Clinton administration during their campaign to sell the North American Free Trade Agreement (NAFTA).

For years, Mexico increased its foreign borrowing—and thereby its foreign debt—to cover consumer imports, capital flight, and debt-service payments. This borrowing took many forms, including selling high-risk, high-interest bonds to foreigners; selling public corporations to private foreign interests; and attracting foreign money with the speculative binge that sent Mexico's stock market skyrocketing.

As little as 10 percent of the $70 billion in foreign "investment" funds that flowed into Mexico over the previous five years actually went into the creation of capital goods to expand productive capacity and thereby create a capacity for repayment. Prices of many of the assets transferred to foreign ownership were based on fictitiously inflated balance sheets. Projected debt-service payments alone came to exceed the country's projected export revenues. Mexico's "economic miracle" was little more than a giant Ponzi scheme.[21]

Who benefited from these inflows? A few Mexicans built huge fortunes during this period. *Forbes* identified fourteen Mexican billionaires in its 1993 survey of the world's billionaires. It identified twenty-four in its 1994 survey.[22]

The bubble burst in December 1994. The Mexican stock market lost more than 30 percent of its money value in peso terms as speculators rushed to pull their money out. Downward pressure on the overvalued peso due to the flight of money out of Mexico pushed the Mexican government into a deep financial crisis and forced it to devalue a highly overvalued peso. This resulted in a dramatic shift in the terms of trade between the United States and Mexico and priced most US imports out of reach of the Mexican market.

When it appeared that the Mexican government might be forced to default on its foreign obligations, the Wall Street investors who held Mexican bonds ran to the US government with cries that the sky would fall unless US taxpayers financed a bailout. President Clinton responded by circumventing a reluctant Congress to put together a bailout plan totaling more than $50 billion in taxpayer money to ensure that the Wall Street banks and investment houses would recover their money. Critics of the bailout noted that not a penny of this money would go to the millions of poor and middle-class Mexicans who bore the major burden of the crisis.[23]

Neither the bailout nor interest rates as high as 92 percent on Mexican government securities had stemmed the peso's continuing decline by mid-March 1995.[24] Austerity measures imposed by the Mexican government were expected to put 750,000 Mexicans out of work during the first four months of 1995, and interest rates of 90 percent or more on mortgages, credit cards, and car loans would push many families into insolvency.[25] Estimates of the number of US jobs that would be lost due to the related drop in exports to Mexico ran as high as 500,000.[26]

Shock waves from the Mexican crisis reverberated throughout the world's interlinked financial markets as speculators scurried to move their money to safer havens. When the Mexican stock market bubble burst, speculators with holdings in other Latin American countries got nervous and quickly pulled out their money, resulting in a fall of more than 30 percent in one month in the per-share value of the leading Latin

American stock funds.[27] When the US bailout linked the dollar to the falling peso, wary currency speculators sold dollars to buy German marks and Japanese yen, further weakening the dollar in international currency markets.[28]

How did this look to the Stratos dwellers from high above the clouds? I happened to be flying from New York to San Francisco in the midst of the Mexican peso debacle. The March 1995 issue of the United Airlines magazine *Hemispheres,* placed in every seat pocket, featured an article praising the success of the NAFTA and calling for its extension to the rest of the Western Hemisphere.[29]

The ability to move massive amounts of money instantly between markets has given speculators a weapon by which to hold public policy hostage to their interests, and they are increasingly open about calling attention to this fact. The economist Paul Craig Roberts of the Cato Institute, a Washington, DC, think tank devoted to the propagation of corporate libertarianism, lectured President Clinton in a *Business Week* op-ed piece:

> The dollar is also under pressure because investors have realized that Clinton favors big government "solutions," while other parts of the world, especially Asia and Latin America, are curtailing the scope of government and growing rapidly as a result. Equity investors have developed a global perspective, and they prefer markets where government is downsizing and the prospects for economic growth are good. . . . It would also help if Congress were to repeal hundreds of ill-considered laws that benefit special interests at the expense of the overall performance of the economy, and if thousands of counterproductive rules in the Code of Federal Regulations were removed.[30]

The process is simple. If the speculators who are shuffling hundreds of billions of dollars around the world decide that the policies of a government give preference to "special interests"—by which they mean groups such as environmentalists, working people, or the poor—over the interests of financial speculators, they take their money elsewhere, creating economic havoc in the process.

In the minds of the speculators, the resulting economic disruption only confirms their thesis that the policies of the offending government were unsound. The view expressed to the *Washington Post* by a New York foreign exchange analyst is typical: "A lot of central banks love to blame it on the speculators. I think it's more a question of their gross incompetence in managing their monetary policy than a speculative attack."[31]

The fact that most of these financial movements occur in a globalized cyberspace makes oversight or regulation by any individual government extremely difficult. Those who profit handsomely from the resulting lack of public oversight are quick to assure lawmakers and the public that the system is working in the public interest. They maintain that the only threat to the public good is from regulation itself.

Typical is the position articulated by Thomas A. Russo, the managing director and chief legal officer of Lehman Brothers, a major investment house, in a *New York Times* op-ed piece:

> Derivatives play a key role in the formation of capital and the management of risk by helping governments, manufacturers, hospitals, utilities and fast-food chains deliver the best products and services at the lowest cost. . . . The evolution of financial products has not been followed by a regulatory evolution, and the mismatch has created problems. . . . The system's artificial distinctions create legal uncertainty, hamper, and distort the development of new products and encourage self-interested tinkering with product definitions. In the fast-moving field of derivatives, these failings inflict great harm, including chasing the American derivatives business offshore.
>
> To add more rules to a system that was never designed for derivatives can only enlarge these problems. On the other hand, a complete overhaul of the system is politically unrealistic. The only remaining remedy: derivatives dealers and regulators should jointly formulate principles of good business practice for the industry.
>
> . . . New derivatives should be evaluated for risk not only by the people who develop and trade them, but also by an independent group within the company. Another principle might advise that traders—the first line of defense in managing risk—be urged to admit mistakes quickly and be fired for hiding them.[32]

Russo's observation that the financial system has acquired such political power as to virtually preclude its reform is, of course, accurate. Regulation is made all the more difficult by the fact that, in the words of James Grant, the editor of *Grant's Interest Rate Observer,* "The markets are global and sleepless and will flow to the area of least regulation."[33] As for Russo's argument that derivatives and other speculative financial tools strengthen the productive economy and that the system is capable of self-regulation, the most polite thing that can be said is that it demonstrates the extent to which Stratos dwellers have become detached from reality.

Almost coincidentally with the publication of Russo's op-ed piece touting the adequacy of self-regulation, Kidder, Peabody & Company—an investment house that prides itself on integrity and tight controls—

announced that one of its senior traders had, over a more than two-year period, single-handedly recorded trades totaling $1.76 *trillion*—nearly 10 percent of total annual global economic output—and reported profits on those trades of $349.7 million.

Yet no one in the firm had noticed that only $79 billion of these trades had ever actually been made or that these trades had cost the firm $85.4 million in losses. Accepting the trader's report, management had given him $11 million in bonuses, a promotion, and a chairman's award and reported his false profits as real profits to General Electric, the firm's parent company. It took more than two years for either his supervisors or the firm's accounting and internal audit systems to pick up the discrepancies.

Edward A. Cerullo, the $20-million-a-year head of the Kidder, Peabody division in which the fraud had occurred, gave the following explanation of his failure to detect the problem earlier: "Somehow, to single out one supervisor as singularly responsible for a department with 700 or 800 people, $100 billion in assets and $20 billion in daily transactions and earnings of $1 billion is totally unrealistic."[34] So much for the system's capacity for self-regulation.[35]

It is worth a passing note that while this was going on, senior officers of Kidder, Peabody were engaged in pitting Connecticut, New Jersey, and New York City against one another in a bidding war for the company's headquarters. According to Michael A. Carpenter, Kidder, Peabody's chairman, New York City's offer of subsidized electricity, sales tax breaks on equipment and services, and property tax reductions worth a total of $31 million would "enable Kidder, Peabody to continue to operate in Manhattan on a cost-competitive basis."[36]

The reality that the Stratos dwellers are loath to acknowledge is that financial institutions once dedicated to mobilizing funds for productive investment have transmogrified into a predatory, risk-creating, speculation-driven, global financial system engaged in the unproductive extraction of wealth from taxpayers and the productive economy.

This system is inherently unstable and is spiraling out of control, spreading economic, social, and environmental devastation and endangering the well-being of every person on Earth. Among its more specific sins, the transmogrified financial system is cannibalizing the corporations that once functioned as good local citizens, making socially responsible management virtually impossible and forcing the productive economy to discard people as costly impediments to economic efficiency.

CHAPTER 16

Corporate Cannibalism

> Mergers, acquisitions, and leveraged buyouts completed in 1988 cost a staggering $266 billion. . . . None of this . . . paid for as much as a single connecting bolt in a new machine . . . for an ounce of new fertilizer nor a single seed for a new crop. . . . A corporation that takes the long view of its profits and the broad view of its social responsibilities is in great danger of being acquired by an investors group that can gain financially by taking over the corporation and turning it to the pursuit of more immediate profit.
>
> **—WILLIAM M. DUGGER**

Finding ways to create new value in a sophisticated modern economy is seldom easy. Finding ways to create new value that will produce returns in the amount and with the speed demanded by a predatory financial system many times larger than the productive economy is virtually impossible.[1] The quickest way to make the kind of profit the system demands is to capture and cannibalize existing values from a weaker market player.

In a "free" market, the "weaker" player is often the firm that is committed to investing in the future; providing employees with secure, well-paying jobs; paying a fair share of local taxes; paying into a fully funded retirement trust fund; managing environmental resources responsibly; and otherwise managing for the long-term human interest. Such companies are a valuable community asset. In a healthy economy, they pay their shareholders solid and reliable—but not extravagant—dividends over the long term. They do not, however, yield the instant shareholder gains that computerized trading portfolios demand.

As Joel Kurtzman points out, by current market logic such firms should sell their assets and pay out the proceeds to shareholders.

Companies dismembering themselves look good on the computerized maps in the investors' nose cones. They pay rich rewards, their stock prices remain high, and they have virtually no investment in the future in research and development. This sort of company would be all payoff, and the computers would fight one another to buy it.[2]

When responsible managers are disinclined to cannibalize their own companies, the financial system stands eager to fund a buyout by those who will. In consequence, a predatory financial system teams up with a predatory market to declare responsible managers "inefficient" and purge them from the system, making the socially responsible corporation an endangered species.

Raiding the "Inefficient" Corporation

A special breed of extractive investor, the corporate raider, specializes in preying on established corporations. The basic process is elegantly simple and profitable, though the details are complex and the power struggles often nasty. The raider identifies a company traded on a public stock exchange that has a "breakup" value in excess of the current market price of its shares. Sometimes they are troubled companies. More often, they are well-managed, fiscally sound companies that are being good citizens and looking to the long term. They may have substantial cash reserves to cushion against an economic downturn and may have natural resources holdings that they are managing on a sustainable yield basis. Often the raider is looking specifically for companies with reserves and long-term assets that can be sold off and that have costs that can be externalized onto the community.

Once such a company is identified, the prospective raider may form a new corporation as a receptacle for the acquired company. Often the receptacle corporation is financed almost entirely with debt and has little or no equity. The borrowed funds are used to quietly buy shares of the target company on the public stock exchanges at the prevailing market price up to the maximum allowed by law. An offer is then tendered to the company's board of directors to buy the outstanding shares of the company's stock at a price above the going market price, but below its breakup value. If the takeover bid is successful, the acquiring company consolidates the purchased company into itself, thus passing to the acquired company the debt that was used to buy it. Through a bit of financial sleight of hand, the acquired company has been purchased by using its own assets to secure the loans used to buy it.

Those who organize the deal ensure virtually risk-free gains for themselves by collecting large fees for their "services" in putting the deal together. Since the deals are financed mostly with money from banks or investment funds, the risks are borne largely by others, including the public that insures the bank deposits and gives up tax revenues to subsidize interest payments on the loan financing, and the small investors and pensioners whose money is at stake.

The "new" company now has considerable additional debt. To pay off that debt, the new management may draw down its cash reserves and pension funds, sell off profitable units for quick cash returns, bargain down wages, move production facilities abroad, strip natural resource holdings, and cut back maintenance and research expenditures. Thus they increase short-term gain at the expense of long-term viability. Nearly 2,000 cases have been identified in which the new owners have virtually stolen a total of $21 billion they declare to be "excess" funding from company pension accounts to apply to debt repayment.[3]

Once the debt is paid down and the company is reporting rapid growth in annual profits, the firm may be sold back to the public through a stock offering at a significant premium. The raider congratulates himself or herself for "increasing economic efficiency" and "adding value" to the economy and seeks another target. These are the essentials of the leveraged buyout, a form of corporate cannibalism.

The key to the leveraged buyout is the ability to assemble the financing package. One might think that responsible bankers and investment brokers would shun such deals, which involve making huge unsecured loans to newly formed companies with no assets. To the contrary, since the deal makers offer unusually high interest rates to offset the lack of collateral, banks and investment houses often compete with one another for the opportunity to participate.

During the 1980s, some large banks, awash in the same petrodollars that they were lavishing on indebted Southern countries in the 1970s, sought out the deal makers with offers of financing at the first rumor of a new takeover strike. Normally, the final financing package involves a combination of bank loans and funds realized from the sale of high-interest bonds, commonly called "junk bonds" because they are issued by shell corporations with no assets.

All this is played out with a chilling sense of moral detachment. In the words of Dennis Levine, a Wall Street highflier who was imprisoned for insider trading:

> We had a phenomenal enterprise going on Wall Street, and it was easy to forget that the billions of dollars we threw around had any material impact upon the jobs and, thus, the daily lives of millions of Americans.

All too often the Street seemed to be a giant Monopoly board, and this game-like attitude was clearly evident in our terminology. When a company was identified as an acquisition target, we declared that it was "in play." We designated the playing pieces and strategies in whimsical terms: white knight, target, shark repellent, the Pac-Man defense, poison pill, greenmail, the golden parachute. Keeping a scorecard was easy—the winner was the one who finalized the most deals and took home the most money.[4]

What happens all too often after the buyout is complete is illustrated by the acquisition of the Pacific Lumber Company and its holdings of ancient redwoods on the California coast by corporate raider Charles Hurwitz. Before Hurwitz acquired it in a hostile takeover, the family-run Pacific Lumber Company was known as one of the most economically and environmentally sound timber companies in the United States.

It was exemplary in its pioneering development and use of sustainable logging practices on its substantial holdings of ancient redwood timber stands, was generous in the benefits it provided to its employees, overfunded its pension fund to ensure that it could meet its commitments, and maintained a no-layoffs policy even during downturns in the timber market.[5] These practices made it a prime takeover target.

After establishing control of the company, Hurwitz immediately doubled the cutting rate of the company's thousand-year-old trees. According to *Time*, "In 1990, the company reamed a broad, mile-and-a-half corridor into the middle of the Headwaters forest and called it, with a wink and a snicker, 'our wildlife-biologist study trail.'"[6]

On a visit to Pacific's mills at Scotia, Hurwitz told the employees, "There's a story about the golden rule. He who has the gold rules." With that pronouncement, he drained $55 million from the company's $93 million pension fund.[7] The remaining $38 million was invested in annuities of the Executive Life Insurance Company that had financed the junk bonds used to make the purchase—and which subsequently failed.[8]

The hypocrisy of some corporate raiders is even more outrageous than their actions. To justify his role in the mass firings and wage cuts that followed the takeover of the Safeway supermarket chain, investor George Roberts told the *Wall Street Journal* that the supermarket chain's employees "are now being held accountable. . . . They have to produce up to plan, if they are going to be competitive with the rest of the world. It's high time we did that."[9]

Roberts and his principal partner, each of whom is worth more than $450 million, had taken over Safeway along with three other partners.

Together, the group put up roughly $2 million of their personal money to complete the deal. *Forbes* magazine heralded it in a headline as "The Buyout That Saved Safeway" by freeing the company "from the albatross of uncompetitive stores and surly unions."[10]

The pay of Safeway workers in Denver was cut by 15 percent, and truck drivers complained of being forced to work sixteen-hour shifts. Some $500 million was shifted from taxes to interest payments, and the hundreds of millions in taxes formerly paid by tens of thousands of Safeway employees simply evaporated. For their contribution to making America more competitive by stemming the greedy impulses of Safeway's stock clerks, the five partners reaped a profit of more than $200 million.[11]

The fact that interest payments are tax deductible helps make all this possible. Since operating profits that would have been taxable are turned into deductible interest payments, the public subsidizes the cannibalizing of the nation's productive corporate assets.

The effect on the US taxpayer is far from trivial. During the 1950s, American corporations paid out $4 in taxes for every $1 in interest. During the 1980s, the increase in debt financing reversed the ratio, with corporations paying out $3 in interest for every $1 in taxes. One study concluded that $92 billion a year was thus shifted from taxes to interest payments. Whereas corporations paid 39 percent of all taxes collected in the United States in the 1950s, they paid only 17 percent in the 1980s. The share paid by individuals rose from 61 percent to 83 percent. Many corporations even collected refunds on taxes paid in the years before a takeover![12]

Corporate raiding and other forms of predatory extractive investment have become a source of handsome rewards for those with the stomach for it.

In 1982, making the *Forbes* magazine list of the four hundred wealthiest Americans required assets of $100 million. Only nineteen of those who made the 1982 list had made their fortunes in finance. Just five years later, in 1987, the smallest fortune that qualified for the list was $225 million, and sixty-nine of the four hundred who qualified were from finance—most of them having cashed in on the wave of corporate takeovers.[13]

The corporate raiders boldly assert that they are performing an important service to the American economy by eliminating inefficiency and restoring American competitiveness in the global economy. A compliant press dutifully reports their claims with minimal challenge. "The twisted logic of the robber barons of the Reagan era," writes Jonathan Greenberg, a financial journalist, "is that the living wage of middle America had decimated our economy." As Greenberg concludes, "The truth of the era of corporate takeovers has little to do with economic competitiveness. It's this simple: we've been robbed."[14]

Weeding Out Social Responsibility

Members of the corporate establishment insist that the problems of corporate excess can be dealt with through self-regulation without the need for public oversight or enforcement. This is rather like recommending that police departments and the courts be disbanded in favor of calling on compulsive street criminals to police themselves.

Others argue that the socially responsible action is usually the more profitable and therefore the logical choice purely on economic grounds. They overlook the fact that while responsible action may be the more profitable over the long term, financial markets demand instant returns and corporate raiders are standing by to trash any company that isn't responding.

Still others argue that corporations are simply collections of people and that raising their awareness of the social and environmental consequences of their actions will correct any problems. They overlook the fact that there are a great many socially and environmentally conscious managers. The problem is that they work within a predatory system that demands they ask not, "What is the right thing to do?" but rather, "What is the most immediately profitable thing to do?" This creates a terrible dilemma for managers with a true social vision of the corporation's role in society. They must either compromise their vision or risk being expelled by the system.

The Stride Rite Corporation, a shoe company, provides an example.[15] In addition to its generous contributions to charitable causes, it became known for its policy of locating plants and distribution facilities in some of America's most depressed inner cities and rural communities to revitalize them and provide secure, well-paying jobs for minorities. The policy was a strong personal commitment of Arnold Hiatt, Stride Rite's chief executive officer, who believed that business could and should contribute more to community life than simply generating profits for its stockholders. As CEO, Hiatt was able to hold his board of directors in line behind this policy until 1984.

In that year, a 68 percent drop in income, the first drop in thirteen years, convinced the company's directors that the firm's survival depended on moving production abroad. They were concerned, among other things, that if they did not make that move, the company would become a takeover target. Hiatt fought the board of directors on this policy for as long as he could and ultimately resigned. According to Myles Slosberg, a director and former executive vice president of Stride Rite, the pursuit of low-cost labor bargains has since become something of a holy grail for the company.

The systemic forces bearing on Stride Rite were enormous. Its US workers averaged $1,200 to $1,400 a month for wages alone, plus fringe benefits. The skilled workers in China now hired by contractors to produce Stride Rite's shoes earn $100 to $150 a month, working fifty to sixty hours a week. In addition to moving its plants abroad, Stride Rite moved its national distribution center in the United States from Massachusetts to Louisville, Kentucky, to take advantage of lower-cost US labor there and an offer of tax abatements from the state valued at $24 million over ten years.

Stride Rite sales doubled, and the price of its stock increased sixfold, making it a favorite on the New York Stock Exchange, including among socially conscious investors impressed by its record of corporate giving. According to Ervin Shames, Stride Rite's current chairman, "Putting jobs into places where it doesn't make economic sense is a dilution of corporate and community wealth.[16]

The Stride Rite experience presents a chilling example of the inexorable workings of a predatory global economy, and the distortions of a self-justifying logic that ignores the distinction between corporate wealth and community wealth. By bidding down Stride Rite's share of the public tax burden and the shifting jobs from well-paid to poorly paid workers, the actions of Stride Rite's management resulted in a massive upward wealth redistribution from those producing real wealth to passive investors.

By the rules of the system, Stride Rite's management had no real choice. If Hiatt, as Stride Rite's CEO, had carried the day, stuck to his convictions, and refused to move production abroad, a hovering group of investment bankers most certainly would have acquired the company through a hostile takeover, fired Stride Rite's socially concerned management, and moved the production abroad far more abruptly and with even worse consequences for the workers and the community.

Some investment funds specialize in buying and selling companies in labor-intensive industries that have resisted moving to low-wage countries. The AmeriMax Maquiladora Fund, a group of US and Mexican investors initially backed by Nafinsa, Mexico's largest national development bank, was formed specifically to target US companies that have resisted the move abroad. According to its prospectus:

> The Fund will purchase established domestic United States companies suitable for maquiladora acquisitions, wherein a part or all of the manufacturing operations will be relocated to Mexico to take advantage of the cost of labor. The Fund will seek to acquire companies where labor is a significant component of a company's cost of goods sold. It is anticipated that within six to 18 months after a company has been acquired by the

Fund, the designated portion of the company's manufacturing operations will be relocated to Mexico to take advantage of reduced labor costs.

We anticipate that manufacturing companies that experience fully loaded, gross labor costs in the $7–$10 per hour range in the US may be able to utilize labor in a Mexican maquiladora at a fully loaded, gross labor cost of $1.15–$1.50 per hour. Though each situation may vary, it is estimated that this could translate into annual savings of $10,000–$17,000 per employee involved in the relocated manufacturing operations. It is anticipated that most investments will be retained for three to eight years.[17]

The potential profits from reselling such relocated companies are substantial. At a savings of $17,000 per employee, shifting 1,000 jobs from the United States to Mexico creates a potential increase of $17 million in annual profits. Assuming that the company's stock normally sells for ten times the company's annual earnings, this translates to an increase of $170 million in the market value of the company's stock.[18] Clearly those who invest in such schemes are not doing so from a desire to provide secure and well-paying jobs to needy Mexican workers.

A rogue financial system is actively cannibalizing the productive corporate sector. In the name of economic efficiency, it is rendering responsible management ever more difficult. Those who call on corporate managers to exercise greater social responsibility miss this basic point. Corporate managers live and work in a system that is virtually feeding on the socially responsible. That system is transforming itself into a two-tiered structure, creating a world that is deeply divided between the privileged and the dispossessed, between those who have the power to place themselves beyond the prevailing market forces and those who have become sacrificial offerings on the altar of global competition.

CHAPTER 17

Managed Competition

The business system is increasingly taking the form of lean and mean core firms, connected . . . to networks of other large and small organizations, including firms, governments, and communities . . . [These] networked forms of industrial organization . . . exhibit a tendency to reinforce, and perhaps to worsen, the historic stratification of jobs and earnings.

—BENNETT HARRISON

On September 14, 1993, E. I. du Pont de Nemours and Company announced it would dismiss 4,500 employees in its US-based chemical business by mid-1994 to cut costs. While 4,500 families struggled to adjust to the fact that the economy had labeled their breadwinner a redundant burden, the money markets cheered. This layoff was part of a larger cutback of 9,000 people from DuPont's total worldwide workforce of 133,000—all part of a plan intended to cut the company's costs by $3 billion a year.[1] The price of a share of DuPont stock jumped $1.75 on the day of the announcement. Such announcements have become daily fare in the financial press. Clearly, important changes are occurring in the structure of industry. According to *The Economist*:

> The biggest change coming over the world of business is that firms are getting smaller. The trend of a century is being reversed. . . . Now it is the big firms that are shrinking and small ones that are on the rise. The trend is unmistakable—and businessmen and policy makers will ignore it at their peril.[2]

It is a widespread perception that the massive corporate giants have become too large and bureaucratic to compete against the more nimble and innovative smaller firms that we are told are rapidly gaining the advantage in highly competitive global markets. Proponents of this view point to the fact that large firms are shedding employees by the hundreds of thousands. To back their claim they cite statistics showing that the new employment and technological innovations are being generated primarily by more competitive small and medium-sized firms. Although employment growth and innovation do generally come from the smaller firms, to claim that smaller firms have the advantage in global markets is highly misleading.

Shedding Jobs and Concentrating Power

Although there are regional variations, the world's most successful transnational corporations—whether Japanese, European, or American—are engaged in a process of transforming themselves and the structures of global capitalism to further consolidate their power through complex networking forms of organization. Bennett Harrison, the author of *Lean and Mean: The Changing Landscape of Corporate Power in the Age of Flexibility,* calls it "concentration without centralization." Four elements of that transformation are of particular relevance to our analysis.[3]

Downsizing: Drastic cuts in personnel are the most visible aspect of downsizing, but they are in most instances only one part of a larger organizational strategy. The larger scheme is to trim the firm's in-house operations down to its "core competencies"—generally the finance, marketing, and proprietary technology functions that represent the firm's primary sources of economic power. The staffing of these functions is reduced to the bare minimum and consolidated within the corporate headquarters.

Peripheral functions, including much of the manufacturing activity, is farmed out to networks of relatively small outside contractors—often in low-wage countries. This process involves shifting employment from the corporate core to peripheral contractor organizations that form part of a production network of firms that are dependent on the markets and technology controlled by the corporate core. Peripheral activities that are not contracted out and cannot be automated may be located far away from corporate headquarters. These are, for example, the "back offices" of the big insurance companies and banks, which are generally staffed with poorly paid female clerical workers.

Computerization and automation: The core corporation brings the full capabilities of computerization and automation to bear in whatever manufacturing functions it retains and in the management information systems by which it flexibly coordinates the product network's far-flung activities. Automation has two key purposes: One is to pare down the number of workers to an absolute minimum, such as in AT&T's plans to replace thousands of telephone operators with computerized voice-recognition systems.[4] The second is to minimize inventories by linking dispersed suppliers with marketing outlets using "just in time" delivery of parts and supplies.

Mergers, acquisitions, and strategic alliances: The corporations that stand at the core of a major network pursue a variety of strategies to manage the potentially destructive competition among themselves. One is to meld through mergers and acquisitions. Another is to construct strategic alliances through which they share technology, production facilities, and markets and engage in joint research.

Headquarters teamwork and morale: Substantial attention is given to maintaining conditions that are conducive to high morale and effective teamwork among core personnel.

This restructuring creates a two-tiered or dualistic employment system. Those employees engaged in the core corporate headquarters functions are well compensated, with full benefits and attractive working conditions. The peripheral functions—farmed out either to subordinate units within the corporation or to outside suppliers dependent on the firm's business—are performed by low-paid, often temporary or part-time "contingent" employees who receive few or no benefits and to whom the corporation has no commitment.

The two tiers also differ significantly with regard to competitive pressures. There is considerable, if uneasy, cooperation among the corporations that control the core of a major network to maintain their collective monopoly control over markets and technology. The peripheral units, even those that remain within the firm, function as independent small contractors pitted in intense competition with one another for the firm's continuing business. They are thus forced to cut their own costs to the bone. This dualistic structure is an important part of the explanation for the growing income gap found in the United States and many other countries.

According to Harrison, "It is the strategic downsizing of the big firms that is responsible for driving down the average size of business organizations in the current era [as measured by number of employees], *not* some spectacular growth of the small firms sector, per se."[5] The largest 1,000 companies in America account for over 60 percent of the gross national product (GNP), leaving the balance to 11 million small businesses.[6] The contracting-out process does create new opportunities for smaller firms, but the power remains right where it has been all along—with the corporate giants. Lacking independent access to the market, the smaller firms that orbit core corporations function more as dependent appendages than as independent businesses.

The power relationships between companies of the core and the periphery are remarkably similar to those that prevailed between core and peripheral countries in the days of colonial empires. The dominant players in both systems capture the resources and surpluses of the players at the periphery to maintain the core in relative affluence.

Colonial states crafted alliances of convenience with one another to manage the often-destructive competition between themselves. Present-day strategic alliances among core corporations do much the same. When core corporations buy out and absorb smaller firms it is generally because they control promising technologies or lucrative markets.

The tyranny of state colonialism worked very well for a rather small percentage of the world's population. It was disastrous for the rest. Modern corporate colonialism is little different.

Thus, the seeming paradox that when the world's largest corporations unceremoniously shed well-educated, loyal, and hardworking employees, they are increasing their economic power. From 1980 to 1993, the Fortune 500 industrial firms shed nearly 4.4 million jobs, more than one out of four that they previously provided. During that same period, their sales increased by 1.4 times and assets by 2.3 times. The average annual CEO compensation at the largest corporations increased by 6.1 times to $3.8 million.[7]

Although downsizing has been an unavoidable response to weak markets and lax management for some companies, others have downsized from a position of considerable strength. GTE announced plans on January 13, 1994, to lay off more than 17,000 employees in the face of a strong market and a steady growth in operating income. Other companies enjoying growth in markets and profits announced significant layoffs at the end of 1993 or the beginning of 1994: Gillette (2,000 employees), Arco (1,300), Pacific Telesis (10,000), and Xerox (10,000). Some cut real fat from the payrolls. Other cuts were part of the shift to outsourcing. Many layoffs were made possible by new technologies. Major job cuts commonly follow mergers and acquisitions motivated specifically by a desire to strengthen and consolidate market share while reducing employment costs. After Chevron merged with Gulf in 1984, it reduced the combined workforce by nearly half, to about 50,000 people. It cut another 6,500 people in 1992–93.[8]

General Electric (GE) shed 100,000 employees over eleven years to bring total employment down to 268,000 in 1992. During that same period, its sales went up from $27 billion to $62 billion, and net income from $1.5 billion to $4.7 billion.[9] GE became smaller only in terms of the number of employees who shared the benefits of its growth in profits and market share. It shed its commitment to provide productive and well-remunerated employment for 100,000 people and their families. It retained its technical, financial, and market power.

Within this restructuring drama, we see a secondary drama being played out in a major contest between the manufacturing and retailing giants for control of the core network positions. The growing success of the core retailing giants is revealed in the growing rate of bankruptcy among retailers in the United States. Since 1991, retail firms have been going bankrupt at a rate of more than 17,000 a year, up from approximately 11,000 in 1989. Many of them have been driven out of business by the mega-retailers.[10] According to *Business Week:*

> A vast consolidation in U.S. retailing has produced giant "power retailers" that use sophisticated inventory management, finely tuned selections, and above all, competitive pricing to crowd out weaker players and attract more of the shopper's dollar. . . . They're telling even the mightiest of manufacturers what goods to make, in what colors and sizes, how much to ship and when. . . . Leading the pack, of course, is Wal-Mart Stores. The nation's No. 1 retailer is expected to grow 25% this year, to some $55 billion in sales, at a time when retailers as a whole will be lucky to grow 4%.[11]

When Wal-Mart grows at a rate of 25 percent in an industry that is growing at no more than 4 percent, its growth is clearly at the expense of rivals that lack comparable clout. The smaller retailers that used to be the commercial core of, and major employers in, most towns and cities have been hit particularly hard. It has been predicted that retailers accounting for half of all sales in the United States in 1992 will have disappeared by the year 2000. The systems analyst and syndicated columnist Donella Meadows describes what happens when a Wal-Mart comes to town:

> In Iowa the average Wal-Mart grosses $13 million a year and increases total area sales by $4 million, which means it takes $9 million worth of business from existing stores. Within three or four years of a Wal-Mart's arrival, retail sales within a 20-mile radius go down by 25 percent; 20 to 50 miles away, sales go down 10 percent.

A Massachusetts study says a typical Wal-Mart adds 140 jobs and destroys 230 higher-paying jobs. . . . Despite public investments in restoring downtown business districts, vacancies increase. Rents drop, and the remaining enterprises pay lower wages and taxes. Competing chain stores in existing malls leave and are not replaced.[12]

The mass retailing superpowers—Wal-Mart, Kmart, Toys 'R' Us, Home Depot, Circuit City Stores, Dillard Department Stores, Target Stores, and Costco, among others—are increasingly becoming the core firms in vast consumer goods networks. The mega-retailers are notorious for playing off suppliers against one another and for abruptly shifting their sourcing from domestic firms to low-labor-cost countries such as China or Bangladesh. Many small manufacturers have suddenly found themselves in bankruptcy when the major part of their market evaporated. Even the manufacturing giants, such as Procter & Gamble, that lack their own retail outlets are under intense pressure from the retailing giants to cut their prices and profit margins.

As the big retailers grow, they tend to favor larger suppliers that have the resources and sophistication to meet their demands for customized products and packages, computer linkups, and special delivery schedules. This contributes to further consolidation on the manufacturing side. Only a decade ago, no single toy maker controlled more than 5 percent of the market.[13] Now, in a toy industry dominated by Toys 'R' Us and general discounting giants such as Wal-Mart, Kmart, and Target Stores, the manufacturing side is dominated by just six companies.

While basically applauding this as a move toward greater efficiency, even *Business Week* sounds a cautionary note: "What if the growing clout of power retailers stifles too many small companies and forces too many large ones to dodge risks? The close ties between retailers and their surviving suppliers could ultimately end up raising consumer prices and reducing innovation."[14]

The Growth of Centrally Managed Economies

The scale of the concentration of economic power that is occurring is revealed in the statistics. Of the world's hundred largest economies, fifty are corporations,[15] and the aggregate sales of the world's ten largest corporations in 1991 exceeded the aggregate GNP of the world's hundred smallest countries.[16] General Motors' 1992 sales revenues ($133 billion) roughly equaled the combined GNPs of Bangladesh, Ethiopia, Kenya, Nepal, Nigeria, Pakistan, Tanzania, Uganda, and Zaire. Five hundred fifty million people inhabit these countries, a tenth of the world's population.

The world's five hundred largest industrial corporations, which employ only 0.05 of 1 percent of the world's population, control 25 percent of the world's economic output.[17] The top three hundred transnationals, excluding financial institutions, own some 25 percent of the world's productive assets.[18] The combined assets of the world's fifty largest commercial banks and diversified financial companies amount to nearly 60 percent of *The Economist*'s estimate of a $20 trillion global stock of productive capital.[19] The global trend is clearly toward greater concentration of the control of markets and productive assets in the hands of a few firms that make a minuscule contribution to total global employment. The giants are shedding people but not control over money, markets, or technology.

This concentration of economic power in relatively few corporations raises an interesting contradiction. Corporate libertarians regularly proclaim that central economic planning does not work and is contrary to the broader public interest. Yet successful corporations maintain more control over the economies defined by their product networks than central planners in Moscow ever achieved over the Soviet economy.

Central management buys, sells, dismantles, or closes component units as it chooses, moves production units around the world at will, decides what revenues will be given up by subordinate units to the parent corporation, appoints and fires managers of subsidiaries, sets transfer prices and other terms governing transactions among the firm's component organizations, and decides whether individual units can make purchases and sales on the open market or must do business only with other units of the firm. Unless top management chooses to invite dissenting views, its decisions on such matters are seldom open to question or review by any subordinate person or unit.

Although no global corporation yet manages a planned economy on the scale of the former Soviet economy, they are coming closer. The 1991 sales of the world's five largest diversified service companies (all of which happen to be Japanese) were roughly equivalent to the entire 1988 gross domestic product (GDP) of the former Soviet Union. Cuba, with a GDP of $26.1 billion, now ranks seventy-second among the world's centrally managed economies; the first seventy-one are all global corporations. Tiny North Korea wouldn't even make the list of the world's five hundred largest centrally managed economies.

It is far from an incidental consideration that in its internal governance structures, the corporation is among the most authoritarian of organizations and can be as repressive as the most oppressive totalitarian state. Those who work for corporations spend the better portion of their waking hours living under a form of authoritarian rule that dictates their dress, their speech, their values, their behavior, and their levels of income—with no opportunity for appeal. With few exceptions, their subject employees can be dismissed without recourse on momentary notice.

Market freedom as defined by corporate libertarians turns out to be in practice the most complete and oppressive of authoritarian tyrannies.

Integration and Cooperation at the Core

For all their praise of free-market competition, most corporations seek to insulate themselves from it at every opportunity. As Adam Smith observed in 1776, "People of the same trade seldom meet together, even for merriment and diversion, but the conversation ends in a conspiracy against the public, or in some contrivance to raise prices."[20]

Such cooperation need not be born of evil motives. Competition creates turbulence, which results in uncertainty that for any productive business makes investment planning difficult, disrupts the orderly function of the firm, and can result in serious economic inefficiency. The desire to increase control and predictability by reducing competition might be considered a natural law of the market.

Firms try to reduce competition in the global economy by the same means they have always used, by increasing their control over capital, markets, technology, and competitors. However, the combination of a globalized economy and modern information technologies lets firms consolidate that control on a scale never before possible. The competitive tactics are also familiar. Weaker competitors are absorbed, colonized, or crushed. Accommodation is sought with stronger competitors through strategic alliances, mergers, acquisitions, and interlocking boards of directors.

A favorite corporate libertarian argument for globalization is that opening national markets introduces greater competition and leads to increased efficiency. This neglects the larger reality that when markets are global, the forces of monopoly transcend national borders to consolidate at a global level. As soon as borders are opened, the pressure mounts to allow domestic firms to merge into ever more powerful combinations in order to be "competitive" in the global marketplace. When a Philip Morris acquires a Kraft and a General Foods, as it did in the 1980s to create the United States' largest food company, it does not make US markets more competitive. Rather it creates a strengthened platform from which to create and project monopoly power on a global scale.

As a rule of thumb, economists consider a domestic market to be monopolistic when the four top firms account for 40 percent or more of sales. Through a series of mergers and consolidations, the top four major appliance corporations in the United States (Whirlpool, General Electric, Electrolux/WCI, and Maytag) controlled 92 percent of the US appliance market as of 1990, and four airlines (United, American, Delta, and Northwest) accounted for 66 percent of US revenue passenger miles. Four computer software companies (Microsoft, Lotus, Novell/Digital, and WordPerfect) controlled 55 percent of the US software market in 1990, and two of them (Novell and WordPerfect) merged on June 27, 1994.[21]

When five firms control more than half of a global market, that market is considered to be highly monopolistic. *The Economist* recently reported five-firm concentration ratios for twelve global industries. The greatest concentration was found in consumer durables, where the top five firms control nearly 70 percent of the entire world market in their industry. In the automotive, airline, aerospace, electronic components, electrical and electronics, and steel industries, the top five firms control more than 50 percent of the global market, placing them in the monopolistic category. In the oil, personal computers, and media industries, the top five firms control more than 40 percent of sales, which shows strong monopolistic tendencies.[22]

The argument that globalization increases competition is simply false. To the contrary, it strengthens tendencies toward global-scale monopoly.

Agriculture has been a major subject in trade negotiations, with US trade negotiators making a strong appeal for reducing barriers to free trade in agricultural commodities and eliminating protection for small farmers in Europe and Japan. The story of US agriculture reveals why US agribusiness corporations are so enthusiastically calling for the "freeing" of agricultural markets. It is part of the process of restructuring global agriculture into a two-tiered system controlled by the agribusiness giants.

From 1935 to 1989, the number of small farms in the United States declined from 6.8 million to under 2.1 million; a period during which the US population roughly doubled. As farmers have gone out of business, so too have the local suppliers, implement dealers, and other small businesses that once supported them. Entire rural communities have disappeared. Meanwhile, the major US agribusiness corporations have grown and consolidated their power. The top ten "farms" in the United States are now international agribusiness corporations with names like Tyson Foods, ConAgra, Gold Kist, Continental Grain, Perdue Farms, Pilgrim's Pride, and Cargill—each with annual farm products sales ranging from $310 million to $1.7 billion.

Two grain companies, Cargill and ConAgra, control 50 percent of US grain exports. Three companies—Iowa Beef Processors (IBP), Cargill, and ConAgra—slaughter nearly 80 percent of US beef. One company, Campbell's, controls nearly 70 percent of the US soup market. Four companies—Kellogg, General Mills, Philip Morris, and Quaker Oats—control nearly 85 percent of the US cold cereal market. Four companies—ConAgra, ADM Milling, Cargill, and Pillsbury—mill nearly 60 percent of US flour. This concentration is in part the consequence of 4,100 food industry mergers and leveraged buyouts in the United States between 1982 and 1990—and the consolidation process continues.[23]

Often these core firms find that it is most profitable and least risky to contract out the actual production to smaller producers. These smaller producers hold the major capital investment and bear the risks inherent in agriculture. The large firms control the market and the terms under which the producers operate. It is common for the core firm to force farmers to purchase required inputs—such as fertilizer and feed—from itself, prescribe the production methods, and purchase the crops or animals produced on whatever terms it chooses. The only choice left to farmers is to accept the terms, go out of business, or find another crop whose market is not yet controlled by a core corporation. This restructuring of agriculture has contributed to decreasing the farmers' share of consumers' food dollars from 41 percent in 1910 to 9 percent in 1990.[24]

Figures compiled in 1980 by the US Department of Agriculture revealed that production and marketing contracts covered the production of 98 percent of sugar beets, 95 percent of fluid-grade milk, 89 percent of chicken broilers, 85 percent of processed vegetables, and 80 percent of all seed crops. When a contractor firm controls the market, producers are at its mercy. When Del Monte decided, for example, to transfer the bulk of its peach procurement from Northern California to Italy and South Africa, most of its contract farmers saw their market vanish for reasons that had nothing to do with the local appetite for peaches.[25]

Such conditions mock Adam Smith's notion of a competitive market comprising small buyers and sellers. The farmer receives a lower price and the consumer pays a higher price than either would have obtained under conditions of true competition.[26] This is the system the dominant agribusiness companies hope to extend to the world.

The public is encouraged to believe that the corporate titans of Japan, North America, and Europe are battling it out toe to toe in international markets. This image is increasingly a fiction that obscures the extent to which a few core corporations are strengthening their collective monopoly market power through joint ventures and strategic alliances with their major rivals. Through these arrangements, firms share access to special expertise, technology, production facilities, and markets; spread the costs and risks of research and new product development; and manage relationships with their major rivals.

For example, the American computer giants IBM, Apple Computer, and Motorola formed an interfirm alliance to develop the operating system and microprocessor for the next generation of computers. In 1991, Apple Computer turned to the Sony Corporation to manufacture the cheapest version of its PowerBook notebook computer.[27]

Toyota struck a deal with General Motors to produce Toyota cars in the United States for sale in Japan. General Motors now owns 37.5 percent of the Japanese auto manufacturer Isuzu, which produces automobiles for sale under the GM and Opel brand labels. Chrysler has had an ownership stake in Mitsubishi, Maserati, and Fiat.[28] The Ford Motor Company has a 25 percent stake in Mazda and names three outside directors to the Mazda board. Ford and Mazda jointly own a dealer network in Japan, cooperate in new product design, and share production techniques.[29] *The Economist* suggests the following exercise:

> Take a really big international industry such as cars, in which the products are complicated and fairly expensive. Write down all the manufacturers' names (there are more than 20 large ones for cars) along the four sides of a square. Now draw lines connecting manufacturers that have joint ventures or alliances with one another, whether in design, research, components, full assembly, distribution or marketing, for one product or for several, anywhere in the world. Pretty soon, the drawing becomes an incomprehensible tangle; just about everyone seems to be allied with everyone else. And the car industry is not an exception. It is a similar story in computer hardware, computer software, aerospace, drugs, telecommunications, defense and many others.[30]

Cyrus Freidheim, vice chairman of Booz Allen Hamilton, a management consulting firm, foresees an economic future dominated by what he calls "the relationship enterprise," a network of strategic alliances among firms spanning different industries and countries that acts almost as a single firm. He points to the discussions among Boeing, members of the Airbus consortium, McDonnell Douglas, Mitsubishi, Kawasaki, and Fuji about cooperating on the joint development of a new superjumbo jet and to the group formed by the world's major telecommunications firms to provide a worldwide network of fiber-optic underwater cables.

According to Freidheim, these corporate juggernauts will dwarf existing global corporate giants, with individual relationship enterprises reaching total combined revenues approaching $1 trillion by early next century. That will make them larger than all but the six largest national economies.[31]

The world's corporate giants are creating a system of managed competition by which they actively limit competition among themselves while encouraging intensive competition among the smaller firms and localities that constitute their periphery. The process forces the periphery to absorb more of the costs of the "value added" so that the core can produce greater profits for its own insatiable master, the global financial system.

The underlying patterns of the institutional transformation being wrought by economic globalization persistently move power away from people and communities to concentrate it in mega-corporations that have slipped the bonds of human accountability and delinked from the human interest. We have become captives of the tyranny of a rogue system that is running on autopilot into the face of a great mountain. Driven by its own imperatives, that system has gained control over many of the most important aspects of our lives, constantly demanding that we give ourselves over totally to its purpose: making money.

We now face an even more ominous prospect. Having gained control of the institutions that once served our needs and being intent on eliminating inefficiency to increase profits, the system has found that people are the primary source of economic inefficiency.

PART V

No Place for People

CHAPTER 18

Race to the Bottom

Freer markets and freer trade in the new global economic system are what will ultimately put an end to slow growth and high unemployment in the industrial world. . . . that's what the new economic order is all about.

—BUSINESS WEEK

The recent quantum leap in the ability of transnational corporations to relocate their facilities around the world in effect makes all workers, communities and countries competitors for these corporations' favor. The consequence is a "race to the bottom" in which wages and social conditions tend to fall to the level of the most desperate.

—JEREMY BRECHER

While competition is being weakened at the core, it is intensifying among smaller businesses, workers, and localities at the periphery as they become pitted against one another in a desperate struggle for survival. What the corporate libertarians call "becoming more globally competitive" is for communities and smaller businesses more accurately described as a race to the bottom.

With each passing day, it becomes more difficult to obtain contracts from one of the mega-retailers without hiring child labor, cheating workers on overtime pay, imposing merciless quotas, and operating unsafe facilities. If a contractor does not do it, his or her prices will be higher than those of another who does. With hundreds of millions of people desperate for any kind of job the global economy may offer, there will always be willing competitors. Pressed by predatory financiers to maximize their own margins, the core corporations close their eyes to the infractions and insist that they have no responsibility for working conditions in the factories of their contractors.

Modern Slavery

Descriptions of the working conditions of millions of workers, even in the "modern and affluent" North, sound like a throwback to the days of the early Industrial Revolution. Consider this description of conditions at contract clothing shops in modern, affluent San Francisco:

> Many of them are dark, cramped and windowless. . . . Twelve-hour days with no days off and a break only for lunch are not uncommon. And in this wealthy, cosmopolitan city, many shops enforce draconian rules reminiscent of the nineteenth century. "The workers were not allowed to talk to each other and they didn't allow us to go to the bathroom," says one Asian garment worker. . . .
>
> Aware of manufacturers' zeal for bargain-basement prices, the nearly 600 sewing contractors in the Bay Area engage in cutthroat competition—often a kind of Darwinian drive to the bottom. . . . Manufacturers have another powerful chip to keep bids down. Katie Quan, a manager of the International Ladies Garment Workers Union in San Francisco, explains, "They say, 'If you don't take it, we'll just ship it overseas, and you won't get work and your workers will go hungry.'"
>
> In 1992 a [Department of Labor] investigation of garment shops on the U.S. protectorate of Saipan found conditions akin to indentured servitude: Chinese workers whose passports had been confiscated, putting in eighty-four-hour weeks at subminimum wages.[1]

The line between conditions in the South and the North as defined by geography becomes ever more blurred. Dorka Diaz, a twenty-year-old textile worker who formerly produced clothing in Honduras for Leslie Fay, a US-based transnational, testified before the Subcommittee on Labor-Management Relations of the US House of Representatives that she worked in Honduras alongside twelve- and thirteen-year-old girls locked inside a factory where the temperature often hit 100 degrees and there was no clean drinking water. For a fifty-four-hour week, she was paid a little over $20. She and her three-year-old son lived at the edge of starvation. In April 1994, she was fired for trying to organize a union.[2]

When the black women who toiled over knitting machines in a Taiwanese-owned sweater factory in South Africa for fifty cents an hour made it known that with the election of Nelson Mandela they expected "a union shop, better wages and a little respect," the Taiwanese owners responded by abruptly closing their seven South African factories and eliminating 1,000 jobs. Low as the wages were, the cost of labor in South Africa is twice that of labor in Brazil or Mexico and several times that in Thailand or China.[3]

Noting that prospective foreign investors have turned wary of South Africa, the *New York Times* suggests, "There are doubts about the Government's long-term commitment to capitalism, about whether Mr. Mandela can contain the expectations of the impoverished majority."[4] In the world of big money and multimillion-dollar compensation packages, greed is a worker who wants a living wage.

In many Southern countries, to say that conditions verge on slavery is scarcely an exaggeration. China has become a favorite of foreign investors and corporations seeking labor at rock-bottom prices. *Business Week* described the prevailing conditions of Chinese factory workers:

> In foreign-funded factories, which employ about 6 million Chinese in the coastal provinces, accidents abound. In some factories, workers are chastised, beaten, strip-searched, and even forbidden to use the bathroom during work hours. At a foreign-owned company in the Fujian province city of Ziamen, 40 workers—or one-tenth of the work force—have had their fingers crushed by obsolete machines. According to official reports, there were 45,000 industrial accidents in Guangdong last year, claiming more than 8,700 lives. . . . Last month . . . 76 workers died in a Guangdong factory accident.[5]

Although the Chinese government is reportedly trying to tighten up on standards, it has faced enormous problems of unemployment since its decision to free up market forces. Tens of millions of rural workers are streaming to the cities. Urban unemployment stood at 5 million in mid-1994, a 25 percent increase in a year. Two million workers lost their jobs in Heilongjiang province in 1993 alone. Millions more urban workers face pay cuts, and half of the government-owned enterprises that employ approximately half of the urban workforce are losing money, creating the prospect of massive layoffs and plant closings.[6] Government efforts to tighten up on standards in this "free-market miracle" are also hampered by skyrocketing rates of crime and corruption.[7]

In Bangladesh, an estimated 80,000 children under age fourteen, most of them female, work at least sixty hours a week in garment factories. For miscounting or other errors, male supervisors strike them or force them to kneel on the floor or stand on their heads for ten to thirty minutes.[8]

It isn't only in the garment industry. In India, an estimated 55 million children work in various conditions of servitude, many as bonded laborers—virtual slaves—under the most appalling conditions. Each child has his or her own story. A few months after his rescue from forced labor, Devanandan told a reporter that he had been coaxed to leave home by a promise of wages up to $100 a month for working at a loom two hours a day while going to school. When he agreed, he found himself locked up in a room where he ate, slept, and was forced to work knotting carpets from four in the morning till late evening for pennies in pay.[9]

Former Indian chief justice P. N. Bhagwati has publicly testified to observing examples of boys working fourteen to twenty hours a day: "They are beaten up, branded [with red-hot iron rods] and even hung from trees upside down." The carpet industry in India exports $300 million worth of carpets a year, mainly to the United States and Germany. The carpets are produced by more than 300,000 child laborers working fourteen to sixteen hours a day, seven days a week, fifty-two weeks a year. Many are bonded laborers, paying off the debts of their parents; they have been sold into bondage or kidnapped from low-caste parents. The most unfortunate are paid nothing at all. The carpet manufacturers argue that the industry must have child laborers to be able to survive in competition with the carpet industries of Pakistan, Nepal, Morocco, and elsewhere that also use child laborers.[10]

As we rush to enter the race to the bottom in a globally competitive world, it is sobering to keep in mind just how deep the bottom is toward which we are racing.

The Limits of Social Responsibility

Within the apparel industry, a few socially concerned firms such as Levi Strauss, Esprit, and The Gap are attempting to live by their values. They are proving that a responsible, well-managed company need not tolerate the worst of the conditions described above, but they face the same competitive pressures as others in their industry. Almost inevitably, such firms find themselves developing a split personality. In the end, they finance their public good works and the good pay and conditions of their headquarters staffs by procuring most of the goods they sell through contractors that offer low wages and substandard working conditions.

Consider specifically the case of Levi Strauss, a company widely claimed as a leader in the realm of corporate responsibility. In April 1994, the Council on Economic Priorities gave Levi Strauss an award for its "unprecedented commitment to non-exploitative work practices in developing countries."[11] In 1984, the company was named one of the hundred best companies to work for in America. In June 1992, *Money* magazine ranked it first among all US companies for employee benefits.[12] Bob Haas, the CEO of Levi Strauss, was featured in the August 1, 1994, cover story of *Business Week* titled "Managing by Values," which emphasized his belief that social responsibility and ethical practice are good business.

In 1985, Haas, as CEO and a member of the Levi Strauss family, led a $1.6 billion leveraged buyout of the company, taking it private specifically to prevent a takeover by outside speculators. The fact that 94 percent of the stock is in Haas family hands has given the company more flexibility in maintaining its social commitment than a publicly held company might have in an era of hostile takeovers.

Under Haas's leadership, Levi Strauss has set strict standards with regard to the work environment. As evidence that they mean it, the Levi Strauss board of directors voted unanimously to close out $40 million a year in production contracts in China in protest of human rights violations. When the company found that its contractor in Dhaka, Bangladesh, was hiring girls as young as eleven as full-time seamstresses, it worked out an agreement by which Levi Strauss would continue to pay the wages of these girls while sending them to school and paying for their uniforms, books, and tuition. When they reach age fourteen, the minimum employment age set by International Labor Organization standards, they will return to work.[13] By the standards of the industry, Levi Strauss is a candidate for sainthood. But it is sobering to see how low the standards for such candidacy have become and how constrained even a truly committed company can be.

Although Haas asserts that Levi Strauss has made every effort to keep as many of its production jobs in the United States as possible, during the 1980s, it closed fifty-eight US plants and laid off 10,4000 workers. According to Haas, if the company had made its decisions on purely economic grounds, its remaining thirty-four production and finishing plants would all have been closed in favor of overseas production.

Even at its plants in the United States, the core-periphery phenomenon is evident. When the authors of *The 100 Best Companies to Work for in America* visited the Levi Strauss plant in El Paso, Texas, they found that *Money* magazine had ranked the company number one on the basis of the benefits enjoyed by its headquarters staff, not by staff at its plants. The benefits received by the El Paso production workers were little different from the marginal conditions at other local textile factories. The authors decided not to include the company among the 100 best in the book's revised edition.[14]

A Spreading Cancer

We have focused here on US-based transnationals, because their dysfunctions seem to be spreading through the world like a cancer. By May of 1994, a binge of corporate restructuring in Europe, similar to that in the United States, had pushed Europe's unemployment rate to 10.9 percent.[15] Even these rates, high as they are, may mask a much-deeper dysfunction. In Belgium, unemployment was 8.5 percent in 1992, but 25 percent of the workforce was living on public assistance.[16]

Persistent joblessness is resulting in growing social unrest, exacerbating racial tensions, and sparking a vicious backlash against immigrants. Joblessness is especially acute among youth, whose unemployment rate is twice that of the general population and still rising. On March 25, 1994, 50,000 students marched down a Paris boulevard, "taunting police and chanting slogans demanding jobs." A survey of 3,000 European teenagers found them "confused, vulnerable, obsessed with their economic futures."[17]

Pointing out that the unemployment rate in Europe has averaged about 3 percentage points higher than in the United States, *The Economist* cautioned "no trade barrier will keep out the technological changes that are revolutionizing work in the rich world; and a trade war is sure to destroy more jobs than it saves."[18] It counseled Europe to respond by emulating the United States to reduce the social safety net benefits that "give the unemployed little incentive to seek work," minimum wage laws that "cost young workers their jobs," employer social security contributions that reduce demand for labor, and "strict employment-protection rules" that discourage firms from hiring by making "it hard, if not impossible, to lay off workers once they are on the payroll."

To those who point out that the quality of jobs in America has deteriorated as a consequence of such policies, *The Economist* has a ready answer:

> Too many [of the jobs being created in America], say the merchants of gloom, are part-time, temporary and badly paid. The real wages of low-skilled workers have fallen over the past decade. Yet in comparison with Europe, this should be seen as a sign of success, an example—of a well-functioning labour market—not a failure. As manufacturing has declined, America and Europe have both faced shrinking demand for low-skilled labour. In America, the relative pay of these workers was allowed to fall, so fewer jobs were lost. European workers, by contrast, have resisted the inevitable and so priced themselves out of work.[19]

In short, according to the corporate press, Europe's unemployment problem is a result of overpaying the poor, taxing the rich, and imposing regulations that limit the ability of corporations to get on with serious downsizing. *The Economist* editorial pointed to moves by various European countries to reduce minimum wages, cut payroll taxes, and loosen employment-protection laws as signs of hope for Europe.[20] *Business Week* offered similar counsel:

> To ensure it remains competitive once the down-cycle wanes, Europe must be willing to see more of its low-value-added manufacturing jobs move to Eastern Europe and elsewhere. . . . And it must reduce farm subsidies while continuing to hammer away at high wages and corporate taxes, short working hours, labor immobility, and luxurious social programs. If Europeans don't follow these prescriptions, this recession may be doomed to be more than just a cyclical one. . . . Putting up trade barriers will only insulate Europeans from the discipline they need to maintain.[21]

Although they are running a bit behind the United States, the evidence suggests that European companies and governments are increasingly heeding this advice, which means that the unemployment, racial tension, and social unrest currently plaguing Europe are almost certain to spiral upward. We may presume that *The Economist* will then praise Europe for its success.

Japan, with unemployment below 3 percent, continues to be the full-employment champion of the industrial world. There is evidence, however, that Japan's commitment to lifetime employment has begun to break down and that a growing number of Japanese are experiencing the pinch of joblessness.[22] A series of economic shocks has led Japanese managers to look to the United States for lessons on increasing efficiency. According to Michael Armacost, former US ambassador to Japan:

> Japanese business leaders—who just a few years ago thought they had nothing further to learn from us—are examining American business practices with renewed interest and emulating some with interesting results. . . . Daiei, one of the country's largest chain stores, says it will seek to reduce retail prices by 50 percent over three years. . . . Wal-Mart Stores recently established links with two of Japan's supermarket chains. . . . Japanese executives are now studying America's experience with corporate downsizing, merit-pay packages and investment practices.[23]

Armacost goes on to urge American trade negotiators to focus on pushing for regulatory reforms to accelerate these processes.

With or without US tutelage, it is already happening. Domy, a discounter, is importing Safeway cola for sale in Japan at forty-seven cents a can, undercutting the price of local beverages by 5 percent. It sees great potential for imports of Safeway lemon-lime soda, cookies, and bottled water.

The Japanese government has relaxed size limits on new retail outlets as well as limits on store hours and business days—with the consequence that retailers are seeking the wide-open spaces of the suburbs, and strip malls are springing up throughout the countryside. Retailers are turning to cheap imports, with China as a preferred source. The burgeoning discount retailers have become the darlings of the Japanese stock market. Faced with the price cutting based on low-cost imports, Japanese companies have been restructuring to "increase their efficiency."[24]

In January 1995, an accord was announced between the United States and Japan under which US investment houses would have the right to participate in the management of Japanese pension funds.[25] Wall Street investment managers may soon be positioned to give the Japanese lessons in their home territory on the money game, predatory finance, corporate cannibalism, and managed competition.

The trend toward concentration in the retail sector is spreading rapidly to other countries as well, partly as a consequence of changes in trade rules that open domestic markets to the large retail chains. On January 14, 1994, only two weeks after the North American Free Trade Agreement (NAFTA) went into effect, Wal-Mart announced its move into Canada, which began with the purchase of 120 Woolco discount department stores from Woolworth Canada. *Business Week* called it "a full-scale invasion of the Canadian market." Investors rushed to sell holdings of Canada's major retail chains, which were believed to be ill-equipped to meet Wal-Mart's price competition.[26] Canadian retailing consultant John Winter predicted that by the late 1990s, "half of the Canadian retailers you see up here now may not be in business."[27]

With the signing of NAFTA, US retailing giants were poised to quickly "conquer retailing" in Mexico as well, but according to *Business Week,* "Mexico's army of bureaucrats, steeped in protectionist habits, is plaguing them with mountains of paperwork, ever-changing regulations, customs delays, and tariffs of up to 300 percent on low-priced Chinese imports favored by the discounters."[28]

Mexico thought that it had a free trade agreement with the United States to become the major low-wage supplier of the US market. It seems to have balked when confronted with the reality that US retailers intended to use NAFTA to open Mexico to goods produced by even-lower-paid Chinese workers.

The complaints of the US retailing giants aside, we might conclude that the Mexican government showed better sense in putting up a few roadblocks to slow the assault of the mega-retailers than it did in spending millions to promote NAFTA in the first place.

The dream of the corporate empire builders is being realized. The global system is harmonizing standards across country after country—ever downward toward the lowest common denominator. Although a few socially responsible businesses are standing against the tide with some limited success, theirs is not an easy struggle. We must not kid ourselves. Social responsibility is inefficient in a global free market, and the market will not long abide those who do not avail themselves of the opportunities to shed their inefficiency. Let us be clear as to the meaning of efficiency.

To the global economy, people are not only increasingly unnecessary; they and their demands for a living wage are a major source of economic inefficiency. Global corporations are acting to purge themselves of this unwanted burden. We are creating a system that has ever fewer places for people.

CHAPTER 19

The End of Inefficiency

We are entering a new phase in human history—one in which fewer and fewer workers will be needed to produce the goods and services for the global population.

—JEREMY RIFKIN

Throughout the previous chapters, we have seen a pattern repeated at all levels of society and in every corner of the world. In the name of increasing efficiency, hundreds of millions of people are being discarded by a global economy that has no need for them.

In Mexico, small farmers are displaced to make way for mechanized agriculture. In India, they are forced off their lands by massive new dams needed to produce electricity so that factory workers can be replaced by more efficient machines.

On Wall Street, the human traders who key decisions into computer terminals to execute trades in global money markets are replaced by more efficient computer programs. Small-town merchants are driven out by superstores run by mega-retailers, who in turn are threatened by dot-com retailers. Voice-recognition and automated answering devices replace telephone operators. Multimedia education tools replace teachers. Corporate downsizing is eliminating "redundant" workers and middle managers.

Corporate mergers and consolidation eliminate middle, and even top, managers. There is no end in sight.

First the Muscle, Now the Brain

We are crossing the threshold into the second Industrial Revolution. The first Industrial Revolution exploited a newfound human mastery of energy to give machines enormous muscle power and greatly reduced the demand for physical human labor. Machines, however, could not calculate, reason, discriminate visual patterns, or recognize and interpret human speech.

Every machine required a human operator to provide it with a brain and a human intermediary to serve as its eyes and ears. The greater the number of machines, the greater the number of people needed to tend them. The more sophisticated the machines, the greater the skills their operators required and the higher the wages they could command.

The second Industrial Revolution is exploiting major advances in information technology that use computers and electronic sensors to give machines eyes, ears, and brains to see and hear, interpret, and act on their own.

Economists with secure tenured positions at leading universities assure us that we have no need to worry. The increases in productivity will spur economic growth, and growth will mean more jobs, they tell us, just as happened in the first Industrial Revolution.

They fail to note that when the British textile industry was mechanized during the first Industrial Revolution, Britain shifted much of the resulting unemployment to India. It placed prohibitive tariffs on textiles imported from India to Britain, and British colonial administrators in India virtually eliminated the tariff on British textiles imported to India and levied taxes on Indian cloth produced domestically for domestic sale and on household spinning wheels.[1]

Workers surplus to European economies were exported to the colonies, where they commandeered the best lands to grow export crops, such as cotton, to feed the mother-country industries.

The second Industrial Revolution, based on a process of colonization defined by class rather than geography, is creating a global class division between colonizers and the colonized.

Efficiency is about producing greater output with less input. When we increase the productive output per hour of human labor, we call it increasing productivity. In the simplified examples of the sort favored by economics texts, it seems quite a good thing.

A farmer who buys a small tractor can cultivate more acres to provide more food and income for her family or devote fewer hours to toiling in the fields. Either way the farmer gains, no one loses, and the society is enriched in a variety of ways.

Unfortunately, the real world isn't like such simplified textbook examples. Note that in our example, the manager, the owner, and the laborer are one and the same person—Adam Smith's ideal enterprise. She makes the decision, bears the costs, and decides whether the productivity gain will go toward increasing production or reducing work time.

In the real world, the decision is likely to be made by an agribusiness corporation based solely on profitability. A few favored workers will be required to increase their output; the remainder will lose their jobs, with few alternative prospects.

It seems that the only certain beneficiaries of large-scale productivity increases in a nonunionized, labor-surplus world are the owners of capital. Yet, as the management analyst William Dugger suggests, we may be on the way to displacing them as well:

> The corporation is a true Frankenstein's monster—an artificial person run amok, responsible only to its own soulless self. Some fascinating possibilities present themselves. Corporations have already begun to buy up their own stock, holding it in their treasury. Taken to the logical conclusion, when 100 percent of the stock is treasury stock the corporation will own itself. It will have dispensed entirely with shareholders from the species *Homo sapiens*. To whom or to what would it then be responsible? Take these speculations about organized irresponsibility a bit further. . . . Could a corporation entirely dispense with not only human ownership but also human workers and managers? . . . What would it be then? . . . It would exist physically as a network of machines that buy, process, and sell commodities, monitored by a network of computers. Its purpose would be to grow ever larger through acquiring more machines and to become ever more powerful through acquiring more computers to monitor the new machines. It would be responsible to no one but itself in its mechanical drive for power and profit. It would represent capitalism at its very purest, completely unconcerned with anything save profit and power.[2]

Perhaps one day, if allowed sufficient freedom to follow its own unrestrained tendencies, a global corporation will achieve the ultimate in productive efficiency, an entity made up solely of computers and machines busily engaged in the replication of money. We might call it the perfectly efficient corporation. Although this is surely not what anyone intends, we are acting as though this is the world we seek.

Pain at the Top

Behind their bold public defense of an economic system in an advanced stage of self-destruction, there are growing reports of unease and concern even among the elite of the Stratos dwellers. In 1980–82, 79 percent of managers reported that their job security was "good" or "very good." By 1992–94, that figure had fallen to 55 percent.[3] It is not simply that their own positions are increasingly at risk. It is a sense that something simply isn't right, that they are leaving their children a deeply troubled world. Many corporate managers face growing conflicts between their personal values and what their corporate positions demand of them.

When justifying outrageous executive salaries, the press commonly notes such rewards are necessary to motivate the heads of corporations to exert their best efforts. When William A. Anders, the chairman of General Dynamics Corporation, was granted a $1.6 million bonus for having kept his company's stock price above $45 for ten days, a company spokesperson told the *Washington Post* that the bonus plan was needed to give top executives the incentive to change the company's business strategy and focus on maximizing returns to shareholders.[4] It is an extraordinary claim that the most privileged and well-paid professionals in the world require million-dollar bonuses to motivate them to do their job.

Derek Bok, the former president of Harvard University, offers a telling explanation. He suggests that top corporate executives must be paid such outrageous sums to ensure that they place the short-term interests of shareholders above all other interests that they might otherwise be tempted to consider—such as those of employees, the community, and even the corporation's own long-term viability.[5] In short, top executives have to be paid outrageous salaries to motivate them not to yield to their instincts toward social responsibility. Viewed from this perspective, these salaries indicate how distasteful the job of top corporate managers has become in the era of corporate downsizing.

With no end to the bloodletting in sight, a growing number of managers are losing their enthusiasm for their job, as *Fortune* reported in its July 25, 1994, cover story, "Burned-Out Bosses":

> Managers who were trained to build are now being paid to tear down. They don't hire; they fire. They don't like the new mandate, but most have come to understand that it's not going to change. That realization makes the daily routine different: Work no longer energizes; it drains.
>
> Under the circumstances it seems almost immoral to take much joy in work. So they become morose and cautious, worrying that they will be washed away in the next wave of discharges. Meanwhile, they work harder and longer to make up for the toil of those who have left. Fatigue and resentment begin to build.[6]

Unlike the financial speculators who move billions of dollars around the world from computer terminals detached from human reality, the managers of companies that produce real things deal every day with flesh-and-blood humans. They are the ones who must respond to the demands of the money managers for greater "efficiency" by imposing on their former friends and colleagues an experience almost as devastating as the loss of a loved one. As one CEO related to *Fortune*, "You get through firing people the first time around, accepting it as part of business. The second time I began wondering, 'How many miscarriages is this causing? How many divorces, how many suicides?' I worked harder so that I wouldn't have to think about it."[7]

An executive recruiter reported visiting a manager who had just gone through several rounds of firing immediate subordinates. Previously a strong, take-charge executive, he was now smoking, had lost weight, was unable to look the recruiter in the eye, and seemed extremely nervous. For another executive who had previously eliminated thousands of jobs, the need to put several thousand more former colleagues out on the street resulted in a loss of appetite and difficulty sleeping. He began breaking out in spontaneous fits of crying and one day couldn't get out of bed.

Those who achieve the pinnacles of financial and professional success in America seldom lack for physical comforts. They are learning, however, that no amount of money can buy peace of mind, a strong and loving family, caring friends, and a feeling that one is doing meaningful and important work.

The world is changing even for managers who were once at the pinnacle of power and prestige within their industries. Richard E. Snyder, one of the best known and most powerful figures in the publishing business, had a key role during his thirty-three-year career in building Simon & Schuster into a major US communications firm with an annual gross income of $2 billion. On June 14, 1994, he was abruptly and summarily sacked as chairman and CEO during a five-minute meeting with the CEO of Viacom, which had recently taken over Simon & Schuster's parent company Paramount Communications. The reason given was simply "a difference in styles."[8]

Under the leadership of its chairman Kay R. Whitmore, Eastman Kodak reported 1992 profits of $1.14 billion—a margin of roughly 5 percent on sales. On August 6, 1993, he was fired by the company's outside directors on the grounds that he was moving too slowly on cost reduction. He had announced 1992 layoffs of only 3,000 of Kodak's 132,000 employees. Institutional shareholders were clamoring for cuts of at least 20,000. Financial analysts heralded his firing as clear evidence that the outside directors were committed to placing the interests of investors ahead of those of management and employees. Kodak stock closed up $3.25 at the end of the day.[9]

No one is immune. There is no longer security at any level of the pyramid. *The Economist* recently noted:

Being the boss of a big American firm has been one of the safest and most richly rewarded jobs in the world. Until recently, that is. Last week the bosses of IBM, Westinghouse and American Express lost their jobs. A few months earlier Robert Stempel was unceremoniously removed as chairman of General Motors. . . . Now those at the top of big companies are wondering who will be next.[10]

The Economist attributes the phenomenon to a shift of shareholder power from the individual investor to performance-oriented investment funds that are flexing their muscles to kick out top managers of corporations that they consider to be "underperforming." There is no need for takeover battles as fund managers realize they can simply fire managers whose performance is lagging.

Limiting Commitment

Corporate restructuring is not simply about the drastic elimination of jobs; it is also about downgrading those that remain. The white-collar labor market is becoming more like the labor exchanges where jobless day laborers gather, hoping to hire out for the day. The "just in time" inventory concept now applies to people too.

The number of workers employed by temporary agencies has increased 240 percent in ten years. Manpower, the largest of 7,000 US temp agencies with 600,000 temporary workers on its rolls, is now America's largest private employer. Although some workers are part time or temporary by choice, in 1993 nearly a third of the 21 million part-time workers in the United States said that they would prefer full-time jobs.

Many displaced workers become self-employed, contracting out individually for temporary work. Most of these have suffered a sharp decline in income. Although much of the evidence is anecdotal, Census Bureau statistics reveal that from 1989 to 1992, the real median income of Americans who worked for themselves fell 12.6 percent to $18,544. Many of the newly self-employed workers are earning well below $18,000 a year—a level that makes supporting a family in the present American economy difficult, if not impossible.[11]

Young professionals are now actively counseled to plan career paths independently of their companies, to build their résumés and their outside contacts so that they are ready to move on when a new opportunity arises or when their companies abandon them. The advice to young people starting their careers: treat every job as though you are self-employed.[12]

Not so long ago, the firm for which a person worked was almost like family. It was a primary support system in an otherwise often impersonal and transient world. A good job was far more than an income. It was a source of identity and of valued and enduring relationships. Those days are no more. Increased stress in the workplace spills over to marriage and family life.

In the present job market, the distinction between white-collar and blue-collar workers is less significant than the distinction between those who have permanent jobs and those who don't. The system nurtures an attitude of "Get what you can from the system while you can. Look out for yourself, because no one else will."

Adjusting to Diminished Prospects

Those forced out of their existing jobs seldom find new ones with comparable pay. Starting pay is dropping rapidly. Six hundred new United Airlines reservation agents hired in July 1994 faced a permanent pay ceiling of $18,000, whereas an agent doing the same job but hired only six months earlier had prospects of earning up to $34,000 after ten years on the job.[13] Those workers who manage to hang on to their jobs often face a choice between giving up salary and benefits or seeing their jobs disappear entirely. In the United States, average hourly wages for production and nonsupervisory workers fell from $11.37 in 1973 to $10.34 in 1992 (in constant 1991 dollars), whereas average annual hours worked increased from 1,683 hours in 1973 to 1,781 hours in 1990.[14]

A declining percentage of full-time jobs pay a living wage. The US Census Bureau reported that in 1992 the wages received by 18 percent of full-time workers in the United States were not adequate to maintain a family of four above the official poverty line of $13,091—compared with 12 percent of full-time workers in 1979. Among full-time workers in the age group eighteen to twenty-four, the report found that 47 percent earned less than a poverty-level wage, up from only 25 percent in 1979. The usually understated Census Bureau referred to this rapid and dramatic shift as "astounding."[15] Some experts say that the census figures seriously understate the number of America's working poor, because an income of at least $20,000 is now required to provide basic necessities for a family of four.[16]

Even the fortunes of upper-middle-class professionals took a turn for the worse in the 1990s. According to *Business Week*, "just as the last decade was defined by yuppies and their flamboyant material excesses, the 1990s may come to be the age of 'dumpies'—downwardly mobile professionals."[17]

The US Labor Department reports that 20 percent of graduates from US universities in the 1984–90 period took jobs in which they were "underutilized" and predicts that 30 percent of those graduating between 1994 and 2005 will join the ranks of the unemployed or underemployed.[18] The phenomenon of the hotel bellboy with a bachelor's degree has become commonplace. *Time* recently noted one bright spot on the horizon—growing opportunities for prison guards.[19]

Even households with two wage earners in what used to be considered good middle-class white-collar jobs are struggling to make ends meet. Take the case of Paul and Jane Lambert, both of whom have full-time jobs. She is an office manager and he is a Sears phone order taker. Their combined income doesn't allow them to buy new clothes, health insurance, or dental care, let alone go to a movie, fix the car, or eat out. They are able to provide their family with regular meals only because Jane's parents give them money.[20]

Craig Miller was once a unionized sheet-metal worker for TWA. His $15.65-an-hour job gave his family an income of over $36,000 a year. With two cars in the garage and a swing set in the yard, they were a solid middle-class family living the American dream. Miller was laid off in the summer of 1992. He now hustles hamburger orders at McDonald's, drives a school bus, and has started a small business changing furnace filters. He gets home from his school bus duties at 5 p.m. After a hurried dinner, his wife leaves for her six-to-midnight job at Toys 'R' Us, restocking the shelves while her husband watches the children at home. She also works at the same McDonald's as her husband one day a week. Their total income from these jobs comes to about $18,000. They look to a bleak future.

One of Miller's buddies who was also laid off from TWA was unable to find a job paying more than $6 an hour and, at age thirty-nine, moved back in with his parents, abandoning hope for marriage and children. Another former colleague works as a janitor. Marriages have collapsed. Alcoholism has taken its toll. Union officials say that of the several hundred workers TWA dismissed, perhaps a dozen have committed suicide.[21] The tales read like ones from the Great Depression. However, they are tales from what conventional indicators suggest is a robust economy.

In an economy that measures performance in terms of the creation of money, people become a major source of inefficiency—and the economy is shedding them with a vengeance. When the institutions of money rule the world, it is perhaps inevitable that the interests of money take precedence over the interests of people. What we are experiencing might best be described as a case of money colonizing life. To accept this absurd distortion of human institutions and purpose should be considered nothing less than an act of collective, suicidal insanity. It is not an entirely new phenomenon, however. We can gain insights into the nature and consequences of our current situation from the experience of the historical colonialization of traditional societies.

CHAPTER 20

People with No Place

We must find new lands from which we can easily obtain raw materials and at the same time exploit the cheap slave labour that is available from the natives of the colonies. The colonies would also provide a dumping ground for the surplus goods produced in our factories.

—CECIL RHODES, the "founder" of Rhodesia

Those of us who have grown up in societies in which survival depends on money easily accept this dependence as a natural part of the human condition. To fully appreciate the extent to which this dependence is a largely artificial condition, we must revisit earlier societies in which relationships were defined by enduring family and community ties.

Although we now tend to associate pre-monetized societies with primitive cultures and harsh living conditions, some such societies had highly advanced cultures and provided their members with socially and spiritually secure and meaningful lives. Although people in these societies at times endured serious hardships, they seldom experienced the sense of deprivation, insecurity, and isolation that is the daily lot of those who find themselves without money in a monetized society. Indeed, it is likely that in today's monetized world, from 2 to 3 billion people live less secure and less prosperous lives than did their ancestors whose livelihoods were predominantly nonmonetized.

In the Name of Development

Most of the world has now been drawn so far into the globalized money economy that few among us have had the opportunity to experience any other way of living. The anthropologist Helena Norberg-Hodge is an exception. She had the privilege of coming to know life in the traditional villages of Ladakh, a trans-Himalayan region of Kashmir in India, when the area was first opened to outsiders some twenty years ago. Her moving accounts of what she found speak of human possibilities now largely forgotten:

> In traditional Ladakh to link happiness to income or possessions would have been unthinkable. A deep-rooted respect for each other's fundamental human needs and an acceptance of the natural limitations of the environment kept the Ladakhi people free from misplacing values of worth. Happiness was simply experienced. Though not an easy lifestyle by western standards, people met their basic physical, social, spiritual and creative needs within the security of a caring, sharing community and an abundant agrarian subsistence economy—and experienced evident joy.

Norberg-Hodge has made regular visits to the region, observing and documenting the subsequent changes as the intrusion of Western-style development has "created a void in people's lives, an inferiority in their self-perceptions and a greed for material wealth." The contemporary colonization of Ladakh has been advanced by a combination of Western tourists, media, educational models, and technology.

> A western tourist can spend more in one day than what a Ladakhi family might in one year. Seeing this, Ladakhis suddenly feel poor. The new comparison creates a gap that never existed before because in traditional Ladakh, people didn't need money in order to lead rich, fulfilling lives. Ladakhi society was based on mutual aid and cooperation; no one needed money for labor, food, clothing or shelter. . . .
>
> In the traditional economy, Ladakhis knew that they had to depend on other people, and that others in turn depend on them. In the new economic system, local interdependence disintegrates along with traditional levels of tolerance. In place of cooperative systems of meeting needs, competition and scarcity become determinants for survival. Passivity also develops, as reliance upon distant government bureaucracies increases. The more government becomes involved in village activities for the sake of "development," the less villagers feel inclined to help themselves.
>
> The Indian government's effort to industrialize the Ladakh region has meant that men leave their families in rural areas to become wage earners in the city. Since the modern world recognizes only wage earners as "productive" members of society—housewives, traditional farmers and the elderly suddenly become identified as "unproductive"—in complete contrast to their roles in traditional Ladakh. The weakening

of family and community ties increases individual insecurity, which in turn contributes to a hunger for material status symbols.[1]

We can learn a great deal about the range of human possibilities from memories of highly culturally evolved pre-monetized societies such as Ladakh without presuming that the answer to our current crisis lies in returning to a premodern past. Studies of their subsequent transformation provide useful—if disturbing—insights into the nature and destructive consequences of conventional economic development introduced into traditional communities.

After more than thirty years as a dedicated development professional, I've only recently come to see the extent to which the Western development enterprise has been about separating people from their traditional means of livelihood and breaking down the bonds of security provided by family and community to create dependence on the jobs and products that modern corporations produce.

It is an extension of a process that began with the enclosure, or privatization, of common lands in England to concentrate the benefits of their production in the hands of the few rather than the many.[2] The colonial era extended the process to the people of nonindustrial lands. Post–World War II development assistance and investment continued the same basic process—under a subtler and friendlier guise—monetizing the production and service functions of the social economy, replacing locally controlled systems of agriculture, governance, health care, education, and mutual self-help with systems more amenable to central control and the expropriation necessary to support a ruling class.

It is also instructive to characterize the era of modern development as expanding opportunities for workers whose functions are exclusive to the money economy—such as corporate executives, marketing specialists, lawyers, bankers, accountants, investment brokers, and others. These "money workers" produce nothing of intrinsic worth yet receive handsome financial compensation for performing functions that did not exist in premonetized societies. They have arguably been the major beneficiaries of development—more accurately described as corporate colonialism.

Noted earlier was an estimate of the globalization guru Kenichi Ohmae: that in the modern global economy, production accounts for only about 25 percent of the selling price of a typical product. Another way to put it is that most of the value created by those who produce real goods and services is now being captured by those who do only money work.

One of the major challenges faced by colonial administrators was to force those who obtained their livelihood from their own lands and common areas to give up their lands and labor to plantation development, that is, to make them dependent on a money economy so that their resources, labor, and consumption might yield profits to the colonizers. A first step was usually to declare all "uncultivated" lands—generally common lands—to be the property of the colonial administration. "At one stroke, local communities were denied legal title to lands they had traditionally set aside as fallow and to the forests, grazing lands and streams they relied upon for hunting, gathering, fishing and herding."[3]

Then vast tracts of forestland were declared "reserve forests." Traditional rights of access were curtailed as the lands were sold to European settlers or leased to commercial concerns for plantations, mining, and logging. The Boer settlers in South Africa justified their expulsion of subsistence farmers from their tribal lands with the claim that they were not engaged in any systematic forms of agriculture and therefore were little more than squatters.[4] Forced labor was piously justified as developmentally beneficial to the enslaved. As the French minister of commerce stated in 1901:

> The black does not like work and is totally unaccustomed to the idea of saving; he does not realise that idleness keeps him in a state of absolute economic inferiority. It is therefore necessary to use . . . slavery to improve his circumstances and afterwards lead him into an apprenticeship of freedom.[5]

In many colonized countries, the imposition of taxes payable only in cash was used to force people into the cash economy. By requiring the village elders to collect the tax, the credibility and legitimacy of traditional local governance structures were undermined.

Taxes were placed on whatever villagers would find it most difficult to do without. In Vietnam, the French imposed taxes on salt, opium, and alcohol. The British in Sudan taxed crops, animals, houses, and households. In their West African colonies, the French punished tax evasion by holding wives and children hostage, whipping men, burning huts, and leaving people tied up without food for several days.[6] Development was a hard sell in those early days.

Traditional colonialism came to an end after World War II, and the new corporate colonialism—presented as economic development through foreign aid, investment, and trade—stepped into the breach. Colonization as economic development is more subtle, more sophisticated, and more appealing than traditional colonialism. In the battle for the souls of the colonized, economic conversion replaced religious conversion and economic growth became the path to eternal salvation. The methods varied; the consequences were strikingly similar. Alienate people from their traditional means of living and create dependence on money to transfer power to an occupying country or corporation seeking to extract labor and resources for its own exclusive benefit.

People were pushed off their farms—often by convincing them to convert to seeds, fertilizers, and pesticides purchased from foreign corporations on credit—which were converted into foreign-owned or foreign-controlled plantations financed with foreign money. The displaced provided a cheap labor pool for the plantations and for urban factories also financed with foreign money. Countries became increasingly dependent on expensive foreign technologies and expertise—financed by foreign borrowing. The plantations and factories produced primarily for export to obtain the foreign exchange required to pay interest and principle on foreign loans and repatriate the profits of foreign investors.

Multilateral banks and aid agencies dictated the economic policies that drove this "liberation." Military assistance missions and clandestine political operatives shaped their politics as transnational corporations expropriated their resources and penetrated their markets.[7] Money was the enticement—grant money, loan money, trade money, investment money. To every need and crisis, money was the answer, more specifically foreign money that bought foreign goods from foreign companies.

At each step of the way, the social fabric was weakened and dependence on the money economy, especially the foreign-money economy, was strengthened. Governments were encouraged and supported in creating vast public bureaucracies that displaced traditional education, health care, and welfare services.

Then came structural adjustment, and the poor who had become dependent on these services were told that the services had become too expensive and a drain on the economy's ability to meet its needs for foreign exchange, especially to pay its obligations to foreign banks. People would have to do without this extravagance. Moreover, they must transfer still more of their agricultural lands to export crops, import more of their own food, and attract foreign investors with offers of tax holidays, cheap access to timber, prime agricultural lands, mineral and petroleum reserves, and cheap labor. They must also offer them subsidized electricity and physical infrastructure paid for with still more foreign borrowing.

As monetization of the economy grows GDP, and the displaced manage to eke out incomes of a dollar a day working under slave-like conditions, development economists tout to the world the success of development in liberating the poor from extreme poverty.

From colonialism to development to structural adjustment, the people of Southern countries have been integrated into the new colonialism of the corporate-ruled global economy, step by wrenching step. Development has elevated a fortunate few among the Southern elites to the ranks of the world's richest people. Millions whose service the system particularly values now enjoy middle-class incomes and support thriving enclaves of affluent consumerism.

The majority of people in the geographical South, however, have been systematically deprived of the livelihoods and social support once provided by their now-disrupted social economies and reduced to lives of violent servitude and extreme deprivation.

Free Markets, Open Borders

The fate of societies in which the exclusionary processes of colonialism, both old and new, have progressed to their ultimate conclusion is vividly documented in Robert Kaplan's *Atlantic Monthly* article "The Coming Anarchy." The place is West Africa, and Kaplan sees its experience as a premonition of a human future—a place of "disease, overpopulation, unprovoked crime, scarcity of resources, refugee migrations, the increasing erosion of nation-states and international borders, and the empowerment of private armies, security firms, and international drug cartels."[8] In short, it is the ultimate expression of a borderless free-market economy.

In Kaplan's account, the government of Sierra Leone is run by a seventeen-year-old army captain and a ragtag group of followers in the military who control the capital city and, by day, rule parts of the rural interior—making their presence visible mainly by threatening travelers to extract tribute at checkpoints. At night, an opposing army of rebels moves in when the national army moves out. Renegade government military commanders align themselves with disaffected village chiefs. Two separate units from the war in Liberia maintain bases within Sierra Leone's borders.

> As a consequence, roughly 400,000 Sierra Leonians are internally displaced, 280,000 more have fled to neighboring Guinea, and another 100,000 have fled to Liberia, even as 400,000 Liberians have fled to Sierra Leone. The third largest city in Sierra Leone, Gondama, is a displaced-persons camp. With an additional 600,000 Liberians in Guinea and 250,000 in the Ivory Coast, the borders dividing these four countries have become largely meaningless. Even in quiet zones, none of the governments except the Ivory Coast's maintains the schools, bridges, roads, and police forces in a manner necessary for functional sovereignty.[9]

Deforestation is progressing at a devastating rate, with consequent soil erosion, flooding, and mosquitoes. Malaria is almost universal. Violence, volatility, and disease are isolating the rural areas from the cities. The Ivory

Coast's once-thriving cocoa economy makes it a magnet for migrant workers from other countries of West Africa. As much as half of the country's population is now non-Ivorian, with estimates of the foreign population of Abidjan running as high as 75 percent of the total. Shantytowns occupy ever more of the city amid the skyscrapers that maintain the façade of prosperity in what was formerly known as the "Paris of West Africa." The inhabitants of these shantytowns live in shelters made of scrap materials; they defecate in streams filled with garbage and pigs as women do the wash in the same water among swarms of malarial mosquitoes. The young men drink beer, palm wine, and gin while gambling by day and rob houses in more prosperous neighborhoods by night.

The people of traditional Ladakh may have endured their own hardships, and few of us living in modern Western societies would wish to trade our lives for theirs. Yet life within the cohesive communities of Ladakh was a paradise compared with life in places like West Africa, where social structures have been torn asunder by successive waves of colonial intrusion.

Kaplan observes that the West African experience is a spreading phenomenon. He cites Martin van Creveld, a military historian at Hebrew University, who paints the following scenario of an emergent world of extreme inequality, scarcity, and weak states that have lost their capacity to maintain civil order:

> Once the legal monopoly of armed force, long claimed by the state, is wrested out of its hands, existing distinctions between war and crime will break down much as is already the case today in . . . Lebanon, Sri Lanka, El Salvador, Peru, or Colombia. [Urban crime may] develop into low-intensity conflict by coalescing along racial, religious, social, and political lines.[10]

It is an apt description of the violence that has turned many American ghettos into virtual war zones. Kaplan's apocalyptic vision is an alarmingly credible projection of current trends and the dynamics that underlie them. For growing numbers of people around the world, especially youth, minorities, and women, there is no longer a dream of a more prosperous and secure future, only the bleak prospect of exclusion, despair, deprivation, shame, and brutalizing violence.

United Nations refugee statistics offer one of the most frightening indicators of the accelerating rate of global social disintegration and exclusion. In 1960, the UN classified 1.4 million people as international refugees. By 1970, the number had risen to 2.5 million, by 1980 to 8.2 million, and by 1992 to 18.2 million. The substantial majority subsist in refugee camps in Asia and Africa, with an average of nearly 10,000 people join-ing their ranks each day.[11] In 1994, in one 48-hour period, more than a million Rwandans fled the bloody battles in their devastated country into neighboring Zaire, bringing the total number of Rwandan refugees to an estimated 2.1 million.[12]

The UN estimates that more than 24 million additional people are cur-rently displaced within the borders of their own countries. This means that roughly one of every 130 people on Earth lives involuntarily separated from the place they consider home. The words of Sadako Ogata, the UN high commissioner for refugees, echo those of Kaplan:

> Flight is more than ever before the product of vicious internal conflicts. Nationalistic, ethnic or communal tensions have become the predomi-nant factor in refugee movements around the world, be it in the Horn of Africa and the Sudan, the former Soviet Union and the Balkans or in the Middle East and parts of the Asian subcontinent. . . . The loosening grip of authoritarian regimes and the destructive effects of civil war are straining fragile state structures. This has led, in cases such as Somalia and Bosnia and Herzegovina, to the disintegration of states into ter-ritories controlled by competing factions.[13]

Millions are also forced from their homes because natural or manmade disasters have made the land on which they live uninhabitable or reduced its ability to sustain the number of people who depend on it. Environ-mental stresses may in turn contribute to internal armed conflicts, which are commonly associated with a combination of declining economic cir-cumstances, a lack of strong representative political institutions, and the disruption of traditional processes of mediation.

Under such circumstances, political conflict readily degenerates into anarchy, leaving the state in the position of being simply one of many contenders for the dwindling spoils and leaving the population without any form of national security. The conflict disrupts food production and distribution, which accounts for the fact that in conflict situations, it is common for far more deaths to result from starvation and disease than from the actual conflict itself. It is scarcely a fit world for either people or corporations—yet it is the world toward which the forces of corporate colonization inexorably move us.

Alternatives for the Excluded

The excluded, for whom a globalized money economy offers no employ-ment whatever, have three basic choices: (1) give in to the inevitable and live on scraps scavenged from relief agencies or refuse piles, slowly starve, or commit suicide; (2) seek the comradeship of violence and live from the spoils of crime and pillage; or (3) join with others in the re-creation of human communities delinked from the global economy. The first of these options needs no elaboration. The latter two define competing visions of the human future: one of doom and one of hope.

Kaplan points to a terrible and disturbing truth. For people whose lives are a collage of brutality and deprivation, organized violence brings a sense of relief:

> A large number of people on this planet, to whom the comfort and stability of a middle class life is utterly unknown, find war and a barracks existence a step up rather than a step down. . . . Where there has always been mass poverty, people find liberation in violence.[14]

We are learning that much the same can be said for membership in ghetto gangs. They fill a need for companionship and provide a sense of belonging otherwise denied. Organized violence fills a void by creating an opportunity to be part of a larger human whole, to find companions who provide social support and legitimacy for the venting of one's rage at an otherwise uncaring world.

Violence can be for some an almost religious experience, heightening a sense of consciousness and being by focusing the senses on the here and now and freeing the mind of the distractions of deprivation. So long as forced physical, social, and spiritual deprivation exists among us, violence will be an almost inevitable consequence.

Fortunately, there is a third path for the excluded, the re-creation of communities delinked from a corporate-dominated global economy. As a counterpoint to his descriptions of terrifying anarchy in the slums of West Africa, Robert Kaplan describes the social strength of a shantytown in the Turkish capital of Ankara. Financially poor and materially deprived, its residents maintain a strong cultural identity, values, and social fabric. Crime against persons and alcoholism are rare. The insides of makeshift shelters are spotless, and the children are in school.

It should now be clear that the cure for the deprivations of poverty will not—cannot—be found in the economic growth of a globalized free market that weakens and destroys the bonds of culture and community to the exclusive benefit of global corporations. The necessary cure lies instead in restoring and strengthening these bonds. Our collective survival—not only of the poor and excluded but also of the relatively affluent and not yet excluded—depends on creating an institutional and values framework that advances this restoration.

PART VI

To Reclaim Our Power

CHAPTER 21

The Ecological Revolution

By deliberately changing the internal image of reality, people can change the world.

—WILLIS HARMAN

I believe that the world has moved closer to oneness and more people see each other as one with the other. . . . It is possible to have new thoughts and new common values for humans and all other forms of life.

—WANGARI MAATHAI,
coordinator, Kenya Green Belt Movement

No sane person seeks a world divided between billions of people living in absolute deprivation and a tiny elite guarding their wealth and luxury behind fortress walls. No one rejoices at the prospect of life in a world of collapsing social and ecological systems. Yet we continue to place human civilization and even our species' survival at risk mainly to allow a few million people to accumulate money beyond any conceivable need. We continue to go boldly where no one wants to go.

Many are awakening to the reality that economic globalization has come at an intolerable price. In the name of modernity we create dysfunctional societies that breed pathological behavior—violence, extreme competitiveness, suicide, drug abuse, greed, and environmental degradation—at every hand. Such behavior is the inevitable consequence of a society's failure to meet the needs of its members for social bonding, trust, affection, and shared sacred meaning.[1] Yet the madness of pursuing policies that deepen economic, social, and environmental dysfunction is not inevitable. The idea that we are caught in the grip of irresistible historical forces and inherent, irreversible human imperfections to which we must adapt is pure fabrication. Corporate globalization is advanced by the conscious choices of those who view the world through the lens of corporate interest. Human alternatives do exist, and those who view the world through the lens of a healthy society have both the right and the power to choose them.

Liberation from corporate rule requires that we shed the illusions of our collective cultural trance, reclaim the power we have yielded to failing institutions, take back responsibility for our lives, and reweave the basic fabric of caring families and communities to create places for people and other living things. These actions are within our means—including the transformation of the dominant belief systems, values, and institutions of contemporary society—an Ecological Revolution comparable to the Copernican Revolution that ushered in the scientific-industrial era. The parallels are instructive.

Competing Visions of Reality

The Copernican Revolution was grounded in a basic change in the prevailing perception of the nature of reality. The issues involved bear examination, because they go to the root of our present crisis and help define the challenge of the Ecological Revolution.[2]

Transcendental monism (the view that consciousness or spirit gives rise to matter) has formed the philosophical foundation of many Eastern cultures, at least until the recent onslaught of Western science, industrialization, global competition, and consumerism. Adherents to this tradition believe that consciousness is the primary reality and that matter is a creation of consciousness or spiritual energy.

Based on the belief that all consciousness, as well as the material manifestation of consciousness, originates from the same underlying unity, transcendental monism considers inner wisdom, accessed through our spiritual connection with the infinite, to be the primary source of valid knowing. This tradition was commonly associated with a denial of things material, a fatalistic acceptance of one's material condition, a strong sense of community, and a deep reverence for nature.

In the West, the Judeo-Christian tradition took quite a different course, personifying God as a being who lives in a distant and separate realm and whose attention is centered on Earth and its human inhabitants. In this tradition, God's will and wisdom were revealed through prophets, such as Moses, or through his incarnation as Jesus. Earth was believed to be the center of the universe, with the sun, stars, and planets revolving around it. These beliefs remained the foundation of scientific thought and moral and political authority in Europe until as recently as five hundred years ago.

Then in 1543, Nicolaus Copernicus published *Revolution of the Celestial Spheres,* setting forth the thesis that Earth is only one among the planets that revolve around the sun, itself one of countless such stars of the cosmos. This led to a historic confrontation between science and the church as to whether scientific observation or divine revelation is the more valid source of human knowledge.

Materialistic monism (the view that matter gives rise to consciousness or spirit) became the image of reality embraced by science and unleashed what historians refer to as the Copernican Revolution. Adherents to this tradition believe that matter is the primary reality, physical measurement is the one valid source of knowledge, and the experience of consciousness is only a manifestation of the material complexity of the physical brain.

For this tradition it is inconceivable that any form of consciousness exists independently of a physical presence. Materialistic monism has been the foundation of Western scientific training and culture throughout most of the scientific-industrial era. It has commonly been associated with a denial of the spiritual and an emphasis on materialism, individualism, and the exploitation of nature.

According to the historian Edward McNall Burns, the significance of the Copernican Revolution lies in the fact that "reason was now held to be the solitary fount of knowledge, while the whole idea of spiritual meaning in the universe was cast aside like a worn-out garment."[3] The intellectual and moral authority of the church was greatly weakened.

The idea that only those things that can be measured are suitable subjects for scientific study and that the only acceptable explanation for observed phenomena is material causation allowed science to distinguish "scientific explanations from such prescientific interpretations as the whims of the gods or the intervention of divine grace."[4] However, it also meant that consciousness, values, aesthetics, and other aspects of human experience were excluded from consideration in scientific inquiry. By rejecting free will and moral choice as acceptable explanations for human behavior, science effectively exempted itself from moral responsibility for the application of scientific knowledge.

The seventeenth-century philosopher Thomas Hobbes took materialistic monism to its ultimate extreme. He maintained that absolutely nothing exists except matter. If there is a God, he must have a physical body. In Hobbes's view, good is merely that which gives us pleasure, evil that which brings pain, and the only meaningful purpose in life is to pursue pleasure[5]—a value system that now serves as the implicit moral premise of corporate globalization.

The institutions of religion and science—each with its own view of reality—henceforth competed for the soul of Western societies. Dualism (the view that matter and spirit are two distinct and independent aspects of reality) provided the basis for an uneasy accommodation between religious and scientific worldviews. While the church ministered to a constricted spiritual life, secular society came to embrace the material world as the primary reality, materialism as the dominant value, and ultimately economic growth as the primary human purpose.

As a philosophy of science, materialistic monism made possible the scientific and technological accomplishments of the scientific-industrial era. As a philosophy of life deeply embedded in modern culture, it has led us to the brink of self-destruction, because it leads so naturally to the embrace of Hobbesian values that alienate us from any higher meaning or purpose. Having embraced material self-indulgence as our purpose, an appeal to limit indulgence in the interest of economic justice or concern for future generations becomes a call to sacrifice the only thing that gives life meaning. It follows, as corporate libertarians sometimes maintain, that it is most rational for those who have the financial means to continue to enjoy the party for as long as it lasts. If they sacrifice these pleasures and the environmentalists are ultimately proved wrong, they will have sacrificed their reason for living to no end. If the environmentalists are proved right and the party ends in self-destruction, then at least they enjoyed it while they could.

Materialistic monism also prepared the way for an economics that, intent on achieving the status of a true science, embraced market prices, which can be observed and measured, as the sole arbiter of human values. It is impossible to understand or explain anything more than purely habitual human behavior without addressing the values, loyalties, aspirations, love, psychological conflicts, altruism, spirituality, conscience, and even metaphysical beliefs that inform our choices as living choice-making beings. Although central to our experience and well-being, they are often difficult to observe, let alone measure. Thus, as science defines itself, the term *social science* is a contradiction, because we lack the means to directly observe or measure many of the most important "causes" of social behavior.

This presses the social scientist to either redefine the prescriptions of scientific inquiry to fit the human reality or deny the qualities that make us truly human. Intent on raising their discipline to the stature of a science, economists chose the latter by postulating a hypothetical economic man who mechanistically seeks only his own pleasure, defined in terms of measurable economic gain. Whenever a model requires a human decision maker—irrespective of gender—the economist thus substitutes the imaginary, decidedly nonhuman, economic man, who evaluates every choice on the basis of its financial return.

Having eliminated the human, economists then eliminated the behavior. Finding the interactions among people too hopelessly complex and difficult to measure, economists chose to observe the behavior of markets rather than the behavior of people. Market behavior involves prices and flows of money, which are more easily observed and measured.

Since a science must be objective and value-free, economists chose to reduce all values to market values as revealed in market price. Thus air, water, and other essentials of life provided freely by nature are treated as valueless until scarcity and privatization render them marketable. By contrast, gold and diamonds, which have almost no use in sustaining life, are valued highly. The value of a human life is arrived at by calculating a person's lifetime earning potential or "economic contribution." As a cynic once accurately noted, "Economists know the price of everything and the value of nothing."

The partial and materialistic view of our human nature embodied in the materialistic monism of classical physics was extended to an absurdity by economists seeking to raise their status in the academy by denying that which makes us human. By the economist's calculation, our financial worth is the measure of our human worth. This fallacy has become so embedded in modern culture that we have come to equate success of a person's life with their financial success. As noted by the contemporary philosopher Jacob Needleman in *Money and the Meaning of Life:*

> In other times and places, not everyone has wanted *money* above all else; people have desired salvation, beauty, power, strength, pleasure, propriety, explanations, food, adventure, conquest, comfort. But now and here, *money*—is what everyone wants. The outward expenditure of mankind's energy now takes place in and through money.[6]

It seems odd that we would voluntarily redirect our life energy from the pursuit of life to the pursuit of money and do so in ways so inherently detrimental to our own well-being—until we realize that in a modern monetized society survival itself depends on having money to buy those essentials of life we once obtained directly through our own labor in co-productive partnership with the rest of nature.

As Joe Dominguez and Vicki Robin point out in their *New York Times* best-seller *Your Money or Your Life,* money becomes "something we all too often don't have, which we struggle to get, and on which we pin our hopes of power, happiness, security, acceptance, success, fulfillment, achievement and personal worth."[7]

Beyond meeting our survival needs, we have come to look to money to provide all these intangibles of good living—forgetting the simple reality that only forgeries of the real thing are up for sale. The real thing must be earned by investing ourselves in loving relationships, being good friends and neighbors, living by ethical principles, and developing and engaging our abilities in ways that contribute to the life of the community.

Marketing experts surround us with a different cultural message. They don't sell laundry soap; they sell acceptance, achievement, and personal worth. They don't sell automobiles; they sell the sense of freedom, success, joy, and control of our lives that we really want. To buy what the marketers offer, we need money, so we sell ourselves to jobs we may hate in order to obtain it. Dominguez and Robin sum it up:

> Money is something we choose to trade our life energy for. . . . Our allotment of time here on earth, the hours of precious life available to us. When we go to our jobs, we are trading our life energy for money. This truth, while simple, is profound.[8]

Money is not an ordinary number after all. It is our ticket to the same things that people have wanted in other times and places. It is a measure of the life energies expended in its acquisition. It has become our answer to the question "What am I worth?" and the measure of our collective worth and accomplishment as a nation.

Professional charities have even made money the measure of our compassion: "Make a difference. Send us your check today." Defining ourselves in terms of money, we become trapped in a downward spiral of increasing alienation from living, from our own spiritual nature (see figure 21.1).

Rather than teaching us that the path to fulfillment is to experience living to the fullest through our relationships with family, community, nature, and the living cosmos, the corporate media continuously repeat a false promise: whatever our longings, the market is the path to their instant gratification. Our purpose is to consume—we are born to shop. Entranced by the siren song of the market, we consistently undervalue the life energy that we put into obtaining money and overvalue the expected psychic rewards obtained by spending it.

The more we give our life energies over to money, the more power we yield to the institutions that control our access to money and to the things it will buy. Yielding such power serves the corporate interest well, because corporations are creatures of money. It serves our human interest poorly, because we are creatures of nature and spirit.

Forced to reexamine who we are by the limits of the planet's ability to accommodate our greed, we find ourselves confronted with a beautiful

Figure 21.1 Downward Spiral of Deepening Alienation

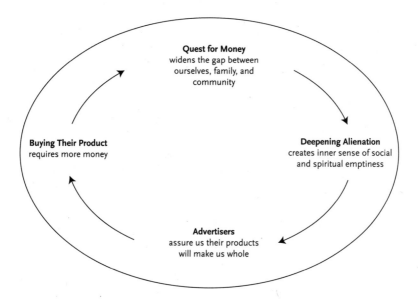

truth: Whereas our pursuit of material abundance has created material scarcity, our pursuit of life may bring a new sense of social, spiritual, and even material abundance.

People who experience an abundance of love in their lives rarely seek solace in compulsive, exclusionary personal acquisition. For the emotionally deprived, no extreme of materialistic indulgence can ever be enough, and the material world becomes insufficient to our wants. A world starved of love becomes one of material scarcity. In contrast, a world of love is also one of material abundance. When we are spiritually whole and experience the caring support of community, thrift is a natural part of a full and disciplined life. That which is sufficient to one's needs brings a fulfilling sense of nature's abundance.

The implications are profound. Our seemingly insatiable quest for money and material consumption is in fact a quest to fill a void in our lives created by a lack of love. It is a consequence of dysfunctional societies in which money has displaced our sense of spiritual connection as the foundation of our cultural values and relationships. The result is a world of material scarcity, massive inequality, overtaxed environmental systems, and social disintegration. So long as we embrace moneymaking as our collective purpose and we structure our institutions to give this goal precedence over all others, the void in our lives will grow and the human crisis will deepen.

There is an obvious solution: create societies that give a higher value to nurturing life than to making money. Idealistic as this may sound, it is entirely within our means. The key is a shift in consciousness already being created through an emerging synthesis of scientific and religious knowledge that embraces the integral connection between reality's material and spiritual dimensions.[9]

The Copernican Revolution ushered in the scientific-industrial era by freeing us from one set of misperceptions about ourselves and the nature of our reality. An Ecological Revolution, based on a more holistic integration of the spiritual and material, may usher in an ecological era that will open currently unimagined opportunities for our social and spiritual development. To realize this goal, we must reclaim for people the power that we have yielded to money and a corporate-dominated global economy.

Our Human Nature

Although a competitive instinct forms an important part of our nature, there is substantial evidence that competition is a subtheme to the more dominant theme of the bonding, caring, and cooperation essential to our species' survival. According to the cultural anthropologist Mary Clark:

> The early human species could not have survived without the expanded social bonding beyond parent and offspring needed to protect helpless human infants—a job that mothers alone could not accomplish. Social bonding to one's group was a biological necessity—for adults as well as infants.[10]

Things haven't really changed so much. Social bonding is as essential to the healthy functioning of a modern society as it was to more traditional or tribal societies. Harvard University political scientist Robert Putnam refers to the bonding that characterizes a strong civil society as *social capital* and has shown its importance in a study of local government effectiveness in Italy.

Beginning in 1970, Italy created twenty regional governments. Their formal structures were identical. There were dramatic differences, however, in the social, economic, political, and cultural context in which these structures were planted. The localities ranged "from the pre-industrial to the post-industrial, from the devoutly Catholic to the ardently Communist, from the inertly feudal to the frenetically modern." In some localities, the new government structures were "inefficient, lethargic, and corrupt." In others, they were dynamic and effective, "creating innovative day care programs and job training centers, promoting investment and economic development, pioneering environmental standards and family clinics."[11]

Putnam found only one set of indicators that consistently differentiated those localities in which the government worked from those in which it didn't. These were indicators of a strong and active civil society, as measured by "voter turnout, newspaper readership, membership in choral societies and literary clubs, Lions Clubs and soccer clubs." Localities high on these indicators had highly developed social capital. Rich networks of nonmarket relationships built a general sense of trust and reciprocity that increased the efficiency of human relationships.[12]

Contemporary economic theory and practice gives no more than passing lip service to the importance of social capital to the healthy functioning of societies and ignores the impact of economic structures and policies on its formation or depletion.

How about your community? Does it contain small local shops run by merchants you know by name? Or are your choices limited to mega-shopping malls and large retail chain outlets that send their profits elsewhere and are staffed by part-time temporary workers you've never met and are unlikely ever to see again?

Is there a thriving farmers' market where you can get to know the people who produce your food? Or only a supermarket selling food imported from thousands of miles away? Are farms small, individually owned, and family operated, or are they controlled by huge corporate enterprises and worked mainly by itinerant landless laborers?

Do people devote their free time to Little League baseball, community gardens, local theater, community choirs, community centers, and school boards, or to sitting alone watching TV? Are there credit cooperatives and local banks committed to supporting local enterprises, or only branches of large urban banks that package local deposits into loans to international hedge funds?

Do residents consider the area their permanent home, or are working and professional people largely itinerant? Are productive assets owned locally or by distant corporations? Are local forests harvested selectively and sustainably by local firms to provide sustainable material inputs for local industry? Or are they being stripped bare by huge global corporations to export raw timber to distant lands?

The answers to such questions are powerful predictors of the sense of dignity, freedom, responsibility, prosperity, and security of local people and the extent to which relationships are characterized by trust, sharing, and cooperation.

Think Globally, Act Locally

We humans have a distinctive ability to anticipate the consequences of our individual actions for our collective future and to change our behavior accordingly. We also have the capacity to discern repeating patterns in evolutionary processes and to distill from those patterns insights into how to maximize our own evolutionary potentials. One such regularly repeated pattern in the self-organizing growth and evolution of crystals, biological organisms, social organizations, and consciousness is a persistent advance toward higher orders of complexity.[13] Systems with the highest evolutionary potential are those that nurture rich diversity within coherent unifying community structures. The greater the diversity, the greater the evolutionary potential—if the unifying structure is maintained.

Arnold Toynbee found this pattern in his epic study of the growth and decline of the world's greatest civilizations. Civilizations in decline were consistently characterized by a "tendency toward standardization and uniformity." This pattern contrasted sharply with "the tendency toward differentiation and diversity" during the growth stage of civilizations.[14] It appears to be a near-universal truth that diversity is the foundation of developmental progress in complex systems, and uniformity is the foundation of stagnation and decay.

Standardization and uniformity seem to be almost inevitable outcomes of a globalized economy dominated by massive globe-spanning corporations geared to mass production and marketing in a rootless, culturally homogenized world. It is difficult to imagine a civilization moving more totally toward standardization and uniformity than one unified by Coca-Cola and MTV. The processes of corporate globalization are not only spreading mass poverty, environmental devastation, and social disintegration; they are also weakening our capacity for constructive social and cultural innovation at a time when such innovation is needed as never before. Corporate globalization is leading us to an evolutionary dead end.

By contrast, economic systems composed of locally rooted, self-reliant economies create in each locality the political, economic, and cultural spaces within which people can find the path to a future consistent with their distinctive aspirations, history, culture, and ecosystems. A global system composed of local economies can accomplish what a single global economy cannot—encourage the rich and flourishing diversity of robust local cultures and generate the variety of experience and learning that is essential to the enrichment of the whole.

Economic globalization deepens the dependence of localities on detached global institutions that concentrate power, colonize local resources, and have no loyalty to any place. The greater a locality's external dependence, the less its ability to find within its own borders satisfactory solutions to its own problems. Although advocates of economic globalization commonly argue that globalization creates interdependence and shared interests, the argument is a misrepresentation. What actually happens is a growing dependence of people and localities on global corporations and financial markets. The consequence of this dependence is to pit people and localities against one another in a self-destructive competition for the favor of global corporations, thus yielding ever more power to them.

The power of the center stems from a number of interrelated sources: its power to create money, its ownership of the productive assets on which each locality depends, and its control of the institutional mechanisms that mediate relationships among localities. This power resides increasingly in global financial markets and corporations, which have established themselves as the de facto governance institutions of the planet. The more global the economy, the greater the dependence of the local on the world's ruling corporations and the greater the power of these corporations relative to that of democratic governments.

A globalized economic system delinked from place has an inherent bias in favor of the large, the global, the competitive, the resource extractive, the short term, and the wants of those with money. Our challenge is to create a locally rooted planetary system biased toward the small, the local, the cooperative, the resource conserving, the long term, and the needs of everyone—a system that empowers all people to create a good living in balance with nature. The goal is not to wall each community off from the world but rather to create zones of local accountability and responsibility within which people can reclaim the power that is rightly theirs to manage their economies in the common interest.

It is a fundamental paradox of our time that in the name of market competition we have created a system that unifies corporations while dividing people and forcing them to compete for corporate favor. The human purpose is better served by a system that divides corporations and forces them to compete for the favor of people, in the true spirit of a competitive market. Let corporations compete to earn their profits. Let people and communities cooperate to create a good living for all.

In the ecological era, people will be unified globally not by the mutual insecurity of global competition, but by a global consciousness that we share one Earth and a common destiny. This consciousness is already emerging and has three elements unique in human history: First, the formative ideas are the intellectual creations of popular movements involving millions of ordinary people who live and work outside the corridors of elite power. Second, the participation is truly global, bringing together people from virtually every nation, culture, and linguistic group. Third, the new consciousness is rapidly evolving, adapting, and taking on increasing definition as local groups meld into global alliances, ideas are shared, and consensus positions are forged in meetings and via the Internet.

This process is creating a growing web of understanding, shared interests, and mutual compassion that is the proper foundation of a global community of people. The strength and vitality of this web arise because its members—unlike the Stratos dwellers who live in splendid, wealthy isolation—are rooted in real-world communities of place. They experience directly the consequences of the spreading crisis. Their experience is real, and they are naturally inclined to the human rather than the corporate interest.

By participating in the social movements that are the driving force of the Ecological Revolution, growing numbers of citizens are committing themselves to rebuilding their local communities and reaching out to others engaged in similar efforts. They actively recognize the need to act cooperatively in the global human interest through voluntary processes based on consensus and shared power.

These efforts are building the foundations of new human societies for an ecological era based on local economies unified by a global consciousness.

Four Guiding Truths

Although issues of class and political power figure prominently in its agenda, the Ecological Revolution is less a class struggle than a struggle of people against a rogue economic system that diminishes our humanity and threatens our collective survival. It is in the larger interest of all people, including the Stratos dwellers, that we join as the people of Earth to transform our culture and institutions through a social learning process grounded in four truths:

1. **Sovereignty resides in people**—all people, real people who need fresh air to breathe, clean water to drink, nutritious food to eat, and a means of livelihood by which they earn their keep. Governments and corporations are human creations. Neither can usurp the sovereignty of the people if we the people choose not to yield it.

2. **Corporations have no natural or inalienable rights**. The corporation is a public body created by a public act through issuing a public charter to serve a public purpose. We, the sovereign people, have the inalienable right to determine whether the intended public purpose is being served and to establish legal processes to amend or withdraw a corporate charter at any time we so choose. We need only decide.

3. **The current societal failures are systemic.** Incremental changes within individual corporations or political institutions cannot provide an adequate solution. The whole system of institutional power must be transformed.

4. **The Ecological Revolution is a revolution of ideas, not guns.** The Ecological Revolution is inclusive and invites the participation of all who seek to create healthy societies in which life may flourish. The human interest is not the corporate interest, but it is the interest of all people.

Six Organizing Principles

The formative ideas of the Copernican Revolution were produced by the scientific observation of physical bodies and can be traced to a handful of prominent scholars from the physical sciences. In contrast, the formative ideas of the Ecological Revolution are products of the collective human experience and the study of both living and nonliving systems.

The underlying values and principles are articulated in countless consensus documents and declarations of citizen movements. They find theoretical grounding in the intellectual treatises of scholars from diverse academic disciplines, including history, sociology, ecology, economics, biology, physics, general systems theory, and ecological economics. Together they reveal a convergence on a number of guiding principles for the creation of healthy twenty-first-century societies.

The principle of environmental sustainability. Healthy societies are environmentally sustainable, which means their economies must satisfy three conditions:[15]

1. Rates of the use of renewable resources do not exceed the rates at which the ecosystem can regenerate them.

2. Rates of the consumption or irretrievable disposal of nonrenewable resources do not exceed the rates at which renewable substitutes are developed and phased into use.

3. Rates of pollution emissions into the environment do not exceed the rates of the ecosystem's natural assimilative capacity.

Any use of environmental resources or sink capacities greater than these rates is by definition unsustainable and compromises the opportunities available to future generations. The principle of environmental sustainability thus defines a collective property right of future generations that takes natural precedence over the individual property rights of the current generation.

The principle of economic justice. Healthy societies provide all their members, present and future, with the essentials for a healthy, secure, productive, and fulfilling life. There is nothing wrong with additional rewards for those who contribute more, but only if everyone's basic needs are met, the options of future generations are not impaired, and there are strict limits on the concentration of economic power.

The principle of biological and cultural diversity. Healthy societies nurture Earth's biological and cultural diversity. Diversity is the foundation of evolutionary potential. Nurturing biological and cultural diversity is fundamental to our constructive participation in the evolutionary process.

The principle of people's sovereignty (also known as the principle of subsidiarity). In healthy democratic societies, sovereignty resides in people. The purpose of the human economy is to meet human needs—not the needs of money, corporations, or governments. It is the inalienable sovereign right of the people to decide how to use their local resources to best nourish their bodies and their spirit within the limits of the first three principles. People are best able to exercise this right when:

- The ownership and control of productive assets is locally rooted, thus increasing the likelihood that important decisions are made by those who will live with the consequences.

- Governance authority and responsibility are located in the smallest, most local system unit possible to maximize opportunity for direct, participatory democracy.

- More central-system levels define their roles as serving and supporting the local in achieving self-defined goals.

The principle of intrinsic responsibility. Healthy societies assign the full costs of resource-allocation decisions to those who participate in making them—an essential requirement for efficiency in a self-regulating economic system. This principle applies to individual persons, enterprises, and political jurisdictions. No entity has the right to externalize the costs of its consumption to another. The goal is to structure economic relationships so as to encourage each locality to live within its sustainable environmental means. Much as a global economic system supports and encourages the privatization of economic gains and the socialization of economic costs, so a localized system of self-reliant local economies supports and encourages internalizing costs, because both costs and benefits of economic activity fall on the same community and its members.

The principle of common heritage. Healthy societies recognize that Earth's environmental resources and the accumulated knowledge of the human species are common-heritage resources, and it is the right of every person—indeed of every living being both present and future—to share in their beneficial use. No one has the right to monopolize or use common-heritage resources in ways contrary to the broader interest of present and future generations. Indeed, it is the rightful responsibility of any who own environmental resources to serve as trustees in the interest of future generations and of those who possess special knowledge to share it with all who might benefit.

Healthy social function depends on giving the rights and responsibilities defined by these principles precedence over all other rights, including the property rights of individuals, corporations, and governments. Being life and people centered rather than corporate and money centered, these principles offer a clear alternative to corporate libertarianism's preserip-tion for social dysfunction. They are also essential principles of sound and healthy market economies.

Healthy societies seek balance in all things. They recognize a role for both government and locally accountable businesses, and they resist domination by powerful distant governments and corporations. Similarly, they seek local self-reliance while freely sharing information and technology, avoiding both external dependence and local isolation.

The appropriate organizational form for the ecological era is likely to be a multilevel system of nested economies, with the household as the basic economic unit, up through successive geographical aggregations to localities, districts, nations, and regions (see figure 21.2).[16] Embodying the principle of intrinsic responsibility, each level seeks to function as an integrated, self-reliant, self-managing political, economic, and ecological community and supports each subordinate level in doing the same. Starting from the base unit, each system level seeks to achieve the optimal feasible ecological self-reliance, especially in meeting basic needs with the support of superordinate levels.

To compensate for imbalances in natural environmental endowments, units at each level engage in selective exchanges (trade) with other units within their cluster, keeping those exchanges as balanced as possible—consistent with David Ricardo's principles of mutually beneficial trade. Households exchange with other households in their locality, localities with other localities in their district, and so on. The smaller the system unit, the greater its need for exchange. Thus, a substantial portion of a household's economic activity necessarily involves external exchanges in local markets. Although many households may grow some of their own food, it is rare for any household to be self-sufficient. Community economies are relatively more self-reliant, and so on, with regions striving for total self-reliance.

Figure 21.2 Nested Economics

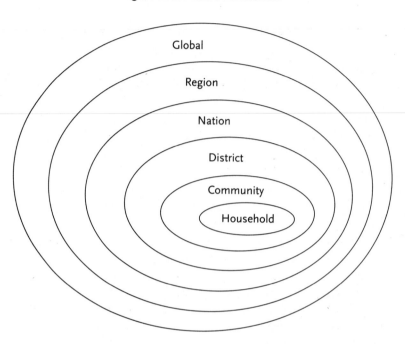

Organizing to meet economic needs as close to the local level as feasible enables the application of the principle of subsidiarity, which calls for vesting governance authority and responsibility in the smallest, most local unit possible. This makes it possible to maintain a system in which market power is balanced with political power at each level. Local firms enjoy a natural advantage, and there is less long-haul movement of people and goods.

Less trade and greater local self-reliance may mean less consumer choice. In the Northern climates, we would eat winter or preserved vegetables and might put apples rather than bananas on our cereal. People in forested areas would construct their houses of wood, and those in hot, dry climates would build houses of earthen materials. Some prices might be higher, but so would wages. Overall, the sacrifices would be small compared with the prospects of greater economic security, caring communities in which people can walk the streets at night without fear, a healthy natural environment, the survival of our species, and the creation of new evolutionary potential.

As we reorganize ourselves into a multilevel system, it is likely that we will continue the present process of redrawing national boundaries. Countries that have grown too large and complex to be manageable may break up into smaller countries, as happened with the USSR and has been debated in Canada.

The present political movement in the United States toward greater local authority and autonomy is in part a response to the United States having reached an unmanageable size and complexity—even without the North American Free Trade Agreement, the Asia-Pacific Economic Cooperation, and the General Agreement on Tariffs and Trade. It makes good sense to devolve to the individual states more of the powers once lodged at the national level, including the power to regulate their commerce and trade. Conversely, many smaller countries may find that they are too small to be viable and decide to undertake some form of merger. In the not-too-distant future, we may look back on the present, almost frantic press to form ever-larger economic blocs through regional and global trade agreements as the last desperate gasp of a dying era.

The principles of the Ecological Revolution point toward a global system of local economies that distribute and localize both power and responsibility, create places for people, encourage the nurturing of life in all its diversity, and limit the opportunity for one group to externalize the social and environmental costs of its consumption onto others. Instead of forcing localities into international competition as a condition of their survival, a localized global system encourages self-reliance in meeting local needs. Instead of monopolizing knowledge for private gain, it encourages sharing knowledge and information. Instead of promoting a homogeneous globalized consumer culture, it nurtures cultural diversity. Instead of measuring success in terms of money, it encourages measuring success in terms of healthy social function.

CHAPTER 22

Economies Are for Living

Our village was prosperous. . . . The real foundation of our prosperity . . . was the deep and enduring sense of community that enabled us to make the best use of these resources. . . . We had all the things we needed—well-crafted, beautiful things that lasted a long time— but we did not do much "consuming."

—EKNATH EASWARAN

We were taught to see the world as a great machine. But then we could find nothing human in it. Our thinking grew even stranger—we turned this world-image back on ourselves and believed that we too were machines. . . . But the world is not a machine. . . . As we change our images of the world, as we leave behind the machine, we welcome ourselves back.

—MARGARET J. WHEATLEY and MYRON KELLNER-ROGERS

By organizing societies around the pursuit of material gratification, we have made a virtue of social dysfunction, diminished the quality of our living, and threatened our viability as a species.

We humans are complex creatures. History and daily life demonstrate both our capacity for hatred, violence, competition, and greed and our capacity for love, tenderness, cooperation, and compassion. Healthy societies nurture the latter and make it easy to live in balance with one another and nature. In consequence, they enjoy an abundance of what is most important to human happiness and well-being. Dysfunctional societies nurture the former and in consequence suffer scarcity and deprivation.

The choice is ours. The world's major religions have for millennia taught love, cooperation, and compassion. Then economics became our religion.

Money became our object of worship and sacred veneration. Economists taught us that individualistic greed and competition define our human nature and that their ruthless expression will lead us to a paradise of universal prosperity.

We forgot that humans were not created to serve the economy. We humans created the economy to serve our living. It is time to rediscover our nature as living beings; rebuild our social, institutional, and physical infrastructure; and come back to life. Here are some thoughts on what that means.

The Goldilocks Rule

In the classic children's story of Goldilocks and the three bears, Goldilocks sought the porridge that was not too hot and not too cold and the bed that was not too hard and not too soft—but just right. It is a story by which we teach our children the wisdom of pursuing all things in moderation, a basic rule of healthy living and a key to true happiness.

Capitalism follows a different rule: If a little is good, more is better. The actual result is not the promised paradise of prosperity for all. It is a world divided between the desperately gluttonous and the desperately deprived.

Alan Durning, the director of Sightline Institute, observes in *How Much Is Enough?* that some 80 percent of global environmental damage is caused by 20 percent of the world's population—1.1 billion *overconsumers* who organize their lives around cars, meat-based diets, and the use of prepackaged and disposable products. Meanwhile, 1.1 billion *excluded* suffer absolute deprivation.[1] In between are 3.3 billion *sustainers*, 60 percent of the world's people who meet most of their needs sustainably. (See Table 22.1.)

Sustainers travel by foot, bicycle, and public surface transport; eat a healthy diet of grains, vegetables, and some meat; buy few prepackaged goods; and recycle most of their waste. Although their lifestyles do not correspond to our vision of consumer affluence, neither do they evoke a vision of hardship. In a properly organized society, sustainer lifestyles can be far happier and more fulfilling than overconsumer lifestyles.

Life in a community organized around properly designed walking, bicycling, and public transportation with ample green spaces is generally healthier and happier than life in a community that sacrifices spaces for walking, biking, public transit, and nature to meet the needs of cars for roads and parking—and bears the resulting congestion, noise, and pollution as a necessary cost of "progress." An environmentally friendly, low-meat, low-fat diet based on natural foods results in better health and increased mental and physical vitality than a diet high in animal fats and

Table 22.1 Earth's Three Socioecological Classes

Overconsumers	Sustainers	Excluded
1.1 billion	*3.3 billion*	*1.1 billion*
> US$7,500 per capita	*US$700–$7,500 per capita*	*≤ US$700 per capita*
(cars, meat, disposables)	*(living lightly)*	*(absolute deprivation)*
Travel by car and air	Travel by bicycle and public surface transport	Travel by foot or donkey
Eat high-fat, high-calorie, meat-based diets	Eat healthy diets of grains, vegetables, and some meat	Eat nutritionally inadequate diets
Drink bottled water and soft drinks	Drink clean water plus some tea and coffee	Drink contaminated water
Use throwaway products and discard substantial wastes	Use unpackaged goods and recycle wastes	Use local biomass and produce negligible wastes
Live in spacious, climate-controlled, single-family homes	Live in modest, naturally ventilated homes, with extended or multiple families	Live in rudimentary shelters or in the open; usually lack secure tenure
Maintain image-conscious wardrobes	Wear functional clothing	Wear secondhand clothing or scraps

Source: Based on data in Alan Durning, "Asking How Much Is Enough," in Lester R. Brown et al., *State of the World 1991* (New York: W. W. Norton, 1991), 153–69.

junk food. A life free from fashion fads, impulse buying, useless gadgets, and the long hours of work required to buy them is a life free from much of the stress and depression that are hallmarks of overconsumer societies.

Herein we see the tragedy of nearly fifty years of misguided economic policies that embrace ever-increasing overconsumption as their ideal. As a society restructures its physical, social, cultural, and institutional infrastructure to support an overconsumer lifestyle, it makes sustainer lifestyles ever more difficult. Growing numbers of sustainers are either recruited to the ranks of the overconsumers or pushed into the ranks of the excluded. The ever more recklessly wasteful consumption of a minority of the population drives environmental devastation, a growing wealth gap, violent social breakdown, and the political corruption that blocks effective corrective public action.

More Living, Less Consuming

We commonly assume that moving from an overconsumer to a sustainer lifestyle requires giving up the things that make our lives comfortable and satisfying. It need not be so. The move that Fran (my spouse) and I made to New York City in 1992—where we lived until 1998—helped us see the possibilities.

Although New York is deeply afflicted with crime, poverty, and other manifestations of the inequities of modern economic life, we did not experience the cold, impersonal city we had expected. Instead, we found a city of ethnically diverse local neighborhoods and small family shops that throbs with a human energy and vitality beyond anything we experienced in any of the other places we have lived. New York is far from a model of sustainability and has much that detracts from the quality of life, but we have come to appreciate living in New York in ways we had not anticipated.

With a high residential population density—an average of 5,000 people per square block, housed in multifamily dwellings—a functioning subway system, and shopping facilities within walking distance of most residences, New York's per capita energy consumption is half the average for the United States as a whole. For the first time in forty years, Fran and I do not have a car. We have no need for one. My office is in our apartment, and Fran commutes to work on the subway. We meet more than 90 percent of our shopping needs within a three-block radius of our apartment door: pharmacy, hardware, electronics, books, groceries, clothing, housewares—all in abundant selection. For my office needs, there is an ecologically conscious printing shop directly across the street, a software store around the corner, and two office supply stores within a five-minute walk.

Similarly, we have a vast array of restaurants of every conceivable ethnicity and price range, jazz clubs, theater, opera, dance, art galleries, museums, free public concerts, and health clubs—easily accessible on foot or by subway. An extraordinary system of parks and botanical gardens provide access to nature, even within the city boundaries. When we need to get out of the city, we take the train or rent a car from a neighborhood agency. Rather than feeling deprived of a car, we feel liberated—no commutes in heavy traffic, parking problems, insurance hassles, or auto repair rip-offs. The thousands of dollars we save each year help make it possible for me to devote my life to the things I want to do, like write this book.

We especially enjoy the Union Square farmers' market, just half a block from our front door. Here, four days a week, people who operate neighboring small farms, dairies, cottage wineries, and kitchen bakeries sell their wares—eggs and poultry from free-range chickens, milk from cows that have never experienced a bovine growth hormone injection, organically grown fruits and vegetables, fresh meat and fish, all free of additives and artificial hormones.

Most of the year, I prepare our meals mainly from what is available at the market. Eating nutritious, flavorful, unprocessed, chemical-free foods, we find ourselves feeling healthier and more vital, sleeping better, and thinking more clearly. We enjoy getting to know the farmers and are pleased that our food purchases support environmentally responsible, local family farms.

Carrying home fresh unpackaged foods from the market in our own shopping bag means we have little packaging waste. The city recycles cans, glass, plastic, and newspapers. At the Saturday and Wednesday markets, a local voluntary organization collects organic wastes for composting. We send very little garbage to the landfill.

On the whole, we are leading healthier, happier, and more environmentally responsible lives than we ever have before—not because we are being heroically virtuous, but because the place where we live is organized in a way that makes it easy and enjoyable to do so. This experience helps us see the impact of the way communities are organized on the quality of social and environmental relationships and thereby of our living. Many things could be done to make New York City even more livable and sustainable—starting with banning personal automobiles from Manhattan—but there is a lot on which to build.

A major part of the burden we overconsumers place on Earth comes from our use of automobiles, airplanes, and throwaway products that come in unnecessary packaging. And from our consumption of unhealthy foods produced by methods that destroy Earth and leave what we eat poisoned with toxic residues.

Few of us would find it a burden to give up long commutes on crowded freeways, constant noise, job insecurity, gadgets we never use, clothes we seldom wear, unhealthy fatty diets, chemically contaminated fruits and vegetables, products that don't last, useless packaging, tiring business trips, and drafty energy-inefficient homes and buildings. By learning to resolve our disputes by nonmilitary means, we would eliminate the approximately 30 percent of all global environmental degradation that results from military operations.[2]

Individual choices can make a difference. We can reduce the amount of meat in our diet. We can buy a water filter to reduce our dependence on bottled water and soft drinks. We can buy fewer clothes or a more gas-efficient car. There are countless such positive choices to be made. However, we must also organize as place-based communities that make the responsible choices easy and economical.

Let's take a quick look at how changes in three major systems—urban habitat, food and agriculture, and materials management—can improve the quality of our lives while at the same time increasing justice and sustainability.

Urban Habitat

In *Reclaiming Our Cities and Towns,* David Engwicht reminds us that people invented cities as places devoted to human interaction. The purpose of cities is to "facilitate exchange of information, friendship, material goods, culture, knowledge, insight, [and] skills" with little need for travel.[3] Cities once consisted primarily of exchange spaces for people—places such as shops, schools, residences, and public buildings. The pathways that connected exchange spaces were also places to meet and reaffirm our relationships with neighbors.

The automobile has changed our cities in fundamental ways, colonizing ever more of the spaces that were once devoted to human exchange and transforming them into systems of parking lots connected by highways. Thus, many of the spaces that once brought us together have been converted into noisy, congested, polluting places that isolate us from one another and destroy the quality of city life. The faster and more densely the traffic flows through our neighborhood, the less we feel at home there and the less likely we are to relate to and befriend our neighbors.[4]

The automobile is not only one of our least energy-efficient modes of transportation but also one of our least space efficient. When we take into account the multiple parking spaces that each car must have at home, office, shopping center, church, recreational facilities, and school, plus the amount of road space required for its movement, the total space required by each family car is typically three times the space occupied by the average family home.[5]

One reason people flee to the suburbs is to escape the environmental and social consequences of giving cities over to automobiles. When productive agricultural lands are paved over for suburban development, we become separated from nature and one another by even greater distances, our dependence on automobiles increases, and per capita energy consumption skyrockets, both for transportation and to heat and cool the detached single-family dwellings in which suburbanites live. There is sound foundation for the conclusion of urban ecologists William Rees and Mark Roseland that "sprawling suburbs are arguably the most economically, environmentally, and socially costly pattern of residential development humans have ever devised."[6]

Automobile companies sell their products as tickets to freedom, defined in many auto ads as the escape by automobile from city and suburbs to the unspoiled countryside. It is ironic, because the automobile has been perhaps the single greatest contributor to making our urban areas unlivable, turning our countryside into sprawling suburbs and strip malls, and making us more dependent on cars to survive the consequences of this affliction.

In 1950, the average American drove some 3,800 kilometers (2,356 miles). That figure had risen to 9,700 kilometers (6,014 miles) by 1990. Greater freedom? Roughly half of the miles driven by Americans involve commuting to work on congested roadways. Between 1969 and 1990, the number of miles traveled to work by the average American household increased 16 percent.

The second major use of cars is for shopping. The average distance traveled for shopping increased by 88 percent. A third use—up 135 percent—is for matters such as business travel, delivering children to and from school, doctor's visits, and church attendance.

Social and recreational travel actually declined by 1 percent, perhaps because we had less time left for it. It is estimated that in the largest US urban areas, 1 billion to 2 billion hours a year are wasted due to traffic congestion. In Bangkok, the average worker loses the equivalent of forty-four working days a year sitting in traffic.[7] Mostly these lost hours would otherwise be available for family, community, recreation, and relaxation.

It is not difficult to figure out who benefits from this damage to the quality of our living. In terms of sales, the three largest corporations in America are General Motors Corporation (cars), Exxon Corporation (oil), and Ford Motor Company (cars). Mobil Corporation (oil) is number seven.

In 1992 Groningen, a Dutch city of 170,000 people, dug up its city-center highways and took a variety of steps to make the bicycle the main form of transportation. As a consequence, business has improved, rents have increased, and the flow of people out of the city has been reversed. Local businesses that once fought any restraint on the automobile are now clamoring for more restraint.[8]

It is a step that many more cities should take. Few measures would do more to improve the quality of our living and the health of our environment than organizing living spaces to reduce our dependence on the automobile. Other actions to help accomplish this include planning and controlling the use of urban space to increase urban density and the proximity of work, home, and recreation; restricting parking facilities; increasing taxes on gasoline; and investing in public transit and facilities for pedestrians and cyclists.

"Hold on," says the corporate libertarian. "What about the impact on the economy? One job in six in the United States is linked to the auto industry. In Australia, it is one in ten.[9] Unemployment would skyrocket and stock prices would plummet if we were to reorganize space to do away with the automobile. It would be an economic disaster."

This important point is best answered with another question. Is it rational to structure an economy so that investors profit from socially harmful investments and the only employment people can find involves doing things that reduce our quality of life? An intelligent species can surely find a better way to provide people with a means of livelihood doing needed work that improves rather than diminishes the quality of our lives. We will return to the jobs issue in a moment.

Food and Agriculture

Our food and agriculture system is similarly designed to generate profits for giant chemical and agribusiness corporations with little regard for the health of people and the ecosystem. This system features chemical-intensive, mechanized production; long-distance shipping; captive contract producers; migrant laborers paid bare subsistence wages; and large government subsidies for giant corporations. It is suited to the profitable mass production of standardized food products, but it comes at the cost of depleting soils and aquifers, contaminating water with chemical runoff, and driving out the small family farms that were for many years the backbone of strong rural communities.

For the consumer, it delivers highly processed, wastefully packaged foods of dubious nutritional value contaminated with chemical residues. Although the system abundantly fills supermarkets, it features misleading nutritional claims; strongly resists efforts to inform consumers about additives, synthetic hormones, genetically modified organisms, and toxic residues; and gives consumers little option of choosing organically grown, unprocessed foods produced by local farmers. Our food choices have largely been reduced to whatever big corporations find it most profitable to offer.

Even though we may be intent on exercising healthful and responsible choice, we seldom have any way of knowing whether the piece of fish we are about to buy was caught by a massive foreign factory trawler sweeping the ocean bare with fine-mesh drift nets or harvested by a local fisherman using environmentally responsible gear. We have no way of knowing whether a piece of meat is from an animal raised on sustainably managed, natural rangelands or from one raised on unstable lands from which tropical forests were recently cleared and fattened in feedlots on grain that might otherwise have fed hungry people.

If our goal is to provide a good living for people, we need to transform our food and agriculture system much as we must transform our habitats and transportation systems. Our goal must be to optimize the use of land and water resources to meet an expanding population's needs for a nutritionally adequate diet. And we must do it in an environmentally sustainable way.

An appropriate system would most likely be composed of millions of intensively managed, small family farms producing a diverse range of food, livestock, fiber, and energy products for local markets. Farming practices would use biodynamic methods to maintain soil fertility, retain water, and control pests. The food system would be designed to limit, contain, and recycle contaminants—including human waste—and would depend primarily on renewable solar-generated energy sources—including animal power and biogas—for preparation, production, processing, storage, and transport.[10]

Steps that can be taken toward such a system include carrying out agrarian reform to break up large corporate agricultural holdings, providing adequate credit facilities for small farmers, creating farmer-based research and extension systems oriented to bio-intensive methods, requiring the full and accurate labeling of food products, eliminating financial and environmental subsidies for agricultural chemicals, developing appropriate processing and marketing facilities, increasing the costs of food transport by eliminating energy and other transportation subsidies, and creating locally accountable watershed-management authorities to coordinate measures for soil and water protection.

Although moving toward more localized food and agriculture systems and healthier, less fatty diets would require adjustments in our eating habits, this is not a vision of sacrifice and deprivation. Rather, it is a vision of a fertile Earth and of vibrant and secure human communities populated by people with healthy bodies and minds nourished by wholesome, uncontaminated foods. The elements of this vision are technically and socially feasible. They simply require restructuring the relevant systems to support healthful living rather than corporate profits.

Materials Management

To achieve true sustainability, we must reduce our "garbage index"—that which we permanently throw away into the environment that nature cannot readily recycle—to near zero. Productive activities must be organized as closed-loop systems. Minerals and other nonbiodegradable resources, once taken from the ground, must become a part of society's permanent capital stock and be recycled in perpetuity. Organic materials may be disposed into the natural ecosystems, but only in ways that assure that they are absorbed back into the natural production system.

Individual consumers are regularly urged to sort and recycle discards—an important but insufficient measure. Many of the most important decisions are out of our hands, and much of the garbage related to our individual consumption is created and discarded long before any product reaches us. The market rarely offers us a choice of a daily newspaper printed on recycled paper using nontoxic, biodegradable ink. Nor can we ensure that the dutifully bundled newspapers we place at curbside for recycling will indeed be recycled. Such decisions lie in the hands of publishers, paper manufacturers, politicians, and government bureaucrats.

Over a twenty-year period, assuming current levels of recycling, the typical American household "consumes" the equivalent of roughly 100 trees in the form of newsprint. Of that newsprint, 60 to 65 percent is devoted to advertisements.[11] Even though we may never read those ads, we are not given the option of subscribing to a paper without them.

According to the Worldwatch Institute, "Most materials used today are discarded after one use—roughly two thirds of all aluminum, three fourths of all steel and paper, and an even higher share of plastic."[12] The physical environment is disrupted to extract the materials involved, vast amounts of garbage are generated, we work extra hours to earn the money to keep replacing what is discarded, and we become beasts of burden endlessly toting replacements from the store to our homes and then out to the garbage. This may be good for the economy, corporate profits, and executive salaries; but it degrades the quality of our living.

Recycling not only reduces the environmental costs of resource extraction but also saves energy. Producing steel from scrap requires only a third as much energy as producing it from ore, reduces air pollution by 85 percent, reduces water pollution by 76 percent, and eliminates mining wastes. Making newsprint from recycled paper takes 25 to 60 percent less energy than producing it from virgin wood pulp, while reducing the release of air pollutants by 74 percent and water pollutants by 35 percent. Reuse produces even more dramatic gains. Recycling the glass in a bottle reduces energy consumption by a third, while cleaning and reusing the bottle itself can save as much as 90 percent of the energy required to make a new bottle.[13]

Germany has pioneered the idea of life-cycle product planning and responsibility. Government-mandated programs encourage manufacturers of automobiles and household appliances to assume responsibility for the disassembly, reuse, and recycling of their products. Besides being environmentally sound, this practice relieves the consumer of the burden of disposing of those items at the end of their useful lives.[14] Life-cycle management can be carried out through lease arrangements in which the ownership of the item remains with the manufacturer, which becomes responsible for both maintenance and disposal and thus has an incentive to design products for maximum durability and ease of recycling.

Governments can encourage producers to design their products and packaging to reduce waste by charging them a fee to cover the estimated public cost of the products' eventual disposal to be included in the selling price consistent with the foundational market principle of cost internalization. Governments can also require that multi-sized and odd-shaped beverage and other containers be replaced with standardized, durable glass containers that can be reused many times by any food-processing business simply by washing and relabeling.[15]

Making a Living

An important part of the demand for economic growth comes from the carefully cultivated myth that the only way people can meet their needs is with a paid job and that jobs must be created faster than corporations can eliminate them with labor-saving technology. We neglect an important alternative: to redefine the problem and to concentrate on creating livelihoods rather than jobs, on creating jobs that address otherwise unmet needs, and on sharing and enjoying more free time once all the needs for paid work are met.

A job is defined by *Webster's New World Dictionary* as "a specific piece of work, as in one's trade, or done by agreement for pay; anything one has to do; task; chore; duty."[16] A livelihood is defined as "a means of living or of supporting life."[17] A job is a source of money. A livelihood is a means of living. Speaking of jobs evokes images of people working in the factories and fast-food outlets of the world's largest corporations. Speaking of sustainable livelihoods evokes images of individuals and families working together in community to meet their needs in ways that share the burdens and benefits and assure environmental health.

We could be using advances in technology to give everyone more options for good, sustainable living. If we so choose, instead of demanding that those fortunate enough to have jobs sacrifice their family and community lives on the altar of competition while others languish in the ranks of the unemployed, we could be organizing our societies around a twenty- to thirty-hour workweek to assure secure and adequately compensated employment for almost every adult who wants a job. The time thus freed could be devoted to the social economy in activities that meet unmet needs and rebuild a badly tattered social fabric.

The possibilities are extraordinary once we acknowledge that many existing jobs not only are unsatisfying but also involve producing goods and services that are either unnecessary or cause major harm to society and to the environment. This includes a great many of the jobs in the automobile, chemical, packaging, and petroleum industries; most advertising and marketing jobs; the brokers and financial portfolio managers engaged in speculative and other extractive forms of investment; ambulance-chasing lawyers; 14 million arms-industry workers worldwide; and the 30 million people employed by the world's military forces.[18]

This leads to a startling fact: Societies would be better off if, instead of paying millions of people sometimes outrageous amounts to do work that is harmful to the quality of our lives, we gave them the same pay to sit home and do nothing. Although far from an optimal solution, it would make more sense than the wholly irrational practice of organizing societies to pay people to do things that result in a net reduction in real wealth and well-being.

Why not organize to support people instead to engage in activities that meet critical needs using environmentally benign methods? The many examples include providing loving care and attention to children and the elderly, operating community markets and senior citizen centers, educating our young people, counseling drug addicts, providing proper care for the mentally ill, maintaining parks and commons, participating in community crime watch, organizing community social and cultural events, registering voters, cleaning up the environment, replanting forests, doing public-interest political advocacy, caring for community gardens, organizing community recycling programs, and retrofitting homes for energy conservation. Similarly, many of us could use more time for recreation, quiet solitude, and family life and for practicing the disciplines and hobbies that keep us physically, mentally, psychologically, and spiritually healthy.

Our problem is not too few jobs; it is an economic structure that creates too much dependence on paid employment and then pays people to do harmful things while neglecting so many activities that are essential to a healthy society. It is instructive to remember that until the past ten to twenty years, most adults even in the most "developed" societies—the substantial majority of them women—served society productively in unpaid work in the social economy.

Generally, as a society, we enjoyed a stronger social fabric and a greater sense of personal security and fulfillment. We can recover much of the benefit in gender-balanced ways by sharing both paid and unpaid work as we address the needs and possibilities outlined above.

We can organize around rural and urban villages that bring residential, work, recreation, and commercial facilities together to meet most mobility needs by foot and bicycle and facilitate cooperative and efficient self-organization around sustainable production to meet local needs with a substantial degree of self-reliance. These villages can feature green spaces and intensive human interaction and can optimize self-reliance in energy, biomass, and materials production.

Human and environmental productive activities can be melded into local closed-loop co-production processes that recycle sewage, solid waste, and even air through fishponds, gardens, and green areas to continuously refresh and regenerate them. Urban agriculture and aquaculture, repair and reuse, and intensive recycling can provide abundant livelihood opportunities in vocations that increase sustainability.

Organizing these activities around neighborhoods that are also largely self-reliant in social services helps to renew family and community ties, decentralize administration, and increase the sharing of family responsibilities between men and women. The need for transporting people and goods is reduced. Nutritional needs are met with fresh, unpackaged, and locally produced foods.

We can have a wide range of traditional and electronic-age cottage industries, many involved in various kinds of recycling, existing side by side with urban agriculture. Family-support services such as community-based day care, family counseling, schools, family health services, and multipurpose community centers can become integral neighborhood functions, engaging people in useful and meaningful work within easy walking distance of their homes.

Most adults can divide their time between activities relating to the money economy and those relating to the social economy. We can have multifamily, multifunctional residences that serve as centers of family and community life and drastically reduce our dependence on automobiles and other energy-intensive forms of transportation. We can line our byways with trees rather than billboards. We can limit advertising to product information that is available on demand, only when we want it.

On the path to true social efficiency, we can have ample time for recreation, cultural expression, intellectual and spiritual development, and political participation. We can use video calls to maintain friendships and collegial relations with others around the world. We can conference via computer to share our exotic recipes, ideas on how to organize a local food co-op, and experiences in campaigning to improve public transit service. We can network internationally to shape new trade rules to protect living communities from corporate predators. Or we can tune in to news broadcasts from Russia, India, and Chile to see how people there are reacting to election results in South Africa.

We have the right and the means to create healthy societies that support us in living whole lives. It is time to reclaim our power and get on with it.

CHAPTER 23

An Awakened Civil Society

Our historic challenge is to add, sift, stir, spice, knead, and otherwise blend ourselves together, over time, into a genuine people's political power.

—JIM HIGHTOWER

We, the people of the world, will mobilize the forces of transnational civil society behind a widely shared agenda that bonds our many social movements in pursuit of just, sustainable, and participatory human societies. In so doing we are forging our own instruments and processes for redefining the nature and meaning of human progress and for transforming those institutions that no longer respond to our needs.

—"The People's Earth Declaration,"
UNCED NGO Forum

January 1, 1994, was the inaugural day of the North American Free Trade Agreement, an agreement intended to complete the integration of the economies of Mexico, Canada, and the United States. Business leaders throughout North America welcomed the opportunities for corporate expansion afforded by the merger. The indigenous peoples of Chiapas state in southeastern Mexico took a strikingly different view. They had for generations endured similar economic "advances," each time losing more of their land and finding their livelihood opportunities ever more limited. Calling NAFTA a death sentence for the people of Chiapas, some 4,000 Indians launched an armed rebellion against the Mexican government.

The Mexican political analyst Gustavo Esteva called the Chiapas rebellion the "first revolution of the twenty-first century." Whereas the revolutions of the twentieth century were contests for state power, the Chiapas people sought greater local autonomy, economic justice, and political rights within the borders of their own communities.[1] They did not call on their fellow Mexicans to take up arms against the state but rather to join them in a broad social movement calling for the liberation of local spaces from colonization by alien political and economic forces. Their battle cry— "Basta!" (Enough!)—resonated with popular movements all across Mexico and the world.[2]

Each day, more people are saying no to the forces of corporate colonialism, reclaiming their spaces, taking back responsibility for their lives, and working to create real-world alternatives to the myths and illusions of economic globalization.

Saying No

The journalist Dai Qing is a courageous and outspoken opponent of the Three Gorges Dam in China that threatens to displace 1.2 million people, flood 100,000 hectares of the country's most fertile agricultural land, inundate a magnificent stretch of canyons, and destroy the habitat's endangered species. In her words, "The highest expression of dignity can be summed up in the single word 'No!'"[3]

The democratic legitimacy of the institutions to which we yield power derives from their (1) being duly constituted by, and accountable to, the sovereign people, (2) conducting operations according to an appropriate code of morals and ethics, and (3) producing desirable consequences for the whole.[4] Most institutions fail on all three counts, not because the individuals who head them are corrupt, but because these institutions have become too big, too distant, and too captive to special interests. Capturing state power in the name of popular rule, whether by election or revolution, does not change this. Nor do reforms that simply chip away at the edges of an established imperial system. This is why elections have come to have so little meaning.

We must transform the system itself by reclaiming the power that we have yielded to corrupted institutions and take back responsibility for our own lives—exactly what millions of people are doing at this moment everywhere on Earth.[5] As this process continues, we redefine the relationships of power between the global, the national, and the local. The power of once-seemingly invincible institutions evaporates.

In 1986, the Philippine people took to the streets in massive demonstrations to say no to the corrupt Marcos dictatorship. The military sided with the people, Marcos fled the country in disgrace, and democracy was restored with scarcely a shot fired. The world saw an even more dramatic demonstration of this truth in 1989 in Eastern Europe and in 1991 in the former Soviet Union.

In Canada, France, Hungary, India, Tasmania, Thailand, and elsewhere, people are joining Dai Qing in saying no to dam projects that threaten their homes, livelihoods, and wild places. The women of India's Chipko movement are wrapping themselves around threatened trees to save them from loggers; the Penan tribal people of Sarawak, Malaysia, are blockading logging roads with their bodies; and the 1 million strong Future Forest Alliance is organizing demonstrations and media campaigns in Canada.

People are mobilizing to protect mangroves in the Ivory Coast, reef systems in Belize, and wildlife in Namibia. They are opposing toxic dumping in the United States and campaigning to protect Antarctica as a natural preserve. Japanese citizens are pressuring Japanese logging companies to change their practices abroad. Germans are calling for an end to foreign aid that destroys primary forests. Indigenous pocket miners, farmers, and fisherfolk in the Philippines are mobilizing to challenge the right of a few powerful mining corporations to permanently destroy the livelihood of thousands of people for a quick profit.

The ideologues of corporate libertarianism tell us that environmentalism is a middle- or upper-class issue—a luxury that the poor cannot afford. Yet we find with increasing frequency that the most heroic actions to save the environment are being taken by the poor. They know from harsh experience the costs of allowing the plunder of the natural resources upon which their existence depends.

Indigenous peoples are often at the forefront. In Ecuador, they have organized to reclaim their lands, protect the Ecuadoran rain forests from foreign oil companies, and block a government agricultural "modernization" program that would drive them off their farms. In Peru, they have formed a 300,000-member alliance to initiate projects that combine environmental and indigenous land objectives. National Indian organizations from Bolivia, Brazil, Colombia, Ecuador, and Peru have formed an international alliance representing over a million people to press for Indian land rights. Native Americans blocked a Honeywell plan to create a nuclear weapons testing site in the sacred Black Hills of South Dakota and rejected offers from Amcor to build a 5,000-acre landfill and incinerator on tribal lands. In southern Panama, indigenous peoples have organized to prevent the completion of the Pan-American Highway through the tropical forests of their homelands—well aware that the highway would lead to the devastation of their forests, the expropriation of their land, and the destruction of their culture.

In the Philippines and Colombia, people are saying no to violence, declaring their villages to be zones of peace and telling both government and insurgent combatants to fight their wars elsewhere. The Women's Action Forum in fundamentalist Islamic Pakistan has brought women out from the seclusion of their homes and veils to join in mass public demonstrations to say no to the curtailment of women's rights.

There are costs to saying no. Many of the nonviolent warriors of the Ecological Revolution have suffered public ridicule, threats, the loss of jobs and businesses, imprisonment, torture, and death at the hands of those who do not share their vision of life-centered societies. They bear the burdens of the political and spiritual awakening that must precede the transformational changes on which our collective future depends.

Creating the building blocks of healthy societies is an important part of saying no. The women of Kenya's Green Belt Movement have set up 1,500 grassroots nurseries and planted over 10 million trees. Other African women are following their lead. The fisherfolk of Kerala state in India have organized to protect their coastal fisheries.

In the United States the Quinault Indians on the west coast of Washington State are buying back reservation lands acre by acre to carry out plans for their sustainable management. Nearby, the people of Willapa Bay, a major salmon and oyster fishery, have formed an alliance of environmentalists, loggers, local businesspeople, politicians, fisherfolk, landowners, and members of the Shoalwater Bay Indian tribe to regenerate their once dynamic and biodiverse ecosystem as the foundation of a prosperous, diversified, and sustainable local economy. In Washington, a group of citizen leaders has formed Sustainable Seattle to pioneer the development of indicators of progress toward sustainability.

Japanese women operate a 200,000-household Seikatsu Club Consumers' Cooperative, which works with suppliers to assure that they provide safe and healthful products and treat workers and nature properly. The 23,000 members of the Spanish Mondragón cooperatives grossed $3 billion in sales in 1991 and provide the world with a model of the potential of dynamic worker-owned, community-based enterprises. In hundreds of communities in Argentina, Australia, Canada, New Zealand, the United States, and elsewhere, people are creating their own community currencies—known variously as local exchange tradition system (LETS), green, or time dollars—to free themselves from colonization by the global financial system, revitalize their communities, and build economic self-reliance.[6]

Over 7,500 households representing some 20,000 people in thirteen European and North American countries participate in Global Action Plan International (GAP) to support one another and monitor their individual and joint progress toward more sustainable lifestyles. Students in the

United States have organized to make their schools advertising-free zones. Five hundred Philippine citizen organizations have formed a National Peace Conference to develop an agenda to end the long-standing armed conflict in their country. In Israel, the Re'ut-Sadaka Jewish-Arab Youth Movement encourages Arab and Jewish youth to live and study together.

Each such initiative reclaims previously colonized space, advances the rebuilding of human communities and natural ecosystems, and serves as an inspiration for others.

The Power of Citizen Networking

When citizen volunteers organize to oppose powerful institutions that command billions of dollars and access to the most privileged inner sanctums of political power, it seems a highly uneven contest. The institutions of transnational capital are highly visible, their power is concentrated in an identifiable corporate core, and they command enormous amounts of money. Yet the ability of these institutions to command the life energies of people depends on paying them to act in ways contrary to the natural values and inclinations that motivate the energy that fuels effective citizen movements.

The power of civil society rests with its enormous capacity to rapidly and flexibly link diverse and dispersed individuals and organizations that are motivated by voluntary commitments. Effective citizen networks have many leaders—each able to function independently of the others. The diversity and independence of their members allow them to examine problems from many different perspectives and bring a broad range of abilities to bear.[7] Their use of the same communications technologies—phone and Internet—that corporations use to extend their global reach allows them to move quickly and flexibly in joint actions at local, national, and global levels.

The lack of a defined hierarchy can render citizen networks incoherent and difficult to sustain, but it also gives them the ability to surround, infiltrate, and immobilize the most powerful institutions. These same characteristics make them virtually impervious to attacks by the more centralized, money-dependent global institutions of business and finance. Any one node in the network can be immobilized and isolated. Key actors have been assassinated. High-energy networks have the ability to adjust almost instantaneously.

Well-networked citizen movements are much like holograms for which the image of the whole resides in each of its parts. Indeed, an attack on a citizen network may expose the ill will of the perpetrators, offend moral sensibilities, increase the network's visibility, attract new recruits, and strengthen resolve.

There are many contemporary examples of the ability of citizen movements to make a difference at both the national and the global level. In the former Soviet Union, grassroots environmentalists held the government accountable for widespread environmental degradation and built a movement that helped spark the region's democratic transformation. These groups are now allied under the politically powerful Socio-Ecological Union to advance a broad environmental and human rights agenda.

In South Korea, the Citizen Coalition for Economic Justice helped establish democratic rule and now works for economic justice and environmental sustainability. In Finland, 2,300 committees of the Village Action Movement have affected the lives of some 500,000 people and restored rural areas to a central place in national life.

A social movement in Sweden called the Natural Step is building a consensus around a commitment to make Sweden a model of sustainability by achieving near 100 percent recycling of metals, eliminating the release of compounds that do not break down naturally in the environment, maintaining biological diversity, and reducing energy use to levels of sustainable solar capture. Some 10,000 professionals, business executives, farmers, restaurateurs, students, and government officials are active in sixteen specialized networks developing and carrying out action plans. Forty-nine local governments, members of the Swedish Farmers Federation, and twenty-two large Swedish companies are working to align themselves with the rigorous Natural Step standards.

A broadly based US citizens' alliance of farmer, consumer, environmental, animal welfare, religious, labor, and other public interest organizations is working on an agenda to transform US agriculture to restore small farms, eliminate the use of toxic chemicals, and make land management practices sustainable.[8] New initiatives in the US labor movement—largely spearheaded by women and minority groups—have more of the community-oriented, participatory, and open quality of social movements than conventional hierarchically organized craft or industrial unions. They seek alliances with small farmers and small-business owners who share a stake in strong local economies.[9] Local African American groups are reclaiming their power and taking back responsibility for their communities by mobilizing to steer their young men away from drugs and guns and build more economic opportunity for African American people.[10]

One of the most dramatic national-scale citizen initiatives is Citizenship Action against Hunger and Poverty and for Life—Brazil's grassroots movement spearheaded by Herbert "Betinho" de Souza of the Brazilian Institute for Social Analysis and Economics. It is an outgrowth of the broadly based Brazilian citizen movement that led to the 1993 impeachment of Fernando Collor de Mello, the president whose corruption grew to exceed even the tolerance of Brazil's jaded middle and upper classes.

Once the new government was installed, de Souza capitalized on his reputation as a leader of the impeachment movement and the resulting sense of civic empowerment. He mobilized Brazilians behind a commitment to end a national disgrace—32 million of Brazil's 156 million people living in perpetual hunger on incomes of less than $120 a year in a country with one of the world's most modern and dynamic economies.[11]

A 1994 survey estimated that some 2.8 million Brazilians, roughly 10 percent of the population over sixteen years old, were active participants in neighborhood hunger committees made up of workers, students, housewives, businesspeople, artists, and others. Roughly a third of Brazil's adult population has made some kind of personal contribution to the campaign.[12] Three key elements make the Brazilian hunger movement distinctive:

1. **The problem is broken down into manageable pieces.** Members of the middle and upper classes were admonished to go into their immediate neighborhoods, find one person who was hungry, and do something about it. An individual feels overwhelmed and disempowered by the hunger of 32 million people, but doing something about the hunger of one or two people who live within a block of home is possible—and deeply fulfilling. Each individual has the empowering experience of being able to make a difference. When millions of people share this experience, it can create a new civic culture.

2. **It involves direct human engagement.** People are not asked to send money to a relief agency so that professional hunger workers can feed the needy in some safely distant place. They are challenged to go into their own neighborhoods and build human relationships, to allow themselves to be touched by the life of a poor and hungry person whom the system has excluded, to hear that person's story, share in the burden of his or her suffering, and serve as a bridge to make society whole again.

3. **It builds toward a new political and spiritual consciousness.** People are encouraged to reflect on the act of befriending and improving the life of a hungry person as both a political and a spiritual experience and as a source of insight into the cause of the dysfunctions of Brazilian society. Through media presentations and local meetings, citizens are led to a growing awareness of the dynamics of inequality and exclusion that flow from the concentration of economic power in a few giant corporations.

International citizen advocacy has come into its own in the past twenty to thirty years. Global alliances such as Amnesty International have long been at the forefront of the international struggle to recognize basic human rights. In the late 1960s and early 1970s, the International Planned Parenthood Federation led a global transformation in attitudes toward family planning and a woman's right to control her fertility.

In the 1980s, while US president Ronald Reagan was characterizing the Soviet Union as the evil empire and Soviet leaders were characterizing Americans as barbaric monsters, thousands of private American and Soviet citizens were engaged through groups such as the Institute for Soviet-American Relations, the Esalen Institute, the Natural Resources Defense Council, and the Context Institute in building foundations for peace, mutual understanding, and democratization.[13] The Philippine Development Forum, with offices in Washington and Manila, helped block multilateral funding of destructive energy projects, exposed toxic wastes at US military bases, and advanced creative funding mechanisms to promote sustainable development in the Philippines. A coalition of Canadian, Mexican, and US groups formed to oppose NAFTA is coordinating citizen proposals for people-centered economic cooperation among the countries of North America. When Honeywell and General Electric fired union organizers at their plants in Juarez and Chihuahua, Mexico, unions in the United States and Canada representing workers employed by these transnationals joined to act against these companies in support of their Mexican counterparts.[14]

In 1979, the Malaysian consumer activist Anwar Fazal, then president of the International Organization of Consumer Unions (IOCU), convened the International Baby Food Action Network (IBFAN), an international alliance of citizen advocacy groups, to boycott Nestlé products. Responding to evidence that bottle-feeding was causing thousands of infant deaths each year in poor countries, the boycotters demanded that Nestlé stop the aggressive promotion of its infant formula as a modern and nutritious substitute for breast-feeding. Nestlé launched a vicious counterattack, which spurred the rapid growth of IBFAN into a coalition of more than 140 citizen groups in seventy countries. As a result of the IBFAN efforts, the World Health Organization issued a code of conduct in 1981 governing the promotion of baby formula, and Nestlé made a promise—subsequently dishonored—to follow the code.

Building on the IBFAN experience, the IOCU regional office in Penang, Malaysia, launched other citizen networks to counter threats to human health, safety, and pocketbooks from the activities of transnational corporations dealing in pharmaceuticals, tobacco, toxic wastes, chemical agriculture, biotechnology, and food irradiation. The Third World Network, an important Southern citizen advocacy group led by former university professor Mohamed Idris, was also born in Penang—making this coastal city a global focal point of citizen resistance to the new colonialism.[15]

The way in which citizen networks with modest resources are able to surround and infiltrate the most powerful international institutions is demonstrated by the Fifty Years Is Enough campaign organized by citizen groups on the occasion of the fiftieth anniversary of the World Bank and the International Monetary Fund (IMF). The Bank and the IMF command massive financial resources, leverage the world's largest financial markets, and virtually dictate the policies of many governments. They can mobilize thousands of highly paid staff to generate statistics and policy papers favoring their positions, buy media reach through the world's most prestigious public relations firms, and co-opt influential nongovernmental organizations (NGOs) with offers of grants, contracts, and foreign travel.

Citizen groups in nearly every country in which these two institutions operate rose to the challenge of this highly unequal contest, even eliciting cooperation from sympathetic staff within these secretive institutions. The Bank and the IMF are now never certain what internal documents will find their way into citizen hands and publications or where protest banners, mass demonstrations, op-ed pieces, advertisements, and special issues of citizen journals and newsletters will appear challenging their claims of effectiveness and calling for cuts in their funding. No more than three years ago, the suggestion that the World Bank should be shut down seemed naive and even a bit frivolous. Now the Bank's funding replenishments are in jeopardy, and its closure is discussed as a serious proposal.

This is only a small illustrative sampling of the countless initiatives being undertaken by ordinary people everywhere. Together they represent the awakening of civil society and the emergence of the social and political forces of the Ecological Revolution.

Globalizing Consciousness

Citizen networking is a crucial part of the process of creating a globalized human consciousness. In countless forums, people from every corner of the world are meeting to share their experiences with an errant global system and build a cooperative agenda.[16] The United Nations Conference on Environment and Development (UNCED), or Earth Summit, held in Rio de Janeiro in June 1992 was a defining moment in the global citizen dialogue. While the official meetings were going on in the grand and heavily guarded Rio Centro convention center, some 18,000 private citizens of every race, religion, social class, and nationality gathered in tents on a steamy stretch of beachfront on the other side of town for the NGO Global Forum to draft citizen treaties setting agendas for cooperative voluntary action.

The two gatherings could hardly have been more different. The official meetings were tediously formal and tightly programmed. They largely affirmed the status quo and carefully avoided most of the fundamental issues, including planetary limits to economic growth, unaccountable corporate power, and the consequences of economic globalization. The citizen deliberations were chaotic, free-floating, and contentious. They directly confronted the fundamental issues and called for sweeping transformational change. In the end, it was evident that behind the cacophony of discordant voices were important elements of consensus manifesting a new global political, environmental, and spiritual consciousness.

At UNCED, citizen organizations worked largely at the periphery of the official discussions, but the citizen treaty process made a major contribution to putting in place the foundation of a consensus and helped prepare the way for more substantive input to future global meetings. At subsequent official international conferences, citizen groups have become more familiar with and skilled in dealing with official UN processes—especially key organizations within the women's movement, such as Development Alternatives with Women for a New Era (DAWN) and the Women's Environment and Development Organization (WEDO).

By the time of the 1994 International Conference on Population and Development in Cairo, the women's movement demonstrated that it was the first among the citizen movements to truly master the UN meeting process. Working with and through national governments and the UN secretariat, women's groups set the basic frame of the official conference document. Dissenting governments and the Catholic Church were the ones placed in the position of seeking adjustments in the nuances of phrases to which they objected. Bearing a disproportionate share of the human burden of the global human crisis, women are now taking the leadership in crafting a gender-balanced human development agenda to benefit all people.[17] The women's movement is rapidly emerging as the political vanguard of the Ecological Revolution.

Doing the Impossible

We live in an era in which the potential for rapid change on a global scale far exceeds that of any previous period in human history. During my lifetime, I have witnessed the end of traditional colonialism and a transportation and communications revolution that virtually eliminated geography as a barrier to human communication and exchange.

The civil rights, environment, peace, women's, and gay rights movements transformed many of our collective perceptions and values regarding human and environmental relationships. Though much remains to be done, each has made its contribution to replacing the materialistic dominator culture of the global capitalist society with the spiritually grounded partnership cultures of civil societies.

Such experience teaches that the underlying forces for powerful social change often build silently and invisibly over decades, even centuries, until at a moment of dramatic breakthrough the seemingly impossible dreams of millions of people become a new social reality. We have seen it, for example, in the collapse of the Soviet Union and in South Africa in the sudden dissolution of apartheid and the peaceful election of Nelson Mandela to the presidency. As late as 1988 no one was even considering the possibility that by 1991 the Soviet Union would peacefully dissolve itself, Germany would be reunited, the Berlin Wall would be gone, and the leadership of the former "evil empire" would invite the United States to help dismantle its nuclear arsenal. The extraordinary events in South Africa were similarly unanticipated as little as three years before they occurred.[18]

Perhaps even more remarkable than the fact that these events occurred at all is that we already take most of them for granted, quickly forgetting what extraordinary events they were and how rapidly impossible dreams can become accomplished fact. Born of a confluence of necessity and possibility, similar forces are now building toward the completion of a historic transition to true democracy grounded in one-person, one-voice popular sovereignty.

As a species we now find ourselves confronted with a choice either to take the step to a new level of understanding and function in service to the whole of life—to consciously and intentionally reinvent human society—or to risk our own extinction. We have the knowledge, the technology, and the necessity to rethink and intentionally re-create humanity's economic, political, and cultural institutions to achieve peace, justice, and prosperity for all as a collective creative act. This powerful combination of imperative and opportunity presents us with the most compelling creative challenge in all of human history—an unprecedented opportunity to create the truly civil society of which philosophers, religious prophets, and countless millions of others have dreamed for millennia.

CHAPTER 24

Agenda for Democracy

A political community cannot be healthy if it cannot exercise a significant measure of control over its economic life.

—HERMAN DALY and **JOHN COBB JR.**

I sympathize, therefore, with those who would minimize, rather than with those who would maximize, economic entanglement between nations. Ideas, knowledge, art, hospitality, travel—these are the things which should of their nature be international. But let goods be homespun whenever it is reasonably and conveniently possible, and above all, let finance be primarily national.

—JOHN MAYNARD KEYNES

Democracy turns on a question of power. Does power reside in the people, based on one person, one voice? Or does it reside with distant rulers and institutions over which the individual has no meaningful influence? When corporations rule over our political, cultural, and economic spaces, democracy is at best an illusion. Now even the illusion is fading.

Corporate rule is antithetical to democracy and to human viability. We the people must strip corporations of their power and claim our right to organize as caring, sustainable communities able to make our own political, cultural, and economic choices.

This chapter deals with specific measures to reclaim our colonized political and economic spaces and restore the rights of people. Many of the measures suggested below can be phased in over time and adjusted based on experience. The idea here is not to provide a prescriptive blueprint but rather to illustrate policies that support sound economic practice in healthy societies. What is right for a given community may differ by local circumstance.

The underlying aim is to limit the power and freedom of powerful corporations in order to restore democracy and the rights and freedoms of people and communities. To those who claim this agenda is anti-business, anti-market, and protectionist, the answer is straightforward.

It is against predatory businesses that destroy nature, exploit people, corrupt democracy, and come only to extract as much wealth from the community as quickly as they can. It is for businesses that have strong roots in, and are committed to serving, a community by providing quality goods and services, offering good family-wage jobs to local people, sourcing locally, paying their fair share of local taxes to maintain the local infrastructure and social services, maintaining high environmental standards, and competing fairly alongside similar businesses.

It is against markets dominated and manipulated by ruthless monopolistic corporate predators. It is for rule-based markets populated by human-scale businesses that play by the rules within a framework of moral values.

If defending democracy, human values, economic justice, and livelihoods from invasive predator corporations is protectionist, then let us all proudly proclaim ourselves to be protectionists.

Reclaiming Our Political Spaces

Political rights belong to people, not to artificial legal entities. The claim by corporations to the same constitutional rights as natural-born persons is a legal perversion without moral or logical foundation. Corporations are instruments of public policy, not its purpose. It is up to corporations to obey the law as determined democratically by the citizenry, not to write those laws. The corporate claim to a free-speech right to lobby and fund political candidates and actions without limit or restriction is particularly pernicious. Paul Hawken observes that by invoking this right, "corporations achieve precisely what the Bill of Rights was intended to prevent: domination of public thought and discourse."[1]

We must give high priority to legislative and judicial action to reestablish the legal principle that corporations are public bodies created by issuing a public charter to serve public needs. Corporations have no inherent rights and only those privileges explicitly extended to them by charter or law. Furthermore, these privileges are properly subject to withdrawal or revision at any time through popular referendum or legislative action. If a corporation persistently seeks to exceed the privileges granted by its charter—such as knowingly selling defective products—or fails to honor its obligations under the law—such as consistently violating laws regarding toxic dumping—it is the right of citizens, acting through their government, to disband it by withdrawing its charter. It is the same as the people's right to abolish any public body that, in their judgment, no longer serves the public interest.[2]

Shareholders, managers, employees, consumers, and others have every right in their capacity as private citizens to express their political views for or against the corporate interest. They also have the right to form not-for-profit organizations to advance any cause they choose to support in their private capacity using their personal funds. Corporations have no such natural right. They simply do not belong in people's political spaces.

Corporations have become particularly active in creating not-for-profit organizations to serve as fictitious citizen fronts for political lobbying. Even corporate giving to true public charities and the arts comes with strings. For example, when New York City proposed a sweeping smoking ban in public places in the fall of 1994, the Philip Morris Corporation made known to the city's many arts organizations it had funded that it expected their support in opposing the ban.

A publicly traded corporation will almost inevitably align its charitable giving with its own financial interests. There is little other basis on which it can justify allocating shareholder profits for charitable purposes within the existing system. If corporations truly care about the communities in which they reside, let them provide good, secure jobs and safe products, maintain a clean environment, obey the law, and pay their rightful share of taxes. Let their managers, shareholders, and employees contribute to charitable and educational causes of their individual choice from their share of the corporation's distributed wages, salaries, and profits.

Prohibiting corporate political participation is an essential step toward reclaiming our political spaces. It is not, however, sufficient. The *New York Times* columnist Russell Baker all too accurately described the 1994 US congressional elections as an auction, more of a bidding war to outspend opponents on negative campaign ads than a contest of vision, issues, and competence.[3] This trend has left American voters increasingly disillusioned with democracy and outraged at a government controlled by big-money interests.

Politics in America has been reduced to a system of legalized bribery. If democracy is to survive, reforms must get corporations out of politics. The ability to spend millions of dollars to saturate the electronic media, especially television, with negative messages about one's opponent has become a key to winning elections. So long as winning an election is excessively expensive and the only sources of adequate funding are powerful financial interests, policy will favor financial interests over the public interest. Setting term limits or voting incumbents out of office will accomplish very little. Three deep and sweeping campaign reforms are necessary:

1. **Publicly fund public elections.** Abolish political action committees and prohibit corporations from making any kind of political contribution or using corporate resources to favor any candidate or issue in an election campaign. When corporate-funded nonprofit organizations with corporate boards raise public monies, issue public statements, or make presentations to public bodies, they should be required to identify themselves as such.

2. **Limit total campaign expenditures.** Let candidates concentrate on competing to get their messages out as effectively as possible within a set spending limit—a better measure of their ability to spend public funds responsibly.

3. **Require television and radio stations to provide public-service exposure for all qualified candidates.** This should be done on issues-oriented interview programs and debates on an equal-time basis. Informing the public about the views and qualifications of candidates is one of the most basic responsibilities of the news media in a democracy. They should be held accountable for fulfilling it in return for the privilege of using public airways.

Reclaiming Our Cultural Spaces

With their dominance of the mass media and their growing infiltration of the classroom, corporations increasingly control and shape our primary institutions of cultural reproduction, constantly reinforcing the values of consumerism and the basic doctrines of corporate libertarianism in an effort to align mainstream culture with the corporate interest. To reclaim our colonized political spaces, we must reclaim our colonized cultural spaces. Three measures merit serious consideration:

1. **Media antitrust laws.** Special legislation for the media should establish that it is prima facie evidence of monopolistic intent for a single corporation to own more than one major public media outlet, whether a newspaper, radio station, TV station, or home cable service. Furthermore, the operation of a media outlet should be the primary business of the corporation that owns it. This would ensure that the outlet is not used primarily as a means to advance other corporate interests.

   No individual should be allowed to have a majority holding in more than one such media corporation. This would enhance the free-speech rights of the public by limiting the ability of a few powerful individuals and corporations to dominate access to the major means of public communication.

2. **Limits on advertising subsidies.** In classical market economics, the role of business is to respond to market demand, not to create it. Factual, informative advertising based on verifiable facts regarding the uses, specifications, and availability of a product serves a legitimate business and public need, and it is wholly appropriate that businesses deduct the cost of providing it from their taxes as a necessary and appropriate business expense. Such product information is best provided on demand through product directories, including directories that are accessible through computer services and interactive TV.

Saturating public and private spaces with advertising aimed at enticing people to buy things they do not want or need is actively detrimental to the health of society and Earth and should not be supported by a public subsidy tax exemption of hundreds of billions of dollars a year. Not only should such expenditures not be tax deductible, it would be appropriate to assess a public fee on advertising in outdoor and public spaces as a measure to control visual pollution, with the proceeds used to fund public interest consumer education.

3. **Elimination of advertising in schools.** Declare schools advertising-free zones, assure that the administration of public schools remains a public-sector function, and ban corporate-sponsored teaching modules from classroom use under the ban on in-school advertising.

Reclaiming Our Economic Spaces

Both capitalism and communism acknowledge a basic truth expressed by the popular aphorism, "He who has the gold rules." Communist theory explicitly calls for worker ownership of the means of production. Adam Smith implicitly assumed worker ownership in his vision of an ideal market economy composed of small farmers and artisans, a circumstance in which owner, manager, and worker are commonly one and the same.

In practice, both communism and capitalism have failed to live up to their expressed ideals. Communism vested property rights in a distant state in the name of the people, but denied the people any means of holding the state accountable for its exercise of those rights. Capitalism persistently transfers property rights to giant corporations and financial institutions that are mostly owned by other corporations in a system ultimately accountable only to impersonal financial markets.

There is an important structural alternative: a market economy composed primarily of family enterprises, cooperatively owned enterprises, and neighborhood and municipal corporations. The Malaysian consumer activist Bishan Singh calls it the community enterprise economy, as it melds the market forces of the money economy with the community forces of the social economy.[4]

The historian and political economist Gar Alperovitz argues that just such a major restructuring of the American economy is already under way. It is led

> by civic-minded entrepreneurs, innovative labor unions and effective local governments. . . . The number of firms now experimenting with worker-ownership approaches 10,000, involving perhaps 12 million people—more than the entire membership of private-sector trade unions. There are also more than 30,000 co-ops, including 4,000 consumer goods co-ops, 13,000 credit unions, nearly 100 cooperative banks and more than 100 cooperative insurance companies. Add to this 1,200 rural utilities and nearly 5,000 housing co-ops, plus another 115 telecommunication and cable co-ops.[5]

A common element of these ownership innovations is that they establish local control of productive assets through institutions that are anchored in and accountable to the community.[6] This tends to make capital patient and rooted, an essential condition of stable, healthy communities. Such initiatives are vitally important in building the foundations of healthy societies, but they are seriously disadvantaged by economic policies and institutions that favor the large, the global, and the predatory.

Reclaiming our economic spaces requires us to transform such policies and institutions to shift the advantage to the small and locally accountable. To do so, we will need to restore the integrity and proper function of our financial institutions and systems, shift the social and environmental costs of production to producers and the users of their products, eliminate subsidies to big business, localize markets, deconcentrate capital ownership, establish corporate accountability, and restore market competition.

The term *transform* is used advisedly. If these measures seem to run counter to the current trend toward the big and the global, that is precisely the intent. The goal is to transform an undemocratic and rapacious capitalist economy into a democratic and socially efficient market economy. The following are specific proposals worthy of consideration.

Financial transactions tax. A small 0.5 percent tax on the purchase and sale of financial instruments such as stocks, bonds, foreign currencies, futures contracts, and derivatives, among others, would be a disincentive to very short-term speculation and arbitraging and remove an important source of unearned profit while having no consequential impact on real investing.[7]

Graduated surtax on short-term capital gains. Capital gains on assets held only for a brief time are usually a form of unearned income and are appropriately taxed at a rate higher than the rate of tax on earned income. A surtax on net short-term capital gains above and beyond the normal income tax would make many forms of speculation unprofitable, stabilize financial markets, and lengthen investment perspectives without penalizing long-term productive investment. The capital gains surtax on the sale of an asset held less than a week might be as high as 80 percent on the otherwise untaxed portion, falling to 60 percent on assets held more than a week but less than six months, 50 percent on those held for more than six months but less than three years, 35 percent for assets held from three to six years, and 20 percent beyond that.[8]

One hundred percent reserve requirement on demand deposits. As far back as 1948, Henry C. Simons, founder of the conservative University of Chicago school of economic monetarism, argued for a 100 percent reserve requirement on any amount payable to a depositor immediately on demand, such as funds in a checking account. This would preclude lending these funds. Thus banks could lend only funds deposited in interest-bearing savings accounts and CDs for which the bank would have the right to require advance notice to withdraw. Many economists have since called for a similar measure.[9] The reserve requirement on demand deposits in the United States currently averages less than 10 percent. Phased in over several years to allow the financial system to adjust, raising this requirement to 100 percent would deflate the borrowing pyramid and help restore the connection between the creation of money and the creation of real wealth.

Tight regulation of financial derivatives. Many forms of derivatives are basically high-risk gambling instruments that serve primarily to generate fees for the investment houses that package and sell them while creating dangerous financial instability. Like any other form of gambling, their creation, sale, and purchase should be tightly regulated and heavily taxed. Pension funds and other funds managed as public trusts should be strictly prohibited from trading in instruments so classified and from investing in companies that do. All publicly held corporations that engage in trading derivatives should be required to file a full report each quarter on that activity, report their potential financial exposure on such instruments, and reveal the proportion of their financial assets held in derivatives.

Preferential treatment of community banks. The US banking system was once made up of unitary or community banks that collected local savings deposits, made loans to local businesses, and financed mortgages to expand local homeownership. Successive changes in banking regulations have allowed the former community banks to be colonized by gigantic money-center banks that channel local deposits into the global money system.

If the banking system is to serve local economies, the system of community banks must be restored by requiring money-center banks to divest their branches and by tightening community investment laws to require that a substantial majority of the investment portfolio of any bank covered by federal deposit insurance be invested within its service area and that all its investments meet federally mandated standards.

The large, global money-center banks that wish to speculate with their depositors' money in risky investments around the world should be required to obtain deposit insurance from private insurers, with the premiums determined by the risks involved. Federal insurance should be reserved for community banks that serve community needs and play by community rules.[10]

Rigorous enforcement of antitrust laws. Vigorous legal action should be taken to break up concentrations of corporate power. There should be a legal presumption that any acquisition or merger reduces competition and is contrary to market principles and the public interest. The burden of proving otherwise to skeptical regulators should fall squarely on those presenting such proposals.

Worker and community buyout options. In most instances, the human interest is best served by patient, rooted capital. Most businesses have many investors in addition to the formal shareholders, and this investment should be recognized in the law. To this end, worker and community buyouts of corporate assets should be supported by public policy. For example, before a major corporation is allowed to close a plant or undertake a sale or merger, the affected workers and community should have the legal right of first option to buy the assets on preferential terms. The terms should reflect the workers' years of personal investment of labor in the company and the local community's collective investment in public infrastructure that have made its local operations possible.

Bankruptcy rules should be structured similarly to give employees and communities the option of taking possession, on preferential terms, of the corporation's remaining assets after bankruptcy proceedings. Similarly, when a company is required to divest parts of its operation under antitrust laws, its employees or the community or both should have first option to buy the divested units. Rules governing company pension funds might allow their use by employees to purchase voting control of the firm's assets. Government oversight should structure worker and community buyouts so that workers and communities have real control—in contrast to many employee stock ownership plans (ESOPs) that vest control in management.

Tax shift. One of the most basic, but often violated, principles of tax policy is that taxes should be assessed against activities that contribute to social and environmental dysfunction, such as resource extraction, packaging, pollution, imports, corporate lobbying, and advertising—and be considered a fee. Such fees would cascade through the system to encourage more social and environmentally responsible behavior and discourage the use of harmful products. The fees can offset by reducing taxes on activities that benefit society, such as employment (including employer contributions to social security, health care, and workers' compensation).

A carbon emissions fee at the source on coal, oil, gas, and nuclear energy would increase end-user prices and encourage conservation and conversions to energy sources such as solar, wind, hydro, photovoltaic, and biomass. The resulting increases in transportation costs would provide a nondiscriminatory natural tariff to encourage the localization of markets. The added cost of automobile commuting would encourage taking public transit and locating closer to one's work. A fee on the extraction of virgin materials would encourage a conversion to less polluting, less materials-intensive product designs and modes of production and a greater reliance on recycled materials. Assessing manufacturers a fee sufficient to cover the estimated costs of disposing of their product packaging would discourage unnecessary packaging. Import fees would encourage economic self-reliance and discourage long-distance shipping.

Required annual profit payouts. Instead of taxing corporate profits, corporations might be required to pay out their profits each year to their shareholders. Profits would thus be taxed as shareholder income at the shareholder's normal marginal rate—much like mutual fund earnings are now taxed. The double taxation of corporate profits—once to the corporation and once to the shareholder—would be eliminated, along with the deferral of shareholder taxes and the many distortions that the corporate income tax introduces into corporate decision making. If this provision were applied globally, corporations would have no incentive to shift profits around the world to the jurisdiction with the lowest tax rate.

Under this arrangement, interest payments on debt financing would come directly out of dividends to shareholders rather than out of taxes, thus discouraging the use of debt and encouraging greater reliance on equity financing. Many leveraged buyouts that depend on the tax deductibility of interest to make them profitable would be discouraged.

Corporations would reimburse the public for services and benefits provided to them through the assessment of fees at the source on specific activities such as the use of carbon fuels, resource extraction, and speculative financial transactions. Global corporate expansion would become more difficult and less profitable—a step toward keeping markets more competitive—because a company would not be able to grow simply because management decided to reinvest its profits rather than paying them out to shareholders. If a corporation wanted funds to expand, it would need to raise money in the financial markets and make its case accordingly. Shareholders would have the option to roll over their dividends into additional stock, much like the current US procedure on the taxation of earnings from mutual funds.

Corporate welfare reform. Get corporations off the welfare rolls. Corporate subsidies range from resource-depletion allowances to subsidized grazing fees, export subsidies, and tax abatements. Such subsidies should be systematically eliminated. Exceptions might be considered for locally owned, community-based enterprises.

Intellectual property. Information is the only resource we have that cannot be depleted and can be freely shared without depriving anyone of its use. Every contemporary human invention necessarily builds on the common heritage of knowledge accumulated over thousands of years and countless generations. This is the information commons of the species.

The justifiable purpose of intellectual property right protection is to provide incentives for research and creative contribution, not to create protected information monopolies. Laws relating to intellectual property rights should be reformed to conform to this principle. Such rights should be defined and interpreted narrowly. They should be granted only for the minimum time necessary to allow those who have invested in for-profit research to recover their costs and a reasonable profit.

The patenting of life-forms or genetic processes, discoveries funded with public monies, or processes or technologies that give the holder effective monopoly control over a type of research or class of products should be precluded by law. As with any common heritage resource, when there is a conflict between an exclusive private interest and a community interest, the community interest should prevail.

Sharing the Wealth

As our current experience demonstrates, justice and sustainability are virtually impossible to achieve in a world divided between extreme wealth and extreme poverty. In such a world the economically powerful colonize the environmental resources of the weak to consume beyond any reasonable need at the expense of others who depend on those resources for their basic living.

This deprives the economically weak of their basic means of livelihood and delinks the economically strong from the environmental consequences of their actions. The excluded poor respond to their resulting insecurity by having many children—the one thing they can call their own and their only prospective source of care in their hour of need.

The rich expand their consumption. The poor produce more children. The human burden on the environment becomes more than Earth can bear.

A more equitable sharing of wealth will eliminate the most extreme forms of overconsumption, increase justice, and reduce the incentive to seek security through having large families. In addition to actions aimed at broadening participation in ownership, measures such as the following will secure a more equitable distribution of income.

Guaranteed income. An idea long popular with both conservative and progressive economists, a guaranteed income merits serious consideration. It involves guaranteeing every person an income adequate to meet his or her basic needs. The amount would be lower for children than for adults but would be unaffected by a person's other income, wealth, work, gender, or marital status. It could replace existing welfare programs and allow for a downward adjustment in social security payments. Since guaranteed payments would be modest and be independent of earned income, there still would be substantial incentive to work for pay, though employers might have to pay more to attract workers for unpleasant, menial tasks.[11] If some people choose not to supplement their guaranteed income with paid work, this should not be considered a problem in a surplus-labor world. Hopefully many will use their freedom to make financially uncompensated contributions to society in the many ways people always have, such as caring for children, volunteering for community service, engaging in artistic, intellectual, and scientific expression, and assuring the accountability of public and private institutions.

Such a scheme would be expensive but could be supported in most high-income countries by reducing military spending, corporate welfare, and existing entitlement programs while increasing taxes on unearned income and luxuries and user fees on pollution, resource extraction, and other activities a sustainable society seeks to discourage. Combined with an adequate program of universal publicly funded health insurance and merit-based public fellowships for higher education, a guaranteed income would greatly increase the personal financial security afforded by more modest incomes and provide greater scope for those who wish to do unpaid work in the social economy. In low-income countries, agrarian reform and other measures to assure equitable access to land from which families can meet their own needs might appropriately substitute for a guaranteed income.

Progressive income and consumption taxes. Taxes on incomes up to the level required to meet basic needs in a comfortable, satisfying, and responsible way should be eliminated, as should sales or value-added taxes on basic food, clothing, shelter, health, personal hygiene, educational, and entertainment or recreational expenditures needed to sustain good living. There should, however, be a sharply graduated tax on incomes above this level—going as high as 90 percent on top income brackets. In addition to a tax of at least 50 percent on estates over a million dollars, inheritance or trust income should be taxed to the receiving individual the same as any other personal income. Appropriate exceptions may be provided for family farms and businesses.

There should be a substantial luxury tax on nonessential consumption items that are socially harmful or environmentally wasteful or destructive. Personal charitable contributions, including to family foundations, should be fully tax exempt, thus providing a substantial incentive for individuals with excess incomes to support a strong independent sector as a counter to the power of the state and the corporation. Such measures would move us toward more equitable and sustainable societies while maintaining incentives to do socially useful work.

Pay equity. The performance of an effective organization depends on the productive contribution of all its members. It is perfectly reasonable that those who carry more responsibility and bring more experience and skills to the organization be compensated accordingly. But how much more? What is a proper ratio between the compensation of the highest- and lowest-paid workers in an organization? Two to one? Ten to one? A hundred to one? A thousand to one?

Ratios of well over a thousand to one are common in US corporations, even if we limit the comparison to US workers and CEOs. A healthy society must establish a reasonable balance between economic incentive and economic justice. Public policy should provide incentives to keep the ratio within a reasonable limit, say a ratio of no more than fifteen to one. If a company considers its lowest paid worker is worth $10,000, then it could pay its CEO $150,000. If it raised the lowest paid worker to $20,000, then the CEO's pay could go up to $300,000.

If the top jobs in a corporation or other organization are so difficult or distasteful that qualified applicants cannot be attracted for such a sum, then perhaps the job needs to be restructured. If the job is too demanding because the corporation is simply too big, then perhaps the corporation should be broken up to make it more manageable. Society can easily learn to do without the services of those who require compensation packages in the millions of dollars to motivate them to perform their jobs effectively.

Equitable allocation of paid employment. Access to opportunities for paid employment should also be allocated as fairly as possible through measures to reduce the workweek and assure equal employment opportunity regardless of gender, race, or other extraneous considerations.

Localizing the Global System

Transnational corporations have for decades used global institutions and international agreements to circumvent democratic processes, force open national economies, and transfer control over markets, finance, resources, and productive assets to themselves. Any agenda to reclaim economic and political spaces for people must address the need to replace this predatory system of global governance with a system that

- empowers people and institutions at national and local levels to control and manage their economic resources to their own benefit;
- makes it difficult for any locality to externalize its production or consumption costs beyond its borders; and
- encourages cooperation among localities in the search for solutions to shared problems.

These objectives are strongly supported by the application of sound market principles. As we have already seen, to function in the public interest, markets must operate within a framework of enforceable rules that maintain the conditions of socially efficient market allocation. Otherwise, predatory speculation drives out productive investment, responsible cost-internalizing firms are put out of business by predatory cost-externalizing firms, and centrally planned corporate monopolies make a mockery of basic market principles.

To maintain the conditions essential to efficient markets, global institutions should encourage national and local governments to implement market rules that favor local producers using local resources to meet local needs and protect local markets and resources from colonization by economic predators. As business localizes, we can downsize and localize government.

As Paul Hawken insightfully notes, it is big business that creates the need for big government to control its excesses and clean up its messes. Similarly, it is the interference of big business that renders government ineffective. Hawken describes the dynamic:

> Business assumes the role of guardianship vis-à-vis the ecosystem and fails miserably in the task; government steps in to try to mitigate the

damage; business tries to sabotage this regulatory process and nimbly sidesteps those regulations that are put on the books; government ups the ante and thereby becomes a hydra-headed bureaucratic monster choking off economic development while squandering money; business decries "interference in the marketplace" and sets out to redress its grievances by further corrupting the legislative and regulatory process in an attempt to become *de facto* guardian, if not *de jure*.[12]

There is an essential need for global institutions responsible for maintaining mutually beneficial economic exchange among nations, just as there is a need for national institutions to maintain mutually beneficial exchange among local communities. Properly designed, such institutions prioritize community interests over corporate interests. For the most part, existing global institutions do the exact opposite.

Global governance functions related to economic, social, and environmental affairs are divided between the United Nations system and the Bretton Woods system. The Bretton Woods system comprises the World Bank, the IMF, and the World Trade Organization. These well-funded institutions, heavily staffed by neoliberal economists, dominate the economic policy arena, evaluate performance solely by conventional economic indicators, and acknowledge no public accountability for the social and environmental consequences of their policies.

The United Nations system comprises the United Nations secretariat and its specialized agencies (such as the World Health Organization, the International Labour Organization, and the Food and Agriculture Organization) and its various development assistance funds (such as the UN Development Programme, UN Population Fund, UNICEF, and UN Development Fund for Women). The United Nations has virtually no influence over economic policies but is left with the task of cleaning up the social and environmental messes that the flawed policies of the three Bretton Woods institutions leave in their wake.

The founders of the United Nations intended that coordination of international economic, social, cultural, educational, health, and related affairs, including oversight of the Bretton Woods institutions, would rest with the United Nations Economic and Social Council (ECOSOC). Although the World Bank, IMF, and WTO are officially designated specialized agencies of the United Nations, they operate as independent powers and reject any UN effort to coordinate or oversee their activities.

This division of the governance of global affairs between two competing systems, one representing the human interest and the other the corporate interest, has worked well for corporations and badly for people.

The UN system has by far the broader mandate, is more open and democratic, is generally respectful of national sovereignty, and gives serious attention to human, social, and environmental priorities. It has been only marginally effective, however, in part due to underfunding, neglect, and an inability to influence the economic policies of the Bretton Woods institutions.

The secretive and undemocratic Bretton Woods institutions take a narrowly economistic view of the world, run roughshod over national sovereignty and democratic processes, encourage competition among nations, and consistently place financial and corporate interests ahead of human and planetary interests. They have the greater professional competence and enforcement powers.

Corporate interests argue that the Bretton Woods institutions are properly favored because of their ability to get things done. Given that the things they do most effectively are destructive of people and Earth and disregard the democratic will of the people who bear the consequences, their effectiveness is not a benefit.

The more open and democratic decision processes of the United Nations and its greater responsiveness to the will of the people affected generally result in more consensual agendas aligned with human and planetary interests. If we seek to strengthen democracy and give social and environmental goals priority over corporate profits, then it is time to reaffirm the mandate of the United Nations, invest in building its capacity to fulfill its mandate, and decommission the Bretton Woods institutions.

Under a reaffirmed economic mandate the United Nations would support the effort of each member country to regain control of its economy, establish the necessary regulatory regime, and orient the economy toward domestic priorities. In addition to strengthening the mandates and capacities of existing UN agencies in international economic affairs, three new UN agencies are proposed, each with a role nearly the opposite of that of the Bretton Woods institution it would replace.

UN International Insolvency Court (UNIIC). The World Bank has led low-income countries ever deeper into the debt bondage that holds their economies and resources hostage to the predators of the global economy. It should be replaced by a UN International Insolvency Court with a mandate to help countries free themselves from debilitating international debts.

A government that determines that its debt obligations have reached a critical level and cannot be repaid without impairing the well-being of its citizens would voluntarily initiate the insolvency procedure by presenting its case to the court. After a preliminary assessment, the debtor country would be granted a stay on its repayments for a period sufficient to complete the court's review and decision process. In the meantime, it would also agree to incur no new debt.

An assessment process would determine how much a country owes and is able to pay over time without compromising its ability to perform essential governmental functions, including the delivery of necessary social services. The court would also review the country's debt portfolio to identify odious debts that were not legitimately contracted—which would include many World Bank and IMF loans—or were used for purposes that yielded no public benefit—such as World Bank projects that failed to produce the projected benefits due to faulty design or negligent oversight. The UNIIC would sanction the repudiation of such odious debts using international legal precedents.[13]

Funds borrowed in financial markets by the World Bank and IMF to finance the loans they make to borrowing countries are guaranteed by the governments of the high-income countries that sponsor these institutions. The repudiation of odious debts owed to them by borrowing governments would force the World Bank and IMF to call the guarantees from their member countries. In addition to properly penalizing these institutions for past harms and negligence, this would build political support to decommission them.

A negotiated debt-relief plan would provide for the rescheduling, reduction, and cancellation of the remaining debt on terms that would allow the indebted government to continue carrying out necessary functions, including the delivery of essential social services. Such plans would ideally take into account wealth previously extracted by creditor nations from the indebted nation without proper compensation. Debt-relief plans should include implementation of mechanisms to keep its international accounts in balance.

UN International Finance Organization (UNIFO). The International Monetary Fund has forced countries to deregulate the flow of money and goods across their borders and to bear the consequences of resulting trade imbalances, international indebtedness, exploitation, and financial instability.

The proposed UNIFO, which would replace the International Monetary Fund, would work with UN member countries to establish and implement international rules to maintain balance in international financial relationships, limit the accumulation of international indebtedness, promote productive domestic investment and domestic ownership, and support nations and localities in securing an equitable and sustainable livelihood for all.

Lacking lending capacity and enforcement powers, the UNIFO would be limited to maintaining a central database of international accounts, flagging problem situations, and facilitating negotiations among trading partners to correct imbalances. The UNIFO would provide advisory services on request. It would also facilitate the negotiation and implementation of international agreements that support joint action by national governments to prevent the use of offshore banks and tax havens for money laundering and tax evasion.

UN Organization for Corporate Accountability (UNOCA). The World Trade Organization regulates national and local governments to prohibit them from regulating transnational corporations, trade, and finance in the public interest.

The UNOCA, which would replace the World Trade Organization, would assist governments in establishing sensible and appropriate regulatory regimes to assure the public accountability of international corporations and finance. It would provide information and advisory services, facilitate the negotiation of relevant international agreements, and coordinate actions by national governments to break up concentrations of corporate power (especially in banking, media, and agribusiness), prevent unfair competitive practices, decharter corporations with a history of regulatory violations and repeat convictions for criminal behavior, enable persons harmed by a corporate subsidiary in one country to sue the parent company for damages in another, eliminate corporate subsidies, and prohibit corporations from attempting to influence political processes.

The UNOCA would facilitate the negotiation of international agreements that guarantee the right of countries and localities to maintain balanced and mutually beneficial trading relationships with other countries; set rules and standards for businesses—including international corporations—operating in their jurisdictions;[14] prohibit the patenting of genetic materials, life-forms, living processes, and indigenous knowledge; and facilitate access to beneficial information and technologies from other countries on reasonable terms.

Within this frame, responsibility for trade-related labor, health, food, and environmental standards properly falls within the respective jurisdictions of the United Nations agencies with the relevant mandate and expertise, such as the International Labour Organization, the World Health Organization, the Food and Agriculture Organization, and the UN Environment Programme.

UNEP, for example, might take the lead in developing information systems that call attention to the cross-border shifting of environmental burdens from one nation to another through toxic discharges or imbalances in the trading of environmental resources and wastes. With an appropriate strengthening of its mandate and technical capacities, UNEP might coordinate the development and use of appropriate statistical and accounting methods and facilitate the negotiation of international agreements on standards, monitoring, and dispute adjudication relating to regional and national environmental cost internalization.

Monitoring functions should be decentralized so far as possible, with each locality, district, nation, and region maintaining its own monitoring capability. When disputes regarding the cross-border externalization of environmental burdens cannot be resolved directly through bilateral negotiations, they would be adjudicated by the appropriate judicial bodies, including the International Court of Justice.

Corporate libertarians will doubtless point out that the measures suggested here will significantly interfere with the operations of transnational corporations and financial markets. That, of course, is precisely the intent. Our goal should be to create a system that works well for people. Corporations are only a means of meeting human needs. If, in doing what we believe will best serve our needs, we find useful roles for corporations, then we should make such use of them. But the right to decide must reside with people and their democratically elected governments through transparent and accountable processes.

There may also be complaints that these measures will create large global regulatory bodies at a time when the political sentiment is toward reducing governmental regulation. The intention in all instances is to create a framework in which actual regulatory action is taken at the most local level possible. The function of global- and regional-level institutions in such matters is to support the local.

As noted previously, powerful global corporations create the need for global regulatory bodies of sufficient power to hold them accountable to the public interest. The smaller and less powerful the individual corporations, the less the need for obtrusive global regulatory bodies. By reducing the size and power of global corporations and moving the system toward more rooted and patient capital, we limit the need for international bureaucracies and police powers. The same principle applies at all system levels.

The global institutions of money have only the power we yield to them. It is our power. We have the right to reclaim it.

The decisions that shape humanity's future are being made by a small but powerful corporate oligarchy that has circumvented and corrupted the institutions of democracy to advance a narrow special interest agenda without regard to the consequences for humanity. The reforms outlined in this chapter all serve a common purpose: to restore the democratic accountability of political and economic decision making to the majority who bear the consequences.

As the institutions of corporate globalization tighten their grip over the world's economic resources and deepen the corruption of the institutions of democracy, their excesses become ever more visible and direct our attention to some crucial questions: Will life or money be humanity's defining value? Will people or corporations determine the path to our collective future? Is there sufficient spiritual awareness and political will within the human polity to achieve the necessary reforms to restore the democratic accountability of our institutions before the social and environmental devastation wrought by corporate globalization becomes irreversible?

There are signs of hope, even in the growing excesses of the corporate world, because the more obvious and arrogant the excess, the faster the spiritual and political awakening of the world's people unfolds.

A Living Economy
for Living Earth

When the last tree is cut, the last fish is caught, and the last river is polluted; when to breathe the air is sickening, you will realize, too late, that wealth is not in bank accounts and that you can't eat money.

—ALANIS OBOMSAWIN of the Abenaki tribe

Once an emergent phenomenon has appeared, it can't be changed by working backwards, by changing the local parts that gave birth to it. You can only change an emergent phenomenon by creating a countervailing force of greater strength

—MARGARET J. WHEATLEY

Between impossibility and possibility, there is a door, the door of hope. And the possibility of history's transformation lies through that door.

—JIM WALLIS, *The Soul of Politics*

Twenty years ago, the title *When Corporations Rule the World* evoked for many people a question: Do corporations rule the world? Events of the past twenty years have erased all trace of doubt. Indeed, they do. And the consequences are dire.

Our future depends on replacing a life-destroying capitalist suicide economy with a living economy devoted to life's service. The need is urgent and imperative. The time to debate whether it is necessary or even possible has long passed. We must turn what seems politically impossible into the politically unstoppable. And we must do it in a blink of history's eye.

In 1995, the seeds of resistance to corporate rule—which captured global attention with the 1999 Seattle WTO protest—were just beginning to germinate. Local-economy initiatives were few and scattered and had yet to coalesce into the global new-economy movement now emerging and gaining momentum by the day.

As the momentum builds, corporatists respond with assurances to the public that if government and special interest citizen advocates will just get out of their way, profit-driven corporations will create jobs for all and heal the environment. These assurances wear increasingly thin as the same corporatists spend billions of dollars on PR campaigns and political lobbying to defeat any initiative that might benefit people and the rest of nature at the expense of corporate freedom and profits.

The ruling institutions of the suicide economy cannot reform themselves from within for a simple reason: Their structure limits human decision makers in their service to choices that maximize short-term profits. A system designed to maximize short-term profits free from the expression of moral sensibility drives inevitably toward ever-increasing inequality, environmental destruction, and political corruption. This inherently self-destructive economic system is like a cancer cell. It can destroy itself and the body on which it feeds; it cannot heal or replace itself with a healthy cell.

Even if modest internal reform is possible, marginal reforms can at best slow the damage. Humanity will continue on its suicidal path for so long as we accept the premise that money is wealth and that control of our means of living is best left to a global alliance of "too big to regulate" money-seeking corporate robots devoted to amassing monopoly power to extract unearned profits. Our human future requires a different system based on authentic values and valid assumptions. We are only beginning to recognize the scope and depth of the implications.

To succeed in the daunting task of securing the future of humankind, we must be clear on the magnitude of the challenge, the forces aligned in our favor, and the critical needs and breakthrough opportunities. To this end, I begin this chapter with a brief overview of the need for deep systemic change followed by a review of the growth since 1995 of the global people-power movement for democracy and a new economy that holds the potential to drive that change. I then examine the need for strategic initiatives to replace four pillars of the capitalist suicide economy—the story, the economics, the law, and the structure of ownership—with the corresponding pillars of a living economy for Living Earth.

Institutional Power

My goal in 1995, the year the original edition of *When Corporations Rule the World* launched, was to advance public understanding of the system of corporate rule—its nature, the sources of its power, and the actions required to restrain it, limit its harms, and restore democracy. My focus, as explicated in the introduction to chapter 24, "Agenda for Democracy," was on the need to "strip corporations of their power and claim our right to organize as caring, sustainable communities able to make our own political, cultural, and economic choices." That remains an essential goal, and all the measures suggested in chapter 24 remain relevant today.

The implications of the essential transformation, however, go significantly further than I then realized. It is not sufficient to tame the institutions of the global capitalist suicide economy. The cultural and institutional system must be replaced by the values and institutions of a wholly different system.

A truly democratic, market-based living economy has no place for global corporations, global financial markets, the speculative high-speed trading of securities, banks that trade for their own account, corporations that are too big to regulate or to fail, foreign ownership of national assets, the systemic externalization of costs, unregulated private monopolies, and international debt. In line with basic market principles, ownership must be long-term, domestic, and preferably local.

Once we are clear on the essential distinction between the old and new institutional structures, we can focus our time and energy on strengthening the institutions of a living economy rather than on slowing the damage with marginal adjustments to the institutions of the suicide economy.

Seeds of Transformation

As advances in technology stripped away geographical barriers to communication in the final decades of the second millennium CE, we the people celebrated the possibilities of unleashing human creativity and realizing the dream of a just and sustainable world united in peace, democracy, and prosperity. Meanwhile, corporatists took command of these same technologies to accelerate the spread of a global consumer culture, compile massive data banks on the most intimate details of our private lives, eliminate jobs through automation and robotization, depress wages through outsourcing, and consolidate corporate control of money, markets, politics, natural resources, technology, and information.

We the people have been rather slower to capitalize on the positive potential of these technologies to create an awakened and globalized civil society with a unifying vision of a living economy and the power to liberate ourselves from corporate rule. Fortunately, the awakening is now well advanced, and the foundational pillars of a new economy, a living economy, are taking shape.

It all begins with caring relationships within and between place-based communities. Never before have so many people been in caring relationship with so many others of races, cultures, religions, and nationalities different from their own. This creates a growing awareness that we share one Earth, that our human similarities far outweigh our human differences, that most of us are thoughtful, caring, and generous, and that extremes of greed and violence are indications of serious psychological, cultural, and institutional dysfunction.

Simultaneously we are awakening to the disturbing truth that democracy, as we know it, is largely a charade organized and manipulated by corporate money to convince us that indentured servitude to capitalism and the suicide economy is freedom. The awakened are voting with their heads, hearts, hands, and feet. The processes are chaotic, disparate, and fleeting in their public expression. They defy coherent description. They are also real and radically self-organizing. And they are building a base of unstoppable power.

With few exceptions, the emerging forces of deep transformation get scant mention in the corporate-controlled press or from politicians beholden to corporatist money. Yet examples are everywhere.

People are building new political parties and movements, deepening their spiritual practice, demanding democracy and action on climate change, campaigning to put the rights of nature before the rights of corporations, and insisting that corporations be held accountable for their crimes. They are challenging corrupt governments and political processes while demanding economic justice, the dismantling of institutional racism, the demilitarization of police, and an end to the devastation of traditional lands and waters in the pursuit of a false prosperity.

People are practicing voluntary simplicity, building networks of locally rooted businesses, certifying socially and environmentally responsible products, restoring forests and watersheds, promoting walkable and bikeable neighborhoods and public transportation, and creating living buildings. They are developing holistic health centers, directing their investments to socially responsible businesses, inoculating children against manipulation by advertisers and mass media, organizing zero-waste campaigns, demanding that trade agreements protect the rights of people and the environment rather than the rights of corporations, insisting on living wages, employing restorative-justice circles, and engaging in countless other life-affirming acts.

These initiatives are far too numerous, diverse, and rapidly evolving to document here. They are generally ignored or dismissed by corporate media. They get increasing coverage by independent media. As mentioned in the prologue, I participated in founding YES! Magazine specifically to provide such coverage to build awareness of alternatives within the reach of all.[1]

We find these initiatives in every country, indeed every community. They demonstrate the powerful potential of living democracies in which people take direct responsibility for their communities and their future.

The leaders come from every race, class, religion, and ethnic group. They span the political spectrum. They include illiterate peasants, wealthy philanthropists, youth, ranchers, teachers, persons of faith, artists, house-wives, itinerant farmworkers, elders, small-business owners, farmers, jani-tors, physicians, scientists, corporate dropouts and retired executives, home care workers, local government officials, inner-city kids, loggers, wealthy intellectuals with fancy academic credentials, and former gang leaders with criminal records—even a few former banksters. Together, worldwide, they—we—number in the hundreds of millions.

These initiatives may appear to be separate and scattered, even com-peting. They are best understood, however, as the sprouting seeds of an emerging meta-movement with the potential to turn the human course. It has yet, however, to find its unifying story. That story is emerging as one of the four pillars of a living economy for Living Earth.

Four Pillars of a Living Economy

The power and legitimacy of the institutions of the phantom-wealth suicide economy rest on four defective pillars: a "sacred money and markets" story, a phantom-wealth economics, corporate-rights law, and absentee owner-ship mediated by Wall Street banksters. As the defects of these pillars become ever more visible, new-economy thought leaders are turning their attention to the design of the corresponding pillars of a real-wealth living economy: a "sacred life and living Earth" story, a living Earth economics, living Earth law, and living Earth ownership.

- **A sacred life and living Earth story:** We humans live by shared stories that embody the common values and understanding we require to organize as coherent groups, communities, and societies. Our most important stories are those that express our deepest beliefs about our nature, origin, purpose, and what we hold to be sacred—most essential to our well-being. The suicide economy is supported by a sacred money and markets story. By its telling, money is wealth. Those who make money are society's wealth creators. And free markets channel our competitive human instincts in ways that maximize wealth creation for the common good. This story is fast losing credibility. A sacred life and living Earth story is emerging in its place. By the telling of this story, real wealth is living wealth, money is just a number, and we humans are living beings who survive and thrive only as contributing, cooperative members of a living Earth community.

- **A living Earth economics:** Economics is the branch of knowledge concerned with the production, consumption, and transfer of wealth. By the reckoning of the mainstream phantom-wealth economics that guides and legitimates the suicide economy and corporate rule, money is the defining economic value, financial assets are the defining economic constraint, and the growth of monetary exchange and financial capital is the defining measure of economic performance. By the reckoning of living Earth economics, life is the defining economic value, biosystem capital is the defining economic constraint, and the health and creative potential of living people, community, and Earth are the defining measure of economic performance.

- **Living Earth law:** An essential function of a legal system is to provide for the rule-based resolution of disputes over conflicting rights and interests. The institutions of the suicide economy are supported by a system of corporate-rights law in which the rights of money-seeking corporate robots trump the rights of living people and the rest of nature. A living economy requires the support of a living Earth law grounded in recognition that we humans belong to living Earth and that our survival, health, and well-being depend on her health and well-being.

- **Participatory living Earth ownership:** Who owns and thereby controls access to the sources of the food, water, shelter, energy, transport, recreation, education, health care, and other essentials of a healthy prosperous life controls society, its politics, and its priorities. In the current system, the institutions of the Wall Street casino control much of the world's real capital through the exercise of ownership rights delinked from human moral sensibility. This is the suicide economy's least visible, but most vulnerable, pillar.

Let us now take a deeper look at the contrasting nature and function of each of the suicide-economy pillars and the corresponding living-economy pillars currently in initial design and construction.

A Sacred Life and Living Earth Story

A shared framing story is essential to our human ability to function as organized groups and societies. A society without a shared story is like a ship without a rudder. A story, even a failed story, is so essential to our sense of direction and purpose that we tend to cling to an old story even though we may doubt its credibility, until it is replaced by a story more authentic, credible, and appealing.

Capitalism lures us into lives of indentured servitude with a sacred money and markets story—a story fabricated and propagated by corporate-funded advertising and PR to create and maintain an individualistic money-worshiping consumer culture. That story is losing its hold as hundreds of millions—even billions—of people recognize it as the falsified, manufactured product of a sophisticated corporate propaganda machine. Here are some of its familiar themes.

Time is money. Money is wealth. Making money creates wealth and is the defining purpose of business and the economy.

Those who make money are society's wealth creators. Their affluent lifestyles are their fair and just reward. Material consumption is the path to happiness. Poverty is a consequence of laziness. The Earth belongs to us.

Humans are by nature individualistic, competitive, and acquisitive. These are beneficial traits that, guided by the free market's invisible hand, unleash the creative potential of humanity to grow the economy to create the wealth to end poverty and drive the technological innovation required to eliminate our dependence on nature.

Property rights are an essential foundation of liberty, democracy, and the market economy. They must be held sacred and inalienable. A corporation is just a group of people and is entitled to the same rights as any person. Capitalism is the essential foundation of democracy and freedom. There is no acceptable alternative.

This familiar story is false or misleading on every point. It misdefines our nature, celebrates psychopathic behavior as a virtue, and promotes an addiction to material consumption we might otherwise recognize as the sign of an empty life. For so long as this story defines how we evaluate economic performance and make economic policy, money will win; life will lose.

A very different story—a sacred life and living Earth story, a story with ancient roots—is emerging. It replaces each falsified element of the sacred money and markets story with an authentic truth.

Time is life. Real wealth is living wealth. Money is just a number useful as a medium of exchange in well-regulated markets. We humans are living beings born of and nurtured by Living Earth, itself born of a living universe.

Life exists only in community. We are a part of nature, not apart from nature. Earth does not belong to us. We belong to Earth. Our health and prosperity depend on Earth's health and prosperity.

Our human nature calls us to care and share for the benefit of all. Serving the living community that sustains us is essential to community health and the source of our greatest happiness. Individualistic greed, ruthless competition, and violence against life are indicators of serious psychological and societal dysfunction. Poverty is most often the consequence of a lack of opportunity.

The purpose of any human institution—whether business, government, or civil society—is to support people as productive, contributing, sharing members of a vibrant and prosperous living Earth community.

Corporations that seek to monopolize resources and decision-making power in the pursuit of purely financial ends have no place in a healthy society.

The sacred life and Living Earth story remains largely unspoken. It is implicit, however, in the millions of people-power initiatives that prepare the way for the human step to a living future. This in itself is strong evidence that this story lives in the human heart.

The institutions of empire have throughout history sought to suppress this story. It is a story of liberation that celebrates the possibilities of radical living democracy and strips institutions of imperial rule of their cloak of false legitimacy.

Because our authentic story lives in the human heart, we need only affirm it and encourage one another to live it *and* to speak it. Though a great many people already strive to live the sacred life and Living Earth story, we have yet to give it the coherent expression essential to establishing it as the shared framing story of human society.

Every one of us can contribute to changing global society's shared public

An Honest Story Requires Honest Language

Corporations control our lives partly by controlling the language of daily discourse. Using honest language is part of changing the story.
Here is how we can counter their manipulative deception by using words that say what we mean.

- Maintain a clear distinction between phantom wealth and real wealth. Never say *wealth* or *capital* when we mean *money* or *financial assets*.

- Never speak of a *multinational corporation,* which implies a corporation loyal to the interests of each country in which it does business—a fictional institution that does not exist. Use the more accurate *transnational corporation* or *global corporation,* terms that more clearly communicate the reality of a corporation that considers itself beyond loyalty to the interests of any nation or peoples.

- Never preface a reference to markets or trade with *free* unless you intend to refer to markets or trade free of rules that might limit abuses of corporate power.

- Consistently say *Living Earth* to affirm Earth is a living being, rather than speak of *the planet* or *the Earth*. Instead of saying *people and nature*, which implies separation, say *people and the rest of nature* to make clear that we are part of nature.

story by the language we use and the ideas we express in daily conversation, discussion groups, and through social media. We can do the same through books, articles, and public presentations. (See the text box "An Honest Story Requires Honest Language.")

For those interested in delving deeper into humanity's story problem, I take this inquiry to a deeper level in my most recent prior book, *Change the Story, Change the Future: A Living Economy for a Living Earth.*[2] As I note there, the shared sacred story of a people aligns with their underlying cosmology—their deepest shared beliefs about the nature and origin of the universe and their own origin within it.

For reasons elaborated in *Change the Story, Change the Future,* the three cosmologies familiar to Western culture—the Distant Patriarch cosmology of the Abrahamic religions, the Grand Machine cosmology of Newtonian physics, and the Mystical Unity story of the mystic tradition—are in their most familiar forms partial, dated, in conflict with current knowledge, and inadequate to the needs of our time. Worst of all, they sustain a destructive divide between the spiritual and material dimensions of human experience and understanding. The lack of a credible reality-based cosmology has allowed corporatist interests to slip the fabricated sacred money and markets story into the resulting void.

Providing institutional spaces for ongoing inquiry so we can continually update our shared cultural story is the natural domain of religious and educational institutions. Unfortunately, these institutions have failed to fulfill this essential function. Instead, they ritualize the teaching of badly outdated cosmologies. Even worse, educational institutions have provided a legitimating platform for economists to promote morally and intellectually corrupt money-and-markets idolatry as science. These institutional failures go a long way toward explaining our collective misdirection.

Change is in the air in progressive centers within both religion and academia. It comes from theologians who recognize the powerful contribution of science to deepening our understanding of the miracle of creation and from scientists who recognize that mechanism and chance are inadequate to explain the wondrous creativity exhibited in the unfolding of the universe. The primary locus of such inquiry lies largely outside establishment institutions, but it can be found in selected schools of theology and, perhaps most notably, in leading Jesuit universities.

A unifying living universe cosmology is emerging from this rich inquiry, drawing from all the sources of human knowledge and understanding. It provides the deeper intellectual underpinning of the emerging sacred life and living Earth story—and a living Earth economics.

A Living Earth Economics

In the introduction, I related how a group of mid-nineteenth-century economists turned away from the disciplined reality-based study of the institutional dynamics of political economies and turned economics into a money-focused discipline based on a mathematical formula adapted from physics using bogus assumptions. The resulting phantom-wealth economics values money more than life and organizes around the logic of finance rather than the logic of living systems. Serving as the ideological arm of the suicide economy, phantom-wealth economists teach and celebrate the moral code of the psychopath, consistently put the interests of Wall Street banksters ahead of the interests of living societies and ignore the political implications of economic-policy choices.

Phantom-wealth economists are easily identified. They focus on financial returns rather than returns to the health of people and the rest of nature. They have a short-term time perspective. They use deceptive language. They insist that economics is settled science. And they endlessly recite the capitalist's creed:

> I believe in economic growth, free markets, deregulation, the privatization of public assets and services, the unrestricted global flow of goods and investment, and a reduction of taxes on corporations, investors, speculators, and persons of a high net worth. I believe that money is wealth, inequality is good for growth, corporate mergers and acquisitions create beneficial economies of scale, and unregulated market forces drive the creation and application of beneficial technologies to end human dependence on nature and eliminate nature as a barrier to perpetual economic growth.

A living Earth economics will begin with ten essential, observable real-world truths.

1. The economy's only valid purpose is to serve life.

2. Money is a means, not an end.

3. All real wealth begins with the generative systems of a living Earth. We share one Earth and must live accordingly.

4. Equality is an essential foundation of healthy human societies and a healthy coproductive human relationship with the rest of nature.[3]

5. The first test of an economy's performance is how well it maintains and enhances the health of the biosystem capital on which it depends and on which the health and happiness of humans in turn depends.

6. The household that seeks to secure the well-being of its members is a more appropriate choice as the basic unit of economic analysis than the corporation that seeks to maximize financial returns to its managers and those who trade in its shares.

7. Community-based living economies are most secure, stable, productive, and innovative when they organize to meet their own needs with their own resources while freely sharing ideas and technology and trading their surplus in balanced exchange with their neighbors.

8. Living communities are strongest and healthiest when monetary exchange takes place within a strong framework of relationships based on mutual trust, caring, and sharing.

9. Real investment is long-term and produces real value for society. Speculation is short-term and expropriates for private benefit the wealth created by others while contributing nothing of value to society in exchange.

10. A human-scale business owned by local stakeholders who know and care about one another is more likely to serve the community's interests than a global corporation whose owners trade its shares at light speed in global financial markets.

Embracing these truths as foundational principles, real-wealth economists will favor:

- The evaluation of economic performance based on indicators of individual, community, and living Earth health
- Strict limits on the concentration of economic power
- Relationships based on mutual caring, trust, and responsibility
- Local decision making
- Self-reliant use of local resources to meet local needs
- Stable, long-term local ownership
- Full employment of all who seek employment in family-wage jobs producing goods and services that meet real needs
- An equitable distribution of income consistent with individual contributions to the real health and well-being of the community
- Cooperative worker and community ownership of enterprises to eliminate the division of society into an owning class and a working class with opposing interests
- Tax policies that support an equitable distribution of wealth consistent with contribution, fairly reward productive investment, and discourage predatory investment and speculation

Within the phantom-wealth economics frame such preferences represent threats to progress and prosperity. Within the living Earth economics frame, they are a commonsense foundation of true progress and prosperity.

The phantom-wealth economist gives priority to managing money to maximize financial returns, fails to recognize that money is a claim on real capital—but is not itself capital—and mistakenly treats money as the critical economic constraint.

The living-wealth economist recognizes that for a society that creates its own money supply, money itself is a false constraint. He or she will instead seek to maximize living returns to the various forms of real capital: biosystem, human, social, intellectual, and infrastructure.

Biosystem capital consists of everything produced by Earth's nonhuman biosystems essential to human well-being. This includes a stable climate, breathable air, drinkable water, fertile soils, healthy forests and grasslands, and oceans teaming with fish. Biosystem capital is both a product of life and the foundation of life. Living Earth's capacity to continuously regenerate biosystem capital is the ultimate economic resource constraint. We humans suppress, even destroy, this capacity when we deplete or poison soils, poison beneficial insects, overfish the oceans, pollute lakes and rivers, cut down forests, deplete and contaminate aquifers, and disrupt climate systems.

Earth's nonhuman biosystems have a capacity for remarkably rapid self-recovery—but only for so long as species diversity and climate stability are maintained. Species extinction is forever. Earth's recovery from the loss of species diversity and climate stability will likely take thousands, even millions, of years.

Assuring the health and productivity of Earth's living systems must be a prime directive for a living Earth economics. In a living economy, the goal is not simply to avoid causing living systems harm. It is to work with them in ways that actively increase their health and productivity to the benefit of all species.

Human capital consists of all of the physical, social, and mental capacities human persons bring to economic life. It includes our intellectual and physical capacities, sense of moral and civic responsibility, and skills we bring to our engagement as productive members of a healthy society.

Human capital begins with and depends on biosystem capital. All other forms of *human-created* real capital—social, intellectual, and infrastructure—start with and depend on human capital. Biosystem capital and human capital share the distinctive quality that each—when healthy—self-organizes to reproduce itself.

Social capital consists of the relationships of trust and caring that allow individual humans to function as an organized society. It is an essential foundation of our human capacity to innovate, produce, engage in cooperative problem solving, and responsibly manage our relationships with one another and the other species of Earth's community of life to live and work together for the health and well-being of all.

We build social capital by devoting time and energy to social interactions through involvement in community events, celebrations, voluntary associations, farmers' markets, and a host of other activities that bring us together in all our rich human diversity to discover our commonality.

We deplete social capital when we monetize relationships, promote an individualistic culture of greed and materialism, and deprive all but a privileged minority of access to a secure and dignified means of living. Once depleted, the relationships of trust that are the foundation of social capital can take decades, even generations, to restore.

Intellectual capital consists of humanity's accumulated common heritage of information, knowledge, and technology. Intellectual capital has the distinctive quality that its use by one person does not limit its beneficial use by another

In most instances, intellectual capital provides the greatest benefit to society when freely shared. Privatizing its ownership and restricting its use to those able and willing to pay increases the financial assets of private owners, but reduces its real-wealth benefit to society.

Infrastructure capital consists of all the various forms of human-built and human-manufactured capital, including buildings and transportation systems, tools and machinery, and other human-produced physical structures essential to a healthy and productive human society.

All forms of infrastructure capital require and depend on the availability of the other four forms of real capital. Most require a combination of public and private investments in their production, maintenance, and periodic replacement.

Focused on analyzing and managing financial flows to maximize financial gain, phantom-wealth economists take little interest in the varied forms of real capital. A few acknowledge them. Fewer still take note of their distinctive characteristics, the relationships among them, their essential contributions to real productive output to meet real human needs, and the ways in which the capitalist suicide economy systematically depletes them.

In stark contrast, managing the various forms of real-wealth capital to optimize their health, productivity, and creative potential in perpetuity is a primary focus of the real-wealth economist.

There are hopeful signs of unrest at the margins of the phantom-wealth priesthood. George Soros has funded the Institute for New Economic Thinking "to broaden and accelerate the development of new economic thinking that can lead to solutions for the great challenges of the 21st century."[4]

The International Student Initiative for Pluralism in Economics is an alliance of sixty-five associations of economics students from twenty countries demanding that university economics courses offer a greater variety of perspectives.[5] According to London's *Financial Times*, these students "suspect the material they are taught is designed to offer intellectual cover for rightwing ideology."[6]

The Guardian reports that leading employers, including the Bank of England, complain that recent economics graduates "know very little about the real world." The particular example offered by the article is the inability of economics to describe the behavior of real securities traders—as contrasted to the behavior of the theoretical rational trader.[7] That this is the primary example cited reveals the extraordinarily narrow perspective of both economics graduates and the institutions of the phantom-wealth economy that employ them. We have a long way yet to go in creating and establishing the primacy of a living Earth economics.

Even the most radical calls to reform economics curricula fall far short of the need for a true living Earth economics grounded in a living Earth, living-systems worldview. Meeting this need will require more than reforming university economics curricula to allow for a greater diversity of perspectives. It will require a new economics that begins with living-system principles rather than financial-system principles, manifests authentic values and assumptions, draws on the total range of the intellectual resources of academia, and transcends the narrow mechanistic frame of most of academia's siloed disciplines.

We cannot expect economists who have built their careers and reputations elaborating, teaching, and promoting theories and policies based on mathematical models that bear no relationship to reality to lead the way to a living Earth economics. The perspective of real-wealth living Earth economics is alien to their training and mindset.

Students who seek a new approach are best advised to recognize that they themselves are better equipped to take the initiative to create options for the study and understanding of real-world economies than are the neoliberal economists who are the target of their protests.

The most promising steps toward meeting the need for a real-world living Earth economics are being taken by the living communities in which many millions of people are living a new economy into being. They are in the process growing a living Earth economics and an emerging crop of self-educated living Earth economists—few if any of whom recognize themselves as such.

A great deal of work remains to bring together the lessons of this experience into an organized body of practical applied theory and knowledge that can be taught and continuously tested and updated. Perhaps this work might be undertaken by special institutes associated with departments of ecology, with funding from enlightened philanthropists. These institutions would be properly staffed by scholars who value life for its own sake, not for its market value, and who bring to the work the same passion to observe and understand the real-world political economy exhibited by the classical political economists.

If humanity survives its current capitalist misadventure, the day will come when living-wealth economics will be the standard for university economics courses. The teaching of phantom-wealth economics in any respectable university will be confined to history classes exploring a variety of bogus theories and intellectual misadventures that legitimated slavery, colonialism, racism, sexism, genocide, and other forms of the oppression of one people by another and discussing how and why for nearly two centuries economics became such a badly corrupted discipline.

Living Earth Law

Few would dare in our time to defend a system of law based on the principle of the divine right of kings: the theory that the authority of the monarch derives directly from the will of God and cannot be subject to earthly authority or the will of the people.

Yet contemporary legal practice features a roughly equivalent principle: the divine right of capital—more specifically the divine right of money-seeking corporate robots to rule over people and the rest of nature. Its application gives an artificial legal entity created by living people to serve living communities the right to destroy life to make money for other corporate entities.

It is the product of a series of decisions by a corporatist US Supreme Court, extended and codified by global agreements (misleadingly labeled trade pacts) written and promoted by corporate lobbyists to place corporations ever further beyond the reach of democratic accountability. This illogical, morally perverse, anti-democratic, anti-life legal perversion presents a major barrier to advancing a transition to peace, justice, sustainability, democracy, and a living economy grounded in sound market principles.

As we awaken to the reality that human life, liberty, and happiness all depend on the health and vitality of the living Earth community to which we all belong, our attention is drawn to a self-evident truth: There are no corporations without people, and there are no people without the rest of nature. Nature's law ultimately trumps human law. We have scarcely begun to examine the profound implications of the conflict between this reality and a legal system that gives corporations rights once reserved for kings and regards nature as mere property with no rights at all.

We have long been prone to see a conflict between the rights of people and laws intended to protect nature. Once we recognize that we humans are inextricably a part of nature, the seeming conflict between humans and nature largely disappears. Care for the health of Living Earth and the countless species that create and maintain the conditions essential to life is both a fundamental human responsibility and a foundational matter of human self-interest. Only by saving nature from ourselves can we save ourselves.

Just as a living economy requires a living Earth story and a living Earth economics, so too it requires a living Earth jurisprudence that recognizes our common dependence on the health and integrity of Earth's community of life.[8]

Well-organized citizen campaigns to strip away the legal fiction that corporations are entitled to the same rights as natural-born persons are gaining traction. So too are global campaigns to codify recognition of the rights of nature. Both are essential. Neither is sufficient by itself to bring the law into alignment with the reality that the human right to life, liberty, and the pursuit of happiness is inseparable from our responsibility as the children of Earth to act in defense of the health of our living Earth mother. Some of the more interesting of current local initiatives in the United States combine the two.[9]

The US Endangered Species Act, passed in 1973, has since been a foundation of US environmental law. Somewhat ironically, legal actions based on this act generally center on protecting an ecosystem habitat to save a particular species. We are only beginning to recognize that saving biosystem communities and all the species that they comprise is essential to saving ourselves—which is an explicit basis of more recent rights-of-nature initiatives.

Indigenous peoples and environmental organizations brought this new frame to the debates of the 2012 United Nation's Rio+20 environmental conference. Wall Street interests argued that the best way to save nature is to put a price on natural resources and sell them to wealthy global investors to manage for a private return. This, they claimed, would create an incentive to manage them responsibly for the long term. Leaders from indigenous and environmental communities countered with the ancient wisdom that living Earth is the source of our birth and nurture. As our sacred mother, she is beyond price.[10]

A Rights of Nature provision is included in the Ecuadoran constitution. More than two hundred communities in the United States have passed ordinances granting rights to nature. Similar initiatives are springing up all around the world. Presumptuous though it may be for us, the children of Earth, to grant rights to our sacred Earth mother, it is a necessary step toward creating legal structures that support the transition from corporate rule to democratic self-rule by living people and communities.

As we take a serious look at the conflict between current law and our rights and needs as living beings, we come to a slightly less obvious, but in some ways even more foundational, insight. At its foundation, Western jurisprudence takes an atomistic view of society as an aggregation of discrete individuals, each with individual property rights that entitle them to do with their parcel as they wish so long as it is not specifically prohibited by law.[11]

Little note is taken of the reality that each parcel of private land and its nonhuman natural inhabitants are integral to a larger ecosystem that is in turn integral to Earth's ecosystem and essential to the health and well-being of all. The law protects the right of the individual to compromise the health of Living Earth and the well-being of its many species parcel by parcel. This serves well the suicide economy—with devastating consequences for the living Earth economy.

It is essential that this conflict be resolved in the favor of Living Earth. Destruction of the generative capacities of owned pieces of Living Earth is a crime against both life and humanity and a suicidal act of collective insanity. Our living Earth mother is sacred, beyond price. She cannot be put up for sale. We must rethink and restructure our laws and their administration accordingly—a significant challenge for the legal scholars and citizen activists who act in defense of life and democracy.

In addition to rethinking and restructuring the laws by which we define the rights and responsibilities of ownership, there is a critical need to democratize and humanize ownership through redistribution and institutional restructuring. Here again there are hopeful signs and initiatives.

Living Earth Ownership

Ideally, real-wealth investment involves the direct and stable local ownership of productive real assets by people who seek a reliable long-term flow of income and have a personal stake in the long-term well-being of the community in which their assets are located. Stable, responsible, and broadly participatory local ownership aligns household interests and enterprise interests and provides a bulwark against the tyranny that almost inevitably comes when an individual, a mega-corporation, or a state succeeds in monopolizing ownership of property in which their only interest is financial.

Present-day Wall Street financial institutions have no interest in either real-wealth investment or any living community. Though they may not describe themselves in quite these terms, they pride themselves on their ability to extract quick outsized, unearned profits from computer-driven arbitrage, deception, insider trading, asset bubbles, speculation, corporate-asset stripping, and other socially unproductive financial games unburdened by the obligation to produce anything of value in return.

In control of massive financial assets, they buy and sell the corporations that hold title to a major portion of the world's productive real-wealth resources. They hire and fire managers at will, quickly replacing any far-sighted, socially conscious manager who might be inclined to manage a corporation responsibly for a fair and reliable long-term return to all its stakeholders with one who is willing to manage for the exclusive short-term benefit of Wall Street banksters.

This is a source of the system's worst perversion. It is also the source of what may prove to be its greatest vulnerability.

Adam Smith and Thomas Jefferson were vocal champions of a system of local smallholder ownership in which each individual owns the means of producing his or her own livelihood. Adam Smith considered it an essential foundation of a market economy. Thomas Jefferson considered it an essential foundation of democracy. Both were correct.

Many economic functions in modern society require larger enterprise units, even within a living-economy framework. We can meet this need in ways consistent with broad, equitable, stable, and locally rooted participation in ownership through cooperative ownership models. The worker-owned Mondragón cooperatives in Spain are a leading example of highly successful cooperative worker ownership in large, complex enterprises. US labor unions, led by the United Steel Workers, are now actively promoting cooperative worker ownership as a bold union project.

Cooperative ownership has a long history in the United States. I find it particularly significant that local cooperative ownership of banks, savings and loans, and credit unions was commonplace in the years following WWII. These locally rooted financial institutions supported real-wealth investments that financed the US victory in WWII, built a strong middle class, generated a large trade surplus, and made the United States the world's undisputed industrial power.

Growing support for various forms of local ownership—including cooperative ownership—is foundational to new-economy initiatives around the world. As one example, US community development foundations brought together by the Business Alliance for Local Living Economies and RSF Finance have taken note of the contradiction in their own long-standing investment practice. They invest their endowments in Wall Street hedge funds to generate a 5 percent return, which they then invest in community projects—in many instances to undo social and environmental harms caused by the investment practices of the hedge funds to which they turn over the management of their endowments. They have agreed to work together on programs to invest instead in local small businesses and to encourage all eight hundred community foundations across the United States to do the same.[12]

The contradiction confronted by these particular community development funds is not unique to them. The bulk of the financial assets with which hedge and private equity funds gamble in the Wall Street casino are funds held in trust by retirement, endowment, and local government investment funds for the benefit of the living people who bear the burden of the devastation wrought by Wall Street's assault on life. Turning this money over to Wall Street to manage makes it possible for Wall Street banksters to extract exorbitant fees for corrupting the entire global economy.

A few insightful Wall Street veterans are pointing to this contradiction as a transformational opportunity. Tim MacDonald, who spent his career as a limited-partnership attorney, is a leader among them. His proposal, which he calls the Evergreen Direct Investing method, holds the potential to strip away Wall Street's power, establish human control over those of the corporate robots that produce beneficial goods and services, defund those that don't, and restore a semblance of integrity to the economy.

I learned of MacDonald's idea from my friend and colleague John Fullerton, former JPMorgan managing director and now founder and president of the Capital Institute. Fullerton is working with MacDonald to refine the Evergreen Direct Investing model and adopt it to the sustainability crisis we now face.[13] During his years on Wall Street, Fullerton personally experienced Wall Street's turn from facilitating productive investments for long-term financial returns to gaming the system and corrupting corporate management for unearned personal short-term gains.

This corruption forces those corporate managers who might wish to build solid companies that provide responsibly produced useful products and good jobs for the long term to instead manage their companies to maximize short-term bumps in share price. Worse, it drives responsible managers out of the system in the favor of managers who feel comfortable managing with a ruthless disregard for people and the rest of nature.

Any retirement, endowment, or local government investment fund that turns over its financial assets to Wall Street to manage faces the same conflict faced by the community development foundations. They are financing the economic corruption that is devastating the lives of the very people they have a fiduciary duty to serve.

In Fullerton's words:

Pension funds exist for a defined purpose and have known contractual financial obligations to fulfill to their beneficiaries, in increments, over time. There is little doubt that today's boom-bust cycling capital markets, frequently hi-jacked and manipulated by short-term speculators and algorithmic traders who together account for the vast majority of exchange trading, are no longer well suited to deliver the dependable stream of returns that large, purposeful, powerful and perpetual pension investors, who now account for $30 trillion in investable capital, require to fulfill their fiduciary obligations. . . .

The growing dysfunctionality of the capital markets, coupled with its narrow focus on quarterly earnings and shareholder-value maximization, is depriving enterprise of vital strategic investment partners, and limiting business leaders' ability to undertake the kind of strategic decision-making required to harmonize the long-term interests of people, planet, and profits in the transition to a regenerative economy.[14]

As Fullerton suggests, pension funds can far better fulfill their fiduciary responsibility by taking their funds out of the Wall Street casino. Instead, they can meet their payout obligations by using those funds to directly buy and hold corporations that produce needed goods and services and have the potential, with sound and responsible management, to provide environmental leadership; good, stable, family-wage jobs for workers; and sustained long-term yields. Many of those good, stable, family-wage jobs might well be those of workers whose retirement the pension fund is obligated to secure.

This would take fiduciary responsibility to a new level by recognizing that pensioners are living beings who need more than a reliable stream of income in their retirement years. They and their children also require and benefit from a total-living return on their investments throughout their lives. That return includes a healthy society with a healthy natural environment.

Under the Evergreen Direct Investing model, like-minded funds would form alliances to identify, buy, and hold corporations that fit their social responsibility criteria. Wealthy individual philanthropists might join as well. (See the text box: "Attention, High-Net-Worth Individuals of Conscience.")

Members of an Evergreen Direct Investment alliance would enter into agreements with managers of selected corporations to work together to liberate those corporations from subordination to the Wall Street casino by buying them out and taking them private. Corporate ownership, oversight, and management responsibilities would then reside with funds and managers with similarly aligned investment and management philosophies that embrace the full spectrum of a corporation's responsibilities to its workers and other stakeholders.

If the existing managers of a candidate corporation did not wish to align their company with the Evergreen Direct Investing goals and values,

---

Attention, High-Net-Worth Individuals of Conscience

If you are a billionaire or other high-net-worth individual of conscience who has committed to give away a major portion of your fortune to philanthropic causes during your lifetime, acknowledge that you are likely the beneficiary of a corrupt, life-destroying system. The moral implications of past choices by you or your forebears are as they are.

You now have the opportunity to demonstrate your true values by putting the fruits of your good fortune to work in support of humanity's epic quest to liberate itself from its servitude to a suicide economy and take the historic step to a living Earth future. Participate in forming and investing in an Evergreen Direct Investment alliance with a specific commitment to use your portion of the investment to finance a gradual conversion to cooperative ownership, thereby contributing to the restoration of a strong worker-owner middle class.

---

the members of the alliance would have the option to use the methods of private equity to organize a hostile takeover and replace the recalcitrant managers with managers of conscience.

This proposal has significant practical potential to drive a profound and foundational transformation of finance and ownership beneficial to all except the Wall Street banksters who profit from the current corruption. It could be a defining victory on the path to democracy and a real-wealth market economy. Longer term it may be a step toward breaking up too-big-to-be-accountable corporations and converting them to more human-scale businesses cooperatively owned by workers, communities, and other stakeholders while at the same time providing a fair and reliable financial return to public trust endowments and the multitrillion-dollar pension plans of real people seeking a secure retirement in a healthy society.

Fullerton points out that the same investment logic also applies to sovereign and local funds, university and foundation endowments, and other investment funds whose managers best fulfill their fiduciary responsibility as stewards of the long-term public interest by seeking stable, long-term returns from responsible investments.[15] This logic is particularly relevant to philanthropic enterprises that profess a commitment to advancing the general betterment of society.

Take as a case in point the Gates Foundation, by orders of magnitude the world's largest private philanthropic foundation. As documented by *The Nation*, the Gates Foundation is the poster child of foundations that invest billions of dollars in corporations that through their activities and products actively subvert the foundation's philanthropic goals.[16] If the Gates Foundation were to adopt the Evergreen Direct Investing model, the positive social and environmental returns to society from its investment program could easily exceed by a significant margin any beneficial contribution of its philanthropy.

Once an alliance of retirement and other public trust funds has secured the ownership of a corporation and restructured its mission to align with the interests of its true stakeholders, it would then have the option to take its public trust mission a step further by democratizing and humanizing the corporation. This would involve breaking up the corporation into its component parts and gradually converting each part to cooperative ownership by its workers, suppliers, customers, and other stakeholders who live in the communities in which the component operations are located. This could dramatically advance cooperative ownership, democracy, and economic sanity.[17]

One could argue that the Evergreen Direct Investment proposal demonstrates that, contrary to my basic thesis, the system can indeed reform itself. Partially true. It is best understood, however, as an initiative from the margins of the system that would essentially eliminate much of Wall Street as we know it and put responsible, accountable humans in control of the corporate robots. As an added benefit, it can be accomplished with minimal dependence on government and a corrupted political system.

As we humans awaken to the stark contrast between our true nature, responsibilities, and creative potential and the dark future we have created for ourselves, we embark on the most profound and exciting course change in human history.

Although the outcome is uncertain, the interlocking institutional structures of capitalism and the suicide economy are far more vulnerable than they seem. They are inherently unstable, unable to self-correct, and destined to collapse under the stress of their ever-increasing excess. Furthermore, they are fast losing credibility as awareness spreads that they engage in a war against life for the sole purpose of advancing control by the richest among us of the declining pool of the real wealth of the living Earth they are systematically killing.

In our current end-game encounter with the imperial institutions of elite rule, we the people hold the ultimate advantage: We have the moral authority of an authentic and truthful story that lives in the human heart and calls us to recognize our higher nature. As we frame and take this story public, we unmask the moral and intellectual corruption of the institutions of the suicide economy and of the economic and legal theories that support it.

Our trump card is the clear intellectual, technical, and moral argument that the trustees of many trillions of dollars held in public trust investment funds best fulfill their fiduciary responsibility by investing directly in responsibly managed businesses.

The institutions and theories of the suicide economy have only the power we yield to them. We have every right to reclaim our power and move forward—as many billions of people are already doing—to grow the culture and institutions of a living economy for a living Earth, and ultimately to reclaim the unearned real-wealth assets these institutions have expropriated.

Individually, our actions are only symbolic. Together, we become unstoppable.

People often ask me whether I believe we still have sufficient time to achieve a transformation of the necessary magnitude to transform our economy and save our species. I have certain knowledge of only two things.

First, my generation has experienced many profound shifts that occurred in the historical blink of an eye—including a transformation of deeply cruel, unjust, and dysfunctional relationships between races and genders that previously endured for millennia.

Second, if we assume it is too late to change and we yield to despair, we create a self-fulfilling prophecy. Business will continue as usual. And social and environmental system collapse will follow as certain as night follows day. Our only rational choice is to assume it is both possible and not too late and do all in our power to make the necessary change a reality.

Fortunately, the actions required to avoid ultimate social and environmental collapse are the same as the actions needed to facilitate a recovery by those who might survive it. So let us act with courage and conviction to turn the politically impossible into the politically unstoppable. Together, we can end corporate rule and take the step to a living Earth future of universal democracy, peace, prosperity, creative opportunity, and happiness for all.

EPILOGUE

Our Need for Meaning

> Without a global revolution in the sphere of human consciousness, nothing will change for the better . . . and the catastrophe toward which this world is headed, whether it be ecological, social, demographic, or a general breakdown of civilization, will be unavoidable.
>
> **—VÁCLAV HAVEL**

The spiritual and political roots of our crisis run deep. But because our corporate-dominated public policy discourse is framed by an economics that takes no account of either the spiritual or the political, it remains unproductive. A more realistically grounded perspective is found, however, in the emerging discourse of an awakening civil society.

We are now rousing from a deep cultural trance to rediscover the neglected political dimensions of our societies and spiritual dimensions of our being. If our crisis is a consequence of an excessively partial view of reality, as I believe it is, then this awakening—by bringing us to a more holistic awareness of who we are—may lead to a long overdue acceptance of essential responsibility for how we use our technical and organizational capacities.

As science tells the cosmic story, consciousness is nothing more than an illusion born of chemical reactions. It is a story without meaning or purpose that leaves us with little reason to restrain our hedonistic impulses. As I began writing *When Corporations Rule the World* twenty years ago, I read Thomas Berry's *The Dream of the Earth*.[1] His defining argument struck a deep chord: Our survival as a species depends on discovering a shared story that gives meaning and purpose to our lives—a story that gives us a reason to live more compelling than making money to go shopping.

In late 1993, an autographed copy of Duane Elgin's *Awakening Earth* arrived unsolicited in my mail. Elgin and I had never met and knew each other only through our writing. His book seemed like a divine gift. The story of the of human consciousness, as revealed to him during the course of an extended personal meditation, spoke to my own inner being and awakened a sense that we may exist to serve a divine purpose.

Elgin's essential message is captured in two brief sentences:

> As humanity develops its capacity for reflective consciousness, it enables the universe to achieve self-referencing knowing of itself. Through humanity's awakening, the universe acquires the ability to look back and reflect upon itself—in wonder, awe, and appreciation.[2]

This suggests that we inherit through our birth a responsibility far beyond ensuring our own survival. Our wondrous ability to perceive beauty and feel love is an essential aspect of our being, central to our role in a grand, continuously unfolding cosmic event.

This is a far more logical thesis than the alternative premise: that our experience of consciousness is nothing more than a chance event in an otherwise lifeless universe, or that we were given the miracle of life so that we could destroy the fruits of millions of years of evolution on this unique planet. It is an idea that calls on us to accept responsibility for the impact of our actions on the course of evolution and to assume a responsible role in creating conditions on this planet that advance the continuing evolutionary process.

It suggests as well that our relationship to the larger web of life is neither that of master nor that of servant. Rather, our existence is integral to, and inseparable from, the universal consciousness that manifests itself through our individual being. This suggests to me that we best serve both the whole and ourselves by experiencing with wonder and joy the awesome beauty of a living universe and by living our own lives to the fullest in relation to self, family, community, the planet, and the cosmos.

It suggests as well that although we are neither higher nor lower than other forms of life, we do have our own distinctive capacities and functions in relation to the whole. It is for us to develop these capacities and discover our intended functions.

We unquestionably have more power and greater freedom than other species on this planet. To our own peril, we have confused this power and freedom with the right to dominate, rather than recognizing that it confers on us a greater responsibility for assuring the integrity of the whole.

Of course, this makes no sense whatever within the badly outdated story from Newtonian physics: that we live in a mechanical universe playing out its destiny much like a mechanical clock playing out the tension in its spring. As contemporary science tells the story of creation, however, the universe bears no resemblance whatever to a mechanical clock running down. To the contrary, it bears far greater resemblance to a seed bursting forth to grow into a magnificent flowering tree. It is a trajectory toward ever-greater complexity, beauty, awareness, and possibility. It is a story wondrous in its creative complexity and profound in its implications.

It all began some 13.8 billion years ago in a massive burst that dispersed minute energy particles, the stuff of creation, across the vastness of previously empty space. With the passing of time these particles self-organized into atoms that swirled in great clouds that gradually coalesced into galaxies of countless stars that grew, died, and were reborn as new stars, star systems, and planets. The cataclysmic energies unleashed by the birth and death of billions of suns converted simple atoms into more complex atoms and melded atoms into even more complex molecules, each step opening new possibilities for the growth and evolution of the whole.

Each stage transcended the stage before in definition and capacity. It was as if a great intelligence had embarked on a grand quest to know itself through the discovery and realization of the possibilities of its being.

Billions of years after the quest began there was a truly extraordinary development on a medium-size planet orbiting one of the countless stars in an outer galaxy. Here the cosmos gave birth to living beings. Microscopic in size, they were simple single-celled bacteria. Inconsequential though they seemed, they embodied an enormous creative potential and with time created the building blocks of living knowledge that made possible the incredible accomplishments that followed.

Evolving life discovered the arts of fermentation, photosynthesis, and respiration on which more complex life forms depend. They learned to exchange genetic material through their cell walls to share their discoveries with one another in a grand cooperative enterprise that created the planet's first global communication system. As they evolved, they transformed and stabilized the chemical composition of the entire planet's atmosphere to create conditions that prepared the way for all that followed. As the fruits of life's early learning multiplied, the variety, capacity, and potential of the planet's living cells grew apace.

In due course individual cells discovered the advantages of joining with one another in clusters to create multicelled organisms of ever greater variety and potential. Step by step this extraordinary enterprise converted yet more of the inert matter of the planet into a splendid web of plant and animal life with a growing capacity for innovation and intelligent choice. Continuously experimenting, interrelating, creating, and building, the evolving web of life unfolded into a living tapestry of astonishing variety, beauty, awareness, and capacity for intelligent choice.

Then, a mere 2.6 million years ago, quite near the end of this 13.8-billion-year story, came the creation of a being with the capacity to reflect on its own consciousness; to experience with awe the beauty and mystery of creation; to articulate, communicate, and share learning; to reshape the material world to its own ends; and to anticipate and intentionally choose its own future.

We call ourselves humans. We are the living spirit's most daring experiment: a species possessed of the capacity to shape its own destiny as a conscious collective choice.

We each express as a living body composed of some 30 to 70 trillion individual living, self-regulating, self-reproducing cells. More than half of our individual dry weight consists of the individual micro-organisms we need to metabolize our food and create the vitamins essential to our health and survival.

Think of this body, your body, as a community of tiny living organisms continuously self-organizing in exquisitely balanced union to continually renew and heal the physical body within which our consciousness resides. It is a stunning cooperative achievement that even our most brilliant scientists have barely begun to understand.

We humans are remarkably fast learners in the cosmic scheme of things. During our two and a half million years we developed the capacity for speech, mastered the use of fire, learned to make and use sophisticated tools, express ourselves through art and music, cultivate our food, communicate in written form, live as highly complex societies, and create organized systems of knowledge in botany, zoology, astronomy, and cosmology.

Then, only a few hundred years ago, we began to embrace a scientific paradigm that largely dismissed consciousness and the spiritual aspect of our nature. We focused our life energies on the task of mastering the physical world and building our technical capabilities. These capabilities now open vast opportunities to build healthier societies devoted to advancing our social, intellectual, and spiritual growth.

Our increasing alienation from nature and spirit, however, has led us to use our ever more powerful technologies and institutions not to serve life but to dominate it, even destroy it. In so doing we put our future at risk. Alienation from our spiritual nature has left us exposed to manipulation by advertisers who turn our longing for spiritual connection into an insatiable quest for money to consume that for which we have no need and by political demagogues who align this quest with corporate interests. Tragically misguided, in little more than our most recent hundred years we have destroyed much of the living biosystem capital it took Earth's evolving community of life billions of years to create.

We are now awakening to the beauty, joy, and meaning of life and embarking on the most profound and exciting course change in human history. The Copernican Revolution divided science and religion and initiated an awakening to the potentials of the material side of our existence.

The Ecological Revolution now invites us to experience ourselves as spiritually alive and politically active participants in the unfolding exploration of the potentials of a living universe. It is a challenge that calls us to draw on the full potential of our species and engage in a collective enterprise that requires the creative contribution of every individual.

As the old assumptions crumble, so too will the old political alignments. Traditional distinctions between Left and Right, liberal and conservative, have lost their meaning. Appeals to a political center are futile posturing by those who fail to recognize the significance of the challenges we face. The political future belongs to those who have the courage and vision to form new alliances based on ways of thinking that cannot be defined by the old categories.

We must approach this giant step into the unknown with the mutual caring and tolerance for diversity foundational to the healthy societies we hope to create. Even as we align ourselves with our core values and build alliances with those who share them, we must be constantly aware that we have embarked on a journey for which we have a compass but no map. We are all learners in an unfolding process that requires us to look with a critical eye and an open mind for the spark of goodness in each person and the kernel of truth in each idea.

NOTES

Prologue: A Personal Journey

Epigraph: Václav Havel, on the occasion of the Liberty Medal Ceremony, Philadelphia, July 4, 1994.

1. A leading example is "Rebuilding America's Defenses: Strategy, Forces and Resources for a New Century, (Washington, D.C.: Project for the New American Century, September 2000), http://www.informationclearing house.info/pdf/RebuildingAmericasDefenses.pdf.

Introduction: Capitalism and the Suicide Economy

Epigraphs: George Soros, *Open Society: Reforming Global Capitalism* (New York: Public Affairs, 2000), xi; Johann Wolfgang von Goethe, *Elective Affinities,* http://www.goodreads.com/quotes/103733-niemand-ist-mehr -sklave-als-der-sich-f-r-frei-h-lt.

1. Public Citizen's Global Trade Watch, "NAFTA's 20-Year Legacy and the Fate of the Trans-Pacific Partnership" (February 2014), 2, https://www .citizen.org/documents/NAFTA-at-20.pdf.
2. Ibid., 7.
3. Robert E. Scott, Carlos Salas, and Bruce Campbell, "Revisiting NAFTA: Still Not Working for North America's Workers," Economic Policy Institute, Briefing Paper 173, September 28, 2006, http://s2.epi.org/files/ page/-/old/briefingpapers/173/bp173.pdf.
4. Danielle Kurtzleben, "Report: America Lost 2.7 Million Jobs to China in 10 Years," *U.S. News,* August 24, 2012, http://www.usnews.com/news/ articles/2012/08/24/report-america-lost-27-million-jobs-to-china-in-10 -years.
5. Laura Carlsen, "Under NAFTA, Mexico Suffered, and the United States Felt Its Pain," *International New York Times,* November 24, 2013, http:// www.nytimes.com/roomfordebate/2013/11/24/what-weve-learned-from -nafta/under-nafta-mexico-suffered-and-the-united-states-felt-its-pain.

6. Jose María Imaz, "NAFTA Damages Small Businesses," *El Barzón* (Mexico City), January 1997.

7. Public Citizen's Global Trade Watch, "NAFTA's 20-Year Legacy," 5.

8. John B. Judis, "Trade Secrets," *The New Republic*, April 9, 2008, http://www .newrepublic.com/article/trade-secrets.

9. Public Citizen's Global Trade Watch, "NAFTA's 20-Year Legacy," 21.

10. Carlsen, "Under NAFTA, Mexico Suffered."

11. Adam Liptak, "Review of U.S. Rulings by NAFTA Tribunals Stirs Worries," *New York Times*, April 18, 2004, http://www.nytimes.com/2004/04/18/us/ review-of-us-rulings-by-nafta-tribunals-stirs-worries.html.

12. Public Citizen's Global Trade Watch, "NAFTA's 20-Year Legacy," 17–18.

13. Stefania Vitali, James B. Glattfelder, and Stefano Battiston, "The Network of Global Corporate Control," 6, http://arxiv.org/PS_cache/arxiv/pdf/1107/ 1107.5728v2.pdf.

14. See Nicholas Shaxson, *Treasure Islands: Uncovering the Damage of Offshore Banking and Tax Havens* (New York: Palgrave MacMillan, 2011).

15. Kerry A. Dolan and Luisa Kroll, "Inside the 2014 Forbes Billionaires List: Facts and Figures," *Forbes*, March 3, 2014, http://www.forbes.com/sites/ luisakroll/2014/03/03/inside-the-2014-forbes-billionaires-list-facts-and-figures/.

16. Graham Burton, "The Billionaires," *Forbes*, July 17, 1995, 110–11.

17. "Special Issue: The World Almanac of Wealth," *Forbes* 193, no. 4 (2014): 20, 32.

18. Neil Irwin, "The Benefits of Economic Expansions Are Increasingly Going to the Richest Americans," *New York Times*, September 26, 2014, http://www .nytimes.com/2014/09/27/upshot/the-benefits-of-economic-expansions-are -increasingly-going-to-the-richest-americans.html.

19. Ibid.

20. Credit Suisse Research Institute, *Global Wealth Report 2014* (Zurich, Switzerland: Credit Suisse Research Institute, October 2014), 4, https://publications .credit-suisse.com/tasks/render/file/?fileID=60931FDE-A2D2-F568 -B041B58C5EA591A4.

21. Ibid, 23–24.

22. Ibid., 38.

23. David C. Korten, in *Agenda for a New Economy: From Phantom Wealth to Real Wealth* (San Francisco: Berrett-Koehler, 2010), explores the distinction been phantom wealth and real wealth assets in much greater detail.

24. A 1997 article that reportedly enjoyed wide circulation on Wall Street boldly asserts that producing goods and services is passé. Wealth is created much faster and more easily by issuing securities and pumping up their market prices. The article reads like a parody from *The Onion*, but it is dead serious. John Edmunds, "Securities: The New World Wealth Machine," *Foreign Policy* no. 104 (Fall 1996): 118–38.

25. David Gilson, "Survival of the Richest," *Mother Jones* (September/October 2014): 33.

26. Susan Lund et al., *Financial Globalization: Retreat or Reset? Global Capital Mar-

kets 2013 (McKinsey Global Institute, March 2013), iv, http://www.mckinsey .com/insights/global_capital_markets/financial_globalization.

27. Ibid., 2.

28. William Greider, *One World, Ready or Not: The Manic Logic of Global Capitalism* (New York: Simon & Schuster, 1997), 227.

29. Robert Lenzner, "Warren Buffett Predicts Major Financial Discontinuity Involving Too Big to Fail Banks, Derivatives," *Forbes*, April 30, 2014, http:// www.forbes.com/sites/robertlenzner/2014/04/30/seking-shelter-warren -buffett-limits-receivables-from-major-banks/.

30. Michael Snyder, "The Size of the Derivatives Bubble Hanging over the Global Economy Hits a Record High," *GlobalResearch*, May 27, 2014, http://www.globalresearch.ca/the-size-of-the-derivatives-bubble -hanging-over-the-global-economy-hits-a-record-high/5384096.

31. Richard Wilkinson and Kate Pickett, *The Spirit Level: Why More Equal Societies Almost Always Do Better* (London: Penguin Books, 2009).

32. Intergovernmental Panel on Climate Change, "Summary for Policymakers," in *Climate Change 2014: Impacts Adaptation, and Vulnerability,* http://www.ipcc.ch/ pdf/assessment-report/ar5/wg2/ar5_wgII_spm_en.pdf.

33. World Wildlife Federation, *Living Planet Report 2014,* http://bit.ly/1ssxx5m.

34. Ha-Joon Chang, "This Is No Recovery, This Is a Bubble—and It Will Burst," *The Guardian,* February 24, 2014, http://www.theguardian.com/ commentisfree/2014/feb/24/recovery-bubble-crash-uk-us-investors.

35. D. Joseph Stiglitz, "Moving Beyond Market Fundamentalism to a More Balanced Economy," *Annals of Public and Cooperative Economics* 80, no. 3 (2009): 346.

36. Pope Francis, *Apostolic Exhortation Evangelii Gaudium of the Holy Father Francis to the Bishops, Clergy, Consecrated Persons and the Lay Faithful on the Proclamation of the Gospel in Today's World,* November 24, 2013, paragraph 55, http:// w2.vatican.va/content/francesco/en/apost_exhortations/documents/papa -francesco_esortazione-ap_20131124_evangelii-gaudium.html.

37. Robert L. Nadeau, *Rebirth of the Sacred: Science, Religion, and the New Environmental Ethos* (New York: Oxford University Press, 2013), chapter 7.

38. Philip Morowski, *Against Mechanism* (Lanham, Md.: Rowan and Littlefield, 1988) and Philip Morowski, *More Heat Than Light* (New York: Cambridge University Press, 1989).

39. Nadeau, *Rebirth of the Sacred.*

40. Robert L. Nadeau, personal e-mail communication, January 2, 2015.

Chapter 1. From Hope to Crisis

Epigraph: Jerry Mander, *In the Absence of the Sacred* (San Francisco: Sierra Club Books, 1991), 26.

1. United Nations Development Programme (UNDP), *Human Development Report 1993* (New York: Oxford University Press, 1993), 12.

2. Lester R. Brown, Michael Renner, and Brian Halwell, eds., *Vital Signs 1999* (New York: W. W. Norton, 1999), 65, 69.

3. UNDP, *Human Development Report 1994* (New York: Oxford University Press, 1994), 31.

4. United Nations High Commissioner for Refugees, *The State of the World's Refugees* (New York: Penguin Books, 1993).

5. Gene Stephens, "The Global Crime Wave," *The Futurist* (July–August 1994): 22–28.

6. "Out-of-Wedlock Births Up Since '83, Report Indicates," *New York Times*, July 20, 1994.

7. UNDP, *Human Development Report 1994*, 31.

8. Ibid., 47.

9. United Nations High Commissioner for Refugees, *State of the World's Refugees*.

10. Lester R. Brown, Michael Renner, and Brian Halwell, eds., *Vital Signs 2000* (New York: W. W. Norton, 2000), 98.

11. Gallup poll, June 2, 1990.

12. Harris poll, January 3, 1994.

13. "The New Deal: What Companies and Employees Owe One Another," *Fortune*, June 13, 1994, 44–52.

14. Poll result cited by Robert Reich, U.S. secretary of labor, in a presentation to the Democratic Leadership Council, Washington, D.C., November 22, 1994. The figure for those without college degrees is 68 percent. http://www.dol.gov/dol/aboutdol/history/reich/congress/112294rr.htm.

15. Kettering Foundation, *Citizens and Politics: A View from Main Street America* (Dayton, Ohio: Kettering Foundation, 1991), iii–iv, as quoted in Stephen Craig, *The Malevolent Leaders: Population Discontent in America* (Boulder, Colo.: Westview Press, 1993), 83.

16. Seymour Lipset and William Schneider, *The Confidence Gap: Business, Labor and Government in the Public Mind* (Baltimore: Johns Hopkins University Press, 1987), 410; Elizabeth Hann Hastings and Philip K. Hastings, eds., *Index to International Public Opinion, 1992–1993* (Westport, Conn.: Greenwood Press, 1994).

Chapter 2. End of the Open Frontier

Epigraphs: Royal Society of London and the U.S. National Academy of Sciences, *Population Growth, Resource Consumption, and a Sustainable World* (London and Washington, D.C.: Royal Society of London and the US National Academy of Sciences, 1992), as cited in Lester R. Brown, "A New Era Unfolds," in Brown et al., *State of the World 1993* (New York: W. W. Norton, 1993), 3; Herman E. Daly, "Sustainable Growth: An Impossibility Theorem," *Development* no. 3/4 (1990): 45.

1. Originally published in Henry Jarrett, ed., *Environmental Quality in a Growing Economy* (Baltimore: Johns Hopkins University Press, 1968), 3–14.

2. See the Six Organizing Principles enumerated in chapter 21, 281–83.

3. Lance Davis and Robert Huttenback, *Mammon and the Pursuit of Empire* (New York: Cambridge University Press, 1986), as cited in Richard Douthwaite, *The Growth Illusion* (Tulsa, Okla.: Council Oak Books, 1993), 46.

4. Ibid.

5. These statistics were compiled by William E. Rees and Mathis Wackernagel, "Ecological Footprints and Appropriated Carrying Capacity: Measuring the Natural Capital Requirements of the Human Economy," in A-M. Jannson, M. Hammer, C. Folke, and R. Costanza, eds., *Investing in Natural Capital: The Ecological Economics Approach to Sustainability* (Washington, D.C.: Island Press, 1994), 380. Note that 1 hectare equals 2.47 acres. For further documentation of the thesis that human activities now exceed many of the natural limits of the ecosystem, see Robert Goodland, Herman E. Daly, and Salah El Serafy, eds., *Population, Technology, and Lifestyle: The Transition to Sustainability* (Washington, D.C.: Island Press, 1992), 3–22; Donella H. Meadows, Dennis L. Meadows, and Jorgen Randers, *Beyond the Limits* (Post Mills, Vt.: Chelsea Green Publishing, 1992); Gerald O. Barney, *Global 2000 Revisited* (Arlington, Va.: Millennium Institute, 1993); and Sandra Postel, "Carrying Capacity: Earth's Bottom Line," in Lester R. Brown et al., *State of the World 1994* (New York: W. W. Norton, 1994), 3–21.

6. Alan Durning, *How Much Is Enough? The Consumer Society and the Future of the Earth* (New York: W. W. Norton, 1992), 56.

7. Vandana Shiva, "Homeless in the 'Global Village,'" *Earth Ethics 5* no. 4 (1994): 3.

8. "Aid for Profit: Japanese DDA in Leyte," *Kabalikat* (September 1990): 8–10.

9. "Pollution and the Poor," *The Economist*, February 15, 1992, 16–17.

10. Rees and Wackernagel, "Ecological Footprints and Appropriated Carrying Capacity," 382.

11. Ibid., 374.

12. Manus van Brakel and Maria Buitenkamp, *Sustainable Netherlands: A Perspective for Changing Northern Lifestyles* (Amsterdam: Friends of the Earth, 1992).

13. Alex Hittle, *The Dutch Challenge: A Look at How the United States' Consumption Must Change to Achieve Global Sustainability* (Washington, D.C.: Friends of the Earth, 1994).

14. Van Brakel and Buitenkamp, *Sustainable Netherlands*, 6.

15. David Pimentel, Rebecca Harman, Matthew Pacenza, Jason Pecarsky, and Marcia Pimentel, "Natural Resources and an Optimal Human Population," *Population and Environment* 15, no. 5 (1994): 352.

16. Ibid., 363–64.

Chapter 3. The Growth Illusion

Epigraphs: Mahbub ul Haq, special adviser to the United Nations Development Programme's annual *Human Development Report*, in his Barbara Ward Lecture to the 21st World Conference of the Society for International Development,

Mexico City, April 1994; International Chamber of Commerce (ICC), *The Business Charter for Sustainable Development* (Paris: ICC, 1990), as quoted in Paul Ekins, "Sustainability First," in Paul Ekins and Manfred Max-Neef, *Real-Life Economics: Understanding Wealth Creation* (London: Routledge, 1992), 415.

1. Jan Tinbergen and Roefie Hueting, "GNP and Market Prices: Wrong Signals for Sustainable Economic Success That Mask Environmental Destruction," in Robert Goodland, Herman E. Daly, and Salah El Serafy, eds., *Population, Technology, and Lifestyle: The Transition to Sustainability* (Washington, D.C.: Island Press, 1992), 52–62.
2. Ibid., 52–62.
3. Richard Douthwaite, "The Growth Illusion," in Jonathan Greenberg and William Kistler, eds., *Buying America Back* (Tulsa, Okla.: Council Oak Books, 1992), 92–96.
4. Paul Ekins, ed., *The Living Economy* (London: Routledge, 1986), 8.
5. Herman E. Daly and John B. Cobb Jr., *For the Common Good: Redirecting the Economy toward Community, the Environment, and a Sustainable Future* (Boston: Beacon Press, 1989), 401–55.
6. United Nations Development Programme (UNDP), *Human Development Report 1991* (New York: Oxford University Press, 1991).
7. Richard Douthwaite, *The Growth Illusion* (Tulsa, Okla.: Council Oak Books, 1993), 96–119.
8. Ibid., 33–50.
9. Robin Broad and John Cavanagh, *Plundering Paradise: The Struggle for the Environment in the Philippines* (Berkeley: University of California Press, 1993), 24–31.
10. Broad and Cavanagh, *Plundering Paradise*, 24–31.
11. Eduardo A. Morato, "Far More Destructive Non-Events amidst Us," *Manila Chronicle,* June 18, 1991.
12. Broad and Cavanagh, *Plundering Paradise*, 61–72.
13. Morato, "Far More Destructive Non-Events amidst Us."
14. See John Young, "Mining the Earth," in Lester R. Brown et al., *State of the World 1992* (New York: W. W. Norton, 1992), 111.
15. Edgar Cahn and Jonathan Rowe, *Time Dollars* (Emmaus, Pa.: Rodale Press, 1992).
16. Clarence Shubert, "Creating People-Friendly Cities," PCDForum, Column no. 72, April 5, 1994.
17. Douthwaite, *The Growth Illusion,* 33–50.
18. Edward McNall Burns, *Western Civilizations: Their History and Their Culture,* 5th ed. (New York: W. W. Norton, 1958), 659–60.
19. Douthwaite, *The Growth Illusion,* 50–56.
20. Bennett Harrison, *Lean and Mean: The Changing Landscape of Corporate Power in the Age of Flexibility* (New York: Basic Books, 1994), 191–92.
21. Robert Goodland, Herman E. Daly, and Salah El Serafy, eds., *Population, Tech-*

nology, and Lifestyle: The Transition to Sustainability (Washington, D.C.: Island Press, 1992), xv.

22. Alicia Korten, "Cultivating Disaster: Structural Adjustment and Costa Rican Agriculture," *Multinational Monitor* (July/August 1993): 20–22.

23. Bruce Rich, *Mortgaging the Earth: The World Bank, Environmental Impoverishment, and the Crisis of Development* (Boston: Beacon Press, 1994), 155.

24. Clarence Maloney, "Environmental and Project Displacement of Population in India. Part I: Development and Deracination," *University Field Staff International Report* no. 14 (Indianapolis, Ind.: University Field Staff International, 1990–91), 1.

25. Rich, *Mortgaging the Earth*, 156.

26. *Southeast Asia Regional Consultation on People's Participation in Environmentally Sustainable Development*, vol. 2, *National and Regional Reports* (Manila: Asian NGO Coalition, 1991), 1–2.

27. Walter Hook, "Paving over Bangkok: Development Bank-Funded Highways Will Displace Tens of Thousands," *Sustainable Transport*, no. 2 (September 1993): 7.

Chapter 4. Rise of Corporate Power in America

Epigraph: Richard L. Grossman and Frank T. Adams, *Taking Care of Business: Citizenship and the Charter of Incorporation* (Cambridge, Mass.: Charter, Ink, 1993), 6.

1. K. M. Panikkar, *Asia and Western Dominance* (Kuala Lumpur: The Other Press, 1993), 46; and "Dutch East India Company," *1998 Encyclopaedia Britannica* (CD edition).

2. K. M. Panikkar, *Asia and Western Dominance*, 48.

3. Edward McNall Burns, *Western Civilizations: Their History and Their Culture*, 5th ed. (New York: W. W. Norton, 1958), 467; "The British East India Company," *1998 Encyclopaedia Britannica* (CD edition).

4. "The Opium Wars," *1998 Encyclopaedia Britannica* (CD edition).

5. Douglas Dowd, *U.S. Capitalist Development since 1776: Of, by, and for Which People?* (Armonk, N.Y.: M. E. Sharpe, 1993), 10.

6. Leo Huberman, *We, the People: The Drama of America* (New York: Monthly Review Press, 1960), 50–52.

7. Adam Smith, *An Inquiry into the Nature and Causes of the Wealth of Nations* (1776; New York: Modern Library, 1937), 123.

8. Grossman and Adams, *Taking Care of Business*, 3.

9. Ibid.

10. Ibid., 8–9.

11. Ibid., 11–12.

12. As quoted in Edwin Merrick Dodd, *American Business Corporations until 1860* (Cambridge, Mass.: Harvard University Press, 1934), 130, as cited in Grossman and Adams, *Taking Care of Business*, 13.

13. Harvey Wasserman, *America Born and Reborn* (New York: Collier Books, 1983), 84.

14. As quoted in Wasserman, *America Born and Reborn*, 89–90.

15. Ibid., 90.

16. As quoted in Wasserman, *America Born and Reborn*, 291.

17. As quoted in Wasserman, *America Born and Reborn*, 92–93.

18. Ibid., 108.

19. Grossman and Adams, *Taking Care of Business*, 21.

20. Ibid.

21. Ibid., 18–20.

22. Wasserman, *America Born and Reborn*, 110.

23. Grossman and Adams, *Taking Care of Business*, 18–20.

24. Paul Hawken, *The Ecology of Commerce* (New York: Harper Business, 1993), 108.

25. Wasserman, *America Born and Reborn*, 110.

26. Melvyn Dubofsky, *Industrialism and the American Worker, 1865–1920* (Arlington Heights, Ill.: Harlan Davidson, 1975), 87.

27. Wasserman, *America Born and Reborn*, 110–18; Dubofsky, *Industrialism and the American Worker*, 29–71.

28. Wasserman, *America Born and Reborn*, 110–18.

29. Ibid., 108.

30. Dubofsky, *Industrialism and the American Worker*, 72–108.

31. Wasserman, *America Born and Reborn*, 124; Dubofsky, *Industrialism and the American Worker*, 77–80.

32. Dowd, *U.S. Capitalist Development since 1776*, 157.

33. Robert L. Heilbroner, *The Worldly Philosophers* (New York: Simon & Schuster, 1992), 249–50.

34. Wasserman, *America Born and Reborn*, 140.

35. Ibid., 146–47.

36. Kevin Phillips, *The Politics of Rich and Poor* (New York: Harper Perennial, 1990), 241–42.

37. Walden Bello, with Shea Cunningham and Bill Rau, *Dark Victory: The United States, Structural Adjustment, and Global Poverty* (Oakland, Calif.: Institute for Food and Development Policy, 1994), 4–5.

38. Ibid., 3.

39. Ibid., 5.

40. Ibid.

41. The 1978 figure is from Phillips, *The Politics of Rich and Poor*, 239. The 1994 figure is from the survey of the world's billionaires by *Forbes*, July 18, 1994, 135.

42. *Forbes*, July 18, 1994, 135.

43. Bello, *Dark Victory*, 5–6.

44. Ibid., 3–4.

45. For further development of the autonomous purpose of corporations, see Jerry Mander, "Corporations as Machines," chap. 7 in *In the Absence of the Sacred* (San Francisco: Sierra Club Books, 1991).

46. William Greider, *Who Will Tell the People? The Betrayal of American Democracy* (New York: Simon & Schuster, 1992), 331.

Chapter 5. Assault of the Corporate Libertarians

Epigraphs: Paul Krugman, "Is Free Trade Passe?," *Economic Perspectives* 1, no. 2 (1987): 131; Gar Alperovitz, "Building a Living Democracy," *Sojourners* (July 1990): 16.

1. Michael Pusey, "Reclaiming the Middle Ground . . . From New Right 'Economic Rationalism,'" in Stephen King and Peter Lloyd, eds., *Economic Rationalism: Dead End or Way Forward?* (New South Wales: Allen & Unwin, 1993), 18.

2. Michael Pusey, *Economic Rationalism in Canberra: A Nation-Building State Changes Its Mind* (Sydney: Cambridge University Press, 1991).

3. *Webster's New World Dictionary* (New York: Simon & Schuster, 1980), s.v. "rationalism."

4. David Boaz and Edward H. Crane, *Market Liberalism: A Paradigm for the 21st Century* (Washington, D.C.: Cato Institute, 1993), 23.

5. Adam Smith, *An Inquiry into the Nature and Causes of the Wealth of Nations* (1776; New York: Modern Library, 1937), 60–61.

6. Ibid., 674.

7. A. V. Krebs, *The Corporate Reapers: The Book of Agribusiness* (Washington, D.C.: Essential Books, 1992); and an information sheet, "America's New 'Centrally Planned' Food Economy," prepared by A. V. Krebs and distributed by Prairie Fire Rural Action, Des Moines, Iowa.

8. Neva Goodwin, "Externalities and Economic Power," paper presented to session on "Is It the Economy or the Politics—Stupid?" at the fall retreat of the Environmental Grantmakers Association, Bretton Woods, New Hampshire, October 13–15, 1994, 2.

9. Smith, *Wealth of Nations,* 423.

10. Ibid., 700.

11. United Nations Centre for Transnational Corporations (UNCTC), "Trends in Foreign Direct Investment," E/C.IO/1993/2, March 3, 1993, 8; as reported by John Cavanagh in a May 1, 1993, memo.

12. These arguments are developed in detail by Herman E. Daly and John B. Cobb Jr., *For the Common Good: Redirecting the Economy toward Community, the Environment, and a Sustainable Future* (Boston: Beacon Press, 1989), 209–35.

13. Goodwin, "Externalities and Economic Power," 2.

14. James Stanford, "Continental Economic Integration: Modeling the Impact on Labor," *Annals of the American Academy of Political & Social Science* 526 (March 1993): 92–110.

15. James Stanford, "Free Trade and the Imaginary Worlds of Economic Modelers," PCDForum, Column no. 45, April 5, 1993.

16. Statistics cited by Richard J. Barnet, "Stateless Corporations: Lords of the Global Economy," *The Nation,* December 19, 1994, 754.

17. "Meet the World's Newest Billionaires," *Forbes,* July 5, 1993, 87.
18. "A Millionaire a Minute," *Business Week,* November 29, 1993, 100–102.
19. "21st Century Capitalism," *Business Week,* 1994 special issue, 13, 16.
20. Lawrence Summers, internal World Bank memorandum dated December 12, 1991, 5. The relevant excerpts from this memo were quoted by *The Economist,* February 8, 1992, 62. Summers, a leading proponent of economic rationalism, responded to widespread public criticism of his argument by claiming that he had inserted it into the infamous memo as an ironic counterpoint rather than an actual proposal. It is a classic economic rationalist argument.
21. "Pollution and the Poor," *The Economist,* February 15, 1992, 16–17.
22. The call for the rich to consume more imports from poor countries is a regular theme in the World Bank's World Development Report series. See, for example, World Bank, *World Development Report 1992: Development and the Environment* (New York: Oxford University Press, 1992), 3.

Chapter 6. The Decline of Democratic Pluralism

Epigraphs: Sir James Goldsmith, "Free Trade, Up to a Point," *Times* (London), March 5, 1994, 18; Susan George, Conference on Economic Sovereignty in a Globalising World, Bangkok, March 24–26, 1999, www.millennium-round .org/.

1. Francis Fukuyama, *The End of History and the Last Man* (New York: Avon Books, 1992).
2. The following points are drawn from Herman E. Daly and John B. Cobb Jr., *For the Common Good: Redirecting the Economy toward Community, the Environment, and a Sustainable Future* (Boston: Beacon Press, 1989), 49–60.
3. Based on personal correspondence from Marilyn Mehimann, Swedish Institute for Social Inventions, March 3, 1994.
4. Kenneth Hermele, "The End of the Middle Road: What Happened to the Swedish Model?," *Monthly Review* (March 1993): 14–24.
5. David Vail, "The Past and Future of Swedish Social Democracy: A Reply to Kenneth Hermele," *Monthly Review* (October 1993): 24–31.
6. Hermele, "The End of the Middle Road."
7. Ibid.
8. Vail, "The Past and Future of Swedish Social Democracy."
9. Hermele, "The End of the Middle Road."
10. Ibid.
11. Vail, "The Past and Future of Swedish Social Democracy."
12. Hermele, "The End of the Middle Road."
13. Ibid.
14. Vail, "The Past and Future of Swedish Social Democracy."
15. Larry Diamond, "Beyond Authoritarianism and Totalitarianism: Strategies for Democratization," *The Washington Quarterly* 12, no. 1 (Winter 1989): 141–63.
16. William M. Dugger, *Corporate Hegemony* (New York: Greenwood Press, 1989), 12–15.

17. Ibid., 15.
18. Ibid.

Chapter 7. Illusions of the Cloud Minders

Epigraph: From "The Cloud Minders," *Star Trek,* episode 74, February 28, 1969.

1. Graham Hancock, *Lords of Poverty* (New York: Atlantic Monthly Press, 1989), 38–40.
2. Address by Barber B. Conable to the board of governors of the World Bank and International Finance Corporation, Washington, D.C., September 30, 1986, as quoted in Hancock, *Lords of Poverty,* 38.
3. As reported in Nancy Scheper-Hughes, "The Madness of Hunger," *Why* no. 14 (Fall 1993): 11.
4. Walter Hook, "Paving over Bangkok," *Sustainable Transport* no. 2 (September 1993): 7.
5. Ibid., 6.
6. United Nations Development Programme (UNDP), *Human Development Report 1992* (New York: Oxford University Press, 1992).
7. U.S. data are for families and therefore are not directly comparable with the individual data used by UNDP.
8. Gar Alperovitz, "Building a Living Democracy," *Sojourners* (July 1990): 13.
9. "Executive Pay: The Party Ain't over Yet," *Business Week,* April 16, 1993, 56–64.
10. Ibid.
11. "The Forbes Four Hundred," *Forbes,* October 18, 1993, 110–11.
12. Although net asset values are not directly comparable to gross national product, which is a measure of income, the orders of magnitude are revealing. GNP and population figures are from John W. Wright, *The Universal Almanac, 1994* (Kansas City, Mo.: Andrews and McMeel, 1993).
13. "The Forbes Four Hundred," 111.
14. Lawrence Mishel and Jared Bernstein, *The State of Working America: 1992–1993* (Armonk, N.Y.: M. E. Sharpe, 1993), 256.
15. Ibid., 46; based on data from the House of Representatives Ways and Means Committee, 1991. Figures are in 1992 dollars.
16. James M. Clash, "Reversal of Fortunates," *Forbes,* October 18, 1993, 105–6.
17. Eric Konigsberg, "No Hassles: The Ultimate Perk of the Ruling Class Is Freedom from Pesky Details," *Utne Reader* (September/October 1993): 76.
18. James Bennet, "New Ford Chief Hasn't Bought One. Lately," *New York Times,* October 7, 1993.
19. "CEO Disease: Egotism Can Breed Corporate Disaster—and the Malady Is Spreading," *Business Week,* April 1, 1991, 52–60.
20. Konigsberg, "No Hassles," 76.
21. Richard J. Barnet and John Cavanagh, *Global Dreams: Imperial Corporation and the New World Order* (New York: Simon & Schuster, 1994), 325–29.
22. Ibid. See also Cynthia Enloe, "Globetrotting Sneaker," *Ms.* (March/April 1995): 10–15.

23. "Eisner Pay Is 68% of Profit," *New York Times,* April 16, 1994.
24. "The World's Wealthiest People," *Forbes,* July 5, 1993, 66–111; "The Billionaires," *Forbes,* July 18, 1994, 134–219.
25. Robert B. Reich, *The Work of Nations* (New York: Alfred A. Knopf, 1991), 275.
26. Extensive documentation of this trend within the United States is provided by Reich, *The Work of Nations,* 268–81.

Chapter 8. Dreaming of Global Empires

Epigraphs: "A Survey of Multinationals: Everybody's Favorite Monsters," *The Economist,* March 27, 1993, 7; Richard J. Barnet and Ronald E. Muller, *Global Reach: The Power of the Multinational Corporation* (New York: Simon & Schuster, 1974), 13, 15–16, as cited in Howard M. Wachtel, *The Money Mandarins: The Making of a Supra-national Economic Order* (Armonk, N.Y.: M. E. Sharpe, 1990), 6.

1. Akio Morita, "Toward a New World Economic Order," *Atlantic Monthly* (June 1993): 88.
2. Ibid., 92–93.
3. Ibid., 93.
4. Ibid., 94–95.
5. "Cosmocorp: The Importance of Being Stateless," *Columbia Journal of World Business* 2, no. 6 (November–December 1967), as quoted in Jeff Frieden, "The Trilateral Commission: Economics and Politics in the 1970s," in Holly Sklar, ed., *Trilateralism: The Trilateral Commission and Elite Planning for World Management* (Boston: South End Press, 1980), 63–64.
6. *GATT—The Environment and the Third World, an Overview* (Berkeley, Calif.: Environmental News Network, 1992), 3, as cited in Paul Hawken, *The Ecology of Commerce: A Declaration of Sustainability* (New York: Harper Business, 1993), 101.
7. Rosabeth Moss Kanter, "Transcending Business Boundaries: 12,000 World Managers View Change," *Harvard Business Review* (May–June 1991): 151–65.
8. Calculated from global trade and output tables in Lester R. Brown, Hal Kane, and Ed Ayres, *Vital Signs 1993: The Trends That Are Shaping Our Future* (New York: W. W. Norton, 1993).
9. "A Survey of Multinationals," 7.
10. "The Power of the Transnationals," *The Ecologist* 22, no. 4 (July/August 1992): 159.
11. United Nations, *World Investment Report* (New York: United Nations, 1993), 19, 22.
12. As quoted in Gerald Epstein, "Mortgaging America," *World Policy Journal* 8, no. 1 (Winter 1990–91): 29.
13. *Business Week,* May 14, 1990, 99.
14. Robert B. Reich, "Who Is Us?" *Harvard Business Review,* January–February 1990, 54.

15. Andrew Pollack, "G.M. to Make Toyota Cars for Sale in Japan," *New York Times,* April 16, 1993.
16. "The Stateless Corporation," *Business Week,* May 14, 1990, 98.
17. "The Stateless Corporation," 99–102.
18. Michael E. McGrath and Richard W. Hoole, "Manufacturing's New Economies of Scale," *Harvard Business Review* (May–June 1992): 94–102.
19. "A Survey of Multinationals," 8.
20. Office of Technology Assessment, U.S. Congress, *Multinationals and the National Interest: Playing by Different Rules* (Washington, D.C.: U.S. Government Printing Office, 1993), 1–4, 10.
21. Kenichi Ohmae, *The Borderless World: Power and Strategy in the Interlinked Economy* (London: HarperCollins, 1990), xii.
22. "U.S. Companies Use Affiliates Abroad to Skirt Sanctions," *New York Times,* December 27, 1993.
23. Ohmae, *The Borderless World,* x–xi.
24. Ibid., 19.
25. "Exports Will Fly High, but so Will Imports," *Fortune,* July 25, 1994, 64.
26. Andrew Cohen, "The Downside of 'Development,'" *The Nation,* November 4, 1991, 544–46.
27. This discussion is based on William Greider, *Who Will Tell the People? The Betrayal of American Democracy* (New York: Simon & Schuster, 1992), 378–87; Richard Rothstein, "Continental Drift: NAFTA and Its Aftershocks," *The American Prospect* no. 12 (Winter 1993): 68–84; Ross Perot and Pat Choate, *Save Your Job, Save Our Country* (New York: Hyperion, 1993), 45–47; and Richard J. Barnet and John Cavanagh, "Creating a Level Playing Field," *Technology Review* (May/June 1994): 23–29.
28. As interviewed by and cited in Greider, *Who Will Tell the People?,* 383.
29. "The Boom Belt: There's No Speed Limit on Growth along the South's I-85," *Business Week,* September 27, 1993, 98–104.
30. Robert Reich, *The Work of Nations* (New York: Alfred A. Knopf, 1991), 281.
31. Reported by Robert Reich in a presentation to the Democratic Leadership Conference televised on C-Span, November 29, 1994.

Chapter 9. Building Elite Consensus

Epigraphs: Peter Thompson, "Bilderberg and the West," in Holly Sklar (ed.), *Trilateralism: The Trilateral Commission and Elite Planning for World Management* (Boston: South End Press, 1980), p. 158; Felix Rohatyn, "World Capital: The Need and the Risks," *New York Review of Books,* July 14, 1994, 48.

1. Leonard Silk and Mark Silk, *The American Establishment* (New York: Basic Books, 1980), 183–90.
2. The discussion of these events is based on Laurence H. Shoup and William Minter, "Shaping a New World Order: The Council on Foreign Relations' Blueprint for World Hegemony," in Sklar, *Trilateralism,* 135–56.

3. Silk and Silk, *The American Establishment*, 197–98.
4. Shoup and Minter, "Shaping a New World Order," 135–56.
5. Memorandum E-B32, April 17, 1941, Council on Foreign Relations, War-Peace Studies, NUL, as quoted in Shoup and Minter, "Shaping a New World Order," 145–46.
6. From Memorandum E-B34, July 24, 1941, as quoted in Shoup and Minter, "Shaping a New World Order," 141.
7. Shoup and Minter, "Shaping a New World Order," 141.
8. Bruce Rich, *Mortgaging the Earth* (Boston: Beacon Press, 1994), 49–56.
9. Thompson, "Bilderberg and the West," 157.
10. Statement by John Pomian (secretary to Joseph Retinger, who was a founder of Bilderberg and its first permanent secretary), as quoted in Thompson, "Bilderberg and the West," 169.
11. Thompson, "Bilderberg and the West," 177.
12. As quoted in Thompson, "Bilderberg and the West," 177–78.
13. Sklar, *Trilateralism*.
14. From descriptive materials provided by the Trilateral Commission.
15. Thompson, "Bilderberg and the West," 176.
16. Ibid., 177.
17. From an undated information sheet provided by the Trilateral Commission.

Chapter 10. Buying Out Democracy

Epigraph: William Simon, as quoted in *Justice for Sale: Shortchanging the Public Interest for Private Gain* (Washington, D.C.: Alliance for Justice, 1993), 1.

1. Lewis Powell, as quoted in *Justice for Sale*, 10–11.
2. *Justice for Sale*, 11–12; Mark Megalli and Andy Friedman, *Masks of Deception: Corporate Front Groups in America* (Washington, D.C.: Essential Information, 1991), 153.
3. Megalli and Friedman, *Masks of Deception*, 153.
4. As quoted in *Justice for Sale*, 12.
5. *Justice for Sale*, 5.
6. These and other cases are documented in Megalli and Friedman, *Masks of Deception*.
7. Rosemary Brown, "Unveiling Corporate Front Groups," *Co-Op America Quarterly* (Winter 1994): 14. For a published directory of business-sponsored front groups, see Carl Deal, *The Greenpeace Guide to Anti-Environmental Organizations* (Berkeley, Calif.: Odonian Press, 1993); available from Odonian Press, Box 7776, Berkeley, CA 94707.
8. William Greider, *Who Will Tell the People? The Betrayal of American Democracy* (New York: Simon & Schuster, 1992), 48.
9. *Justice for Sale*, 3.
10. Greider, *Who Will Tell the People?*
11. From a descriptive brochure provided by the Business Roundtable.
12. The ratio is based on the 1992 average annual compensation of $3.84 million

for the CEOs of major U.S. corporations as reported by *Business Week,* April 16, 1993. Since the Roundtable members are the CEOs of the very largest U.S. corporations, we can presume that their average compensation is higher than the average reported by *Business Week.*

13. Sarah Anderson, John Cavanagh, and Sandra Gross, *NAFTA's Corporate Cadre: An Analysis of the USA*NAFTA State Captains* (Washington, D.C.: Institute for Policy Studies, 1993); available from IPS, 1601 Connecticut Ave. NW, Washington, D.C. 20009.

14. Greider, *Who Will Tell the People?,* 35.

15. John Stauber, "Countering the Flack Attack," *Co-op America Quarterly* (Winter 1994): 18.

16. Ibid.

17. Greider, *Who Will Tell the People?,* 253–54.

18. Ibid., 270.

19. Pat Choate, "Political Advantage: Japan's Campaign for America," *Harvard Business Review* (September–October 1990): 87–103; "Is Japan 'Buying' U.S. Politics?" *Harvard Business Review* (November–December 1990): 184–98.

Chapter 11. Marketing the World

Epigraphs: William Leach, *Land of Desire: Merchants, Power, and the Rise of a New American Culture* (New York: Pantheon Books, 1993), xiii; Richard J. Barnet and John Cavanagh, "The Sound of Money," *Sojourners* (January 1994): 12.

1. Paul Hawken, *The Ecology of Commerce: A Declaration of Sustainability* (New York: Harper Business, 1993), 132.

2. Duane Elgin, *Voluntary Simplicity* (New York: William Morrow, 1993), 50–52.

3. Ibid.

4. Leach, *Land of Desire,* xv. For an examination of the intentional development and application of psychological techniques in advertising developed by Freud's nephew Edward Bernays to engineer a new public culture, see the award-winning 2002 BBC television series "The Century of the Self," http://topdocumentaryfilms.com/the-century-of-the-self/.

5. Leach, *Land of Desire,* 11–12.

6. The statistics and analysis of television are from Jerry Mander, *In the Absence of the Sacred: The Failure of Technology and the Survival of the Indian Nations* (San Francisco: Sierra Club Books, 1991), 75–82.

7. Ibid., 97–98.

8. As cited in Richard J. Barnet and John Cavanagh, *Global Dreams: Imperial Corporations and the New World Order* (New York: Simon & Schuster, 1994), 171–72.

9. United Nations, *Report on the World Social Situation 1993* (New York: United Nations, 1993), 48.

10. Alan Thein Durning, "Can't Live Without It," *World-Watch* 6, no. 3 (May–June 1993): 13.

11. Akio Morita, "Toward a New World Economic Order," *Atlantic Monthly* (June 1993).

12. Robert C. Goizueta, as quoted in Barnet and Cavanagh, "The Sound of Money," 14.

13. Barnet and Cavanagh, "The Sound of Money," 14.

14. Sarah Ferguson, "The Comfort of Being Sad: Kurt Cobain and the Politics of Damage," *Utne Reader* (July/August 1994): 62.

15. *TV Nation*, produced by Michael Moore, NBC Television, August 2, 1994.

16. Except as otherwise referenced, information on corporate advertising in the classroom is from Alex Monar, "Corporations in the Classroom," *Co-op America Quarterly* (Winter 1994): 19–20.

17. Randal W. Donaldson, as quoted in Robert Pear, "Senator, Promoting Student Nutrition, Battles Coca-Cola," *New York Times*, April 26, 1994.

18. "A, B, C, D, Economics," *New York Times*, May 26, 1992.

19. Donella Meadows, "Corporate-Run Schools Are a Threat to Our Way of Life," *Valley News*, October 3, 1992; Monar, "Corporations in the Classroom" (West Lebanon, NH), 20.

20. As quoted in Monar, "Corporations in the Classroom," 20.

21. Hawken, *The Ecology of Commerce*, 129.

22. "Empires of the 21st Century?" *Business Week*, February 21, 1994, 19.

Chapter 12. Adjusting the Poor

Epigraphs: Jesse Jackson, speaking to eleven African heads of state, Libreville, Gabon, May 27, 1993; the ad in *Fortune* was placed by the Philippine government in 1975, as quoted in Elizabeth M. Krahmer and Donella H. Meadows, "Money Flows" (draft paper, March 29, 1994), 19.

1. Robin Broad, *Unequal Alliance 1979–1986: The World Bank, the International Monetary Fund, and the Philippines* (Berkeley: University of California Press, 1988), 21.

2. Bruce Rich, "The Cuckoo in the Nest: Fifty Years of Political Meddling by the World Bank," *The Ecologist* 24, no. 1 (January/February 1994): 9.

3. Ibid.

4. Ibid.

5. Broad, *Unequal Alliance*, 6–7.

6. Ibid.

7. Ibid.

8. Ibid., 26–27.

9. Rich, "The Cuckoo in the Nest," 9–10.

10. Ibid., 10.

11. Broad, *Unequal Alliance*, 27.

12. As quoted in Robert W. Oliver, *International Economic Cooperation and the World Bank* (London: Macmillan Press, 1977), 160, and cited in Bruce Rich, *Mortgaging the Earth: The World Bank, Environmental Impoverishment, and the Crisis of Development* (Boston: Beacon Press, 1994), 59.

13. *World Debt Tables 1992–93: External Finance for Developing Countries* (Washington, D.C.: World Bank, 1992), 212.

14. Frances Stewart, "The Many Faces of Adjustment," *World Development* 19, no. 12 (December 1991): 1851.

15. *World Debt Tables 1992–93*, 208.

16. Jonathan Cahn, "Challenging the New Imperial Authority: The World Bank and the Democratization of Development," *Harvard Human Rights Journal* 6 (1993): 160.

17. Clay Chandler, "The Growing Urge to Break the Bank," *Washington Post*, June 19, 1994.

18. Rich, *Mortgaging the Earth*, 77.

19. Senate Committee on Banking and Currency, *Participation of the United States in the International Monetary Fund and the International Bank for Reconstruction and Development*, 79th Cong., 1st sess., 1945, S. Rpt. 452, pt. 2, "Minority Views," p. 9, as quoted in Rich, *Mortgaging the Earth*, 62.

20. Senate Committee on Banking and Currency, p. 9, as quoted in Rich, *Mortgaging the Earth*, 61–62.

21. David C. Korten, *Getting to the 21st Century: Voluntary Action and the Global Agenda* (West Hartford, Conn.: Kumarian Press, 1990).

22. Reported by Pratap Chatterjee, "World Bank Failures Soar to 37.5% of Completed Projects in 1991," *Third World Economics*, December 16–31, 1992, 2.

23. Reported by Michael Cernea, "Farmer Organizations and Institution Building for Sustainable Development," *Regional Development Dialogue* 8, no. 2 (Summer 1987): 1–19.

Chapter 13. Guaranteeing Corporate Rights

Epigraphs: Herman E. Daly, farewell lecture to the World Bank, January 1994; William M. Dugger, *Corporate Hegemony* (New York: Greenwood Press, 1989), ix, xiii.

1. Paul Hawken, *The Ecology of Commerce: A Declaration of Sustainability* (New York: Harper Business, 1993), 99–100.

2. Information on the trade advisory committees is from Tom Hilliard, *Trade Advisory Committees: Privileged Access for Polluters* (Washington, D.C.: Public Citizen's Congress Watch, 1991).

3. U.S. Department of Commerce and Office of the U.S. Trade Representative, *Procedures and Rules for the Industry Advisory Committees for Trade Policy Matters*, n.d., 3, as cited in Hilliard, *Trade Advisory Committees*, 9.

4. Hilliard, *Trade Advisory Committees*, 7.

5. "Government Seeks Advice from Industry on U.S. Trade Policy," *Business America*, January 16, 1989, 9, as cited in Hilliard, *Trade Advisory Committees*, 7.

6. Hilliard, *Trade Advisory Committees*.

7. Clayton Yeutter, as quoted in Mark Ritchie, "GATT, Agriculture and the Environment: The US Double Zero Plan," *The Ecologist* 20, no. 6 (November/December 1990): 217.

8. As cited in "Power: The Central Issue," *The Ecologist* 22, no. 4 (July/August 1992): 159.

9. Cited in Ritchie, "GATT, Agriculture and the Environment," 16.

10. From a study by Tim Lang for the United Kingdom National Food Alliance, as reported in Tim Lang and Colin Hines, *The New Protectionism: Protecting the Future against Free Trade* (New York: New Press, 1993), 100–103.

11. In an April 24, 1993, interview with *New Scientist* magazine, cited in Natalie Avery, "How Companies Influence Global Food Standards," news release issued by *Third World Network Features* (87 Cantonment Road, Penang, Malaysia) (January 1994), 7.

12. Hope Shand, "Patenting the Planet," *Multinational Monitor* (June 1994): 9–13.

13. Ibid.

14. As quoted in Vandana Shiva, *Monocultures of the Mind: Perspectives on Biodiversity and Biotechnology* (London: Zed Press, 1993), 122.

15. Shiva, *Monocultures of the Mind*, 122.

16. *The Ecologist, Whose Common Future? Reclaiming the Commons* (Philadelphia: New Society Publishers, 1993), 55–56.

Chapter 14. The Money Game

Epigraph: "Hot Money," *Business Week*, March 20, 1995, 46.

1. The number of participants is an estimate noted by Representative Henry B. Gonzalez, chair of the House Banking Committee of the U.S. Congress, at a hearing on the derivatives market; cited in Thomas L. Friedman, "International Investors Bet Everything on Anything," *New York Times*, April 17, 1994.

2. Diana B. Henriques, "Questions of Conflict Sting Mutual Funds," *New York Times*, August 7, 1994.

3. "Another Year in 'Bank Heaven'?" *Business Week*, January 10, 1994, 103.

4. Pension fund figures are from Randy Barber and Teresa Ghilarducci, "Pension Funds, Capital Markets, and the Economic Future," in Gary A. Dymski, Gerald Epstein, and Robert Pollin, eds., *Transforming the U.S. Financial System: Equity and Efficiency for the 21st Century* (Armonk, N.Y.: M. E. Sharpe, 1993), 288.

5. On an average day in July 1993, $1.087 trillion in dollar-based transactions, most of them currency trades, took place on the New York Clearing House Interbank Payments System alone. Jay Mathews, "Putting Currency on Trial," *Washington Post*, August 22, 1993.

6. Joel Kurtzman, *The Death of Money* (New York: Simon & Schuster, 1993), 64, 149.

7. For more detailed nontechnical discussions of the financial economy, see Kurtzman, *The Death of Money*; Howard M. Wachtel, *The Money Mandarins: The Making of a Supranational Economic Order* (Armonk, N.Y.: M. E. Sharpe, 1990); and Roy C. Smith, *The Money Wars: The Rise and Fall of the Great Buyout Boom of the 1980s* (Plume, N.Y.: Truman Talley Books, 1990).

8. The actual rate varies, depending on such things as the total assets of the bank, but it averages a little under 10 percent.
9. *Report of the Presidential Commission on Market Mechanisms* (Washington, D.C.: U.S. Government Printing Office, 1988), 1–2, as cited in Wachtel, *The Money Mandarin,* 251.
10. Kurtzman, *The Death of Money,* 98.
11. Ibid., 161.

Chapter 15. Predatory Finance

Epigraph: Carmine Rotondo's comment was made about a period of currency stability in March 1987, as quoted in Hobart Rowen, "Wielding Jawbone to Protect the Dollar," *Washington Post,* March 15, 1987, and cited in Howard M. Wachtel, *The Money Mandarins: The Making of a Supranational Economic Order* (Armonk, N.Y.: M. E. Sharpe, 1990), 269.

1. Joel Kurtzman, *The Death of Money* (New York: Simon & Schuster, 1993), 128.
2. Felix Rohatyn, "World Capital: The Need and the Risks," *New York Review of Books,* July 14, 1994, 53.
3. "A Survey of Multinationals: Everybody's Favorite Monsters," *The Economist,* March 27, 1993, 6.
4. Personal communication with J. T. Ross Jackson, president, Gaiacorp, Copenhagen, Denmark.
5. Carol J. Loomis, "Untangling the Derivatives Mess," *Fortune,* March 20, 1995, 50.
6. "Survey: Frontiers of Finance: On the Edge," *The Economist,* October 9, 1993, 4.
7. Saul Hansell, "A Primer on Hedge Funds: Hush-Hush and for the Rich," *New York Times,* April 13, 1994, A-1, D-15.
8. "Excerpts from Soros Testimony," *New York Times,* April 14, 1994.
9. Alien R. Myerson, "When Soros Speaks, World Markets Listen," *New York Times,* June 10, 1993.
10. "Big Winner from Plunge in Sterling," *New York Times,* October 27, 1992.
11. Elizabeth M. Krahmer and Donella H. Meadows, "Money Flows" (prepared for the annual meeting of the Environmental Grantmakers Association, March 24, 1994), 48.
12. Jay Mathews, "Putting Currency Trading on Trial," *Washington Post,* August 22, 1993.
13. Felix Rohatyn, "World Capital: The Need and the Risks," *New York Review of Books,* July 14, 1994, 51–52.
14. Saul Hansell, "A Bad Bet for P. & G.," *New York Times,* April 14, 1994.
15. Rohatyn, "World Captital," 52.
16. Susan Antilla, "A Concealed Danger for Funds," *New York Times,* April 17, 1994.
17. "Today, Orange County: The Muni Mess on Wall Street: How Bad?" *Business Week,* December 19, 1994, 28–30.
18. Saul Hansell, "For Rogue Traders, Yet Another Victim," *New York Times,*

February 28, 1995; "The Lesson from Barings' Straits," *Business Week*, March 13, 1995, 30–32; Richard W. Stevenson, "Young Trader's $29 Billion Bet Brings Down a Venerable Firm," *New York Times*, February 28, 1995.

19. Sheryl WuDunn, "Tokyo Stocks Plunge on British Firm's Collapse," *New York Times*, February 27, 1995.

20. As cited in Joel Kurtzman, *The Death of Money* (New York: Simon & Schuster, 1993), 89–91.

21. Based on an interview with Christopher Whalen, chief financial officer for Legal Research International, by Russell Mokhiber of the Corporate Crime Reporter, January 19, 1995, distributed via the Internet.

22. "The World's Wealthiest People," *Forbes*, July 5, 1993, 66; "The Billionaires," *Forbes*, July 18, 1994, 194–95.

23. "One Year Later: NAFTA Disaster!" Information package prepared and distributed by Public Citizen's Trade Program, Public Citizen, Washington, D.C., March 1995, 1.

24. "Austerity and Rates of 92% Fail to Perk Up the Peso," *New York Times*, March 16, 1995.

25. Anthony DePalma, "Mexicans Ask How Far Social Fabric Can Stretch," *New York Times*, March 12, 1995.

26. Allen R. Nyerson, "Peso's Plunge May Cost Thousands of U.S. Jobs," *New York Times*, January 30, 1995.

27. Anthony DePalma, "Crisis in Mexico Deepens Damage in Latin Markets," *New York Times*, January 11, 1995.

28. Ralph Nader, testimony on the bailout of the Mexican government before the Senate Banking Committee, U.S. Senate, Washington, D.C., March 9, 1995, 4; David E. Sanger, "Dollar Dips as the Peso Falls Again," *New York Times*, March 10, 1995.

29. Harvey D. Shapiro, "After NAFTA: Facing the New Global Economy," *Hemispheres* (March 1995): 74–79.

30. Paul Craig Roberts, "How Clinton Is Bashing the Buck," *Business Week*, August 8, 1994, 14.

31. Mathews, "Putting Currency Trading on Trial."

32. Thomas A. Russo, "Let Wall St. Handle Derivatives Rules," *New York Times*, May 15, 1994.

33. As quoted in Mathews, "Putting Currency Trading on Trial."

34. As quoted in Sylvia Nasar, "Jett's Supervisor at Kidder Breaks Silence," *New York Times*, June 26, 1994.

35. Sylvia Nasar, "Kidder Scandal Tied to Failure of Supervision," *New York Times*, August 5, 1994.

36. As quoted in Thomas J. Lueck, "Incentives of $31 Million Keep Kidder Peabody in New York," *New York Times*, October 30, 1993.

Chapter 16. Corporate Cannibalism

Epigraph: William M. Dugger, *Corporate Hegemony* (New York: Greenwood Press, 1989), x.

1. The meaning of the phrase "creating value" is commonly distorted by corporate libertarians to refer to anything that inflates a price or extracts a profit. I use the term only in reference to adding to the real value of the world's stock of goods, services, and productive assets.

2. Joel Kurtzman, *The Death of Money* (New York: Simon & Schuster, 1993), 164.

3. Data compiled by Donald L. Bartlett and James B. Steele, "America: What Went Wrong? Part 8: The Disappearing Pensions," *Philadelphia Inquirer,* October 27, 1991, as cited in Jonathan Greenberg, "The Hidden Costs of Corporate Takeovers," in Jonathan Greenberg and William Kistler, eds., *Buying America Back* (Tulsa, Okla.: Council Oak Books, 1992), 153.

4. As quoted in "The Power of the Transnationals," *The Ecologist* 22, no. 4 (July/August 1992): 159.

5. Ned Daly, "Ravaging the Redwoods: Charles Hurwitz, Michael Milken and the Cost of Greed," *Multinational Monitor* (September 1994): 12.

6. John Skow, "Redwoods: The Last Stand," *Time,* June 6, 1994, 59.

7. Ibid.

8. Daly, "Ravaging the Redwoods," 13.

9. As quoted in Susan Faludi, "The Reckoning: Safeway LBO Yields Vast Profits but Exacts a Heavy Human Toll," *Wall Street Journal,* May 16, 1990, and cited in Greenberg, "The Hidden Costs of Corporate Takeovers," 159.

10. Gretchen Morgenson, "The Buyout That Saved Safeway," *Forbes,* November 12, 1990, 88, as cited in Greenberg, "The Hidden Costs of Corporate Takeovers," 155.

11. Greenberg, "The Hidden Costs of Corporate Takeovers," 155.

12. Data compiled by Donald L. Bartlett and James B. Steele, "America: What Went Wrong? Part 3: Shifting Taxes from Them to You," *Philadelphia Inquirer,* October 22, 1991, as cited in Greenberg, "The Hidden Costs of Corporate Takeovers," 152.

13. Greenberg, "The Hidden Costs of Corporate Takeovers," 151.

14. Ibid., 159.

15. Based on Joseph Pereira, "Split Personality," as reprinted by *Utne Reader* (September/October 1993): 63–66, from the *Wall Street Journal.*

16. As quoted in Pereira, "Split Personality," 64.

17. As cited in Ross Perot and Pat Choate, *Save Your Job, Save Our Country: Why NAFTA Must Be Stopped—Now!* (New York: Hyperion, 1993), 52–53.

18. Ibid., 52–53.

Chapter 17. Managed Competition

Epigraphs: Bennett Harrison, *Lean and Mean: The Changing Landscape of Corporate Power in the Age of Flexibility* (New York: Basic Books, 1993), 220; Jeremy Brecher, "Global Village or Global Pillage?" *The Nation,* December 6, 1993, 685–88.

1. "Let the Good Times Roll—and a Few More Heads," *Business Week*, January 31, 1994, 28–29.
2. "The Rise and Rise of America's Small Firms," *The Economist*, January 21, 1989, 73–74, as quoted in Harrison, *Lean and Mean*, 13.
3. Based on Harrison, *Lean and Mean*, 9–11.
4. "Let the Good Times Roll," 28–29.
5. Harrison, *Lean and Mean*, 18.
6. Paul Hawken, *The Ecology of Commerce: A Declaration of Sustainability* (New York: Harper Business, 1993), 8.
7. "Executive Pay: The Party Ain't Over Yet," *Business Week*, April 26, 1993, 56–62; "That Eye-Popping Executive Pay: Is Anybody Worth This Much?" *Business Week*, April 25, 1994, 52–58.
8. Brian O'Reilly, "The New Deal: What Companies and Employees Owe One Another," *Fortune*, June 13, 1994, 45.
9. John Naisbitt, *Global Paradox* (New York: William Morrow, 1994), 14.
10. "Learning to Survive in the '90s," *Business Week*, January 10, 1994, 95.
11. "Channeling Big Stores' Awesome Clout," *Business Week*, December 21, 1992, 98.
12. Donella Meadows, "Wal-Mart Should Come on Our Terms, Not at Our Expense," *Valley News*, June 12, 1993 (Lebanon, NH), 26.
13. "Clout! More and More, Retail Giants Rule the Marketplace," *Business Week*, December 21, 1992, 66–73; "Brawls in Toyland," *Business Week*, December 21, 1992, 36–37.
14. "Clout!," 73.
15. This compares 1991 GNP data for countries against total sales of the world's largest corporations for the same year. GNP data are from *The Universal Almanac*, 1994 (Kansas City, Mo.: Andrews and McMeel, 1993) supplemented by *The Economist, Book of Vital World Statistics* (New York: Random House, 1990). Aggregate sales data are from tables in *Hoover's Handbook of World Business 1993* (Austin, Tex.: Reference Press, 1993) for the world's five hundred largest industrial corporations, the world's fifty largest utilities, the world's fifty largest retailing companies, and the world's fifty largest diversified service companies. Many sources indicate that only forty of the hundred largest economies are corporations. This figure is based on the *Fortune* list of the world's hundred largest "industrial" corporations, which excludes nonindustrial corporations.
16. Hawken, *The Ecology of Commerce*, 92.
17. Ibid.
18. "A Survey of Multinationals: Everybody's Favorite Monsters," *The Economist*, March 27, 1993 (special supplement), 6.
19. Asset figures for commercial banks and financial companies are from *Hoover's Handbook of World Business*, 68, 72.
20. Adam Smith, *An Inquiry into the Nature and Causes of the Wealth of Nations* (1776; New York: Modern Library, 1937), 128.
21. "The Age of Consolidation," *Business Week*, October 14, 1991, 86–94. "Making the Perfect Connection," *WordPerfect Report* (Summer/Fall 1994): 2.

22. These estimates are from "A Survey of Multinationals," 17.
23. A. V. Krebs, *The Corporate Reapers: The Book of Agribusiness* (Washington, D.C.: Essential Books, 1992); A. V. Krebs, "America's New 'Centrally Planned' Food Economy" (information sheet distributed by Prairie Fire Rural Action, Des Moines, Iowa), 1992.
24. Joan Dye Gussow, "A Nutrition Policy . . . That Leads to a Food Policy . . . That Leads to an Agricultural Policy," *WHY Magazine* (Summer 1993): 25.
25. Krebs, *The Corporate Reapers*, 102.
26. Ibid., 372–82.
27. "The Virtual Corporation," *Business Week*, February 8, 1993, 100.
28. "The Partners," *Business Week*, February 10, 1992, 102–7.
29. Ibid.
30. "A Survey of Multinationals," 14.
31. "The Global Firm: R.I.P.," *The Economist*, February 6, 1993, 69.

Chapter 18. Race to the Bottom

Epigraphs: "What's Wrong?" *Business Week*, August 2, 1993, 59; Jeremy Brecher, "Global Village or Global Pillage?" *The Nation*, December 6, 1993, 685–88.

1. Laurie Udesky, "Sweatshops behind the Labels: The 'Social Responsibility' Gap," *The Nation*, May 16, 1994, 666–68.
2. Ms. Diaz's testimony before a hearing of the Subcommittee on Labor-Management Relations, Committee on Education and Labor, U.S. House of Representatives, Wilkes-Barre, Pa., June 7, 1994, as cited in an ad placed in the *New York Times*, June 19, 1994, by the International Ladies Garment Workers Union.
3. Bill Keller, "The Revolution Won, Workers Are Still Unhappy," *New York Times*, July 23, 1994.
4. Bill Keller, "In Mandela's South Africa, Foreign Investors Are Few," *New York Times*, August 3, 1994.
5. "Damping Labor's Fires," *Business Week*, August 1, 1994, 40–41.
6. Ibid.
7. "The Wild, Wild East," *Business Week*, December 28, 1992, 50–51.
8. Robert A. Senser, "Outlawing the Crime of Child Slavery," *Freedom Review*, November–December 1993, 29–35.
9. Ibid.
10. Ibid.
11. Udesky, "Sweatshops behind the Labels," 665–68.
12. Robert Levering and Milton Moskowitz, *The 100 Best Companies to Work for in America*, rev. ed. (New York: Penguin Books, 1994), 500.
13. "Managing by Values: Is Levi Strauss' Approach Visionary—or Flaky?" *Business Week*, August 1, 1994, 46–52.
14. Levering and Moskowitz, *The 100 Best Companies to Work for in America*, 501–2.
15. "Slash and Earn on the Continent," *Business Week*, May 2, 1994, 45–46.

16. "Europe's Economic Agony," *Business Week,* February 15, 1993, 49.
17. "Rage in the Streets," *Business Week,* April 11, 1994, 46.
18. "Doleful," *The Economist,* October 9, 1993, 17.
19. Ibid.
20. Ibid.
21. "Europe's Economic Agony," 48–49.
22. "Land of the Rising Jobless," *Business Week,* January 11, 1993, 47.
23. Michael H. Armacost, "Japan Goes to Business School," *New York Times,* July 28, 1994.
24. "A Bargain Basement Called Japan," *Business Week,* June 27, 1994, 42.
25. David Sanger, "New Japan Access for Wall Street," *New York Times,* January 11, 1995.
26. "Wal-Mart Jitters Reach Canada's Stores," *Business Week,* January 31, 1994, 38.
27. "Invasion of the Retail Snatchers," *Business Week,* May 9, 1994, 72.
28. "NAFTA: A Green Light for Red Tape," *Business Week,* July 25, 1994, 48.

Chapter 19. The End of Inefficiency

Epigraphs: Jeremy Rifkin, *The End of Work* (New York: G. P. Putnam's Sons, 1995), xiv; William M. Dugger, *Corporate Hegemony* (New York: Greenwood Press, 1989), ix, xiii.

1. Richard Douthwaite, *The Growth Illusion* (Tulsa, Okla.: Council Oak Publishing, 1993), 24.
2. Dugger, *Corporate Hegemony,* 13.
3. Brian O'Reilly, "The New Deal: What Companies and Employees Owe One Another," *Fortune,* June 13, 1994, 50.
4. John Burgess, "Debate on Executive Pay Moves across the Atlantic," *International Herald Tribune,* October 24, 1991, Business/Finance section.
5. Derek Bok, *The Cost of Talent: How Executives and Professionals Are Paid and How It Affects America* (New York: Free Press, 1993), 108–11.
6. Lee Smith, "Burned-Out Bosses," *Fortune,* July 25, 1994, 44–46.
7. Ibid., 44–46.
8. Sarah Lyall, "Publishing Chief Is Out at Viacom," *New York Times,* June 15, 1994.
9. Alison Leigh Cowan and John Holusha, "Eastman Kodak Chief Is Ousted by Directors," *New York Times,* August 7, 1993.
10. "Getting Rid of the Boss," *The Economist,* February 6, 1993, 13.
11. "The Contingency Work Force," *Fortune,* January 24, 1994, 31.
12. "Planning a Career in a World without Managers," *Fortune,* March 20, 1995, 72–80.
13. Jaclyn Fierman, "The Perilous New World of Fair Pay," *Fortune,* June 13, 1994, 64.
14. Lawrence Mishel and Jared Bernstein, *The State of Working America, 1992–93* (Washington, D.C.: M. E. Sharpe, 1993), 131–34.

15. Jason DeParle, "Sharp Increase along the Borders of Poverty," *New York Times,* March 31, 1994.
16. As summarized in "Lifestyles of the Poor and Working," *Utne Reader* (March/April 1993): 19–20.
17. "Downward Mobility," *Business Week,* March 23, 1992, 57–58.
18. "Bellboys with B.A.," *Time,* November 22, 1993, 36.
19. George J. Church, "Jobs in an Age of Insecurity," *Time,* November 22, 1993, 36.
20. "Lifestyles of the Poor and Working," *Utne Reader* (March/April 1993): 19–20.
21. The Millers's story is reported by Dirk Johnson, "Family Struggles to Make Do after Fall from Middle Class," *New York Times,* March 11, 1994.

Chapter 20. People with No Place

Epigraph: Cecil Rhodes, as quoted in "Development as Enclosure: The Establishment of a Global Economy," *The Ecologist* 22, no. 4 (1992): 131–47.

1. Quoted material is from Helena Norberg-Hodge, "The Psychological Road to 'Development,'" PCDForum, Column no. 62, October 8, 1993. A more detailed account may be found in *Ancient Futures: Learning from Ladakh* (San Francisco: Sierra Club Books, 1991). An excellent video documenting life in Ladakh before and after development is available from the International Society for Ecology and Culture (ISEC), 12 Victoria Square, Clifton, Bristol BS8 4ES, UK; or P.O. Box 9475, Berkeley, CA 94709, USA.
2. For a more detailed account of the history of the land enclosure process, see the special issue of *The Ecologist* 22, no. 4 (July/August 1992) on the theme "Whose Common Future?"
3. "Development as Enclosure: The Establishment of a Global Economy," *The Ecologist* 22, no. 4 (July/August 1992): 134.
4. Ibid., 135.
5. Ibid.
6. Ibid., 135, 137.
7. For a thoroughly documented account of clandestine U.S. political and military interventions throughout the South, see Jonathan Kwitny, *Endless Enemies: The Making of an Unfriendly World* (New York: Congdon & Weed, 1984).
8. Robert D. Kaplan, "The Coming Anarchy," *Atlantic Monthly* (February 1994): 46.
9. Ibid., 48.
10. Martin van Creveld, *The Transformation of War,* as quoted in Kaplan, "The Coming Anarchy," 74.
11. United Nations High Commissioner for Refugees, *The State of the World's Refugees* (New York: Penguin Books, 1993).
12. "Two Million Refugees," *New York Times,* July 20, 1994.
13. United Nations High Commissioner for Refugees, *The State of the World's Refugees,* foreword, iii.
14. Kaplan, "The Coming Anarchy," 72.

Chapter 21. The Ecological Revolution

Epigraphs: Willis Harman, *Global Mind Change: The Promise of the Last Years of the Twentieth Century* (Indianapolis, Ind.: Knowledge Systems, 1988); Wangari Maathai, "All We Need Is Will," in *Can the Environment Be Saved without a Radical New Approach to World Development?* (Geneva: CONGO Planning Committee for UNCED, 1992), 27.

1. Mary E. Clark, "The Backward Ones," PCDForum, Column no. 51, June 25, 1993.
2. The following discussion draws on Harman, *Global Mind Change,* 34–35; Duane Elgin, *Awakening Earth: Exploring the Evolution of Human Culture and Consciousness* (New York: William Morrow, 1993), 15–16; and personal communications with William Ellis.
3. Edward McNall Burns, *Western Civilizations: Their History and Their Culture,* 5th ed. (New York: W. W. Norton, 1958), 520.
4. Harman, *Global Mind Change,* 12.
5. Burns, *Western Civilizations,* 521.
6. Jacob Needleman, *Money and the Meaning of Life* (New York: Doubleday, 1991), 40–42.
7. Joe Dominguez and Vicki Robin, *Your Money or Your Life: Transforming Your Relationships with Money and Achieving Financial Independence* (New York: Viking, 1992), 54.
8. Dominguez and Robin, *Your Money or Your Life,* 54.
9. Fritjof Capra, *The Tao of Physics* (New York: Bantam Books, 1976); Gary Zukav, *The Dancing Wu Li Masters: An Overview of the New Physics* (New York: Bantam Books, 1979). Fritjof Capra, *The Turning Point: Science, Society, and the Rising Culture* (New York: Simon & Schuster, 1982), and Harman, *Global Mind Change,* deal specifically with the implications for society.
10. Mary E. Clark, "The Backward Ones," PCDForum, Column no. 51, June 25, 1993.
11. Robert D. Putnam, "The Prosperous Community: Social Capital and Public Affairs," *The American Prospect* 13 (Spring 1993): 2.
12. Putnam, *The Prosperous Community,* 2.
13. This thesis is developed in George T. Lock Land, *Grow or Die: The Unifying Principle of Transformation* (New York: Dell, 1973).
14. Arnold Toynbee, *A Study of History,* abridgement of vols. 1–6 by D. D. Somerwell (New York: Oxford University Press, 1947), 555.
15. Herman Daly, "Toward Some Operational Principles of Sustainable Development," *Ecological Economics* 2 (1990): 1–6.
16. Based on the discussion of subsidiarity in James Robertson, *Future Wealth: A New Economics for the 21st Century* (London: Cassell Publishers Limited, 1989).

Chapter 22. Economies Are for Living

Epigraphs: Eknath Easwaran, *The Compassionate Universe: The Power of the Individual to Heal the Environment* (Tomales, Calif.: Nilgiri Press, 1989), 73–74; Margaret J. Wheatley and Myron Kellner-Rogers, *A Simpler Way of Life* (San Francisco: Berrett-Koehler Publishers, 1996), 6.

1. Alan Durning, *How Much Is Enough?: The Consumer Society and the Future of the Earth* (New York: W. W. Norton, 1992). Durning's terms for the three socio-ecological classes are consumers, middle income, and poor.
2. Michael Renner, "Assessing the Military's War on the Environment," in Lester R. Brown et al., *State of the World 1991* (New York: W. W. Norton, 1991), 139.
3. David Engwicht, *Reclaiming Our Cities and Towns* (Philadelphia: New Society Publishers, 1993), 17.
4. Ibid., 48–51.
5. Ibid., 45.
6. William E. Rees and Mark Roseland, "From Urban Sprawl to Sustainable Human Communities," PCDForum, Column no. 54, June 25, 1993.
7. Statistics are reported by Marcia D. Lowe, "Reinventing Transport," in Lester R. Brown et al., *State of the World 1994* (New York: W. W. Norton, 1994), 82–84, from a study by the U.S. Federal Highway Commission. For further discussion, see Engwicht, *Reclaiming Our Cities and Towns,* 138–44.
8. Nicholas Albery, Matthew Mezey, and Peter Ratcliffe, eds., *Social Innovations: A Compendium* (London: Institute for Social Innovations), 92–93.
9. Robyn Williams, foreword to Engwicht, *Reclaiming Our Cities and Towns.*
10. Application of these concepts to villages in India is developed in detail in Anil Agarwal and Sunita Narain, *Towards Green Villages: A Strategy for Environmentally Sound and Participatory Rural Development* (New Delhi: Centre for Science & Environment, 1989).
11. Alan Thein Durning and Ed Ayres, "The Story of a Newspaper," *World Watch* (November/December 1994): 30–32.
12. Lester R. Brown, Christopher Flavin, and Sandra Postel, *Saving the Planet: How to Shape an Environmentally Sustainable Economy* (New York: W. W. Norton, 1991), 65.
13. Ibid., 65.
14. Ibid., 68.
15. Ibid., 70.
16. *Webster's New World Dictionary,* 2d college ed. (New York: Simon & Schuster, 1980), s.v. "job."
17. *Webster's New World Dictionary,* s.v. "livelihood."
18. The armed forces and defense worker estimates are from United Nations Development Programme (UNDP), *Human Development Report 1994* (New York: Oxford University Press, 1994), 47, 60.

Chapter 23. An Awakened Civil Society

Epigraph: Jim Hightower, "20 Questions," *Utne Reader* (January–February 1995): 79.

1. Gustavo Esteva, *Proceso,* February 14, 1994, as quoted in "Chiapas and the Americas," *The Nation,* March 28, 1994, 404.
2. Neil Harvey, *Rebellion in Chiapas: Rural Reforms, Campesino Radicalism, and the Limits to Salinismo,* Transformation of Rural Mexico Series no. 5 (San Diego, Calif.: Ejido Reform Research Project, Center for U.S.–Mexican Studies, University of California, 1994), 1.
3. *Goldman Environmental Prize: The First Five Years* (San Francisco: Goldman Environmental Foundation, n.d.), 34.
4. Based on Willis W. Harman, personal communication, September 9, 1993.
5. I can mention here only a few of the millions of examples. The cases cited here are drawn from sources such as Paul Ekins, *A New World Order: Grassroots Movements for Global Change* (London: Routledge, 1992); *Goldman Environmental Prize: The First Five Years* (San Francisco: Goldman Environmental Foundation, 1994); nominee lists from the "We the Peoples: 50 Communities Awards" sponsored by the Friends of the United Nations, 1151 Wellington Crescent, Winnipeg R3N OA1, Canada, fax (204) 487-0149; Robin Broad and John Cavanagh, *Plundering Paradise: The Struggle for the Environment in the Philippines* (Berkeley: University of California Press, 1993); and Julie Fisher, *The Road from Rio: Sustainable Development and the Nongovernmental Movement in the Third World* (Westport, Conn.: Praeger, 1993). Reviews of social movements in India are provided by Smitu Kothari, "Social Movements and the Redefinition of Democracy," in Philipp Oldenberg, ed., *India Briefing* (Boulder, Colo.: Westview Press, 1993), 131–62; and Smitu Kothari, "Incompatibility of Sustainability and Development: In Search of Social Justice," *Journal of Public Administration* (July–September 1993): 12–30.
6. Thomas H. Greco Jr., *New Money for Healthy Communities* (Tucson, Ariz.: Thomas H. Greco Jr., 1994); Edgar Cahn and Jonathan Rowe, *Time Dollars* (Emmaus, Pa.: Rodale Press, 1992).
7. These and other network characteristics are discussed in Jessica Lipnack and Jeffrey Stamps, *Networking: People Connecting with People, Linking Ideas and Resources* (Garden City, N.Y.: Doubleday, 1982), 222–28.
8. For a rich inventory of resources on the sustainable agriculture movement in the United States, see *WHY Magazine* (Summer 1993): 24–25.
9. Peter Rachleff, "Seeds of a Labor Resurgency," *The Nation,* February 21, 1994, 226–29.
10. James L. Tyson, "Young Blacks Get Helping Hand from Chicago Marchers," *Christian Science Monitor,* May 13, 1994.
11. "Hungry," *The Economist,* July 10, 1993.
12. Further information on Citizenship Action against Misery and for Life is available from IBASE, rua Vicente de Souza, 29-Botafogo, 22251 Rio deJaneiro/ RJ, Brazil; fax (55-21) 286-0541.

13. Michael H. Shuman and Hall Harvey, *Security without War: A Post–Cold War Foreign Policy* (Boulder, Colo.: Westview Press, 1993), 90–92; Gloria Duffy, "Transformation in the USSR: The Role of Track-Two Diplomacy," *Surviving Together* (Spring 1993): 3–5; David Ignatius, "Innocence Abroad: The New World of Spyless Coups," *Washington Post,* September 22, 1991, Outlook section.

14. Rachleff, "Seeds of a Labor Resurgency," 226–29.

15. Information on these networks is available from IOCU, P.O. Box 1045, 10830 Penang, Malaysia, fax (60-4) 366-506.

16. Jeremy Brecher, John Brown Childs, and Jill Carter, *Global Visions: Beyond the New World Order* (Boston: South End Press, 1993).

17. Noeleen Heyzer, "Women's Development Agenda for the 21st Century: Unifem as a Vehicle of Change for Sustainable Livelihoods and Women's Empowerment," address by the director, United Nations Development Fund for Women, to the Third Committee of the General Assembly of Nations, United Nations, December 1994.

18. The presentation of these examples is inspired by a presentation made by Paul Hawken at The Learning Center in New York City.

Chapter 24. Agenda for Democracy

Epigraphs: Herman E. Daly and John B. Cobb Jr., *For the Common Good: Redirecting the Economy toward Community, the Environment, and a Sustainable Future* (Boston: Beacon Press, 1989), 174; John Maynard Keynes: as cited in ibid., 209.

1. Paul Hawken, *The Ecology of Commerce: A Declaration of Sustainability* (New York: Harper Business, 1993), 108.

2. Ibid., 120.

3. Russell Baker, "The Big Hog Wallow," *New York Times,* November 1, 1994.

4. Bishan Singh, "A Social Economy; The Emerging Scenario for Change," in Tina Liamzon (ed.), *Civil Society and Sustainable Livelihoods Workshop Report* (Rome: Society for International Development, 1994), 29–37.

5. Gar Alperovitz, "Ameristroika Is the Answer," *Washington Post,* December 13, 1992.

6. For a partial inventory and assessment of this experience, see Jeff Shavelson, *A Third Way: A Sourcebook: Innovations in Community-Owned Enterprise* (Washington, D.C.: National Center for Economic Alternatives, 1990).

7. This would be an extension of a proposal by James Tobin regarding the taxation of international financial transactions. James Tobin, "A Tax on International Currency Transactions," in United Nations Development Programme (UNDP), *Human Development Report 1994* (New York: Oxford University Press, 1994), 70.

8. See Richard J. Barnet and John Cavanagh, *Global Dreams* (New York: Simon & Schuster, 1994), 416. (The suggested percentages are from the author.)

9. Herman E. Daly and John B. Cobb Jr., *For the Common Good: Redirecting the*

Economy toward Community, the Environment, and a Sustainable Future, 2d. ed. (Boston: Beacon Press, 1994), 414–35.

10. See Barnet and Cavanagh, 415–16.

11. James Robertson, *Benefits and Taxes: A Radical Strategy* (London: New Economics Foundation, March 1994), 12–17. A variant of the guaranteed income, a graduated positive income tax, is proposed by Daly and Cobb, *For the Common Good* (1989), 315–23. These two sources discuss the history of such proposals and the support they have enjoyed from across the political spectrum.

12. Hawken, 163.

13. See Patricia Adams, *Odious Debts: Loose Lending, Corruption, and the Third World's Environmental Legacy* (London: Earthscan, 1991).

14. See Tim Lang and Colin Hines, *The New Protectionism: Protecting the Future against Free Trade* (New York: New Press, 1993), 127, for a discussion of positive approaches to protectionism.

Conclusion: A Living Economy for Living Earth

Epigraphs: Generally attributed to Alanis Obomsawin, member of the Abenaki tribe, http://quoteinvestigator.com/2011/10/20/last-tree-cut/; Margaret Wheatley, "Restoring Hope to the Future through Critical Education of Leaders" (2001), http://www.margaretwheatley.com/articles/restoringhope .html; Jim Wallis, *The Soul of Politics* (New York: Harcourt Brace & Company, 1995), 282.

1. YES! Magazine gives voice to the new story tellers, http://www.yesmagazine .org.

2. I develop this theme more fully, including action steps, in *Change the Story, Change the Future: A Living Economy for a Living Earth* (Oakland, Calif.: Berrett-Koehler Publishers, 2015).

3. Brooke Jarvis interview with Richard Wilkinson, "Why Everyone Suffers in Unequal Societies," *YES! Magazine,* March 4, 2010, http://www.yesmagazine .org/happiness/want-the-good-life-your-neighbors-need-it-too.

4. See http://ineteconomics.org/.

5. See http://www.isipe.net/. Among these initiatives, the Adbusters-sponsored student-centered and -led Kick It Over campaign is one of the more radical and creative: http://kickitover.org/tag/isipe/.

6. John Kay, "Angry Economics Students Are Naïve—And Mostly Right," *Financial Times,* May 20, 2014, http://www.ft.com/cms/s/0/23da4f1e-df48 -11e3-86a4-00144feabdc0.html-axzz3OH2r9S9f.

7. Ha-Joon Chang and Jonathan Aldred, "After the Crash, We Need a Revolution in the Way We Teach Economics," *The Guardian,* May 10, 2014, http://www .theguardian.com/business/2014/may/11/ after-crash-need-revolution-in-economics-teaching-chang-aldred.

8. See David Bolier and Burns H. Weston, *Green Governance: Ecological Survival, Human Rights and the Commons* (New York: Cambridge University Press, 2014).

9. See the Global Alliance for the Rights of Nature, http://therightsofnature.org/

united-nations/rights-of-nature-voice-rio20/; Linda Sheehan, "Submission by Earth Law Center to the United Nations Development Program, How to Include the Rule of Law in the Post 2015 Development Agenda," Earth Law Center, August 29, 2013; Simon Davis Cohen, "Hundreds of Communities Are Building Legal Blockages to Fight Big Carbon," October 20, 2014, http:// thischangeseverything.org/hundreds-of-communities-are-building-legal-block ades-to-fight-big-carbon/; and http://www.earthlawcenter.org/static/uploads/ documents/Rule_of_Law_for_Nature_8_29_133.pdf.

10. David Korten, "Rio+20: A Defining Choice," *YES! Magazine,* June 15, 2012, http://www.yesmagazine.org/blogs/david-korten/rio-20-a-defining-choice; and Janet Redman, "10 Things You Should Know about the Rio+20 Earth Summit," *YES! Magazine,* June 14, 2012, http://www.yesmagazine.org/ planet/10-things-you-should-know-about-the-rio-20-earth-summit.

11. Fritjof Capra and Ugo Mattei, *The Ecology of Law: Toward a Legal System in Tune with Nature and Community* (Oakland, Calif.: Berrett-Koehler Publishers, 2015).

12. Michelle Long, "To Find Real Prosperity, Community Foundations Are Exiting Wall Street," *Huffington Post: The Blog,* http://www.huffingtonpost.com/ michelle-long/to-find-real-prosperity-c_b_6457502.html.

13. Capital Institute, Evergreen Direct Investing: The Field Guide to Investing in a Regenerative Economy, no. 5, http://fieldguide.capitalinstitute.org/evergreen -direct-investing.html.

14. Ibid., 4.

15. Ibid., 7.

16. Charles Piller, "How the Gates Foundation's Investments Are Undermining Its Own Good Works," *The Nation,* August 22, 2014, http://www.thenation.com/article/181342/how-gates-foundations -investments-are-undermining-its-own-good-works.

17. For examples of cooperative ownership, see Gar Alperovitz, *What Then Must We Do? Straight Talk about the Next American Revolution* (Burlington, Vt.: Chelsea Green Publishing, 2013); Marjorie Kelly, "The Economy: Under New Ownership," *YES! Magazine,* February 19, 2013, http://www.yesmagazine.org/ issues/how-cooperatives-are-driving-the-new-economy/the-economy-under -new-ownership; and Amy B. Dean, "Why Unions Are Going into the Co-op Business," *YES! Magazine,* March 5, 2013, http://www.yesmagazine.org/issues/ how-cooperatives-are-driving-the-new-economy/union-co-ops.

Epilogue: Our Need for Meaning

Epigraph: Václav Havel, Februrary 21, 1990 address to a joint session of the US Congress, http://vaclavhavel.cz/showtrans.php?cat=projevy&val=322_aj_ projevy.html&typ=HTML.

1. Thomas Berry, *The Dream of the Earth* (San Francisco: Sierra Club Books, 1988).

2. Duane Elgin, *Awakening Earth: Exploring the Evolution of Human Culture and Consciousness* (New York: William Morrow, 1993), 18.

ACKNOWLEDGMENTS

From its inception, *When Corporations Rule the World* has been the product of an international collaboration involving many wonderful colleagues. I am especially indebted to Sunimal Fernando, Chandra de Fonseca, Tony Quizon, Sixto Roxas, Bishan Singh, and Felix Sugirtharaj, with whom I shared a ten-day retreat in Baguio, Philippines, in November 1992. The collective report on our insights from our conversations provided the initial frame for the original edition of *When Corporations Rule the World.*

Krishna Sondhi and Ian Mayo-Smith of Kumarian Press, which had published many of my previous books, prodded me unrelentingly to write what became the classic edition of *When Corporations Rule the World* and gave me extraordinary support to make it happen. They commissioned Henry Berry as editorial and marketing consultant to help me make the transition from writing for a specialized development audience to writing for a broader trade audience. They also developed a unique co-publication partnership with Berrett-Koehler Publishers that brought to this project the creative talents of Steve Piersanti and his colleagues. Jeevan Sivasubramaniam of the Berrett-Koehler staff proposed this 20th anniversary edition and Karen Seriguchi provided exceptional support as copy editor.

Frances Korten helped shape the classic edition's core arguments through many hours of dinner table conversation and with great love, devotion, and an unrelentingly critical eye read and edited every chapter—several times. She did the same for the new introduction and conclusion for this 20th anniversary edition. An editorial advisory board of Anwar Fazal, Robert Gilman, Willis Harman, Stanley Katz, and Donella Meadows provided ideas, inspiration, and advice throughout the writing of the original edition. Michelle Beesten and Claudia Radel provided voluntary research and editorial assistance.

In addition, extensive critical input and feedback was provided by Nancy Alexander, Robin Broad, John Cavanagh, Walter Coddington, Sandy Cohen, Herman Daly, Richard Douthwaite, Neva Goodwin, Jonathan Greenberg, Ross Jackson, Elizabeth Kramer, Mark Leach, Jerry Mander, and Marilyn Mehlmann. Other colleagues who made special contributions to the underlying ideas and analysis include Fatma Alloo, Gar Alperovitz, Roy Anderson, Winifred Armstrong, Tusi Avegalio, Maude Barlow, Patricia Bauman, Walden Bello, David Bonbright, Jeremy Brecher, Ellen Brown, Beth Burrows, Ruth Caplan, Robert Cassani, Mary Clark, Tony Clarke, Clifford Cobb, Chuck Collins, Harriet Crosby, Joëlle Danant, Joe Dominguez, Duane Elgin, Bill Ellis, Linda Elswick, Gustavo Esteva, Joyce Gillilan-Goldberg, Kat Gjovik, Edward Goldsmith, Tom Goldtooth, Alisa Gravitz, Nathan Gray, Leanne Grossman, Richard Grossman, Ted Halstead, Wendy Harcourt, Paul Hawken, Judy Henderson, Noeleen Heyzer, Janet Hunt, John Ickis, Tom Keehn, Danny Kennedy, Martin Khor, Andrew Kimbrell, Alicia Korten, Smitu Kothari, Sigmund Kvaloy, Kathy Lawrence, Michael Lerner, Tina Liamzon, Jerry Mander, Peter Mann, Atherton Martin, Michael McCoy, Donella Meadows, Luis Lopezllera Méndez, Victor Menotti, John Mohawk, Ward Morehouse, David Morris, Shierry Nicholsen, Helena Norberg-Hodge, Michael Northup, Sharlye Patton, David Perrin, George Porter, William Rees, David Richards, Mark Ritchie, Neil Ritchie, James Robertson, Vicki Robin, Atila Roque, Isagani Serrano, Vandana Shiva, Michael Shuman, Greg Thompson, Sally Timpson, Edgardo Valenzuela, Steve Viederman, Paul Wachtel, Lori Wallach, and Paul Wangoola. The extraordinary music of Jeff Clarkson—friend and colleague, New Zealand composer, synthesizer artist, and environmental activist—created a relaxed and reflective mood during the long periods of writing all three editions.

Others who have made important contributions to my thinking and understanding since writing the original edition of *When Corporations Rule the World* include Gar Alperovitz, Sarah Anderson, Mark Anielski, Rod Arakaki, Jean-Bertrand Aristide, Tom Atlee, Jeff Barber, Maude Barlow, Walden Bello, Janine Benyus, Thomas Berry, Elise Boulding, Puanani Burgess, Raffi Cavoukian, John B. Cobb Jr., Richard Conlin, Kevin Danaher, Susan Davis, Charles Derber, Ronnie Duggar, Duane Elgin, Carol Estes, Ralph Estes, Ted Falcon, Keven Fong, Matthew Fox, Susan George, Kat Gjovik, Danny Glover, William Greider, Thom Hartmann, Paul Hawken, Randy Hayes, Colin Hines, Mae-Wan Ho, Charles Holmes, Garry Jacobs, Ian Johnson, Kurt Johnson, Van Jones,

Marjorie Kelly, Satish Kumar, Frances Moore Lappé, Sara Larrain, Annie Leonard, Chee Yoke Ling, Michelle Long, Don Mackenzie, Joanna Macy, Jerry Mander, Denis Meadows, Jason McLennan, Graeme Maxton, Victor Menotti, Dena Merriam, Stacy Mitchell, Robert Monks, Jane Anne Morris, Robert Muller, Ralph Nader, Martin Palmer, Nicanor Perlas, Harry Pickens, Gifford Pinchott, Libba Pinchott, Jamal Rahman, Paul Ray, Anita and Gordon Roddick, Belvie Rooks, Johnathan Rowe, Elisabet Sahtouris, Lucianne Siers, Klaus Schwab, Claude Smadja, Gus Speth, John Stauber, Brian Swimme, Victoria Tauli-Corpuz, Lama Tsomo, Bill and Lynn Twist, Jakob von Uexküll, Steve Usher, Sarah van Gelder, Roberto Vargas, Karl Wagner, Judy Wicks, and Stephen Zarlenga.

All editions of *When Corporations Rule the World* have been prepared as a project of the People-Centered Development Forum (PCDForum), since renamed the Living Economies Forum. Specific financial support for the original edition was provided to the Forum by the Jenifer Altman Foundation.

The Living Economies Forum is a voluntary organization with only one paid staff person: Kat Gjovik, the director of communications and outreach. I received no personal compensation from any source for the preparation of any of the editions of this book, and all royalties go to the Living Economies Forum. Further information on the Forum is available at http://livingeconomiesforum.org.

The views expressed in this book are mine and do not necessarily represent those of the Forum or its contributors. I extend my deepest appreciation to all who helped make this book possible.

INDEX

ABOUT THE AUTHOR

Photo: Paul Dunn

DR. DAVID C. KORTEN worked for more than thirty-five years in preeminent business, academic, and international development institutions before he turned away from the establishment to become a leading critic of what he calls a global capitalist suicide economy. He now devotes his life to advancing the global transition to a living economy organized around deeply democratic self-governing living communities in which people work in co-productive partnership with the rest of nature to meet the needs of all.

He is the co-founder and board chair of YES! Magazine, a co-chair of the New Economy Working Group, the president of the Living Economies Forum, an associate fellow of the Institute for Policy Studies, a member of the Club of Rome, a founding board member emeritus of the Business Alliance for Local Living Economies, and a former founding associate of the International Forum on Globalization. He earned MBA and PhD degrees from the Stanford University Graduate School of Business.

Trained in psychology, organization theory, business strategy, and economics, he devoted his early career to advancing business education in low-income countries. With his wife, Fran Korten, he set up the College of Business Administration in the Haile Selassie I University in Ethiopia, while completing his doctoral studies at the Stanford Business School. He completed his military service during the Vietnam War as a captain in the US Air Force, with duty at the Special Air Warfare School, Air Force headquarters command, the Office of the Secretary of Defense, and the Advanced Research Projects Agency.

After his military service, he served for five years on the faculty of the Harvard Business School, teaching in its MBA, PhD, and middle-management programs and serving as its adviser to the Central American Management Institute in Nicaragua. He then headed a Ford Foundation–funded Harvard Institute for International Development project to strengthen the organization and management of the national family-planning programs throughout the world and taught a course on family-planning management at the Harvard School of Public Health.

In the late 1970s, he and Fran left US academia and moved to Southeast Asia, where they lived for nearly fifteen years. She served as a Ford Foundation program officer. He served first as a Ford Foundation project specialist and later as Asia regional adviser on development management to the US Agency for International Development.

In 1988, he walked away from the establishment to work with leading Asian nongovernmental organizations on identifying the root causes of development failure in the region and building the capacity of civil society organizations everywhere to function as strategic catalysts of positive national and global change. He and his colleagues concluded that the root cause of development failure resides in economic models and policies promoted by the United States to advance the consolidation of global corporate rule. In 1990, he founded the People-Centered Development Forum, now the Living Economies Forum, to engage with colleagues from around the world in exposing the failures of established economic models and defining alternatives to them.

In 1992, he and Fran returned to the United States to share with their fellow Americans the lessons of their years abroad. They settled in a New York apartment near Union Square between Madison Avenue and Wall Street, where he wrote *When Corporations Rule the World*. It launched in 1995 and became an international best seller. In 1994, he participated in the formation of the International Forum on Globalization and in 1995–96 in the founding of YES! Magazine, which he continues to serve as board chair.

In 1998, he and Fran moved to Bainbridge Island, Washington, where Fran became executive director and publisher of *YES! Magazine* and David wrote in succession *The Post-Corporate World: Life after Capitalism; The Great Turning: From Empire to Earth Community; Agenda for a New Economy: From Phantom Wealth to Real Wealth;* and *Change the Story, Change the Future: A Living Economy for a Living Earth.* In 2001, he participated in founding the Business Alliance for Local Living Economies and served as a founding board member through 2012. In 2008 he co-founded the New Economy Working Group, which he co-chairs with John Cavanagh.

David Korten
http://livingeconomiesforum.org
https://facebook.com/davidkorten
Twitter: @dkorten

Also by David Korten

Change the Story, Change the Future
A Living Economy for a Living Earth

This book dares to speak a forbidden but self-evident truth. Seduced by a fabricated Sacred Money and Markets story, we live in indentured service to money-seeking corporate robots and relate to Earth as if it were a dead rock for sale. Hope lies with the truth of a Sacred Life and Living Earth story that lives in the human heart. We are living beings born of and nurtured by a Living Earth itself born of a Living Universe. And that changes everything.

Paperback, 192 pages, ISBN 978-1-62656-290-5
PDF ebook, ISBN 978-1-62656-291-2

Agenda for a New Economy
From Phantom Wealth to Real Wealth, 2nd Edition

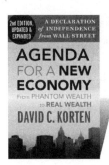

The Wall Street economy has perfected the art of creating "phantom wealth" financial assets without producing anything of real value. Periodic, devastating crashes will continue until it is replaced by a New Economy of locally based, community-oriented, living enterprises that create real wealth in service to people, community, and nature. Korten explains why this is so and provides in-depth advice on how we can bring it about.

Paperback, 336 pages, ISBN 978-1-60509-375-8
PDF ebook, ISBN 978-1-60509-376-5

Berrett–Koehler Publishers, Inc.
www.bkconnection.com

800.929.2929

The Great Turning
From Empire to Earth Community

David Korten exposes the destructive and oppressive nature of "Empire," the organization of society through hierarchy and violence that has held sway since ancient times. Drawing on evolutionary theory, developmental psychology, religious teachings, and other sources, Korten shows that "Earth Community"—an egalitarian, sustainable way of ordering human society—is indeed possible, and he lays out a grassroots strategy for achieving it.

Paperback, 424 pages, ISBN 978-1-887208-08-6
PDF ebook, ISBN 978-1-57675-539-6

The Post-Corporate World
Life after Capitalism

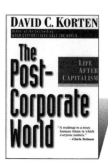

There is a deep chasm between the promises of the new global capitalism and the reality of social breakdown, spiritual emptiness, and environmental destruction it is leaving in its wake. Korten outlines an alternative: a global system of thriving, healthy market economies that organize by living system principles and function as extensions of healthy local ecosystems to meet the livelihood needs of all people and communities.

Paperback, 336 pages, ISBN 978-1-887208-03-1
PDF ebook, ISBN 978-1-60509-396-3

BK Berrett–Koehler Publishers, Inc.
www.bkconnection.com

800.929.2929

Berrett–Koehler
Publishers

A community dedicated to creating
a world that works for all

Visit Our Website: www.bkconnection.com

Read book excerpts, see author videos and Internet movies, read our authors' blogs, join discussion groups, download book apps, find out about the BK Affiliate Network, browse subject-area libraries of books, get special discounts, and more!

Subscribe to Our Free E-Newsletter, the *BK Communiqué*

Be the first to hear about new publications, special discount offers, exclusive articles, news about bestsellers, and more! Get on the list for our free e-newsletter by going to www.bkconnection.com.

Get Quantity Discounts

Berrett-Koehler books are available at quantity discounts for orders of ten or more copies. Please call us toll-free at (800) 929-2929 or email us at bkp .orders@aidcvt.com.

Join the BK Community

BKcommunity.com is a virtual meeting place where people from around the world can engage with kindred spirits to create a world that works for all. BKcommunity.com members may create their own profiles, blog, start and participate in forums and discussion groups, post photos and videos, answer surveys, announce and register for upcoming events, and chat with others online in real time. Please join the conversation!

Certified

Corporation
bcorporation.net

FSC
www.fsc.org
MIX
From responsible
sources
FSC® C113845